Workshop on Simple and Efficient Natural Language Processing (SustaiNLP 2020)

Online
20 November 2020

ISBN: 978-1-7138-2005-5

SustaiNLP 2020

**SustaiNLP: Workshop on Simple and Efficient
Natural Language Processing**

Proceedings of the Workshop

November 20, 2020
Online workshop

Introduction

It is our great pleasure to welcome you to the first edition of SustaiNLP: Workshop on Simple and Efficient Natural Language Processing.

The Natural Language Processing community has, in recent years, demonstrated a notable focus on improving scores on standard benchmarks and taking the lead on community-wide leaderboards such as (Super)GLUE, SentEval or XTREME. While this led to improvements in benchmark performance of (predominantly neural) models, it also resulted in a worrysome increase in model complexity and the amount of computational resources required for training and using the current state-of-the-art models. Moreover, recent research efforts often fail to identify sources of performance gains in models and to justify model complexity beyond benchmark performance.

Because of these trends as well as the worrysome carbon footprint of (pre)training large neural models, we organized SustaiNLP in order to promote simpler and more sustainable NLP research and practices, with two main objectives: (1) encouraging development of more resource-efficient NLP models; and (2) providing simpler architectures and empirical justification of model complexity. For both aspects, we encouraged submissions from all topical areas of NLP.

Besides the original research papers (short and long), we encouraged cross-submissions of work that has been published at other events as well as extended abstracts of work in progress that fit the scope and aims of the workshop (only the original research papers, however, are included in these workshop proceedings).

This first edition of the workshop also included a *shared task* encouraging an optimal trade-off between the model performance and efficiency during inference. The shared task focused on inference efficiency as it can be difficult to fairly evaluate training efficiency in the most general setting. Moreover, as large-scale pretrained models reach production, it is the computational cost of inference that will account for most of the cumulative lifetime environmental cost of these models.

We received overwhelming 48 submissions (and 1 shared task system description), proposing a multitude of viable resource-efficient NLP methods and spanning a wide range of NLP applications. We have selected 28 submissions for presentation at the workshop, yielding an acceptance rate of 58%). Additionally, the workshop will include presentations of 38 papers accepted for publication in EMNLP Findings, the content of which we judged to be in line with the scope and aims of the workshop.

Many thanks to our program committee for their thorough and thoughtful reviews. We would also like to thank to our panelists and invited speakers whose discussions and talks we strongly believe will make the workshop exciting and memorable.

We are looking forward to the first edition of the SustaiNLP workshop!

SustaiNLP Organizers   October 2020

Organizers:

Nafise Sadat Moosavi, TU Darmstadt
Angela Fan, INRIA Nancy & Facebook AI Research Paris
Goran Glavaš, University of Mannheim
Vered Shwartz, Allen Institute for AI (AI2)
Shafiq Joty, Nanyang Technological University
Alex Wang, New York University
Thomas Wolf, Huggingface Inc.

Steering Committee:

Sam Bowman, New York University
Mona Diab, George Washington University
Andrew McCallum, University of Massachusetts Amherst
Alexander Rush, Cornell University
Luke Zettlemoyer, University of Washington & Facebook

Program Committee:

Eneko Agirre, Mikel Artetxe, Dennis Aumiller, Guy Boudoukh, Samuel Cahyawijaya, Elizabeth Clark, Alexis Conneau, Rotem Dror, Gerard Dupont, Nouha Dziri, Kiril Gashteovski, Sebastian Gehrmann, Marjan Ghazvininejad, Samujjwal Ghosh, Andreas Hanselowski, Benjamin Heinzerling, Ari Holtzman, Ozan Irsoy, Srinivasan Iyer, Peter Izsak, Mandar Joshi, Ehsan Kamalloo, Gyuwan Kim, Young Jin Kim, Guillaume Lample, Phong Le, Ji-Ung Lee, Louis Martin, Seyed Abolghasem Mirroshandel, Marius Mosbach, Myle Ott, Daraksha Parveen, Matthew Peters, Jonas Pfeiffer, Mohammad Taher Pilehvar, Barbara Plank, Simone Paolo Ponzetto, Ofir Press, Hannah Rashkin, Siva Reddy, Ines Rehbein, Andreas Rücklé, Victor Sanh, Roy Schwartz, Edwin Simpson, Gabriel Stanovsky, Anders Søgaard, Urmish Thakker, Prasetya Ajie Utama, Ivan Vulić, Moshe Wasserblat, Genta Indra Winata, Sam Wiseman, Caiming Xiong, Canwen Xu

Invited Speakers & Panelists:

Mona Diab, George Washington University
Heng Ji, University of Illinois at Urbana-Champaign
Graham Neubig, Carnegie Mellon University
Alexander Rush, Cornell University
Emma Strubell, Carnegie Mellon University
Armand Joulin, Facebook AI Research
Kyunghyun Cho, New York University
Yejin Choi, University of Washington & Allen Institute for Artificial Intelligence (AI2)
Yoav Goldberg, Bar Ilan University
Iryna Gurevych, TU Darmstadt

Table of Contents

A comparison between CNNs and WFAs for Sequence Classification
Ariadna Quattoni and Xavier Carreras

Counterfactual Augmentation for Training Next Response Selection
Seungtaek Choi, Myeongho Jeong, Jinyoung Yeo and Seung-won Hwang

Do We Need to Create Big Datasets to Learn a Task?
Swaroop Mishra and Bhavdeep Singh Sachdeva

Guiding Attention for Self-Supervised Learning with Transformers
Ameet Deshpande and Karthik Narasimhan

Besides the papers listed above, 38 **EMNLP Findings** papers will be presented at
SustaiNLP as well.

Knowing Right from Wrong:
Should We Use More Complex Models for Automatic Short-Answer Scoring in Bahasa Indonesia?

Ali Akbar Septiandri[1], Yosef Ardhito Winatmoko[2], Ilham Firdausi Putra[3]

[1]Universitas Al Azhar Indonesia, Jakarta, Indonesia
[2]Jheronimus Academy of Data Science, 's-Hertogenbosch, The Netherlands
[3]Institut Teknologi Bandung, Bandung, Indonesia

`aliakbar@if.uai.ac.id`, `yosefardhitowin@gmail.com`
`ilhamfputra31@gmail.com`

Abstract

We compare three solutions to UKARA 1.0 challenge on automated short-answer scoring: single classical, ensemble classical, and deep learning. The task is to classify given answers to two questions, whether they are right or wrong. While recent development shows increasing model complexity to push the benchmark performances, they tend to be resource-demanding with mundane improvement. For the UKARA task, we found that bag-of-words and classical machine learning approaches can compete with ensemble models and Bi-LSTM model with pre-trained word2vec embedding from 200 million words. In this case, the single classical machine learning achieved less than 2% difference in F1 compared to the deep learning approach with $\frac{1}{18}$ time for model training.

1 Introduction

Automated short-answer scoring is the application of computer technologies to assist human grader in evaluating the score of written answers (Dikli, 2006). The first track of UKARA 1.0 is the binary classification version of short-answer scoring, where participants are expected to develop a model that can distinguish right and wrong answers in free text format. The organizer published the questions, the labels' responses, and the guideline on how to determine whether an answer is acceptable.

During a period of five weeks, the training set and the development set were available, and we could validate our model through the score of the development set in a leaderboard. Subsequently, the test set was released, which consists of roughly four times the size of the development set. We are required to submit predicted labels based on the model that we have developed, and the winner was determined by the F1 score of the submitted prediction.

Our final submission to this task consists of feature extraction, such as n-grams and TF-IDF, and classical machine learning algorithms, namely logistic regression and random forest. Moreover, we tested a combination of classical algorithms through ensemble learning and deep learning approach. We have published our implementation for reproduction[1]. We discuss the dataset and our approach in the following sections.

2 Datasets

The dataset consists of two questions and the respective responses collected by the organizer of the challenge. All questions and responses are in Indonesian. The first question ("Task A") asked about the consequence of climate change. Concretely, what are the potential problems faced by a climate refugee when they migrate to a new place? The second question, referred to as task B, is based on an experiment. Potential customers initially wanted to buy clothes, prefer to donate the money instead, when they are presented with videos of the clothes manufacturing worker condition before paying. The respondents were required to give their opinion on why do people decided to change their minds. The responses statistics for both tasks are shown in Table 1.

	Task A	Task B
#Right Ans. Train	191(71%)	168(55%)
#Wrong Ans. Train	77(29%)	137(45%)
Avg. #Char	87.23	97.33
#Dev	215	244
#Test	855	974

Table 1: Summary statistics of the dataset.

---

[1]`https://github.com/aliakbars/ukara`

Proceedings of SustaiNLP: Workshop on Simple and Efficient Natural Language Processing, pages 1–7
Online, November 20, 2020. ©2020 Association for Computational Linguistics

3   Methodology

We split our approach into three categories. Firstly, we have a single classical approach, where we employed simple logistic regression and random forest. Next, we experimented with ensemble learning by combining four different classical machine learning algorithms. Finally, an LSTM-based neural network model is applied. We elaborate on the preprocessing and modeling steps in the following paragraphs.

3.1   Preprocessing

For the preprocessing steps, we first tokenized and lemmatized the text using Bahasa Indonesia tokenizer provided by spaCy (Honnibal and Montani, 2017). We then extracted the features using bag-of-words or TF-IDF. Since the resulting matrix from this feature extraction method tends to be sparse and to encode token relations, we applied Latent Semantic Analysis (LSA) using Singular Value Decomposition (SVD) (Deerwester et al., 1990) on the matrix.

Based on our observation, we noticed that the labels of the provided training set are highly inconsistent. Some responses are clearly labeled incorrectly. For illustration, in task A we found "*untuk pindah ke daerah yang aman*" (to move to a safe place) labelled as 1 (correct) while clearly it does not fit the criteria based on the guideline. The mislabeling was even more prominent in task B: "*karana dengan menyumbang kita bisa membuat produksi pakaian menjadi lebih beretika*" (By donating, we can make clothes production becomes more ethical) is considered wrong while "*agar upaya untuk membuat produksi pakaian menjadi lebih beretika.*" (As an effort to make clothes production becomes more ethical) is approved. To alleviate this issue, we decided to prepare a separate training set with manually corrected labels based on our own judgment. The correction result is shown in Table 2.

Finally, as the responses contain a lot of misspelled and slang words, we also experimented with simple spelling corrector using python difflib package and Indonesian colloquial dictionary (Salsabila et al., 2018). We tried every possible combination of preprocessing steps and whether to use an altered version of the training set with a parameter optimization library described in the following subsection.

	Original Label	Corrected Label	Count
Task A	wrong	right	10
	right	wrong	4
Task B	wrong	right	46
	right	wrong	13

Table 2: Corrected labels of the training set

3.2   Single Classical

After trying several machine learning algorithms, such as k-Nearest Neighbors, Naïve Bayes, logistic regression, and random forest, we found that random forest was the best model for task A. This corroborates what was found by Fernández-Delgado et al. (2014) in their comprehensive comparisons among several machine learning algorithms on different datasets. On the other hand, logistic regression with L2 regularization was the best for task B. The machine learning library used in this study is scikit-learn (Pedregosa et al., 2011). Since the dataset is quite small, we used 10-fold cross validation on the training set to avoid overfitting.

3.3   Ensemble Classical

In parallel, we experimented with ensemble model with a combination logistic regression, random forest, gradient boosting tree, and support vector machine. To find the best configuration for each model, we used hyperopt[2] library, which utilizes sequential model-based optimization (Bergstra et al., 2011). We trained separate voting-based ensemble models for task A and task B. The evaluation metric used for the optimization, including for the voting-ensemble model, is F1 score.

3.4   Deep Learning

Word embedding   We pretrained Word2vec (Mikolov et al., 2013) 100 dimension word embedding using Gensim (Řehůřek and Sojka, 2010) on Indonesian text from Wikipedia dumps[3], Opensubs (Lison and Tiedemann, 2016), and the preprocessed UKARA dataset. For the word count details, see Table 3. The addition of text from Opensubs and UKARA dataset helps in providing informal words that are usually absent in Wikipedia articles. With the additional datasets, we ended up with a total of 420,024 unique vocabularies.

---

[2] http://hyperopt.github.io/hyperopt/
[3] https://dumps.wikimedia.org

Data Source	Word Count
Opensubs	105,348,108
Wikipedia	101,251,643
UKARA	36,930
Total	206,636,681

Table 3: Word counts for each data source

Modelling We used Keras (Chollet et al., 2015) with Tensorflow (Abadi et al., 2015) as the backend to build the model. The text was tokenized and padded into maximum length of 43 (90th percentile of all short-answer length) before it goes into the model. In order to build the embedding layer, we performed a multi-stage text processing using PySastrawi[4] stemmer and a normalizer function (removing duplicate adjacent characters) to minimize the amount of unknown vocabularies. For the known word counts found in each stage, see Table 4. This multi-stage process yields a total of 2.426 known vocabularies and 390 unknown vocabularies. We fit the model with EarlyStopping and ReduceLROnPlateau callbacks and Adam optimizer.

Experiment We ran the experiment on RepeatedStratifiedKFold with 10 split and 10 repeats. For each split and repeat, we predicted the validation and test set. We later normalized the result according to how many predictions made, essentially performing ensemble of 100 different models.

Stage	Known Word Count
1: Raw Word	2310
2: Stemmed	65
3: Normalized	48
4: Stemmed	3

Table 4: The count of known word found in each stage of building the word embedding layer

4 Results

Best Configuration For the single classical approach, we found that setting the `n_estimators` to 200 yielded the best result on the development set. The rest of the hyperparameters followed the default values from the sklearn implementation, including for the logistic regression model. For the ensemble, we used four different algorithms: logistic regression, random forest, XGBoost, and

SVM. In this approach, we leave all the hyperparameters as optimized using hyperopt. We found that hard voting mechanism (weighing based on the binary class) provides better results compared to soft mechanism (weighted average of the predicted probability). Finally, for the deep learning approach, we altered the probability threshold for Task B to 0.48 as they gave better F1 for the development set.

Different preprocessing methods resulted in different performances in the two tasks. Therefore, we varied the use of unigram or TF-IDF, and whether we should apply SVD to the resulting matrix. On the other hand, we found that it is always better to use the lemmatizer built on top of spaCy in this task. Moreover, removing stopwords did not contribute much to the performance on the training set.

Performance The local CV results can be seen in Table 5 and Table 6. As the primary metric of this challenge is the F1 score, it is clear from Table 5 that we should employ the TF-IDF weighting with random forest algorithm for task A. From what we can see in Table 6, TF-IDF + SVD with logistic regression works better for task B. Table 7 shows the performance of our best single models compared to the ensemble approach. We used the optimized ensemble model trained on the original and also the label-corrected training set (Ens+Upd).

Training Time To quantify the required resources of each model, we include the total training time of each method in Table 8. We conducted the training for all models in the following specification: 2-core Intel(R) Xeon(R) CPU @ 2.20GHz and 16GB RAM. As expected, the deep learning method demanded the longest time, almost 6 hours for training word2vec, task A, and task B. Meanwhile, we needed less than 20 minutes to find the best performing single classical models for both tasks.

5 Discussion

Based on the results shown in Table 7, all models perform almost equally well for task A. For task B, the label correction in the Ens+Upd model gives a definite boost on the training set F1 score. This improvement indicates conflicting labeling for task B. However, the difference for the uncorrected development set is just 0.003: even with the corrected labels, the model still perform similarly for the

---

[4] https://github.com/har07/PySastrawi

	Precision	Recall	F1
1-gram+RF	0.830 ± 0.082	0.916 ± 0.057	0.870 ± 0.063
1-gram+logreg	0.850 ± 0.093	0.890 ± 0.084	0.868 ± 0.081
1-gram+SVD+RF	0.794 ± 0.030	$\mathbf{0.984 \pm 0.025}$	0.879 ± 0.021
1-gram+SVD+logreg	$\mathbf{0.858 \pm 0.080}$	0.884 ± 0.074	0.869 ± 0.065
TF-IDF+RF	0.833 ± 0.066	0.963 ± 0.036	$0.892 \pm 0.045^{**}$
TF-IDF+logreg	0.743 ± 0.040	0.979 ± 0.037	0.844 ± 0.035
TF-IDF+SVD+RF	0.778 ± 0.030	$\mathbf{0.984 \pm 0.025}$	0.869 ± 0.020
TF-IDF+SVD+logreg	0.746 ± 0.040	0.979 ± 0.037	0.846 ± 0.036
word2vec+BiLSTM	0.856 ± 0.063	0.934 ± 0.045	$\mathbf{0.900 \pm 0.034}^{*}$

Table 5: 10-fold cross validation results from task A

	Precision	Recall	F1
1-gram+RF	0.699 ± 0.081	0.649 ± 0.123	0.667 ± 0.086
1-gram+logreg	$\mathbf{0.724 \pm 0.072}$	0.732 ± 0.135	0.723 ± 0.087
1-gram+SVD+RF	0.655 ± 0.077	0.768 ± 0.094	0.703 ± 0.065
1-gram+SVD+logreg	0.706 ± 0.055	0.714 ± 0.117	0.707 ± 0.074
TF-IDF+RF	0.693 ± 0.059	0.697 ± 0.125	0.691 ± 0.084
TF-IDF+logreg	0.708 ± 0.082	0.845 ± 0.118	0.767 ± 0.080
TF-IDF+SVD+RF	0.671 ± 0.077	0.850 ± 0.100	0.744 ± 0.047
TF-IDF+SVD+logreg	0.715 ± 0.083	0.839 ± 0.110	$0.768 \pm 0.075^{**}$
word2vec+BiLSTM	0.705 ± 0.077	$\mathbf{0.884 \pm 0.086}$	$\mathbf{0.778 \pm 0.048}^{*}$

Table 6: 10-fold cross validation results from task B

	Train A	Train B	Dev	Test
Single	0.892	0.768	0.793	0.800
Ens+Ori	0.885	0.764	0.799	0.802
Ens+Upd	0.898	**0.831**	0.802	0.804
Deep learning	**0.900**	0.772	**0.806**	**0.811**

Table 7: F1 score comparison with the alternative ensemble models

	Word2Vec	Task A	Task B	Total
Single	—	**8.98**	**10.07**	**19.05**
Ens+Ori	—	36.53	36.70	73.23
Ens+Upd	—	44.45	45.78	90.23
Deep Learning	79.15	132.42	132.06	343.63

Table 8: Total training time for each method (in minutes)

holdout datasets. Since we did not observe significant improvement, we used only original labels to train the deep learning model.

To analyze how hard it is to separate the right from the wrong answers, we reduced the dimensionality of the data into 2D using 1-gram, SVD, and t-SNE (Maaten and Hinton, 2008). Figure 1 suggests that it is harder to separate the two answers in task B. On the other hand, we see more concentrated data points from wrong answers in task A. A similar phenomenon can also be observed in Figure 2 and Figure 3. We can see a lot more data points in the 0.4-0.6 prediction range in Figure 3.

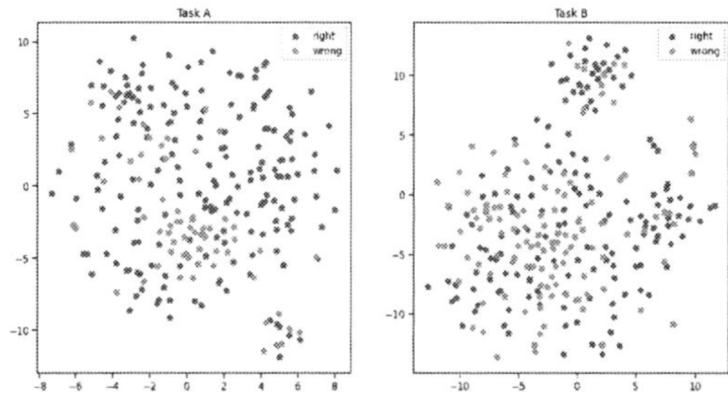

Figure 1: t-SNE visualisation

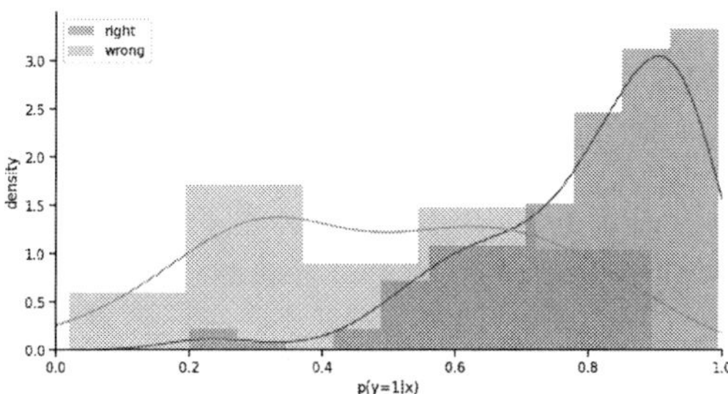

Figure 2: Single model prediction (random forest) with probability on Task A

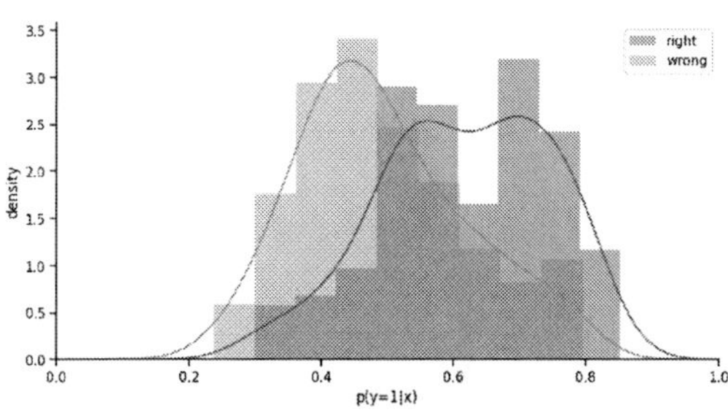

Figure 3: Single model prediction (logistic regression) with probability on Task B

6 Related Work

Studies of short-answer scoring methods range from using pattern matching (Mitchell et al., 2002; Leacock and Chodorow, 2003; Sukkarieh et al., 2004; Nielsen et al., 2009), semantic similarity (Mohler and Mihalcea, 2009; Mohler et al., 2011; Heilman and Madnani, 2013; Jimenez et al., 2013), to neural architectures (Riordan et al., 2017). Note that short-answer scoring tasks usually have shorter response length compared to essay scoring tasks (Riordan et al., 2017). Short-answer scoring focuses on content only instead of broader writing quality, such as elaboration, organization, and grammar (Burstein et al., 2013).

In semantic similarity, Mohler and Mihalcea (2009) compared TF-IDF, WordNet, and LSA-based models for short-answer scoring. Mohler et al. (2011) added graph alignment scores to add syntactic knowledge to improve the LSA-based model in the prior study. Sultan et al. (2016) and Baroni et al. (2014) introduced the use of word embedding using word2vec for this task. Our word2vec model is pretrained using a large collection of Indonesian text from Wikipedia dumps, Opensubs, and the preprocessed UKARA dataset. This makes our word embedding model different from what can be found in the previous work by Riordan et al. (2017).

In this study, we did not use WordNet due to the unavailability of a rich lexical similarity database in bahasa Indonesia. Moreover, in our shared task, the organiser also gave the binary labels for each answer and coding guidelines instead of the expected right answers.

7 Conclusions

In this report, we compare three approaches for automatic Indonesian short-answer scoring using the UKARA 1.0 dataset: single, ensemble, and deep learning. Albeit being more sophisticated, we found that the F1 score difference is insignificant when we compare the single model to the ensemble and the deep learning approach. The 1.1% increment in the deep learning model can help clinch the top position in a competition, but it is not worth the required resources for practical settings. We posit that the primary reason is due to the noisy labels. As the classical models require only $\frac{1}{18}$ of the total time to train deep learning models, we should use simple models and allocate more time for improving dataset quality.

References

Martín Abadi, Ashish Agarwal, Paul Barham, Eugene Brevdo, Zhifeng Chen, Craig Citro, Greg S. Corrado, Andy Davis, Jeffrey Dean, Matthieu Devin, Sanjay Ghemawat, Ian Goodfellow, Andrew Harp, Geoffrey Irving, Michael Isard, Yangqing Jia, Rafal Jozefowicz, Lukasz Kaiser, Manjunath Kudlur, Josh Levenberg, Dandelion Mané, Rajat Monga, Sherry Moore, Derek Murray, Chris Olah, Mike Schuster, Jonathon Shlens, Benoit Steiner, Ilya Sutskever, Kunal Talwar, Paul Tucker, Vincent Vanhoucke, Vijay Vasudevan, Fernanda Viégas, Oriol Vinyals, Pete Warden, Martin Wattenberg, Martin Wicke, Yuan Yu, and Xiaoqiang Zheng. 2015. TensorFlow: Large-scale machine learning on heterogeneous systems. Software available from tensorflow.org.

Marco Baroni, Georgiana Dinu, and Germán Kruszewski. 2014. Don't count, predict! a systematic comparison of context-counting vs. context-predicting semantic vectors. In *Proceedings of the 52nd Annual Meeting of the Association for Computational Linguistics (Volume 1: Long Papers)*, pages 238–247.

James S Bergstra, Rémi Bardenet, Yoshua Bengio, and Balázs Kégl. 2011. Algorithms for hyper-parameter optimization. In *Advances in neural information processing systems*, pages 2546–2554.

Jill Burstein, Joel Tetreault, and Nitin Madnani. 2013. The e-rater automated essay scoring system. *Handbook of automated essay evaluation: Current applications and new directions*, pages 55–67.

François Chollet et al. 2015. Keras. `https://keras.io`.

Scott Deerwester, Susan T Dumais, George W Furnas, Thomas K Landauer, and Richard Harshman. 1990. Indexing by latent semantic analysis. *Journal of the American society for information science*, 41(6):391–407.

Semire Dikli. 2006. An overview of automated scoring of essays. *The Journal of Technology, Learning and Assessment*, 5(1).

Manuel Fernández-Delgado, Eva Cernadas, Senén Barro, and Dinani Amorim. 2014. Do we need hundreds of classifiers to solve real world classification problems? *The Journal of Machine Learning Research*, 15(1):3133–3181.

Michael Heilman and Nitin Madnani. 2013. Ets: Domain adaptation and stacking for short answer scoring. In *Second Joint Conference on Lexical and Computational Semantics (* SEM), Volume 2: Proceedings of the Seventh International Workshop on Semantic Evaluation (SemEval 2013)*, pages 275–279.

Matthew Honnibal and Ines Montani. 2017. spaCy 2: Natural language understanding with Bloom embeddings, convolutional neural networks and incremental parsing. To appear.

Sergio Jimenez, Claudia Becerra, and Alexander Gelbukh. 2013. Softcardinality: Hierarchical text overlap for student response analysis. In *Second Joint Conference on Lexical and Computational Semantics (* SEM), Volume 2: Proceedings of the Seventh International Workshop on Semantic Evaluation (SemEval 2013)*, pages 280–284.

Claudia Leacock and Martin Chodorow. 2003. C-rater: Automated scoring of short-answer questions. *Computers and the Humanities*, 37(4):389–405.

P. Lison and J. Tiedemann. 2016. OpenSubtitles2016: Extracting Large Parallel Corpora from Movie and TV Subtitles. In *Proceedings of the 10th International Conference on Language Resources and Evaluation (LREC 2016)*.

Laurens van der Maaten and Geoffrey Hinton. 2008. Visualizing data using t-sne. *Journal of machine learning research*, 9(Nov):2579–2605.

Tomas Mikolov, Kai Chen, Greg Corrado, and Jeffrey Dean. 2013. Efficient estimation of word representations in vector space.

Tom Mitchell, Terry Russell, Peter Broomhead, and Nicola Aldridge. 2002. Towards robust computerised marking of free-text responses. In *Proceedings of the 6th CAA Conference*. Loughborough University.

Michael Mohler, Razvan Bunescu, and Rada Mihalcea. 2011. Learning to grade short answer questions using semantic similarity measures and dependency graph alignments. In *Proceedings of the 49th annual meeting of the association for computational linguistics: Human language technologies*, pages 752–762.

Michael Mohler and Rada Mihalcea. 2009. Text-to-text semantic similarity for automatic short answer grading. In *Proceedings of the 12th Conference of the European Chapter of the Association for Computational Linguistics*, pages 567–575. Association for Computational Linguistics.

Rodney D Nielsen, Wayne Ward, and James H Martin. 2009. Recognizing entailment in intelligent tutoring systems. *Natural Language Engineering*, 15(4):479–501.

F. Pedregosa, G. Varoquaux, A. Gramfort, V. Michel, B. Thirion, O. Grisel, M. Blondel, P. Prettenhofer, R. Weiss, V. Dubourg, J. Vanderplas, A. Passos, D. Cournapeau, M. Brucher, M. Perrot, and E. Duchesnay. 2011. Scikit-learn: Machine learning in Python. *Journal of Machine Learning Research*, 12:2825–2830.

Radim Řehůřek and Petr Sojka. 2010. Software Framework for Topic Modelling with Large Corpora. In *Proceedings of the LREC 2010 Workshop on New Challenges for NLP Frameworks*, pages 45–50, Valletta, Malta. ELRA.

Brian Riordan, Andrea Horbach, Aoife Cahill, Torsten Zesch, and Chungmin Lee. 2017. Investigating neural architectures for short answer scoring. In *Proceedings of the 12th Workshop on Innovative Use of NLP for Building Educational Applications*, pages 159–168.

Nikmatun Aliyah Salsabila, Yosef Ardhito Winatmoko, Ali Akbar Septiandri, and Ade Jamal. 2018. Colloquial indonesian lexicon. In *2018 International Conference on Asian Language Processing (IALP)*, pages 226–229. IEEE.

Jana Z Sukkarieh, Stephen G Pulman, and Nicholas Raikes. 2004. Auto-marking 2: An update on the ucles-oxford university research into using computational linguistics to score short, free text responses. *International Association of Educational Assessment, Philadephia.*

Md Arafat Sultan, Cristobal Salazar, and Tamara Sumner. 2016. Fast and easy short answer grading with high accuracy. In *Proceedings of the 2016 Conference of the North American Chapter of the Association for Computational Linguistics: Human Language Technologies*, pages 1070–1075.

Rank and run-time aware compression of NLP Applications

Urmish Thakker
SambaNova Systems
uthakker@cs.wisc.edu

Jesse Beu
Arm ML Research

Dibakar Gope
Arm ML Research

Ganesh Dasika
AMD Research

Matthew Mattina
Arm ML Research

Abstract

Sequence model based NLP applications can be large. Yet, many applications that benefit from them run on small devices with very limited compute and storage capabilities, while still having run-time constraints. As a result, there is a need for a compression technique that can achieve significant compression without negatively impacting inference run-time and task accuracy. This paper proposes a new compression technique called Hybrid Matrix Factorization that achieves this dual objective. HLF improves low-rank matrix factorization (LMF) techniques by doubling the rank of the matrix using an intelligent hybrid-structure leading to better accuracy than LMF. Further, by preserving dense matrices, it leads to faster inference run-time than pruning or structure matrix based compression technique. We evaluate the impact of this technique on 5 NLP benchmarks across multiple tasks (Translation, Intent Detection, Language Modeling) and show that for similar accuracy values and compression factors, HLF can achieve more than $2.32\times$ faster inference run-time than pruning and 16.77% better accuracy than LMF.

1 Introduction

Sequence based (LSTMs/GRUs) NLP Applications are being increasingly run on mobile phones and smart watches. They are typically enabled by querying a cloud-based system to do most of the computation. The energy, latency, and privacy implications associated with running a query on the cloud is changing where users run a neural network application. We should, therefore, expect an increase in the number of NLP applications running on embedded devices. Due to the energy and power constraints of edge devices, embedded SoCs frequently use lower-bandwidth memory technologies and smaller caches compared to desktop and server processors. Thus, there is a need for good compression techniques to enable large NLP models to fit into an smaller edge device or ensure that they run efficiently on devices with smaller caches (Thakker et al., 2019b). Additionally, compressing models should not negatively impact the inference run-time as these tasks may have real-time deadlines to provide a good user experience.

In order to choose a compression scheme for a particular network, one needs to consider 3 different axes – the compression factor, the inference run-time speedup over the baseline, and the accuracy. Ideally, a good compression algorithm should not sacrifice improvement along one axis for improvement along another. For example, network pruning (Han et al., 2016) has shown to be an effective compression technique, but pruning creates a sparse matrix representation that is inefficient to execute on most modern CPUs. Our analysis shows that pruned networks can achieve a faster run-time than the baseline only for significantly high compression factors. Low-rank matrix factorization (LMF) is another popular compression technique that can achieve speedup proportional to the compression factor. However, LMF has had mixed results in maintaining model accuracy (Grachev et al., 2017; Chen et al., 2018; Lu et al., 2016). This is because LMF reduces the rank of a matrix significantly, reducing its expressibility (Yang et al., 2018). Lastly, structured matrices (Ding et al., 2018) can also be used to compress neural networks. While these techniques show a significant reduction in computation, this reduction only translates to a realized run-time improvement for large matrices (Thomas et al., 2018) or while using specialized hardware (Li et al., 2018; Sindhwani et al., 2015). For benchmarks evaluated in this paper, HLF gets $30\times$ speed-up improvement over structured matrix based technique (Sindhwani et al., 2015).

Proceedings of SustaiNLP: Workshop on Simple and Efficient Natural Language Processing, pages 8–18
Online, November 20, 2020. ©2020 Association for Computational Linguistics

Given LMF's good run-time characteristics, it can potentially act as an alternative to pruning. However, LMF leads to an accuracy loss. **To overcome the problem of finding an alternative to pruning, which preserves the run-time benefit of dense structures of LMF and the accuracy benefits of pruned networks, we introduce a new compression technique called Hybrid Matrix Factorization (HLF). HLF can act as an effective compression technique for NLP edge use cases on embedded CPUs.** The results are very promising – HLF achieves iso-accuracy for a large compression factor ($2\times$ to $4\times$), improves the CPU run-time over pruning by a factor of $2.32\times$ and can achieve 16.77% better model accuracy than LMF and 9% better accuracy than smaller baselines.

2 Related Work

Pruning (Han et al., 2016; Zhu and Gupta, 2017; Sanh et al., 2020) has been the most successful compression technique for all types of neural networks. Poor hardware characteristics of pruning has led to research in block based pruning technique (Narang et al., 2017). However, block based pruning technique also requires certain amount of block sparsity to achieve faster run-time than baseline. Having a strict compression factor requirement to get better run-time is a stringent constraint that HLF manages to avoid.

Structured matrices have shown significant potential for compression of NN (Sindhwani et al., 2015; Ding et al., 2018; Wang et al., 2018; Ding et al., 2017; Cheng et al., 2015; Thakker et al., 2020). Block circular compression is an extension of structured matrix based compression technique, converting every block in a matrix into structured matrix. We will show in this paper that HLF is a superior technique than block circular decomposition.

Tensor decomposition (CP decomposition, Kronecker, Tucker decomposition etc) based methods have also shown significant reduction in parameters (Tjandra et al., 2017; Thakker et al., 2019c,a). Matrix Factorization (Kuchaiev and Ginsburg, 2017; Chen et al., 2018; Grachev et al., 2017; Thakker et al., 2019) can be categorized under this topic. We will show in this paper that HLF can lead to better accuracy than LMF compressed RNNs.

Quantization is another popular technique for compression (Hubara et al., 2017, 2016; Gope et al., 2020a; Sanh et al., 2019; Liu et al., 2018; Gope et al., 2020b, 2019). Networks compressed using HLF can be further compressed using quantization.

Dynamic techniques are used to improve inference run-time of RNNs by skipping certain RNN state updates (Campos et al., 2018; Seo et al., 2018; Yu et al., 2017; Tao et al., 2019). These techniques are based on the assumption that not all inputs to a RNN are needed for final classification task. Thus we can learn a small and fast predictor that can learn to skip certain inputs and its associated computation. HLF technique is orthogonal to this technique and networks compressed using HLF can be further optimized using this technique.

Design of efficient structures for LSTM/GRU cells like SRU (Lei et al., 2018), QRNN (Bradbury et al., 2016) and PRU (Mehta et al., 2018) have also led to networks with faster inference run-time benefits or lesser number of parameters. These structures are different from structured matrices and are hand-crafted after better understanding the application domain. HLF can be further used to optimize the matrices in these architectures to make the resultant network more parameter and run-time efficient.

Finally, any technique used to reduce the parameter footprint of embedding matrices in NLP can further optimize RNN networks optimized using HLF (Acharya et al., 2019; Mehta et al., 2019). In this paper, we show that HLF can compress networks with compressed word embedding layers.

3 Hybrid Matrix Factorization

3.1 Why LMF can potentially lead to loss in accuracy

LMF (Kuchaiev and Ginsburg, 2017) expresses a larger matrix $A \in R^{m \times n}$ as a product of two smaller matrices $U \in R^{m \times r}$ and $V \in R^{r \times n}$, respectively. Parameter r controls the compression factor. Unlike pruning, matrix factorization is able to improve the run-time over the baseline for most compression factors. Unfortunately, compression via LMF can lead to loss in accuracy. We believe, this is because of two closely related reasons:

- **Rank-Loss**: The rank of a matrix is a measure of the expressibility of a matrix. A lower rank matrix means less expressibility, limiting its learning capacity. This can potentially lead to some accuracy loss. LMF compression leads to a lower ranked matrix. While before compression, the rank of matrix **A** is $min(m, n)$, after compression, it becomes $min(m, n, d)$. Eg - If A $\in R^{256 \times 256}$, compression using LMF by a factor of 2 leads to $U \in R^{256 \times 64}$ and $V \in R^{64 \times 256}$. The resultant compressed matrix A $(= U * V)$ is a 64 rank matrix. Thus, in order to compress the matrix by a factor of 2, LMF reduces the rank of a matrix by a factor of 4.

- **Less expressive output features**: A closely related argument can be viewed when we extend the idea of low-rank matrix and its impact on the output features. Without loss of generality, an LSTM/GRU layer calculates a matrix-vector product during inference. If we assume the parameters of a LSTM/GRU layer are represented by a matrix $A \in R^{m \times n}$ and the input to the matrix is $x \in R^{n \times 1}$, then the output feature calculated is -

$$y = f(A * x)$$
$$where, \ y \in R^{m \times 1}$$

. f is a non-linear function. Thus, each element of y is a dot product of a row of A and the vector x followed by non-linearity. LMF expresses A in a lower dimensional space using the U and V matrix. If we rewrite the equation to calculate y, when **A** is expressed using LMF, we get -

$$y = f(U * V * x) \tag{1}$$
$$y = f(U * k) \ (assuming \ k = V * x) \tag{2}$$
$$where, \ k \in R^{r \times 1} \tag{3}$$

Generally, for compression $r < m, n$. Thus, x $\in R^{n \times 1}$ is projected to a lower dimensional embedding of size $R^{d \times 1}$ and expanded again to $R^{m \times 1}$ to create y. Thus, compressing **A** to a lower rank leads to output features calculated from a lower dimension embedding vector.

3.2 Hybrid Matrix Factorization

This paper introduces a new compression technique that uses dense matrix representation to ensure fast run-time properties and avoids making the strong assumptions made by LMF. This technique is based on three assumptions -

- **A1:** Rank of a matrix is important to create a high-task accuracy LSTM/GRU network (Yang et al., 2018)

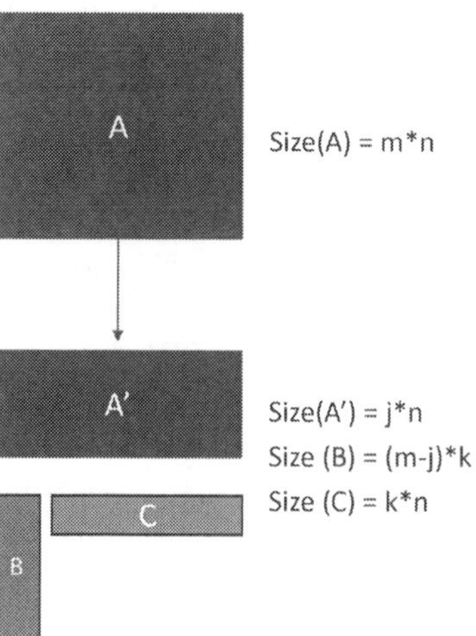

Figure 1: Representation of a matrix using hybrid factorization

- **A2:** LMF makes a strong assumption that all the elements of the output feature vector of a LSTM/GRU Cell can be expressed from a low-dimensional embedding vector (Equation 2). HLF is based on the assumption that a more relaxed constraint of having a hybrid output feature vector, where some elements are calculated from a lower dimensional embedding space and other's from a higher dimensional embedding space can lead to better accuracy.

- **A3:** Most LSTM/GRU networks are followed by a fully-connected softmax layer or another LSTM/GRU layer. Even if the order of the elements in the output of a particular RNN layer changes, the weights in the subsequent fully connected or LSTM/GRU layers can adjust to accommodate that. Thus, the order of the elements of the output vector of LSTM/GRU layer is not strictly important.

These three intuitions of a LSTM/GRU layer can be used to create a more hardware-friendly compression scheme. This paper introduces one such scheme – Hybrid Matrix Factorization.

Hybrid Matrix Factorization (HLF) splits the input and recurrent matrices in an LSTM/GRU layer into two parts – a fully parameterized upper part and low-rank lower part.

Figure 1 shows the strategy we use to decompose the matrix - an unconstrained upper half A' and a lower half that is composed of k rank-1 blocks. If we decompose the weight matrix using this tech-

Algorithm 1 Matrix vector product when a matrix uses the HLF technique

---

Input 1: Matrices A' of dimension $j \times n$, B of dimension $(m - j) \times k$, C of dimension $k \times n$)
Input 2: Vector I of dimension $n \times 1$
Output: Matrix O of dimension $m \times 1$

1: $O_{1:j} \leftarrow A' \times I$
2: $Temp1 \leftarrow C \times I$
3: $O_{j+1:m} \leftarrow B \times Temp1$
4: $O = concatenate\{O_{1:j}, O_{j+1:m}\}$

Matrix of Size (256,256)		
Compression Factor	LMF	HLF
1.25	102	103 - 204
1.67	76	78 - 153
2.50	51	52 - 101
5.00	25	26 - 50

Table 1: The maximum possible rank of a 256×256 sized matrix after it is compressed by 4 different factors using 3 different compression techniques. To compress a matrix by a given compression factor, HLF has 2 different parameters j and k to regulate the rank of the matrix. Hence, we see a range of rank values. Maximum rank is achieved when k=1. The value for j when k=1 can be calculated for different compression factors using equation 4.

nique, the parameter reduction is given by:

$$\frac{m \times n}{(j \times n) + k \times (m - j + n)} \quad (4)$$

Thus, the maximum rank of the matrix becomes $j + k$. Different values of j and k can be used to control the amount of compression and the rank of the matrix.

Structuring a matrix as shown in Figure 1 can lead to significant increase in maximum rank of the compressed matrix. Table-1 shows the maximum possible rank of a 256×256 matrix compressed to the same number of parameters using the two compression techniques - LMF and HLF. As shown, HLF can effectively double the rank of the matrix for the same number of parameters. To compress a matrix by a given compression factor, HLF has 2 different parameters, j and k, to regulate the rank of the matrix. Hence, we see a range of rank values. Maximum rank is achieved when k=1. The value for j when k=1 can be calculated for different compression factors using equation 4.

Apart from the storage reduction, HLF also leads to a reduction in the number of computations. Assuming a batch size of 1 during inference, HLF leads to inference speed-up by using the associative property of matrix products to calculate the matrix-vector product - Algorithm 1 shows how to calculate the matrix vector product when the matrix is represented using HLF. This algorithm avoids expanding the matrix A', B and C into A.

Algorithm 1 uses the associative property of matrix products to gain the computation speedup. For a matrix vector product between a matrix of size $m \times n$ and a vector of size $n \times 1$, the number of operations required to compute the product is $m \times n$ (Trefethen and Bau, 1997). Referring to Algorithm 1, number of operations required to calculate $O_{1:j}$ is $j \times n$. The Temp1 variables need $k * n$ operations and calculating $O_{j+1:m}$ needs k*(m-j) operations. Thus, the reduction in number of operations when we use Algorithm 1 is:

$$\frac{m \times n}{j \times n + k \times n + k \times (m - j)} \quad (5)$$

3.2.1 Impact on output feature vector

Algorithm 1 shows that, HLF divides the output into two stacked sub-vectors. One is a result of a fully-parameterized multiplication, $A' \times I$ (Line 1, Algorithm 1). The other is the result of the low rank multiplication : $B \times C \times I$ (Line 2-3, Algorithm 1). Thus, the upper sub-vector has "richer" features created from a higher dimensional embedding, while the lower sub vector has "constrained" features created from a lower dimensional embedding. By incorporating the HLF structure during training, we force an RNN to learn "richer" features in the upper sub-vector and the "constrained" features in the lower sub-vector. Because a RNN is followed by another RNN or a softmax layer, this restructuring should not impact the subsequent layers. *Thus, HLF structure combines the assumptions A2 and A3 that were discussed previously.*

3.3 Why HLF leads to larger rank than LMF for same number of parameters?

HLF is an extension of LMF. To understand this, let us revisit Figure 1, where the matrix

$$A = [A' \; ; \; BC]$$

where $A \in R^{m \times n}$, $A' \in R^{j \times n}$, $B \in R^{(m-j) \times k}$ and $C \in R^{k \times n}$. Then we can rewrite the matrix as,

$$A = [I \, , \, \mathbf{0_1}; \mathbf{0_2} \, , \, B][A' \, ; \, C]$$

where $I \in R^{j \times j}$, $\mathbf{0_1} \in R^{j \times k}$ and $\mathbf{0_2} \in R^{(m-j) \times j}$. The above equation could be re-written as -

$$A = U'V'$$

where $U' \in R^{m \times (j+k)}$ and $V' \in R^{(j+k) \times n}$. Both U' and V' can have a maximum rank of $j + k$. The maximum value of this rank is achieved when k=1 and j is calculated as discussed in Table 1. Let this value be d. A standard LMF decomposition of A will also lead to a representation of the form UV, but this representation will have same parameters as HLF only if the rank of both U and V is at most $(d+1)/2$. Thus, HLF can be regarded as a $(d+1)$ ranked LMF of A, with a sparsity forcing mask that reduces the number of parameters to express the $(d+1)$ ranked matrix significantly. **This is why HLF can double the rank of the matrix when compared to an iso-parameter LMF matrix.**

Neural networks seldom learn structured sparsity unless they are forced to (Narang et al., 2017), thus, an RNN trained with the LMF structure will rarely end up learning the same structure as HLF. **The pre-determined HLF structure effectively creates a sparsity forcing mask.** Such a sparsity forcing mask also leads to creation of the decoupled output feature vectors as described in section 3.2.1.

4 Results

We compare HLF with LMF and 3 other compression techniques – model pruning, small baseline and a structured matrix based technique called block circular decomposition. These techniques and why they need to be considered are discussed below:

- Pruning: Model pruning (Zhu and Gupta, 2017) induces sparsity in the matrices of a neural network, thereby reducing the number of non-zero valued parameters that need to be stored. Pruning creates sparse matrices which are stored in a specialized sparse data structure such as CSR. The overhead of traversing these data structures while performing the matrix-vector multiplication can lead to poorer inference run-time than when executing the baseline, non-sparse network. *Thus, while pruning*

is an effective compression technique, its runtime performance on CPUs can make it a less appealing choice for compression. We use the magnitude pruning framework provided by (Zhu and Gupta, 2017). While there are other possible ways to prune, recent work (Gale et al., 2019) has suggested that magnitude pruning provides state-of-the-art or comparable performance when compared to other pruning techniques (Neklyudov et al., 2017; Louizos et al., 2018).

- Small Baseline: Additionally, we train a smaller baseline with the number of parameters equal to that of the compressed baseline. This serves as a useful point of comparison because of two reasons.

  - First, to check if compression of a larger network leads to better accuracy than compressing a network by reducing its dimensions (size of hidden layer or number of layers). **This can help us verify if the network was originally overparameterized.**
  - Second, **to establish the hypothesis whether HLF's creation of a stacked output feature vector as described in section 3.2.1 adds any useful information in the network.** Smaller baseline creates output feature vector that is created from a high-dimensional embedding only. HLF, additionally concatenates the output features created from lower dimensional embedding. Thus, comparing the accuracy of HLF with Smaller baseline helps evaluate the usefulness of the output features created using lower dimensional embedding.

Given the significant slow-down of inference of BCD compressed networks, we do not discuss the results sing BCD compression in the rest of the paper.

4.1 Experiment Setup

Measuring inference run-time: In order to compare the inference run-time of RNN cells compressed using pruning, LMF and HLF, we implemented these cells in C++ using the Eigen library. This paper focuses on inference on an edge device. As a result, we make the assumption that the batch size of the application will be 1 while

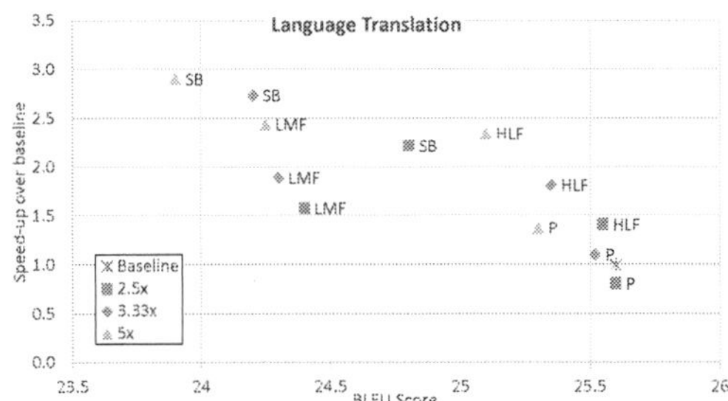 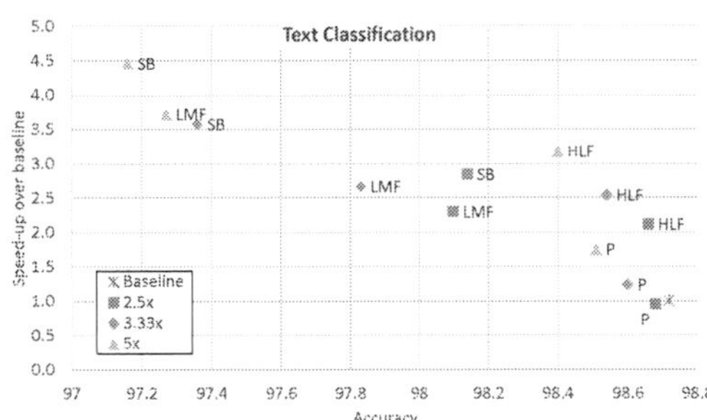

(a) For both figures, HLF exists in the top-right corner, providing the best trade-off in terms of accuracy, compression and speed-up. For all 3 compression points, HLF provides better accuracy than LMF and SB and better run-time than pruning. *(Left) Language Translation:* **HLF improves the BLEU score achieved by LMF by 2.3% to 4.5% and by Small Baseline by 2.8% to 4.1%. At the same time, HLF improves the inference run-time over pruning by** $1.5 - 1.74\times$. *(Right) Text Classification:* **HLF can improve the accuracy achieved by LMF by up-to 1.2% and SB by up-to 1.3% and improve the run-time achieved by pruning by up-to** $1.2\times$

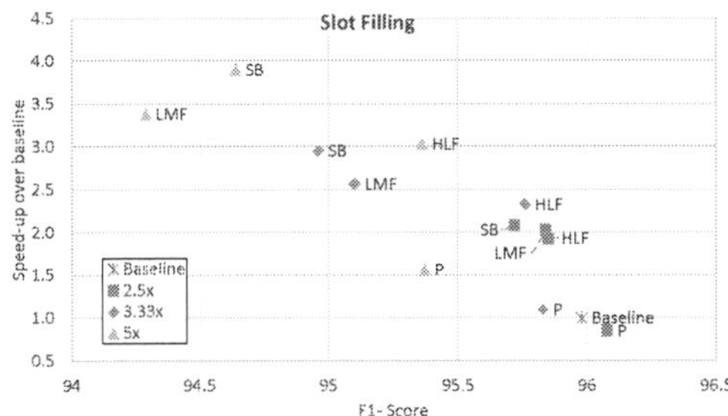 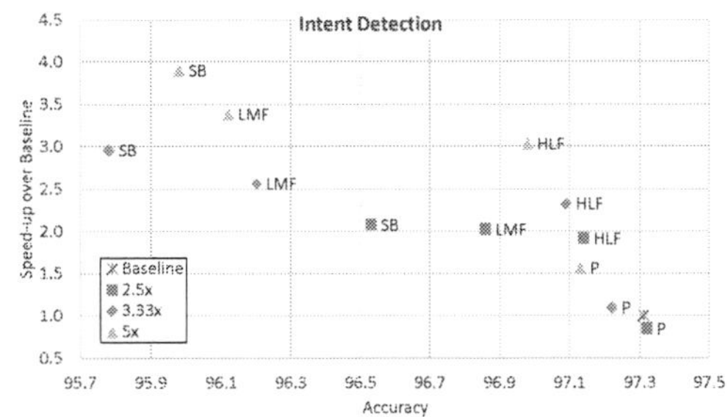

(b) For both figures, HLF exists in the top-right corner, providing the best trade-off in terms of accuracy, compression and speed-up. *(Left) Slot Filling:* For all 3 compression points, HLF provides better accuracy than LMF and SB and better run-time than pruning. **HLF can improve the accuracy achieved by LMF and SB by up-to 1.2% and improve the run-time achieved by pruning by up-to** $1.26\times$. *(Right) Intent Detection:* For all 3 compression points, HLF provides better accuracy than LMF and SB and better run-time than pruning. **HLF can improve the accuracy achieved by LMF and SB by up-to 1% and improve the run-time achieved by pruning by up-to** $1.26\times$

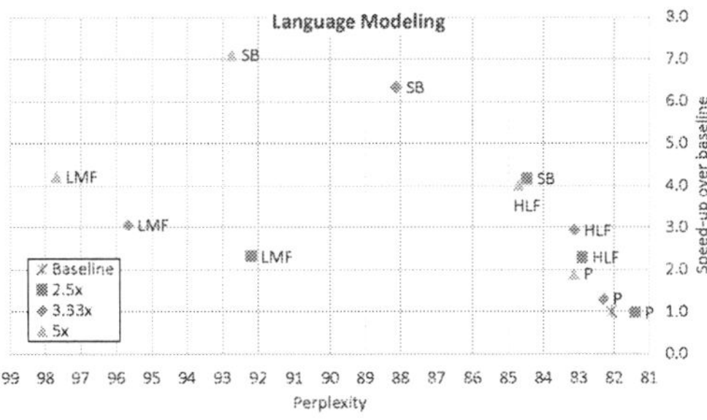

(c) Language Modeling: For LM, lower values of perplexity are better. HLF provides a viable alternative to both pruning and LMF at compression factors of 2.5x, 3.0x and 5x. **HLF can achieve 17% better perplexity than LMF, 9% better perplexity than small baseline and** $2.32\times$ **better inference run-time than pruning.**

Figure 2: Speed-up over baseline vs Accuracy comparing the baseline with a smaller baseline and the baseline compressed using different compression schemes at varying compression factors. Speed-up values > 1 indicate a decrease in inference run-time and values < 1 indicate an increase in inference run-time. **For each compression factor, the compression scheme that is most to the top-right is the ideal choice.** *In case of perplexity, lower values are better.* Thus, the graphs are plotted in a slightly different way to still adhere to the fact that the most ideal choice of compression is in the top-right corner. P = Pruning, LMF = Low rank matrix factorization, HLF = Hybrid matrix decomposition, SB = Smaller baseline. **The best way to view this figure is to either focus on a compression point and see how the Pareto curve of speed-up vs accuracy changes as we add HLF or focus on an accuracy region and see what compression schemes provides the best run-time at highest compression factor.**

13

measuring the run-time of an application. However, the observations regarding run-time should remain consistent for larger batch sizes as well. We ran our experiments on a single cortex-A73 core of the Hikey 960 board. The size of L3 cache is 2MB.

Training infrastructure: We use Tensorflow 1.14 to train our networks on a cluster of 2 RTX 2080 Ti NVidia GPUs with 11 GB Memory. The training settings for the benchmarks evaluated can be found in the reference paper for each benchmark.

What do we compress? We compress the LSTM/GRU layers in each application. We do not compress the embedding layers using HLF.

The amount of compression determines the rank of the compressed matrices when we use LMF to compress an NLP application and the sparsity of the pruned matrix when we use pruning as our choice of compression technique. Similar to LMF, the amount of compression determines the rank of the compressed matrices when we use HLF as our choice of compression. However, for HLF two parameters j and k control the rank of the matrix. We use a sweep starting with k=1 to determine the exact values of j and k that help us achieve a good accuracy.

What do we compare?: We compare the accuracy and inference run-time of all compression technologies at iso-compression factors for various compression techniques.

4.2 Comparison of compression techniques across different ML tasks

The impact of compression on accuracy is compared for 5 benchmarks – machine translation, natural language understanding (intent detection and slot filling), text classification and Language Modeling. These tasks are some of the most important NLP applications that run on edge and embedded devices like smart phones, smart watches and smart homes.

4.2.1 Language Translation

We use the English to Vietnamese translation model in (Luong et al., 2017). The model uses 2-layer LSTMs of size 512 units with bidirectional encoder (i.e., 1 bidirectional layers for the encoder), embedding of dim 512 and an attention layer. We used the hyper-parameters in (Luong et al., 2017) to train the network while modifying the learning rate values used. We sweep the learning rates values from

$\times 0.1$ to 3.0 in multiples of 3. For HLF, we used the value of k=2.

Figure 2a shows the results of compressing the LSTM layers in the NMT_VIEN baseline by $2.5\times$, $3.33\times$ and $5\times$. **HLF improves the BLEU score achieved by LMF by 2.3% to 4.5% and by Small Baseline by 2.8% to 4.1%. At the same time, HLF improves the inference run-time over pruning by** $1.5 \times -1.74\times$.

4.2.2 Language Modeling

We use the medium LM model from (Zaremba et al., 2014) as our baseline. The PTB (Medium) baseline has 2 LSTM layers each with a hidden vector of size 650 with a vocabulary size of 10,000 words from the English vocabulary. We used the hyper-parameters in (Zaremba et al., 2014) and train the compressed networks for 50 more epochs than in baseline. The baseline network is trained for 39 epochs. For the first 6 epochs the learning rate used is of value 1, and after that we decrease it by a factor of 1.2 after each epoch. We clip the norm of the gradients at 5 and use dropout of value 0.35. For HLF, we used the value of k=4.

Figure 2c shows the results of compressing the LSTM layers in the PTB (Medium) baseline by $2.5\times$, $3.33\times$ and $5\times$. Lower the perplexity, better the model. Pruning achieves the same (sometimes better) perplexity than baseline and other compression techniques. LMF leads to significant loss in perplexity for all compression factors while HLF achieves better perplexity than LMF and faster inference run-time than baseline and pruned networks for all compression factors. **In fact, HLF can achieve 17% better perplexity than LMF, 9% better perplexity than small baseline and** $2.32\times$ **better inference run-time than pruning**. The preferred choice of compression scheme for different compression factors will depend on whether slight loss in perplexity can be accommodated for faster inference run-time or not. However, HLF still manages to serve as a more viable alternative to pruning than LMF for inference on edge CPUs.

4.2.3 Text Classification

We use the text classification network in (Zhou et al., 2016) evaluated on the SemEval-2010 dataset. The baseline network has 1 bidirectional LSTM layers with hidden vector of size 256. We used the hyper-parameters in (Zhou et al., 2016) to train the baseline and as the initial hyperparameters explored for the compressed networks. We trained the compressed networks for additional 20 epochs while exploring learning rates of $10\times$ and $1/10$ than the baseline learning rate. The baseline model was trained using AdaDelta with a learning rate of 1.0. The model parameters were regularized with L2 regularization strength of $10^{-}5$.

Figure 2b shows the results for compressing the text classification network by $2.5\times - 5\times$. **HLF can improve the accuracy achieved by LMF by up-to 1.2%, by SB by up-to 1.3% and improve the run-time achieved by pruning by almost** $1.20\times$.

4.2.4 Intent Detection and Slot Filling

We used the benchmark published in (Liu and Lane, 2016). This benchmark is trained on the ATIS dataset and jointly trains for intent detection and slot filling. The benchmark uses 1 LSTM layer of size 128 along with attention layers. For HLF, we used the value of k=1.

Figure 2b shows the results for slot filling task. **HLF can improve the F1-accuracy achieved by LMF and SB by up-to 1.2% and improve the run-time achieved by pruning by up-to** $1.26\times$. Figure 2b shows the result for the intent classi-fication task. Due to joint training, the network used for slot filling and intent classification is the same. As a result, the runtime improvement of HLF over pruning is exactly the same as for the slot filling task. **Additionally, HLF improves the intent classification accuracy by up to 1% over LMF and small baseline.**

4.3 Ablation Studies

4.3.1 Compressing Word Embedding layers using HLF

We compressed the input word-embedding layers in the PTB-LM model discussed in section 4.2.2, without compressing other layers in the network. However, even $3\times$ compression using HLF led to 8% loss in perplexity score.

4.3.2 Orthogonality of word embedding compression methods and HLF

We ran experiments where we prune the word em-bedding layers in the PTB-LM model in section 4.2.2 by $2\times$ while keeping the LSTM layers uncom-pressed, leading to 83.1 perplexity score. We were able to further compress this network by $2\times$ using HLF with only 1 point loss in perplexity score, in-dicating that HLF is compatible with techniques used for compressing word-embedding layers.

5 Discussion

Effectively, HLF acts as an alternative to LMF whenever compression using pruning does not lead to the required run-time benefit and LMF leads to loss in accuracy. HLF has a better accuracy than LMF for most evaluation points, validating the as-sumption in the paper that rank of a matrix in a RNN is important for better task accuracy in NLP applications. Additionally, HLF has a better ac-curacy than smaller baseline. This validates the assumption of the importance of constrained fea-tures in addition to the richer features in a Small Baseline network.

6 Limitations

While HLF provides significant benefits over LMF, there are two limitations associated with the tech-nique:

- The unique nature of RNNs (Assumption A1-A3) makes HLF a natural fit for LSTM/GRU layers. However, these assumptions are not valid for the final classification layer. In clas-sification layer, HLF will lead to more expres-sive output for certain classes (the top part of HLF matrix) in the dataset and less expressive output for the rest of the classes (bottom part of HLF matrix).

- HLF is a training aware compression and can-not be applied to a pre-trained network.

7 Conclusion

Choosing the right compression technique requires looking at three criteria – compression factor, accu-racy, and run-time. Pruning is an effective compres-sion technique, but can sacrifice speedup over base-line for certain compression factors. LMF achieves better speedup than baseline for all compression factors, but leads to accuracy degradation. This paper introduces a new compression scheme called HLF, which preserves the dense structures of LMF while effectively doubling the rank of the matrix using an intelligent structure by design. This leads to $2\times$ faster inference run-time than pruning and up-to 16% better accuracy than LMF.

References

Anish Acharya, Rahul Goel, Angeliki Metallinou, and Inderjit Dhillon. 2019. Online embedding compres-sion for text classification using low rank matrix factorization. In *Proceedings of the AAAI Conference on Artificial Intelligence*, volume 33, pages 6196–6203.

James Bradbury, Stephen Merity, Caiming Xiong, and Richard Socher. 2016. Quasi-recurrent neural networks. *CoRR*, abs/1611.01576.

Víctor Campos, Brendan Jou, Xavier Giró-i Nieto, Jordi Torres, and Shih-Fu Chang. 2018. Skip rnn: Learning to skip state updates in recurrent neural networks. In *International Conference on Learning Representations*.

Ting Chen, Ji Lin, Tian Lin, Song Han, Chong Wang, and Denny Zhou. 2018. Adaptive mixture of low-rank factorizations for compact neural modeling. *Advances in neural information processing systems (CDNNRIA workshop)*.

Y. Cheng, F. X. Yu, R. S. Feris, S. Kumar, A. Choudhary, and S. Chang. 2015. An exploration of parameter redundancy in deep networks with circulant projections. In *2015 IEEE International Conference on Computer Vision (ICCV)*, pages 2857–2865.

Caiwen Ding, Siyu Liao, Yanzhi Wang, Zhe Li, Ning Liu, Youwei Zhuo, Chao Wang, Xuehai Qian, Yu Bai, Geng Yuan, Xiaolong Ma, Yipeng Zhang, Jian Tang, Qinru Qiu, Xue Lin, and Bo Yuan. 2017. Circnn: Accelerating and compressing deep neural networks using block-circulant weight matrices. In *Proceedings of the 50th Annual IEEE/ACM International Symposium on Microarchitecture*, MICRO-50 '17, pages 395–408, New York, NY, USA. ACM.

Caiwen Ding, Ao Ren, Geng Yuan, Xiaolong Ma, Jiayu Li, Ning Liu, Bo Yuan, and Yanzhi Wang. 2018. Structured weight matrices-based hardware accelerators in deep neural networks: Fpgas and asics. In *Proceedings of the 2018 on Great Lakes Symposium on VLSI*, GLSVLSI '18, pages 353–358, New York, NY, USA. ACM.

Trevor Gale, Erich Elsen, and Sara Hooker. 2019. The state of sparsity in deep neural networks. *CoRR*, abs/1902.09574.

Dibakar Gope, Jesse Beu, Urmish Thakker, and Matthew Mattina. 2020a. Ternary mobilenets via per-layer hybrid filter banks. In *Proceedings of the IEEE/CVF Conference on Computer Vision and Pattern Recognition (CVPR) Workshops*.

Dibakar Gope, Jesse G. Beu, Urmish Thakker, and Matthew Mattina. 2020b. Aggressive compression of mobilenets using hybrid ternary layers. *tinyML Summit*.

Dibakar Gope, Ganesh Dasika, and Matthew Mattina. 2019. Ternary hybrid neural-tree networks for highly constrained iot applications. In *Proceedings of Machine Learning and Systems 2019*, pages 190–200.

Artem M. Grachev, Dmitry I. Ignatov, and Andrey V. Savchenko. 2017. Neural networks compression for language modeling. In *Pattern Recognition and Machine Intelligence*, pages 351–357, Cham. Springer International Publishing.

Song Han, Huizi Mao, and William J Dally. 2016. Deep compression: Compressing deep neural networks with pruning, trained quantization and huffman coding. *International Conference on Learning Representations (ICLR)*.

Itay Hubara, Matthieu Courbariaux, Daniel Soudry, Ran El-Yaniv, and Yoshua Bengio. 2016. Binarized neural networks. In *Proceedings of the 30th International Conference on Neural Information Processing Systems*, NIPS'16, page 4114–4122, Red Hook, NY, USA. Curran Associates Inc.

Itay Hubara, Matthieu Courbariaux, Daniel Soudry, Ran El-Yaniv, and Yoshua Bengio. 2017. Quantized neural networks: Training neural networks with low precision weights and activations. *J. Mach. Learn. Res.*, 18(1):6869–6898.

Oleksii Kuchaiev and Boris Ginsburg. 2017. Factorization tricks for LSTM networks. *CoRR*, abs/1703.10722.

Tao Lei, Yu Zhang, Sida I. Wang, Hui Dai, and Yoav Artzi. 2018. Simple recurrent units for highly parallelizable recurrence. In *Proceedings of the 2018 Conference on Empirical Methods in Natural Language Processing*, pages 4470–4481, Brussels, Belgium. Association for Computational Linguistics.

Zhe Li, Shuo Wang, Caiwen Ding, Qinru Qiu, Yanzhi Wang, and Yun Liang. 2018. Efficient recurrent neural networks using structured matrices in fpgas. 6th International Conference on Learning Representations, ICLR 2018 ; Conference date: 30-04-2018 Through 03-05-2018.

Bing Liu and Ian Lane. 2016. Attention-based recurrent neural network models for joint intent detection and slot filling. In *Interspeech 2016*, pages 685–689.

Xuan Liu, Di Cao, and Kai Yu. 2018. Binarized LSTM language model. In *Proceedings of the 2018 Conference of the North American Chapter of the Association for Computational Linguistics: Human Language Technologies, Volume 1 (Long Papers)*, pages 2113–2121, New Orleans, Louisiana. Association for Computational Linguistics.

Christos Louizos, Max Welling, and Diederik P. Kingma. 2018. Learning sparse neural networks through L_0 regularization. In *6th International Conference on Learning Representations, ICLR 2018, Vancouver, BC, Canada, April 30 - May 3, 2018, Conference Track Proceedings*. OpenReview.net.

Zhiyun Lu, Vikas Sindhwani, and Tara N. Sainath. 2016. Learning compact recurrent neural networks. *CoRR*, abs/1604.02594.

Minh-Thang Luong, Eugene Brevdo, and Rui Zhao. 2017. Neural machine translation (seq2seq) tutorial. *https://github.com/tensorflow/nmt*.

Sachin Mehta, Rik Koncel-Kedziorski, Mohammad Rastegari, and Hannaneh Hajishirzi. 2018. Pyramidal recurrent unit for language modeling. *CoRR*, abs/1808.09029.

Sachin Mehta, Rik Koncel-Kedziorski, Mohammad Rastegari, and Hannaneh Hajishirzi. 2019. Define: Deep factorized input token embeddings for neural sequence modeling.

Sharan Narang, Eric Undersander, and Gregory F. Diamos. 2017. Block-sparse recurrent neural networks. *CoRR*, abs/1711.02782.

Kirill Neklyudov, Dmitry Molchanov, Arsenii Ashukha, and Dmitry Vetrov. 2017. Structured bayesian pruning via log-normal multiplicative noise. In *Proceedings of the 31st International Conference on Neural Information Processing Systems*, NIPS'17, page 6778–6787, Red Hook, NY, USA. Curran Associates Inc.

Victor Sanh, Lysandre Debut, Julien Chaumond, and Thomas Wolf. 2019. Distilbert, a distilled version of bert: smaller, faster, cheaper and lighter.

Victor Sanh, Thomas Wolf, and Alexander M. Rush. 2020. Movement pruning: Adaptive sparsity by finetuning.

Min Joon Seo, Sewon Min, Ali Farhadi, and Hannaneh Hajishirzi. 2018. Neural speed reading via skim-rnn. In *6th International Conference on Learning Representations, ICLR 2018, Vancouver, BC, Canada, April 30 - May 3, 2018, Conference Track Proceedings*. OpenReview.net.

Vikas Sindhwani, Tara Sainath, and Sanjiv Kumar. 2015. Structured transforms for small-footprint deep learning. In C. Cortes, N. D. Lawrence, D. D. Lee, M. Sugiyama, and R. Garnett, editors, *Advances in Neural Information Processing Systems 28*, pages 3088–3096. Curran Associates, Inc.

Jin Tao, Urmish Thakker, Ganesh Dasika, and Jesse Beu. 2019. Skipping rnn state updates without retraining the original model. In *Proceedings of the 1st Workshop on Machine Learning on Edge in Sensor Systems*, SenSys-ML 2019, page 31–36, New York, NY, USA. Association for Computing Machinery.

U. Thakker, J. Beu, D. Gope, G. Dasika, and M. Mattina. 2019. Run-time efficient rnn compression for inference on edge devices. In *2019 2nd Workshop on Energy Efficient Machine Learning and Cognitive Computing for Embedded Applications (EMC2)*, pages 26–30.

Urmish Thakker, Jesse G. Beu, Dibakar Gope, Chu Zhou, Igor Fedorov, Ganesh Dasika, and Matthew Mattina. 2019a. Compressing rnns for iot devices by 15-38x using kronecker products. *CoRR*, abs/1906.02876.

Urmish Thakker, Ganesh Dasika, Jesse G. Beu, and Matthew Mattina. 2019b. Measuring scheduling efficiency of rnns for NLP applications. *CoRR*, abs/1904.03302.

Urmish Thakker, Igor Fedorov, Jesse G. Beu, Dibakar Gope, Chu Zhou, Ganesh Dasika, and Matthew Mattina. 2019c. Pushing the limits of RNN compression. *CoRR*, abs/1910.02558.

Urmish Thakker, Paul Whatamough, Matthew Mattina, and Jesse G. Beu. 2020. Compressing language models using doped kronecker products. *CoRR*, abs/2001.08896.

Anna Thomas, Albert Gu, Tri Dao, Atri Rudra, and Christopher Ré. 2018. Learning compressed transforms with low displacement rank. In S. Bengio, H. Wallach, H. Larochelle, K. Grauman, N. Cesa-Bianchi, and R. Garnett, editors, *Advances in Neural Information Processing Systems 31*, pages 9066–9078. Curran Associates, Inc.

Andros Tjandra, Sakriani Sakti, and Satoshi Nakamura. 2017. Compressing recurrent neural network with tensor train. In *Neural Networks (IJCNN), 2017 International Joint Conference on*, pages 4451–4458. IEEE.

Lloyd Trefethen and David Bau. 1997. *Numerical Linear Algebra*. SIAM: Society for Industrial and Applied Mathematics.

Shuo Wang, Zhe Li, Caiwen Ding, Bo Yuan, Qinru Qiu, Yanzhi Wang, and Yun Liang. 2018. C-lstm: Enabling efficient lstm using structured compression techniques on fpgas. In *Proceedings of the 2018 ACM/SIGDA International Symposium on Field-Programmable Gate Arrays*, FPGA '18, pages 11–20, New York, NY, USA. ACM.

Zhilin Yang, Zihang Dai, Ruslan Salakhutdinov, and William W. Cohen. 2018. Breaking the softmax bottleneck: A high-rank RNN language model. In *International Conference on Learning Representations*.

Adams Wei Yu, Hongrae Lee, and Quoc Le. 2017. Learning to skim text. In *Proceedings of the 55th Annual Meeting of the Association for Computational Linguistics (Volume 1: Long Papers)*, pages 1880–1890, Vancouver, Canada. Association for Computational Linguistics.

Wojciech Zaremba, Ilya Sutskever, and Oriol Vinyals. 2014. Recurrent neural network regularization. *CoRR*, abs/1409.2329.

Peng Zhou, Wei Shi, Jun Tian, Zhenyu Qi, Bingchen Li, Hongwei Hao, and Bo Xu. 2016. Attention-based bidirectional long short-term memory networks for relation classification. In *Proceedings of the 54th*

Annual Meeting of the Association for Computational Linguistics (Volume 2: Short Papers), pages 207–212, Berlin, Germany. Association for Computational Linguistics.

Michael Zhu and Suyog Gupta. 2017. To prune, or not to prune: exploring the efficacy of pruning for model compression. *arXiv e-prints*, page arXiv:1710.01878.

Learning Informative Representations of Biomedical Relations with Latent Variable Models

Harshil Shah
University College London
BenevolentAI[*]
h.shah@cs.ucl.ac.uk

Julien Fauqueur
BenevolentAI
julien@benevolent.ai

Abstract

Extracting biomedical relations from large corpora of scientific documents is a challenging natural language processing task. Existing approaches usually focus on identifying a relation either in a single sentence (mention-level) or across an entire corpus (pair-level). In both cases, recent methods have achieved strong results by learning a point estimate to represent the relation; this is then used as the input to a relation classifier. However, the relation expressed in text between a pair of biomedical entities is often more complex than can be captured by a point estimate. To address this issue, we propose a latent variable model with an arbitrarily flexible distribution to represent the relation between an entity pair. Additionally, our model provides a unified architecture for both mention-level and pair-level relation extraction. We demonstrate that our model achieves results competitive with strong baselines for both tasks while having fewer parameters and being significantly faster to train. We make our code publicly available.

1 Introduction

The vast amounts of scientific literature can provide a significant source of information for biomedical research. Using this literature to identify relations between entities is an important task in various applications (van Mulligen et al., 2012; Segura-Bedmar et al., 2013; Bravo et al., 2015; Krallinger et al., 2017).

Existing approaches to biomedical relation extraction usually fall into one of two categories. Mention-level extraction aims to classify the relation between a pair of entities within a short span of text (usually a sentence). In contrast, pair-level extraction aims to classify the relation between a pair of entities across an entire paragraph, document or corpus.

For both mention-level and pair-level relation extraction, recent work has been focused on representation learning. This is considered to be one of the major steps towards making progress in artificial intelligence (Bengio et al., 2013). Representations of relations which understand their context are particularly important in biomedical research, where identifying fruitful targets is crucial due to the high costs of experimentation. Learning such representations is likely to require large amounts of unsupervised data due to the scarcity of labelled data in this domain.

Recent mention-level methods have been based on using large unsupervised models with Transformer networks (Vaswani et al., 2017) to learn representations of sentences containing pairs of entities. These representations are then used as the inputs to much smaller models, which perform supervised relation classification (Lee et al., 2019; Beltagy et al., 2019).

Recent pair-level methods have been based on encoding each mention of a pair of entities, and designing a mechanism to pool these encodings (across a paragraph, document, or corpus) into a single representation. This representation is then used to classify the relation between the entity pair (Verga et al., 2018; Jia et al., 2019).

However, representation learning methods for both mention-level and pair-level extraction typically use a point estimate for each representation. As a result, they may struggle to capture the nature of the true, potentially complex relations between each pair of entities. For example, Figure 1 shows sentences for two entity pairs which demonstrate that relation statements can be very different, typically depending on biological circumstances (*e.g.* anatomical location, experimental details, presence of a disease, *etc*). Such nuanced relations can be difficult to capture with a single point estimate.

We hypothesise that there is a true underlying

---

[*]Work completed during internship at BenevolentAI.

Proceedings of SustaiNLP: Workshop on Simple and Efficient Natural Language Processing, pages 19–28
Online, November 20, 2020. ©2020 Association for Computational Linguistics

Protein Akt and protein GSK3β:

"… Akt negatively regulates GSK3β activity…"
"… Akt phosphorylates GSK3β…"

Protein EAAT2 and disease ALS:

"EAAT2/C1-4 were found to be equally expressed in ALS patients and controls."
"EAAT2 protein is significantly reduced in ALS in the motor cortex and spinal cord."

Figure 1: Two sets of sentences demonstrating the potentially complex nature of the relation between a pair of entities.

relation for each entity pair, and that this relation can be multimodal (because of the aforementioned complexities). The sentences containing each pair are textual observations of these underlying relations.

We therefore propose a probabilistic model which uses a continuous latent variable to represent the true relation between each entity pair. The distribution of a sentence containing that pair is then conditioned on this latent variable. In order to be able to model the complex relations between each entity pair, we use an infinite mixture distribution for the latent representation.

Our model provides a unified architecture for learning representations of relations between entity pairs both at mention and pair level. We show that (an approximation to) the posterior distribution of the latent variable can be used for mention-level relation classification. We also demonstrate that the prior distribution from the same model can be used for pair-level classification. On both tasks, we achieve results competitive with strong baselines with a model which has fewer parameters and is significantly faster to train.

The code is released at `https://github.com/BenevolentAI/RELVM`

2 Model

In this section, we introduce our unified architecture for both mention-level and pair-level relation extraction. Throughout, we use the following notation:

- c represents a 'context', *i.e.* a sentence (or sequence of tokens) containing a pair of entities. c has tokens $c_1, \ldots, c_T$.

  - c_{t_x} and c_{t_y} are the tokens representing the two entities. We replace the actual tokens denoting the two entities with generic $<\text{ENT}>$ tokens. Therefore, a context is given by:

$$c = c_1, \ldots, c_{t_x-1}, <\text{ENT}>, c_{t_x+1}, \ldots,$$
$$c_{t_y-1}, <\text{ENT}>, c_{t_y+1}, \ldots, c_T$$

- x and y are the input representations of the two entities.

  - For pair-level classification, x and y will be unique identifiers for the two entities.
  - For mention-level classification, x and y will be the types of the two entities, *e.g.* GENE and DISEASE. This is done in order to allow for fair comparisons with previous methods, which use the entity types for mention-level classification (see Section 4.2 for further details).
  - x and y always refer to the first and second entities in c respectively.

- $\mathbf{e}(c_t)$ is the embedding of token c_t. $\mathbf{e}(x)$ and $\mathbf{e}(y)$ are the embeddings of the entities x and y.

- r represents the relation label.

Approach Large corpora of labelled relation statements are often scarce, whereas unlabelled sentences are usually plentiful. In order to leverage these unlabelled sentences, we first train an unsupervised model to learn representations of entity pairs and the contexts in which they occur. We then train much smaller models to classify relations using the representations from the unsupervised model.

2.1 Representation learning model

When training the unsupervised representation learning model, we assume access to a corpus of sentences in which entities have been tagged but there are no relation labels. We train the representation model to maximise the conditional log-likelihood $\log p(c|x,y)$. θ will refer to the set of parameters of the representation model which we wish to optimise. A graph of the representation model is shown in Figure 2 and a more detailed explanation is given below.

There are many ways to express the same relation between a given pair of entities. For example, the sentences "*John is Mary's brother*" and "*Mary*

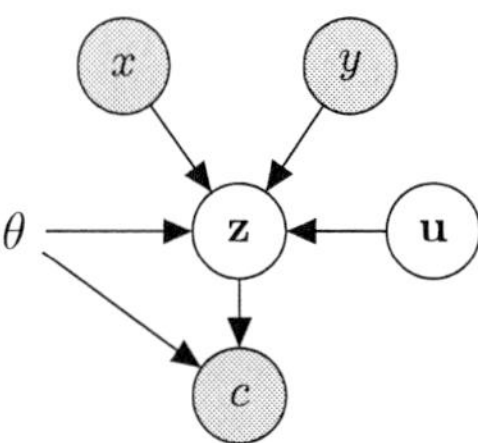

Figure 2: A graph depicting our unsupervised representation learning model. Clear nodes denote latent variables and shaded nodes denote observed variables. Representations from this model are used for both mention-level and pair-level relation classification.

is John's sister" express the same relation in different ways. In order to capture this phenomenon, we introduce a latent variable, $\mathbf{z}$, to represent the true underlying relation. This will be the representation used for mention-level and pair-level relation classification. The conditional distribution is parametrised as:

$$p(c|x,y) = \int_{\mathbf{z}} p_\theta(\mathbf{z}|x,y)p_\theta(c|\mathbf{z}) \quad (1)$$

Intuitively, $p_\theta(\mathbf{z}|x,y)$ captures the true underlying relation between the two entities x and y, and $p_\theta(c|\mathbf{z})$ captures the variation in the multiple possible ways of expressing that relation.

For computational simplicity, we could choose $p_\theta(\mathbf{z}|x,y)$ to be Gaussian. However in reality, the true relation between a pair of entities is probably more complex than can be modelled well with a unimodal distribution. We therefore introduce another latent variable $\mathbf{u}$ such that:

$$p_\theta(\mathbf{z}|x,y) = \int_{\mathbf{u}} p(\mathbf{u})p_\theta(\mathbf{z}|x,y,\mathbf{u}) \quad (2)$$

For $p(\mathbf{u})$, we use a standard Gaussian distribution, $\mathcal{N}(\mathbf{0},\mathbf{I})$. For $p_\theta(\mathbf{z}|x,y,\mathbf{u})$, we again use a Gaussian distribution whose mean and variance are a function of x, y and $\mathbf{u}$. We concatenate together $\mathbf{e}(x)$, $\mathbf{e}(y)$, $\mathbf{e}(x) \odot \mathbf{e}(y)$ and $\mathbf{u}$, and pass the resulting vector into a feedforward network to output the mean and variance of $p_\theta(\mathbf{z}|x,y,\mathbf{u})$ ($\odot$ denotes element-wise multiplication). Using a nonlinear network allows the marginal distribution $p_\theta(\mathbf{z}|x,y)$ to be an infinite mixture distribution (Mattei and Frellsen, 2018). The objective becomes:

$$\log p(c|x,y) = \log \int_{\mathbf{u},\mathbf{z}} p(\mathbf{u})p_\theta(\mathbf{z}|x,y,\mathbf{u})p_\theta(c|\mathbf{z}) \quad (3)$$

We parametrise $p_\theta(c|\mathbf{z})$ with an LSTM, due to its strong performance in language modelling (Graves, 2013; Bowman et al., 2016; Melis et al., 2018). The conditional probabilities for $t = 1, \ldots, T$ are:

$$p_\theta(c_t = v|c_{1:t-1},\mathbf{z}) \propto \exp((\mathbf{W}\mathbf{h}_t^p) \cdot \mathbf{e}(v)) \quad (4)$$

where $\mathbf{W}$ is a learnable parameter of the model, and $\mathbf{h}_t^p$ is computed as:

$$\mathbf{h}_t^p = \text{LSTM}(\mathbf{z}, \mathbf{h}_{t-1}^p, \mathbf{e}(c_{t-1})) \quad (5)$$

Complete hyperparameter details are provided in Section 4.1.

2.1.1 Training

Because of the nonlinear functions involved in $p_\theta(\mathbf{z}|x,y,\mathbf{u})$ and $p_\theta(c|\mathbf{z})$, the integral in Equation (3) is intractable. We therefore perform approximate maximum likelihood estimation using stochastic gradient variational Bayes (SGVB) (Kingma and Welling, 2014; Rezende et al., 2014).

To do this, we parametrise a Gaussian inference distribution $q_\phi(\mathbf{u}|x,y,c)$ (referred to as $q_\phi(\mathbf{u})$ henceforth, for brevity) with trainable parameters ϕ. This allows us to maximise the following lower bound on the log-likelihood:

$$\log p(c|x,y) \geq \mathbb{E}_{q_\phi(\mathbf{u})p_\theta(\mathbf{z}|x,y,\mathbf{u})}\left[\log \frac{p(\mathbf{u})p_\theta(c|\mathbf{z})}{q_\phi(\mathbf{u})}\right]$$
$$\equiv \mathcal{L}_{\theta,\phi}(c,x,y) \quad (6)$$

This bound can be approximated using Monte Carlo integration. It is optimised with respect to θ and ϕ jointly.

To parametrise $q_\phi(\mathbf{u})$, we use a bidirectional LSTM to encode the context. This is due to its ability to capture useful sentence level information into a low-dimensional vector (Zhou et al., 2016; Peters et al., 2018). It is computed as:

$$\overrightarrow{\mathbf{h}_t^q} = \text{LSTM}(\mathbf{e}(c_t), \overrightarrow{h_{t-1}^q}) \quad (7)$$
$$\overleftarrow{\mathbf{h}_t^q} = \text{LSTM}(\mathbf{e}(c_t), \overleftarrow{h_{t+1}^q}) \quad (8)$$
$$\mathbf{h}^q = [\overrightarrow{\mathbf{h}_T^q}; \overleftarrow{\mathbf{h}_1^q}] \quad (9)$$

We concatenate $\mathbf{h}^q$ to $\mathbf{e}(x)$, $\mathbf{e}(y)$ and $\mathbf{e}(x) \odot \mathbf{e}(y)$ and pass the resulting vector into a feedforward network to output the mean and variance of $q_\phi(\mathbf{u})$.

2.2 Mention-level classification

In this section, we assume that the unsupervised representation model from Section 2.1 has been trained with x and y being the types of the two entities. The representations $\mathbf{z}$ can now be used as the inputs to a supervised mention-level relation classification model.

For mention-level classification, we assume access to a corpus of sentences in which entities have been tagged and there are labels classifying the type of relation between the entity pair in each sentence. We train the mention-level classification model to maximise $p(r|x,y,c)$. λ will refer to the set of parameters of the mention-level classification model which we wish to optimise.

The representation $\mathbf{z}$ of the entity pair and context would ideally be distributed according to the posterior $p(\mathbf{z}|x,y,c)$ from the representation model. We would then optimise the parameters λ using the following objective:

$$p(r|x,y,c) = \int_{\mathbf{z}} p(\mathbf{z}|x,y,c)p_\lambda(r|\mathbf{z}) \tag{10}$$

However:

$$p(\mathbf{z}|x,y,c) = \frac{p_\theta(\mathbf{z},c|x,y)}{p(c|x,y)} \tag{11}$$

$$= \frac{p_\theta(\mathbf{z},c|x,y)}{\int_{\mathbf{u},\mathbf{z}} p(\mathbf{u})p_\theta(\mathbf{z}|x,y,\mathbf{u})p_\theta(c|\mathbf{z})} \tag{12}$$

As mentioned in Section 2.1.1, the integral in the denominator is intractable. Instead, the following approximation to the posterior can be used:

$$p(\mathbf{z}|x,y,c) \simeq \int_{\mathbf{u}} q_\phi(\mathbf{u})p_\theta(\mathbf{z}|x,y,\mathbf{u}) \tag{13}$$

This is an approximation to the posterior because maximising the objective in Equation (6) is equivalent to minimising the KL divergence from $q_\phi(\mathbf{u})p_\theta(\mathbf{z}|x,y,\mathbf{u})$ to $p(\mathbf{z},\mathbf{u}|x,y,c)$ (Kingma and Welling, 2014):

$$\mathcal{L}_{\theta,\phi}(c,x,y) = \log p(c|x,y)-$$
$$D_{\mathrm{KL}}[q_\phi(\mathbf{u})p_\theta(\mathbf{z}|x,y,\mathbf{u})||p(\mathbf{z},\mathbf{u}|x,y,c)] \tag{14}$$

Using this approximation, the mention-level classification objective becomes:

$$p(r|x,y,c) \simeq \int_{\mathbf{u},\mathbf{z}} q_\phi(\mathbf{u})p_\theta(\mathbf{z}|x,y,\mathbf{u})p_\lambda(r|\mathbf{z}) \tag{15}$$

$$= \mathbb{E}_{q_\phi(\mathbf{u})p_\theta(\mathbf{z}|x,y,\mathbf{u})}[p_\lambda(r|\mathbf{z})] \tag{16}$$

Empirically, however, we find that the model trains much more easily using the following objective:

$$\mathbb{E}_{q_\phi(\mathbf{u})p_\theta(\mathbf{z}|x,y,\mathbf{u})}[\log p_\lambda(r|\mathbf{z})] \equiv \mathcal{L}_\lambda(r,c,x,y) \tag{17}$$

This is due, particularly at the start of training, to the values of $p_\lambda(r|\mathbf{z})$ being very small. Note that, due to Jensen's inequality, the objective in Equation (17) is in fact a lower bound on the $\log$ of the objective in Equation (16):

$$\mathcal{L}_\lambda(r,c,x,y) \leq \log \mathbb{E}_{q_\phi(\mathbf{u})p_\theta(\mathbf{z}|x,y,\mathbf{u})}[p_\lambda(r|\mathbf{z})] \tag{18}$$

To parametrise $p_\lambda(r|\mathbf{z})$, we use a shallow feedforward network with a softmax function at the output. Complete hyperparameter details are provided in Section 4.2.

2.3 Pair-level classification

In this section, we assume that the unsupervised representation model from Section 2.1 has been trained with x and y being unique identifiers for the two entities. The representations $\mathbf{z}$ can now be used as the inputs to a supervised pair-level relation classification model.

For pair-level classification, we assume access to a dataset with pairs of entity identifiers, and labels classifying the type of relation between each pair. Instead of learning $p(r|x,y,c)$ as in mention-level classification, we now learn $p(r|x,y)$.

Intuitively, for pair-level classification, we wish to classify the relation between a pair of entities based on everything that the unsupervised model has learned about those entities (through the sentences containing them). This is unlike mention-level classification, where we classify the relation described in a specific sentence.

For pair-level classification, we follow a very similar approach to that described in Section 2.2 for mention-level classification. However we no longer base the input representation on the posterior distribution from the unsupervised model, $p(\mathbf{z}|x,y,c)$. Instead, the representation used will be distributed according to:

$$p_\theta(\mathbf{z}|x,y) = \int_{\mathbf{u}} p(\mathbf{u})p_\theta(\mathbf{z}|x,y,\mathbf{u}) \tag{19}$$

Intuitively, this is the natural distribution to use, because we are interested in the relation between the entities x and y, without a specific context to condition on.

We denote ψ as the parameters of the pair-level supervised model. Then, following the same reasoning as Section 2.2, the objective for the pair-level supervised model is:

$$\mathbb{E}_{p(\mathbf{u})p_\theta(\mathbf{z}|x,y,\mathbf{u})}[\log p_\psi(r|\mathbf{z})] \equiv \mathcal{L}_\psi(r,x,y) \tag{20}$$

To parametrise $p_\psi(r|\mathbf{z})$, we use a shallow feedforward network with a softmax function at the output. Complete hyperparameter details are provided in Section 4.3.

3   Related work

Mention-level relation extraction is typically performed using supervised learning. In the general domain, Zhang et al. (2017) combine an LSTM with a position-aware attention mechanism to perform multiclass relation extraction. Soares et al. (2019) fine-tune the BERT (Devlin et al., 2019) architecture to relation extraction tasks by enforcing similarity between representations of sentences containing the same pair of entities across a corpus. (Zhang et al., 2020) construct a teacher model to generate soft labels which guide the optimisation of a student network via knowledge distillation. In the biomedical and scientific domains, BioBERT (Lee et al., 2019) and SciBERT (Beltagy et al., 2019) train the BERT architecture on domain-specific corpora, achieving state of the art results on mention-level relation extraction tasks. Zhang et al. (2018) combine an RNN over the sentence's words and a CNN over its dependency graph to classify drug-drug and protein-protein interactions.

Pair-level relation extraction usually relies on distant supervision (Mintz et al., 2009). In the general domain, Hoffmann et al. (2011) develop a latent variable model to perform multi-instance learning while handling overlapping relations. Lin et al. (2016) use an attention mechanism to pool the representations of sentences containing a given pair into a single representation, which is then used as the input to a classifier. Quirk and Poon (2017) capture relations across sentences by linking dependency graphs between sentences. Other pair-level methods build representations using unsupervised models. Camacho-Collados et al. (2019) use a latent variable model to learn a point-estimate representation from the unigram distribution of tokens co-occurring in sentences with the given pair. Joshi et al. (2019) learn representations of pairs of entities by maximising their pointwise mutual information (PMI) with the contexts that the entities appear in. In the biomedical domain, Verga et al. (2018) build a paragraph-level representation using a modified Transformer network, and aggregate over mentions using a softmax function. Liang et al. (2019) combine knowledge embeddings and graph embeddings using a cascade learning framework

to predict links in biochemical networks. Percha and Altman (2015) use a distributional semantics approach to cluster together drug-gene pairs which are related in similar ways.

Contrary to our work, there does not appear to be prior research performing both mention-level and pair-level relation extraction with a unified model.

4   Experiments

4.1   Representation learning model

We train the unsupervised representation model described in Section 2.1 using sentences from PubMed abstracts, PubMed Central (PMC) open-access full-text articles, and licensed full-text articles from Wiley and Springer. We take sentences with a maximum length of 140 tokens and tag the entities with their type using a dictionary-based method. Entities are linked to unique identifiers by first disambiguating entity types using a bidirectional LSTM sentence classifier, followed by type-specific term lookups. Note that if a sentence contains three or more entities, it is repeated in order to account for each possible pair of entities.

4.1.1   Architectures and training

To parametrise $p_\theta(\mathbf{z}|x, y, \mathbf{u})$, we use a 2-layer feedforward network with the ReLU nonlinearity. To parametrise $p_\theta(c|\mathbf{z})$, we use a 1-layer LSTM. To parametrise $q_\phi(\mathbf{u})$, we use a 1-layer bidirectional LSTM, the output of which is passed to a 2-layer feedforward network with the ReLU nonlinearity.

In order to evaluate the effect of the number of parameters on performance, we train four different versions of our representation learning model: {X-SMALL, SMALL, MEDIUM, LARGE}. These correspond to respective hidden state sizes of {128, 256, 512, 1024} in the networks. For all of the models, both $\mathbf{u}$ and $\mathbf{z}$, as well as all embeddings, are 300-dimensional.

We train the unsupervised representation models using a single sample approximation of the objective in Equation (6). We train for 400,000 iterations, using a minibatch size of 192 and optimising the parameters using Adam (Kingma and Ba, 2015) with a learning rate of 0.0001.

4.1.2   Optimisation challenges

The unsupervised objective in Equation (6) can be expressed as:

$$\mathcal{L}_{\theta,\phi}(c, x, y) = \mathbb{E}_{q_\phi(\mathbf{u})p_\theta(\mathbf{z}|x,y,\mathbf{u})}[\log p_\theta(c|\mathbf{z})]$$
$$- D_{\mathrm{KL}}[q_\phi(\mathbf{u})||p(\mathbf{u})] \qquad (21)$$

When training latent variable models with autoregressive observation distributions (such as that in Equation (4)), this objective can induce local optima where $q_\phi(\mathbf{u}) = p(\mathbf{u})$. This results in the KL divergence term in Equation (21) collapsing to 0, meaning the model ignores the latent variable altogether. To avoid such local optima, we use the following two methods (Bowman et al., 2016):

KL annealing We multiply the KL divergence term by a constant weight which is linearly annealed from 0 to 1 over the first 10,000 iterations of training. This helps the model to escape local optima where $D_{\mathrm{KL}}[q_\phi(\mathbf{u})||p(\mathbf{u})] = 0$ early in training.

Token dropout In Equation (5), we randomly drop the token embedding being passed to the next LSTM hidden state. We use a dropout rate of 50%. This encourages the LSTM to rely more on the representation $\mathbf{z}$ than the previous tokens when modelling the context.

4.1.3 Computational costs

We show the computational costs of our unsupervised representation models in Table 1. We compare against BioBERT (Lee et al., 2019), a language model with state-of-the-art performance on relation extraction.

All versions of our model have significantly fewer parameters than BioBERT. In terms of 'GPU days'[1], training BioBERT is approximately 25 to 40 times slower than training our model. In addition, inference is an order of magnitude faster with our model compared to BioBERT.

4.2 Mention-level classification

After training the unsupervised representation model (using the entity types for x and y), we use it to perform supervised mention-level relation classification, as described in Section 2.2. We use the EU-ADR (van Mulligen et al., 2012) and GAD (Bravo et al., 2015) datasets. In both datasets, each sentence contains a gene and disease. The task is to classify whether the given sentence either does or does not exhibit a relation between the gene and the disease. Examples from both datasets are shown in Table 2 and dataset statistics are shown in Table 3. As per previous work, we report the performance using 10-fold cross validation on each dataset (Lee et al., 2019).

We compare our results with those of BioBERT as reported by Lee et al. (2019). For a fair comparison, we use the same classifier architecture. This is a single layer network with a softmax nonlinearity. As well as training the parameters λ of the classifier, we also fine tune the parameters θ and ϕ of the representation model. Again, this is done to allow for a fair comparison with BioBERT (which follows the same procedure).

We approximate the objective in Equation (17) using 4 samples during training. We use a minibatch size of 8 and update the parameters using Adam with a learning rate of 0.00001. We train on EU-ADR for 200 iterations and on GAD for 3,000 iterations.

Note that the representations for BioBERT are 768-dimensional. This is in contrast to ours which are 300-dimensional.

4.2.1 Results

We perform 10-fold cross validation, and report the mean precision, recall and F1-score in Table 4. On EU-ADR, all versions of our model outperform BioBERT, with our LARGE model achieving a significantly higher F1-score. On this task, all versions of our model have significantly higher recall than BioBERT, with the precision being similar. On GAD, BioBERT slightly outperforms our LARGE model, thanks to its higher precision. In addition, we find that, on both tasks, the performance monotonically increases with the size of the unsupervised representation model.

These results show that it is possible to achieve results competitive with the state-of-the-art while making significant efficiency gains, both in terms of memory and time.

4.3 Pair-level classification

In this section, we use the LARGE representation model from Section 4.1, trained using the unique entity identifiers for x and y. We fix the parameters of the unsupervised representation model and use it to perform supervised pair-level classification, as described in Section 2.3.

We construct a multiclass classification dataset by combining multiple third-party biomedical datasets. These datasets only provide pairs of entities which are related. Therefore, if an entity pair does not appear in any of the datasets, they are assumed to be unrelated and given the label NO-RELATION. If two entities are related, the label is given by the concatenation of the two

---

[1]GPU days = No. of GPUs $\times$ training time (in days).

MODEL	PARAMS	TRAINING		INFERENCE	
		HARDWARE	TIME	HARDWARE	TIME
BioBERT	110M	8 x V100 GPUs	10 days	1 x V100 GPU	0.0087s/sent.
Ours (X-SMALL)	2M	1 x V100 GPU	2 days	1 x V100 GPU	0.0004s/sent.
Ours (SMALL)	4M	1 x V100 GPU	2 days	1 x V100 GPU	0.0004s/sent.
Ours (MEDIUM)	10M	1 x V100 GPU	3 days	1 x V100 GPU	0.0005s/sent.
Ours (LARGE)	30M	1 x V100 GPU	3 days	1 x V100 GPU	0.0007s/sent.

Table 1: The computational costs of each of the unsupervised representation models we train. The inference time for each model is computed on a V100 GPU.

DATASET	x	y	c	r
EU-ADR	GENE	DISEASE	Based on <ENT> analyses, 41 <ENT> patients and 12 healthy controls were studied.	0
	DISEASE	GENE	<ENT> is associated with decreased expression of mucosal <ENT> .	1
GAD	GENE	DISEASE	A broad protective effect of <ENT> S180L against <ENT> per se is not discernible.	0
	GENE	DISEASE	The <ENT> polymorphism Tyr402His appears indicative of <ENT> pathogenesis.	1

Table 2: Positive ($r = 1$) and negative ($r = 0$) examples from the EU-ADR and GAD datasets.

DATASET	EU-ADR	GAD
# relations	355	5330

Table 3: Number of relations for the EU-ADR and GAD datasets.

entity types. This is therefore a multiclass classification problem, with the set of possible classes being {NO-RELATION, DISEASE-GENE, GENE-GENE, CHEMICAL-GENE, CHEMICAL-DISEASE}. Note that we only include entity pairs that occur in at least one sentence in the dataset used to train the representation learning model.

We randomly split the related entity pairs into training, validation and test sets. The set of entity pairs with label NO-RELATION is extremely large. We randomly assign a proportion of these to the validation and test sets. During training, we randomly sample a proportion of each minibatch from the remaining unrelated entity pairs. The dataset statistics are shown in Table 5.

For the pair-level classifier, we train a 2-layer model which has a 300-dimensional hidden layer with a skip connection. We approximate the objective in Equation (20) using 4 samples during training. We train for 100,000 iterations, using a minibatch size of 512 (of which 448 are sampled from the NO-RELATION set). We optimise the parameters using Adam with a learning rate of 0.0001. When making predictions on unseen data points, we only predict a label other than NO-RELATION if the predicted probability is higher than a threshold. This threshold is tuned to maximise the F1-score on the validation set.

4.3.1 Baselines

We compare our method with the following two baselines:

Co-occurrences For every entity pair that occurs in at least one sentence in the dataset used to train the representation learning model, we predict the relation to be positive (*i.e.* the concatenation of the types of the two entities). By design, this method will have perfect recall.

Attention This method is similar to those presented by Lin et al. (2016) and Verga et al. (2018). For a given pair of entities, we collect every sentence containing the pair from the dataset used to train the representation learning model. Each sentence is passed to an LSTM whose final state is taken as the sentence representation. The representations for all sentences for the given entity pair are pooled together into a single representation us-

MODEL	EU-ADR			GAD		
	P	R	F	P	R	F
BioBERT	80.92	90.81	84.83	**75.95**	88.08	**81.52**
Ours (X-SMALL)	79.62	98.08	87.71	67.83	90.76	77.45
Ours (SMALL)	80.35	98.09	88.14	68.31	91.75	78.16
Ours (MEDIUM)	80.72	98.46	88.59	69.68	91.82	78.72
Ours (LARGE)	**82.34**	**98.85**	**89.67**	72.26	**92.00**	80.79

Table 4: Results using 10-fold cross validation on the EU-ADR and GAD classification tasks. We report the mean precision (P), recall (R) and F1-score (F) over the 10 folds. For all metrics, higher is better.

DATASET	PAIR-LEVEL
Train (excl. NO-RELATION)	263,112
Validation	691,627
Test	692,534

Table 5: Total counts across all relation types for the pair-level classification dataset. The training set excludes NO-RELATION types, as these are sampled during training.

MODEL	P	R	F
Co-occurrences	3.10	100.00	6.02
Attention	11.06	26.97	15.69
Ours	12.54	25.91	16.90

Table 6: Results on the test set of the pair-level classification task. We report the precision (P), recall (R) and the F1-score (F). For all metrics, higher is better.

ing an attention mechanism. This representation is then used as the input to a feedforward network with a softmax function at the output. This method is therefore trained on exactly the same dataset as our pair-level classifier.

The attention model is trained for 1,000,000 iterations using a minibatch size of 100 (of which 50 are sampled from the NO-RELATION set). The parameters are optimised using Adam with a learning rate of 0.000005. As with our model, when making predictions on unseen data points, we only predict a label other than NO-RELATION if the predicted probability is higher than a threshold. This threshold is tuned to maximise the F1-score on the validation set.

4.3.2 Results

The precision, recall, and F1-score on the test set are reported in Table 6. Our model achieves a higher F1-score than the attention model. Unsurprisingly, both the attention model and our model achieve significantly higher precision than the co-occurrence baseline at the expense of lower recall.

In contrast to the attention model, when classifying a new pair, our model does not need to encode all of the sentences containing that pair. This provides significant computational advantages, both in terms of memory and time.

5 Conclusion

We have presented a model for learning representations of pairs of biomedical entities from unlabelled text corpora. We use a latent variable with an arbitrarily flexible distribution in order to be able to capture the complex relations between each pair of entities. The unified architecture can be used for both mention-level and pair-level relation extraction. On both tasks, we achieve results competitive with strong baselines. We also show significant computational gains in terms of the number of parameters and training times.

Our model presents many avenues for future work. The results in Table 4 show that the model's performance improves with the size of the hidden states in the networks; this suggests that there are further gains achievable simply by providing the model with more parameters. The model could be further scaled up by using a hierarchy of latent variables to increase the expressive power of the representations.

Other directions include evaluating the benefits of having a representation which explicitly captures uncertainty about the relations. For example, this can be done by assessing if the model is less confident when making predictions about entity pairs which do not occur frequently in the unlabelled corpus. Additionally, since our model can produce a representation for any pair of entities (even those which do not occur together in the unlabelled corpus), it could be used in a link prediction setting to score unseen entity pairs.

Acknowledgements

We would like to thank our colleagues Sia Togia and Angus Brayne for their thorough feedback on this paper and Rogier Hintzen for his precious help in preparing the datasets.

References

I. Beltagy, K. Lo, and A. Cohan. 2019. SciBERT: A Pretrained Language Model for Scientific Text. In *Proceedings of the 2019 Conference on Empirical Methods in Natural Language Processing*.

Y. Bengio, A. Courville, and P. Vincent. 2013. Representation learning: A review and new perspectives. *IEEE Transactions on Pattern Analysis and Machine Intelligence*, 35.

S. Bowman, L. Vilnis, O. Vinyals, A. Dai, R. Jozefowicz, and S. Bengio. 2016. Generating Sentences from a Continuous Space. In *Proceedings of The 20th SIGNLL Conference on Computational Natural Language Learning*.

À. Bravo, J. Piñero, N. Queralt-Rosinach, M. Rautschka, and L. Furlong. 2015. Extraction of Relations Between Genes and Diseases from Text and Large-Scale Data Analysis: Implications for Translational Research. *BMC Bioinformatics*, 16.

J. Camacho-Collados, L. Espinosa-Anke, S. Jameel, and S. Schockaert. 2019. A Latent Variable Model for Learning Distributional Relation Vectors. In *Proceedings of the Twenty-Eighth International Joint Conference on Artificial Intelligence*.

J. Devlin, M. Chang, K. Lee, and K. Toutanova. 2019. BERT: Pre-training of Deep Bidirectional Transformers for Language Understanding. In *Proceedings of the 2019 Conference of the North American Chapter of the Association for Computational Linguistics*.

A. Graves. 2013. Generating Sequences With Recurrent Neural Networks. *CoRR*, abs/1308.0850.

R. Hoffmann, C. Zhang, X. Ling, L. Zettlemoyer, and D. Weld. 2011. Knowledge-Based Weak Supervision for Information Extraction of Overlapping Relations. In *Proceedings of the 49th Annual Meeting of the Association for Computational Linguistics*.

R. Jia, C. Wong, and H. Poon. 2019. Document-Level N-ary Relation Extraction with Multiscale Representation Learning. In *Proceedings of the 2019 Conference of the North American Chapter of the Association for Computational Linguistics*.

M. Joshi, E. Choi, O. Levy, D. Weld, and L. Zettlemoyer. 2019. pair2vec: Compositional Word-Pair Embeddings for Cross-Sentence Inference. In *Proceedings of the 2019 Conference of the North American Chapter of the Association for Computational Linguistics*.

D. Kingma and J. Ba. 2015. Adam: A Method for Stochastic Optimization. In *International Conference on Learning Representations*.

D. Kingma and M. Welling. 2014. Auto-Encoding Variational Bayes. In *International Conference on Learning Representations*.

M. Krallinger, O. Rabal, S. Akhondi, M. Pérez, J. Santamaría, G. Rodríguez, G. Tsatsaronis, A. Intxaurrondo, J. López, U. Nandal, E. van Buel, A. Chandrasekhar, M. Rodenburg, A. Lægreid, M. Doornenbal, J. Oyarzábal, A. Lourenço, and A. Valencia. 2017. Overview of the BioCreative VI chemical-protein interaction Track. In *Proceedings of the BioCreative VI Workshop*.

J. Lee, W. Yoon, S. Kim, D. Kim, S. Kim, C. So, and J. Kang. 2019. BioBERT: A Pre-Trained Biomedical Language Representation Model for Biomedical Text Mining. *Bioinformatics*.

X. Liang, D. Li, M. Song, A. Madden, Y. Ding, and Y. Bu. 2019. Predicting Biomedical Relationships Using the Knowledge and Graph Embedding Cascade Model. *PLOS ONE*, 14.

Y. Lin, S. Shen, Z. Liu, H. Luan, and M. Sun. 2016. Neural Relation Extraction with Selective Attention over Instances. In *Proceedings of the 54th Annual Meeting of the Association for Computational Linguistics*.

P. Mattei and J. Frellsen. 2018. Leveraging the Exact Likelihood of Deep Latent Variable Models. In *Advances in Neural Information Processing Systems 31*.

G. Melis, C. Dyer, and P. Blunsom. 2018. On the State of the Art of Evaluation in Neural Language Models. In *International Conference on Learning Representations*.

M. Mintz, S. Bills, R. Snow, and D. Jurafsky. 2009. Distant Supervision for Relation Extraction Without Labeled Data. In *Proceedings of the Joint Conference of the 47th Annual Meeting of the ACL and the 4th International Joint Conference on Natural Language Processing of the AFNLP*.

E. van Mulligen, A. Fourrier-Reglat, D. Gurwitz, M. Molokhia, A. Nieto, G. Trifiro, J. Kors, and L. Furlong. 2012. The EU-ADR Corpus. *Journal of Biomedical Informatics*, 45.

B. Percha and R. Altman. 2015. Learning the Structure of Biomedical Relationships from Unstructured Text. *PLoS Computational Biology*, 11.

M. Peters, M. Neumann, M. Iyyer, M. Gardner, C. Clark, K. Lee, and L. Zettlemoyer. 2018. Deep Contextualized Word Representations. In *Proceedings of the 2018 Conference of the North American Chapter of the Association for Computational Linguistics*.

C. Quirk and H. Poon. 2017. Distant Supervision for Relation Extraction beyond the Sentence Boundary. In *Proceedings of the 15th Conference of the European Chapter of the Association for Computational Linguistics*.

D. Rezende, S. Mohamed, and D. Wierstra. 2014. Stochastic Backpropagation and Approximate Inference in Deep Generative Models. In *Proceedings of the 31st International Conference on Machine Learning*.

I. Segura-Bedmar, P. Martínez, and M. Herrero-Zazo. 2013. SemEval-2013 Task 9: Extraction of Drug-Drug Interactions from Biomedical Texts (DDIExtraction 2013). In *Second Joint Conference on Lexical and Computational Semantics (*SEM), Volume 2: Proceedings of the Seventh International Workshop on Semantic Evaluation*.

L. Soares, N. FitzGerald, J. Ling, and T. Kwiatkowski. 2019. Matching the Blanks: Distributional Similarity for Relation Learning. In *Proceedings of the 57th Annual Meeting of the Association for Computational Linguistics*.

A. Vaswani, N. Shazeer, N. Parmar, J. Uszkoreit, L. Jones, A. Gomez, Ł Kaiser, and I. Polosukhin. 2017. Attention is All you Need. In *Advances in Neural Information Processing Systems*.

P. Verga, E. Strubell, and A. McCallum. 2018. Simultaneously Self-Attending to All Mentions for Full-Abstract Biological Relation Extraction. In *North American Chapter of the Association for Computational Linguistics*.

Y. Zhang, H. Lin, Z. Yang, J. Wang, S. Zhang, Y. Sun, and L. Yang. 2018. A Hybrid Model Based on Neural Networks for Biomedical Relation Extraction. *Journal of Biomedical Informatics*, 81.

Y. Zhang, V. Zhong, D. Chen, G. Angeli, and C. Manning. 2017. Position-aware Attention and Supervised Data Improve Slot Filling. In *Proceedings of the 2017 Conference on Empirical Methods in Natural Language Processing*.

Zhenyu Zhang, Xiaobo Shu, Bowen Yu, Tingwen Liu, Jiapeng Zhao, Quangang Li, and Li Guo. 2020. Distilling Knowledge from Well-Informed Soft Labels for Neural Relation Extraction. In *The Thirty-Fourth AAAI Conference on Artificial Intelligence*.

P. Zhou, Z. Qi, S. Zheng, J. Xu, H. Bao, and B. Xu. 2016. Text Classification Improved by Integrating Bidirectional LSTM with Two-dimensional Max Pooling. In *Proceedings of the 26th International Conference on Computational Linguistics*.

End to End Binarized Neural Networks for Text Classification

Kumar Shridhar[1*], **Harshil Jain**[2*], **Akshat Agarwal**[3*], **Denis Kleyko**[4,5]

[1]NeuralSpace, London
[2]Computer Science and Engineering, IIT Gandhinagar, Gujarat, India
[3]Electrical Engineering, Delhi Technological University, Delhi, India
[4]Redwood Center for Theoretical Neuroscience, University of California, Berkeley
[5]Intelligent Systems Lab, Research Institutes of Sweden
kumar@neuralspace.ai, jain.harshil@iitgn.ac.in,
akshat.agarwal0311@gmail.com, denis.kleyko@ri.se

Abstract

Deep neural networks have demonstrated their superior performance in almost every Natural Language Processing task, however, their increasing complexity raises concerns. A particular concern is that these networks pose high requirements for computing hardware and training budgets. The state-of-the-art transformer models are a vivid example. Simplifying the computations performed by a network is one way of addressing the issue of the increasing complexity. In this paper, we propose an end to end binarized neural network for the task of intent and text classification. In order to fully utilize the potential of end to end binarization, both the input representations (vector embeddings of tokens statistics) and the classifier are binarized. We demonstrate the efficiency of such a network on the intent classification of short texts over three datasets and text classification with a larger dataset. On the considered datasets, the proposed network achieves comparable to the state-of-the-art results while utilizing $\sim$ 20-40% lesser memory and training time compared to the benchmarks.

1 Introduction

In recent years, deep neural networks have achieved great success in a variety of domains, but the networks are becoming more and more computationally expensive due to their ever-growing size. This tendency has been noticed in (Strubell et al., 2019; Schwartz et al., 2019) and it has been recommended that academia and industry researchers should draw their attention towards more computationally efficient methods. At the same time, many important application areas such as chatbots, IoT devices, mobile devices, and other types of power-constrained and resource-constrained platforms re-

quire solutions that would be highly computationally and memory efficient. Such use-cases limit the potential use of the state-of-the-art deep networks. One viable solution is the transformation of these high-performance neural networks to a more computationally efficient architecture. Recently, Binarized Convolutional Neural Networks (BNN) (Hubara et al., 2016) have been developed where both weights and activations are restricted to $\{+1, -1\}$. BNN is a highly computationally efficient network with a much lower memory footprint. Tasks like language modeling (Zheng and Tang, 2016) were performed using binarized neural networks, but, to the best of our knowledge, in the area of text classification, no end to end trainable binarized architectures have been demonstrated yet.

In this paper, we introduce an architecture for the tasks of intent and text classifications that fully utilizes the power of binary representations. The input representations are tokenized and embedded in binary high-dimensional (HD) vectors forming distributed representations using the paradigm known as hyperdimensional computing (Kanerva, 2009). The binary input representations are used for training an end to end BNN classifier for intent classification. Classification performance-wise, the binarized architecture achieves results comparable to the state-of-the-art on several standard intent classification datasets. The efficiency of the proposed architecture is shown in terms of its time and memory complexity relative to non-binarized architectures.

2 Proposed Method

Figure 1 presents a schematic overview of the architecture. Given an input text document D, we first pre-process the document. The pre-processed document is then tokenized into the corresponding tokens $< T_1, T_2, ..., T_n >$, which are used as an

---

[*] The authors contributed equally to this research and work was done at NeuralSpace

Proceedings of SustaiNLP: Workshop on Simple and Efficient Natural Language Processing, pages 29–34
Online, November 20, 2020. ©2020 Association for Computational Linguistics

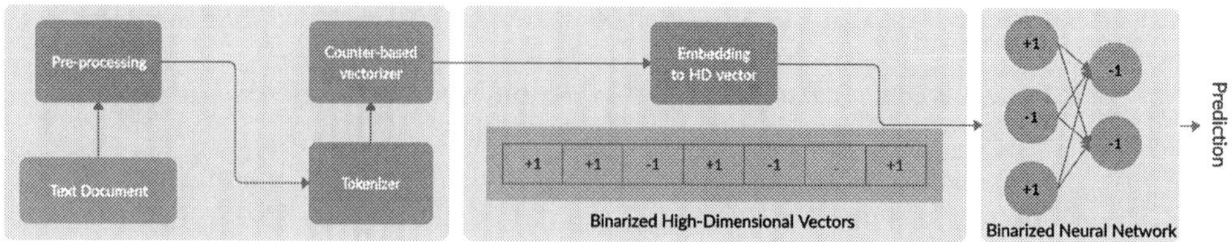

Figure 1: A schematic diagram of the end to end binarized classification architecture for text classification.

input to a count-based vectorizer. The representation of vectorizers, which is sparse and localist, is embedded into an HD vector (distributed representation) using hyperdimensional computing. HD vector representing the counter's content can be binarized. It is used as an input to a classifier. The primary classifier studied in this work is BNN, but other classifiers are also considered for benchmarking.

2.1 High-Dimensional embedding of vectorized representations

In order to reduce the dimensionality of representations, we use hyperdimensional computing (Kanerva, 2009). First, each unique token T_i is assigned with a random d-dimensional bipolar HD vector, where d would be a hyperparameter of the method. HD vectors are stored in the item memory, which is a matrix $\mathbf{H} \in [d \times n]$, where n is the number of tokens. Thus, for a token T_i there is an HD vector $\mathbf{H}_{T_i} \in \{-1, +1\}^{[d \times 1]}$. To construct composite representations from the atomic HD vectors stored in $\mathbf{H}$, hyperdimensional computing defines three key operations: permutation (ρ), binding ($\odot$, implemented via element-wise multiplication), and bundling ($+$, implemented via element-wise addition) (Kanerva, 2009). The bundling operation allows storing information in HD vectors (Frady et al., 2018). The three operations above allow embedding vectorized representations based on n-gram statistics into an HD vector (Joshi et al., 2016).

We first generate $\mathbf{H}$, which has an HD vector for each token. The permutation operation ρ is applied to $\mathbf{H}_{T_j}$ j times ($\rho^j(\mathbf{H}_{T_j})$) to represent a relative position of token T_j in an n-gram. A single HD vector corresponding to an n-gram (denoted as $\mathbf{m}$) is formed using the consecutive binding of permuted HD vectors $\rho^j(\mathbf{H}_{T_j})$ representing tokens in each position j of the n-gram. For example, the trigram '#he' will be embedded to an HD vector as follows: $\rho^1(\mathbf{H}_\#) \odot \rho^2(\mathbf{H}_\text{h}) \odot \rho^3(\mathbf{H}_\text{e})$. In general,

the process of forming HD vector of an n-gram is $\mathbf{m} = \prod_{j=1}^{n} \rho^j(H_{T_j})$, where T_j is token in jth position of the n-gram; the consecutive binding operations applied to n HD vectors are denoted by $\prod$. Once it is known how to form an HD vector for an individual n-gram, embedding the n-gram statistics into an HD vector $\mathbf{h}$ is achieved by bundling together all n-grams observed in the document:

$$\mathbf{h} = [\sum_{i=1}^{k} f_i \mathbf{m}_i = \sum_{i=1}^{k} f_i \prod_{j=1}^{n} \rho^j(H_{T_j})],$$

where k is the total number of unique n-grams; f_i is the frequency of ith n-gram and $\mathbf{m}_i$ is the HD vector of ith n-gram; $\sum$ denotes the bundling operation when applied to several HD vectors; $[*]$ denotes the binarization operation, which is implemented via the sign function. The usage of $[*]$ is optional, so we can either obtain binarized or non-binarized $\mathbf{h}$. If $\mathbf{h}$ is non-binarized, its components will be integers in the range $[-k, k]$, but these extreme values are highly unlikely since HD vectors for different n-grams are quasi-orthogonal, which means that in the simplest (but not practical) case when all n-grams have the same probability the expected value of a component in $\mathbf{h}$ is 0. Due to the use of $\sum$ for representing n-gram statistics, two HD vectors embedding two different n-gram statistics might have very different amplitudes if the frequencies in these statistics are very different. When HD vectors $\mathbf{h}$ are binarized, this issue is addressed. In the case of non-binarized HD vectors, we address it by using the cosine similarity, which is imposed by normalizing each $\mathbf{h}$ by its ℓ_2 norm; thus, all $\mathbf{h}$ have the same norm, and their dot product is equivalent to their cosine similarity.

2.2 Binarized Neural Networks

Based on the work of (Hubara et al., 2016), we construct BNNs capable of working with representations of texts. To take the full advantage of binarized HD vectors, we constraint the weights and

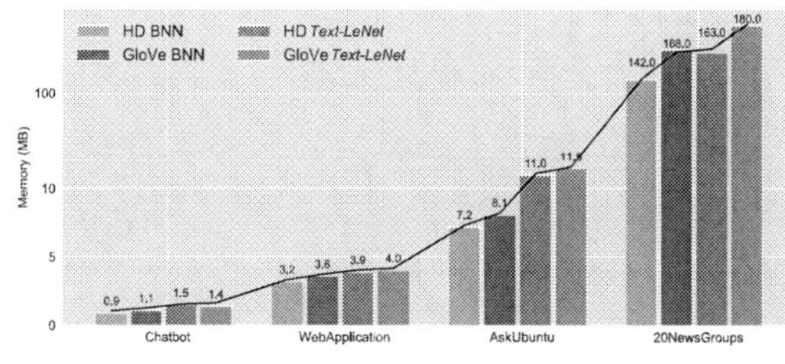

(a) Memory Comparison

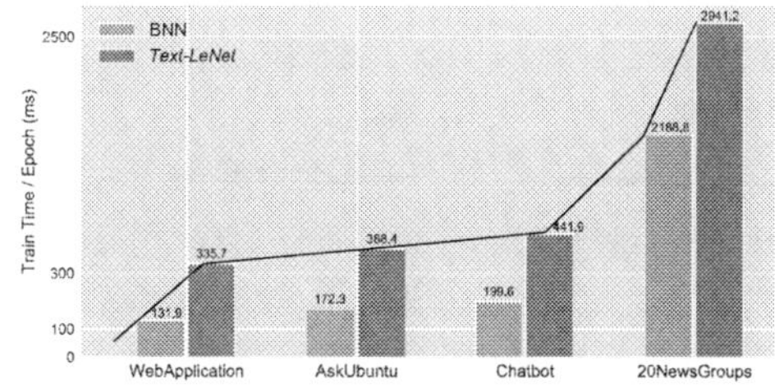

(b) Train Time per epoch Comparison

Figure 2: (a) shows the memory comparisons for all 4 datasets using HD *Text-LeNet*, HD BNN, GloVe *Text-LeNet*, GloVe BNN and (b) shows the training time per epoch comparison for all 4 datasets using BNN and *Text-LeNet*

Tokenizers	Chatbot		AskUbuntu		WebApplication		20NewsGroups	
	Text-LeNet	BNN	*Text-LeNet*	BNN	*Text-LeNet*	BNN	*Text-LeNet*	BNN
Word	**0.80**	0.73	0.51	**0.79**	0.56	**0.78**	0.54	**0.56**
SemHash	**0.94**	0.90	**0.87**	0.84	0.79	**0.83**	**0.78**	0.69
BPE	**0.80**	0.58	0.54	**0.67**	0.52	**0.75**	0.38	**0.42**
Char BPE	**0.92**	0.81	**0.76**	**0.76**	**0.55**	0.53	**0.55**	0.48
SentencePiece	0.80	**0.99**	0.70	**0.72**	0.50	**0.70**	0.41	**0.43**
BERT	**0.89**	0.88	**0.72**	0.71	0.70	**0.77**	**0.60**	**0.60**

Table 1: F_1 performance comparison of binarized *Text-LeNet* (BNN) architecture with non-binarized *Text-LeNet* for the task of intent classification on various datasets.

activations of the network layers to be $\{+1, -1\}$. This constraint is highly efficient in terms of hardware and memory, as bit-wise operations are used instead of multiply-accumulate operations. For example, a multiplication on binary values can be performed using an XNOR logical operation.

The vectorized representations of tokens embedded into HD vectors are binarized with all values $\{+1, -1\}$. In the case of HD vectors, we binarize the result of the bundling operation using the sign function.

Similarly, the sign function is used in the BNN for every weight or activation to restrict them into $\{+1, -1\}$ as follows:

$$b(x) = [x] = \text{sign}(x) = \begin{cases} +1 & \text{if } x \geq 0, \\ -1 & \text{otherwise} \end{cases} \quad (1)$$

where, x can be any weight or activation value.

We further define a convolutional 1D layer that creates a convolution kernel that is convolved with the input HD vector over a single spatial dimension to produce a tensor of outputs. Since gradient descent methods make small changes to the value of the weights, which cannot be done with binary values, we use the straight-through estimator idea, as mentioned in (Yin et al., 2019). We also define a value over which we clip the gradients in the

backward pass:

$$\frac{\delta b(x)}{\delta x} = \begin{cases} +1 & \text{if } |x| < \text{clip value}, \\ 0 & \text{otherwise} \end{cases} \quad (2)$$

This ensures that the entire architecture is end to end trainable using gradient descent optimization.

3 Empirical Analysis

3.1 Datasets

All the experiments are performed on four datasets, namely: the *Chatbot Corpus* (Chatbot), the *Ask Ubuntu Corpus* (AskUbuntu), the *Web Applications Corpus* (WebApplication), and the *20 News Groups Corpus* (20NewsGroups) (Braun et al., 2017).

3.2 Results and Discussions

For CNN-based architecture, 5 hidden layers were used: 3 convolutional 1D layers followed by 2 dense layers. Due to its resemblance to the original LeNet architecture (LeCun et al., 1998), we refer to this architecture as *Text-LeNet*. We compare the results of binarized HD vectors with the binarized *Text-LeNet* (BNN) architecture as the classifier against non-binarized HD vectors with non-binarized *Text-LeNet*. The F_1 scores are compared in Table 1 where BNN performed equally well to a *Text-LeNet* architecture while being 20%

Datasets	Binarized GloVe	Binarized SemHash	Binarized HD vectors
Chatbot	0.74	0.91	**0.99**
AskUbuntu	0.86	**0.87**	0.84
WebApplication	0.66	0.80	**0.83**
20NewsGroups	0.62	0.64	**0.69**

Table 2: F_1 performance comparison of Binarized GloVe vectors, Binarized SemHash vectors and Binarized HD vectors. All vectorizers use the same binarized *Text-LeNet* architecture as classifier.

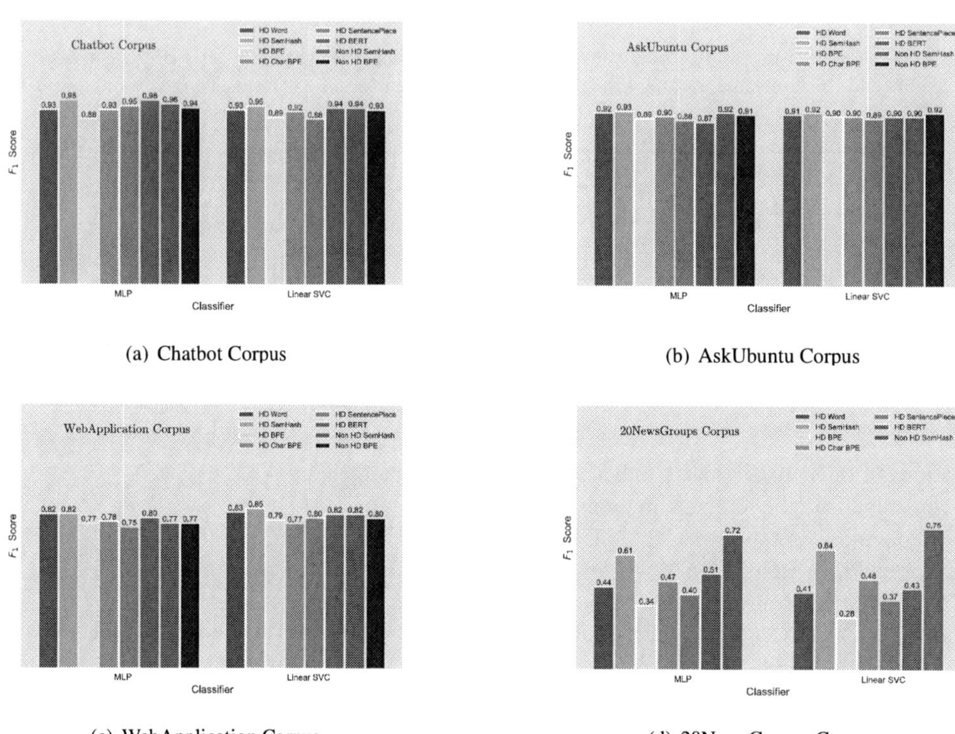

(a) Chatbot Corpus

(b) AskUbuntu Corpus

(c) WebApplication Corpus

(d) 20NewsGroups Corpus

Figure 3: (a), (b), (c) and (d) show the F_1 score comparison of MLP and Linear SVC classifier with HD and non-HD based tokenizers on Chatbot, AskUbuntu, WebApplication and 20NewsGroups corpus respectively.

to 40% more memory efficient, as shown in Figure 2 (a). Note that due to the specifics of implementation, BNNs use 32 bit float values as *Text-LeNet*. The memory efficiency of BNNs can be further improved by 4x when 8-bit representations are used and up to 32x if a single bit representations are used. However, the hardware limitations prevented us from going to that extreme. On the performance side, BNNs outperforms the *Text-LeNet* for AskUbuntu and WebApplication datasets on 4 out of 6 tokenizers. The results reported in Table 1 used 512 dimensional HD vectors for Chatbot, AskUbuntu, and WebApplication corpus, while 1,024 dimensional HD vectors were used for the 20NewsGroups dataset.

One thing to note here is that *Text-LeNet* also used HD vectors with the mentioned tokenizers, but the HD vectors were non-binarized. HD vectors in itself are already faster and much more efficient than counter-based representations, as shown in (Alonso et al., 2020). When experimenting with other embedding methods like GloVe, the training was significantly slower; therefore, HD vectors were used for all the experiments. In addition to that, using the binarized classifier (BNN) further improved the training time up to 50% per epoch when compared to non-binarized classifier on all four datasets, as shown in Figure 2 (b). Furthermore, when compared to GloVe embeddings with *Text-LeNet*, HD BNN used around 20 - 40% lesser

Platform	Chatbot	AskUbuntu	WebApplication	Average
Botfuel	0.98	0.90	0.80	0.89
Luis	0.98	0.90	0.81	0.90
Dialogflow	0.93	0.85	0.80	0.86
Watson	0.97	0.92	0.83	0.91
Rasa	0.98	0.86	0.74	0.86
Snips	0.96	0.83	0.78	0.86
Recast	**0.99**	0.86	0.75	0.87
TildeCNN	**0.99**	0.92	0.81	0.91
FastText	0.97	0.91	0.76	0.88
SemHash (Shridhar et al., 2019)	0.96	0.92	**0.87**	**0.92**
BPE	0.95	**0.93**	0.85	0.91
HD vectors (Alonso et al., 2020)	0.97	0.92	0.82	0.90
Binarized HD vectors with the best classifier	0.98	**0.93**	0.84	**0.92**
HD *Text-LeNet*	0.94	0.87	0.79	0.88
HD BNN	**0.99**	0.84	0.83	0.91

Table 3: F_1 score comparison of various platforms on intent classification datasets of short texts with methods used in the paper. Some results are taken from (Alonso et al., 2020)

memory for all the intent classification datasets.

We also benchmarked the binarized HD vectors with binarized 300-dimensional GloVe vectors and the binarized version of counter-based representation for SemHash tokenizer (Alonso et al., 2020) for all the datasets. Table 2 summarizes the results of the comparison. All the binarized representations were trained with the same BNN classifier. Binarized HD vectors performed significantly better than other binarized methods outperforming binarized GloVe by 4 - 25% and binarized SemHash by 2 - 8% on 2 out of 3 smaller intent classification datasets and achieved comparable results for AskUbuntu dataset. The trend continued for 20NewsGroups with binarized HD achieving 5 - 7% better F_1 scores. Note that for the SemHash counter-based vectorizer, we put a sign function $\text{sign}(x) = +1$ for $x > 0$ and -1 otherwise.

In Figure 3, MLP and Linear SVC with all the tokenizers with HD vectors as representation are compared with MLP and Linear SVC classifiers with SemHash tokenizers and counter-based vectorizer as representation from (Alonso et al., 2020). The F_1 score is comparable to the state-of-the-art for both MLP and SVC. For all small intent classification datasets, binarized HD vectors have achieved better results than non-HD vectors. The proposed architecture beats the non-HD baselines by +2% for AskUbuntu and Chatbot Corpus, and +5% for WebApplication Corpus. However, for 20NewsGroups, the results of binarized HD Vectors are lower than non-HD Vectors. This is mainly due to the large size of the dataset, and simple classifiers like LinearSVC failed to perform with just binarized values. The results for all the other classifiers

are provided in the Appendix.

Table 3 compares the F_1 scores of various platforms on the intent classification datasets. We report the results of binarized HD vectors with the best classifiers from one of the nine classifiers mentioned (Binarized HD vectors with the best classifier), non-binarized HD vectors with *Text-LeNet* (HD *Text-LeNet*) and binarized HD vectors with binarized *Text-LeNet* (HD BNN). Our end to end binarized architecture (HD BNN) achieved the state-of-the-art results for the Chatbot dataset. The approach where only HD vectors were binarized (binarized HD vectors with the best classifier) achieved the state-of-the-art results for the AskUbuntu dataset. The results on the WebApplication dataset are comparable to the state-of-the-art (0.87 with SemHash): 0.84 for binarized HD vectors with the best classifier and 0.83 for HD BNN. The average performance of both binarized HD vectors with the best classifier (0.92) and HD BNN (0.91) was also comparable to the best non-binarized approach (0.92).

4   Conclusion

In this work, we show that it is possible to achieve comparable to the state-of-the-art results while using the binarized representations of all the components of the text classification architecture. This allows exploring the effectiveness of binary representations both for reducing the memory footprint of the architecture and for increasing the energy-efficiency of the inference phase due to the effectiveness of binary operations. This work takes a step towards enabling NLP functionality on resource-constrained devices.

References

P. Alonso, K. Shridhar, D. Kleyko, E. Osipov, and M. Liwicki. 2020. HyperEmbed: Tradeoffs between Resources and Performance in NLP Tasks with Hyperdimensional Computing Enabled Embedding of n-gram Statistics. *arXiv:2003.01821*.

D. Braun, A. Hernandez-Mendez, F. Matthes, and M. Langen. 2017. Evaluating Natural Language Understanding Services for Conversational Question Answering Systems. In *Annual Meeting of the Special Interest Group on Discourse and Dialogue (SIGDIAL)*, pages 174–185.

E. P. Frady, D. Kleyko, and F. T. Sommer. 2018. A Theory of Sequence Indexing and Working Memory in Recurrent Neural Networks. *Neural Computation*, 30:1449–1513.

L. Geiger and P. Team. 2020. Larq: An Open-Source Library for Training Binarized Neural Networks. *Journal of Open Source Software*, 5(45):1746.

G. Hinton, N. Srivastava, and K. Swersky. 2012. Neural Networks for Machine Learning Lecture 6a Overview of Mini-batch Gradient Descent.

I. Hubara, M. Courbariaux, D. Soudry, R. El-Yaniv, and Y. Bengio. 2016. Binarized Neural Networks. In *Advances in Neural Information Processing Systems (NIPS)*, pages 1–9.

S. Ioffe and C. Szegedy. 2015. Batch normalization: Accelerating deep network training by reducing internal covariate shift. *CoRR*, abs/1502.03167.

A. Joshi, J. T. Halseth, and P. Kanerva. 2016. Language Geometry Using Random Indexing. In *Quantum Interaction (QI)*, pages 265–274.

P. Kanerva. 2009. Hyperdimensional Computing: An Introduction to Computing in Distributed Representation with High-Dimensional Random Vectors. *Cognitive Computation*, 1(2):139–159.

Y. LeCun, L. Bottou, Y. Bengio, and P. Haffner. 1998. Gradient-based Learning Applied to Document Recognition. *Proceedings of the IEEE*, 86(11):2278–2324.

R. Schwartz, J. Dodge, N. Smith, and O. Etzioni. 2019. Green ai. *arXiv preprint arXiv:1907.10597*.

K. Shridhar, A. Dash, A. Sahu, G. Grund Pihlgren, P. Alonso, V. Pondenkandath, G. Kovacs, F. Simistira, and M. Liwicki. 2019. Subword Semantic Hashing for Intent Classification on Small Datasets. In *International Joint Conference on Neural Networks (IJCNN)*, pages 1–6.

E. Strubell, A. Ganesh, and A. McCallum. 2019. Energy and Policy Considerations for Deep Learning in NLP. In *57th Annual Meeting of the Association for Computational Linguistics (ACL)*, pages 3645–3650.

P. Yin, J. Lyu, S. Zhang, S. Osher, Y. Qi, and J. Xin. 2019. Understanding Straight-through Estimator in Training Activation Quantized Neural Nets. *arXiv:1903.05662*.

W. Zheng and Y. Tang. 2016. Binarized Neural Networks for Language Modeling. *Technical Report cs224d, Stanford University*.

Exploring the Boundaries of Low-Resource BERT Distillation

Moshe Wasserblat, Oren Pereg, Peter Izsak
Intel AI Lab, Petah Tikva, Israel

{moshe.wasserblat, oren.pereg, peter.izsak}@intel.com

Abstract

In recent years, large pre-trained models have demonstrated state-of-the-art performance in many NLP tasks. However, the deployment of these models on devices with limited resources is challenging due to the models' large computational consumption and memory requirements. Moreover, the need for a considerable amount of labeled training data also hinders real-world deployment scenarios. Model distillation has shown promising results for reducing model size, computational load and data efficiency. In this paper we test the boundaries of BERT model distillation in terms of model compression, inference efficiency and data scarcity. We show that classification tasks that require the capturing of general lexical semantics can be successfully distilled by very simple and efficient models and require relatively small amount of labeled training data. We also show that the distillation of large pre-trained models is more effective in real-life scenarios where limited amounts of labeled training are available.

1 Introduction

In recent years, large pre-trained models such as BERT (Devlin et al., 2019), GPT-2 (Radford et al., 2018) and XLNET (Yang et al., 2019) have demonstrated state-of-the-art performance in many NLP tasks and have become standard. However, the deployment of these models on devices with limited resources is challenging due to the models' large computational consumption and memory requirements. For example, the two variants of BERT, named BERT$_{\text{BASE}}$ and BERT$_{\text{LARGE}}$ consist of approximately 110M and 340M parameters, respectively. Another deployment hurdle in real-world scenarios is the scarcity of labeled data resources.

Model distillation (Ba and Caruana, 2014; Hinton et al., 2015) has shown promising results for reducing model size and computational load while preserving much of the original model's performance. A typical model distillation setup includes two stages; in the first stage, a large, cumbersome and accurate *teacher* neural network is trained for a specific downstream task. In the second stage a smaller and simpler *student* model, that is more practical for deployment in environments with limited resources, is trained to mimic the behavior of the teacher model.

Prior work related to transformer-based model distillation, focused on reducing the number of layers of the original model, obtaining shallower and more efficient student models (Sun et al., 2019; Sanh, 2019; Turc et al., 2019). Tang et al. (2019) proposed a BERT distillation method for single sentence classification tasks and sentence matching tasks using a BiLSTM (Graves, 2012; İrsoy and Cardie, 2014) student model. Our work is closely related to the work of Tang et al. (2019), however, in our work we push the boundaries of BERT model distillation in terms of model size and complexity reduction, computational load and data scarcity for single-sentence classification tasks.

The contribution of this paper is twofold; first, we show that classification tasks that require the capturing of general lexical semantics can be successfully distilled by simple and efficient models while preserving results comparable to those achieved by BERT. Second, building on previous work (Izsak et al., 2019; Mukherjee and Awadallah, 2020), we show that the distillation of large pre-trained models is more effective in real-life scenarios, where a limited amount of labeled training is available. Moreover, we show that in low data resource scenarios, the distillation model size and complexity can be substantially reduced. Specifically, we show that results produced by using a very simple and efficient model such as Continuous Bag of Words (CBoW) with a Feed Forward Network(FFN) are comparable to results produced by using a more complex model such as BiLSTM.

Proceedings of SustaiNLP: Workshop on Simple and Efficient Natural Language Processing, pages 35–40
Online, November 20, 2020. ©2020 Association for Computational Linguistics

2 Approach

The aim of a model distillation process is to use a large pre-trained *teacher* model to train a small and computationally efficient *student* model so it achieves accuracy comparable to that of the teacher model. In this section we describe the teacher and student model architectures (Sections 2.1) and the distillation process (Section 2.2).

2.1 Models Architecture

For the teacher model we chose the popular pre-trained BERT model (Devlin et al., 2019). Specifically, we used BERT$_{BASE}$, consisting of 110M parameters, and added a sentence-level softmax classification layer on top of BERT's CLS token output. The first step of the distillation process is to fine-tune BERT for a specific task using labeled data. In this step, we jointly fine-tune the parameters of BERT and the sentence-level classifier by maximizing the probability of the correct label, using the cross-entropy loss.

For student models we chose two non-transformer-based models whose neural architectures are shallower than BERT, and which contain considerably fewer parameters. The two student models are:

CBoW-FFN This simple student model is often used for very efficient text classification tasks based on sentence representation (Agibetov et al., 2018; Chen et al., 2018). The network consists of an internal embedding layer with embedding vectors of dimension $d_{emb} = 16$, followed by an average pooling layer and a Feed-Forward Network (FFN). The model contains approximately 80K parameters, meaning it is approximately 1375 times more compact than BERT$_{BASE}$.

BiLSTM The BiLSTM network (Graves, 2012; İrsoy and Cardie, 2014) consists of a pre-trained embedding[1] layer followed by two identical BiLSTM layers stacked one on top of another, and where the last hidden state of the second layer is followed by a FFN. The model contains approximately 685K parameters, meaning it is approximately 160 times more compact than BERT$_{BASE}$.

Additional Models We also experimented with Convolutional Neural Networks (CNNs) (Kalchbrenner et al., 2014). However, BiLSTM performed better for the same model size.

---

[1] We used Stanford GloVe embeddings `https://nlp.stanford.edu/projects/glove/`

Dataset	Task	T-train	S-train	Test
AGNews	topic	400	20K	7.6K
Emotion	emotion	1000	50K	2K
IMDB	sentiment	1000	25K	25K
SST-2	sentiment	200	1M*	1.9K
CoLA	acceptability	1000	1M*	516

Table 1: Dataset descriptions and statistics. T-train represents the number of labeled samples used for training the teacher model (step 1) and S-train represent the number of unlabeled samples used for training the student model (step 2). *Obtained using the data augmentation method described by Jiao et al. (2020).

2.2 The Distillation Process

The first step of the training process consists of fine-tuning the teacher model using the available labeled data. The second step of the distillation process is depicted in Figure 1. In this step the student model is trained using the unlabeled data. The unlabeled data is fed in parallel into both the fine-tuned teacher model and to the student model. Following (Tang et al., 2019), we only use the distillation loss which is calculated for each training batch by performing Mean Square Error (MSE) between the soft targets (logits) that are produced by the student and teacher models:

$$L_{distill} = \frac{1}{N} \sum_{n=0}^{N} (y_s - y_t)^2$$

where y_s and y_t are the logits produced by the student and teacher models, respectively.

3 Experimental Setup

3.1 Datasets and Tasks

The goal of our work is to test the distillation boundaries in terms of model size compression, inference computation load and training data size of single-sentence classification tasks. We conducted experiments on five widely-used single-sentence classification datasets, as detailed below.

AGNews A topic classification dataset (Zhang et al., 2015) that consists of internet news titles labeled with four categories: World, Entertainment, Sports and Business.

Emotion An emotion classification dataset (Saravia et al., 2018) that consists of Twitter posts labeled with any of six basic emotion categories: sadness, disgust, anger, joy, surprise, and fear.

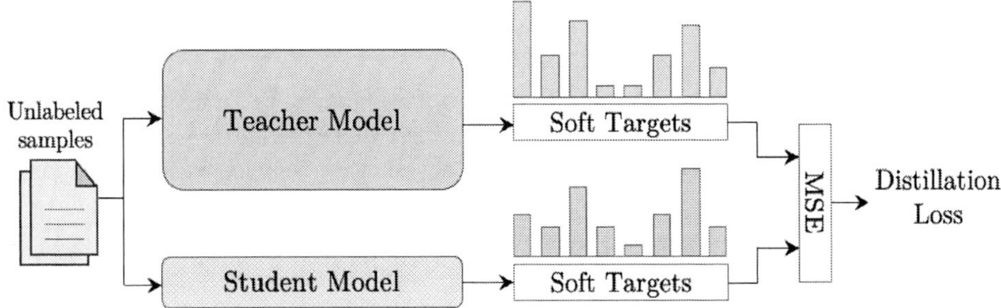

Figure 1: Student model training process. The student and teacher models process the unlabeled samples and generate logits for each example. Distillation loss is produced by calculating the Mean Square Error(MSE) between the logits of both models.

Model	AGnews	Emotion	IMDB	SST-2	CoLA	Comp. ratio	Speedup
BERT$_{BASE}$	87.3	82	88.3	83.5	56	x1	x1
CBoW-FFN	86.3	82	87.6	79.1	10	x1375	x574
BiLSTM	86.4	81.8	85.6	80.7	10	x160	x40

Table 2: Low-data-resource distillation models comparison. For all datasets we report the F1 score except for CoLA, for which we report the Matthews Correlation Coefficient (MCC). Comp. ratio and Speedup[2] represent the model size reduction ratio and inference speedup, respectively, in relation to BERT$_{BASE}$.

IMDB The Internet Movie Database (IMDB; Maas et al. 2011) comprises single sentences extracted from informal movie reviews for binary (positive/negative) sentiment classification.

SST-2 The Stanford Sentiment Treebank 2 (SST-2; Socher et al. 2013) comprises single sentences extracted from movie reviews for binary (positive/negative) sentiment classification. This dataset is part of the widely used General Language Understanding Evaluation (GLUE) benchmark (Wang et al., 2018).

CoLA The Corpus of Linguistic Acceptability (CoLA; Warstadt et al. 2018) consists of English acceptability judgments drawn from books and journal articles on linguistic theory. Each sentence is annotated with whether it is a grammatical English sentence or not. This dataset is also part of the GLUE benchmark.

Table 1 shows the dataset descriptions and statistics. In order to simulate a real-life data-scarce environment, we limited the labeled teacher model training set (T-train) size to no more than a thousand samples. It was shown that large amounts of data are needed for the teacher model to fully express its knowledge (Ba and Caruana, 2014). For AGNews, Emotion and IMDB datasets, we used the available training data which is part of the datasets as unlabeled student training data (S-train). How-

ever, both SST-2 and CoLA datasets, do not contain sufficient amounts of training data, therefore, we use the data augmentation method described by Jiao et al. (2020) for generating unlabeled student training data (S-train).

3.2 Setup

We adopt the HuggingFace (Wolf et al., 2019) implementation of BERT-base (uncased)[3] model for the teacher model. We fine-tune the model for 3 epochs with learning rate of $5e^{-5}$ and batch size of 16. The CBoW-FFN student model was implemented based on the model described by Agibetov et al. (2018) with embedding size of 16 and word vocabulary size of 5000. The BiLSTM student model was implemented in a fashion similar to the model described by Chollet[4] with embedding size of 100 and with vocabulary size of 5000.

4 Results and Discussion

4.1 The Low Resource Scenario

Table 2 shows low-data-resource scenario comparison between the accuracy of the two student

---

[2]Runnig on Intel(R) Xeon(R) CPU @ 2.30GHz, OS: Ubunto 18.04.3 LTS and Tensorflow 2.2
[3]https://github.com/huggingface/transformers
[4]https://keras.io/examples/nlp/bidirectional_lstm_imdb/

Model	SST2-low resource[*]	SST2-high resource[**]
BERT_{BASE}	83.5	91
CBoW-FFN	79.1	82
BiLSTM	80.7	86.1
CBoW-FFN-NoDs[†]	62.8	81.2
BiLSTM-NoDs[†]	63.1	78.8

Table 3: F1 score comparison between low and high data resource scenarios for the SST-2 dataset. [*]Teacher model training size = 200 samples. [**]Teacher model training size = 6920 samples. [†]No distillation.

models and the teacher model across the different datasets and tasks. Overall, the distilled models produced results that are competitive with the teacher model's results across all datasets and tasks except for the CoLA task. An interesting observation is that the relatively lightweight CBoW-FFN model's results are on-par with the BiLSTM results. A possible explanation for these results is that all of the tasks, with the exception of CoLA, require the detection of general lexical semantic features with relatively less emphasis on linguistic structure and contextual relations, therefore BERT's contextual-oriented architecture has no advantage over the student models' architecture. The CoLA task, on the other hand, requires the detection of linguistic structure and contextual relations and this is where BERT's architecture excels and the student models' architectures are lacking.

4.2 Low Resource Vs. High Resource

Table 3 shows an F1 score comparison between the two student models and the teacher model for low and high labeled data resource scenarios for the SST-2 dataset. The table also shows results for the student models when trained directly on the labeled data (non-distilled version).

Distilled Vs. Non-Distilled Models   The results demonstrate that the student models trained using the distillation method (described in Section 2.2), consistently outperform the baseline student models trained directly on the labeled data, proving the effectiveness of the distillation approach. However, and in accordance with the findings of Izsak et al. (2019); Mukherjee and Awadallah (2020), it is also evident that the F1 score enhancement achieved by the distilled student models over the non-distilled models is higher in the low resource scenario than in the high resource scenario. Specifically, the F1 improvement between the distilled and non-distilled versions of the two student models in the low resource scenario are 16.3% and 17.6%, vs. 0.8% and 7.3% in the high resource scenario.

Distilled Models Vs. BERT   The results also show that in the high resource scenario case, where an abundance of labeled training data is available, BERT's accuracy advantage over the distilled models grows larger compared to the low-resource scenario. Specifically, the F1 score gaps between BERT and the student models in the high resource scenario are 9%, and 4.9%, respectively, whereas in the low resource scenario those gaps are only 4.4% and 2.8% respectively.

BiLSTM Vs. CBoW-FFN   Another observation is that in the high resource case, the practical trade-off between model complexity and accuracy becomes more salient. For example, the F1 score gap between CBoW-FFN and BiLSTM is merely 1.6% in the low resource scenario but reaches 4.1% in the high resource scenario. This observation aligns with the basic neural-networks phenomena that larger and deeper neural networks are able to represent the distribution of the data more accurately compared to smaller models when large amounts of data are available (Ng, 2018).

Practical Implications   The practical implications of these results is that distillation is more effective in real-life scenarios where limited amounts of labeled training data are available. In high-resource scenarios, however, where an abundance of labeled training data is available, using deeper and more complex student models such as BiLSTM, or shallower transformer-based models, yields higher accuracies.

5   Conclusion

We showed that in low resource scenarios, it is feasible to distil BERT using very efficient models while preserving comparable results. However, the success of the distillation depends on the dataset and task at hand. Classification tasks that require capturing of general lexical semantics can be successfully distilled by very simple and efficient models; however, classification tasks that require detection of linguistic structure and contextual relations are more challenging for distillation using simple student models. For future work, we aim to explore the impact of the datasets' linguistic structures on the distillation success and to develop dataset-related measurements (Arora et al., 2020) for predicting the success of the distillation in relation to different student models.

References

Asan Agibetov, Kathrin Blagec, Hong Xu, and Matthias Samwald. 2018. Fast and scalable neural embedding models for biomedical sentence classification. BMC Bioinformatics 19, 541.

Simran Arora, Avner May, Jian Zhang, and Christopher Ré. 2020. Contextual embeddings: When are they worth it? In *Proceedings of the 58th Annual Meeting of the Association for Computational Linguistics*, pages 2650–2663, Online. Association for Computational Linguistics.

Jimmy Ba and Rich Caruana. 2014. Do deep nets really need to be deep? In Z. Ghahramani, M. Welling, C. Cortes, N. D. Lawrence, and K. Q. Weinberger, editors, *Advances in Neural Information Processing Systems 27*, pages 2654–2662. Curran Associates, Inc.

Qingyu Chen, Yifan Peng, and Zhiyong lu. 2018. Biosentvec: creating sentence embeddings for biomedical texts.

Jacob Devlin, Ming-Wei Chang, Kenton Lee, and Kristina Toutanova. 2019. BERT: Pre-training of deep bidirectional transformers for language understanding. In *Proceedings of the 2019 Conference of the North American Chapter of the Association for Computational Linguistics: Human Language Technologies, Volume 1 (Long and Short Papers)*, pages 4171–4186, Minneapolis, Minnesota. Association for Computational Linguistics.

Alex Graves. 2012. *Supervised Sequence Labelling with Recurrent Neural Networks*. Studies in Computational Intelligence. Springer, Berlin.

Geoffrey Hinton, Oriol Vinyals, and Jeff Dean. 2015. Distilling the knowledge in a neural network. Cite arxiv:1503.02531 Comment: NIPS 2014 Deep Learning Workshop.

Ozan İrsoy and Claire Cardie. 2014. Opinion mining with deep recurrent neural networks. In *Proceedings of the 2014 Conference on Empirical Methods in Natural Language Processing (EMNLP)*, pages 720–728, Doha, Qatar. Association for Computational Linguistics.

Peter Izsak, Shira Guskin, and Moshe Wasserblat. 2019. Training compact models for low resource entity tagging using pre-trained language models. *ArXiv*.

Xiaoqi Jiao, Yichun Yin, Lifeng Shang, Xin Jiang, Xiao Chen, Linlin Li, Fang Wang, and Qun Liu. 2020. Tiny{bert}: Distilling {bert} for natural language understanding.

Nal Kalchbrenner, Edward Grefenstette, and Phil Blunsom. 2014. A convolutional neural network for modelling sentences. In *Proceedings of the 52nd Annual Meeting of the Association for Computational Linguistics (Volume 1: Long Papers)*, pages 655–665, Baltimore, Maryland. Association for Computational Linguistics.

Andrew L. Maas, Raymond E. Daly, Peter T. Pham, Dan Huang, Andrew Y. Ng, and Christopher Potts. 2011. Learning word vectors for sentiment analysis. In *Proceedings of the 49th Annual Meeting of the Association for Computational Linguistics: Human Language Technologies - Volume 1*, HLT '11, pages 142–150, Stroudsburg, PA, USA. Association for Computational Linguistics.

Subhabrata Mukherjee and Ahmed Hassan Awadallah. 2020. Distilling bert into simple neural networks with unlabeled transfer data. *ArXiv*.

Andrew Ng. 2018. *Machine Learning Yearning*, pages 11–12. deeplearning.ai.

Alec Radford, Jeffrey Wu, Rewon Child, David Luan, Dario Amodei, and Ilya Sutskever. 2018. Language models are unsupervised multitask learners.

Victor Sanh. 2019. Introducing distilbert, a distilled version of bert. Medium.

Elvis Saravia, Hsien-Chi Toby Liu, Yen-Hao Huang, Junlin Wu, and Yi-Shin Chen. 2018. CARER: Contextualized affect representations for emotion recognition. In *Proceedings of the 2018 Conference on Empirical Methods in Natural Language Processing*, pages 3687–3697, Brussels, Belgium. Association for Computational Linguistics.

Richard Socher, Alex Perelygin, Jean Wu, Jason Chuang, Christopher D. Manning, Andrew Ng, and Christopher Potts. 2013. Recursive deep models for semantic compositionality over a sentiment treebank. In *Proceedings of the 2013 Conference on Empirical Methods in Natural Language Processing*, pages 1631–1642, Seattle, Washington, USA. Association for Computational Linguistics.

Siqi Sun, Yu Cheng, Zhe Gan, and Jingjing Liu. 2019. Patient knowledge distillation for BERT model compression. In *Proceedings of the 2019 Conference on Empirical Methods in Natural Language Processing and the 9th International Joint Conference on Natural Language Processing (EMNLP-IJCNLP)*, pages 4323–4332, Hong Kong, China. Association for Computational Linguistics.

Raphael Tang, Yao Lu, Linqing Liu, Lili Mou, Olga Vechtomova, and Jimmy Lin. 2019. Distilling task-specific knowledge from bert into simple neural networks. *CoRR*, abs/1903.12136.

Iulia Turc, Ming-Wei Chang, Kenton Lee, and Kristina Toutanova. 2019. Well-read students learn better: On the importance of pre-training compact models. *arXiv preprint arXiv:1908.08962v2*.

Alex Wang, Amanpreet Singh, Julian Michael, Felix Hill, Omer Levy, and Samuel Bowman. 2018. GLUE: A multi-task benchmark and analysis platform for natural language understanding. In *Proceedings of the 2018 EMNLP Workshop BlackboxNLP: Analyzing and Interpreting Neural Networks for NLP*, pages 353–355, Brussels, Belgium. Association for Computational Linguistics.

Alex Warstadt, Amanpreet Singh, and Samuel R. Bowman. 2018. Neural network acceptability judgments. *CoRR*, abs/1805.12471.

Thomas Wolf, Lysandre Debut, Victor Sanh, Julien Chaumond, Clement Delangue, Anthony Moi, Pierric Cistac, Tim Rault, R'emi Louf, Morgan Funtowicz, and Jamie Brew. 2019. Huggingface's transformers: State-of-the-art natural language processing. *ArXiv*, abs/1910.03771.

Zhilin Yang, Zihang Dai, Yiming Yang, Jaime Carbonell, Ruslan Salakhutdinov, and Quoc V. Le. 2019. Xlnet: Generalized autoregressive pretraining for language understanding. Cite arxiv:1906.08237Comment: Pretrained models and code are available at https://github.com/zihangdai/xlnet.

Xiang Zhang, Junbo Zhao, and Yann LeCun. 2015. Character-level convolutional networks for text classification. In C. Cortes, N. D. Lawrence, D. D. Lee, M. Sugiyama, and R. Garnett, editors, *Advances in Neural Information Processing Systems 28*, pages 649–657. Curran Associates, Inc.

Efficient Estimation of Influence of a Training Instance

Sosuke Kobayashi[1,2]   Sho Yokoi[1,3]   Jun Suzuki[1,3]   Kentaro Inui[1,3]

Tohoku University[1]   Preferred Networks, Inc.[2]   RIKEN[3]

`sosk@preferred.jp`
`{yokoi,jun.suzuki,inui}@ecei.tohoku.ac.jp`

Abstract

Understanding the influence of a training instance on a neural network model leads to improving interpretability. However, it is difficult and inefficient to evaluate the influence, which shows how a model's prediction would be changed if a training instance were not used. In this paper, we propose an efficient method for estimating the influence. Our method is inspired by dropout, which zero-masks a sub-network and prevents the sub-network from learning each training instance. By switching between dropout masks, we can use sub-networks that learned or did not learn each training instance and estimate its influence. Through experiments with BERT and VGGNet on classification datasets, we demonstrate that the proposed method can capture training influences, enhance the interpretability of error predictions, and cleanse the training dataset for improving generalization.

1   Introduction

What is the influence of a training instance on a machine learning model? This question has attracted the attention of the community (Cook, 1977; Koh and Liang, 2017; Zhang et al., 2018; Hara et al., 2019). Evaluating the influence of a training instance leads to more interpretable models and other applications like data cleansing.

A simple evaluation is by comparing a model with another similarly trained model, whose training does not include the instance of interest. This method, however, requires computational costs of time and storage depending on the number of instances, which indicates the extreme difficulty (Table 1). While computationally cheaper estimation methods have been proposed (Koh and Liang, 2017; Hara et al., 2019), they still have computational difficulties or restrictions of model choices. The contribution of this work is to propose an estimation

method, which (i) is computationally more efficient while (ii) useful for applications (iii) without significant sacrifice of model performance.

We propose a trick for enabling a neural network without restrictions to estimate the influence, which we refer to as *turn-over dropout*. This method is computationally efficient as it requires only running two forward computations after training a single model on the entire training dataset. In addition to the efficiency, we demonstrated that it enabled BERT (Devlin et al., 2019) and VGGNet (Simonyan and Zisserman, 2015) to analyze the influences of training through various experiments, including example-based interpretation of error predictions and data cleansing to improve the accuracy on a test set with a distributional shift.

2   Influence of a Training Instance

2.1   Problem Setup

We present preliminaries on the problem setup. In this paper, we deal with the *influence* of training with an instance on prediction with another one, which has been studied in Koh and Liang (2017), Hara et al. (2019) and so on. Let $z := (x, y)$ be an instance and represent a pair of input $x \in X$ and its output $y \in Y$, and let $D := \{z_i\}_{i=1}^N$ be a training dataset. By using an optimization method with D, we aim to find a model $f_D \colon X \to Y$. Denoting the loss function by $L(f, z)$, the learning problem is obtaining $\hat{f}_D = \mathrm{argmin}_f \mathbb{E}_{z_i \in D} L(f, z_i)$.

The *influence*, $I(z_{\mathrm{target}}, z_i; D)$, is a quantitative benefit from z_i to prediction of z_{target}. Let $f_{D \setminus \{z_i\}}$ to be a model trained on the dataset D excluding z_i, the influence is defined as

$$I(z_{\mathrm{target}}, z_i; D)$$
$$:= L(f_{D \setminus \{z_i\}}, z_{\mathrm{target}}) - L(f_D, z_{\mathrm{target}}). \quad (1)$$

Intuitively, the larger this value, the more strongly a training instance z_i contributes to reduce the loss of

Proceedings of SustaiNLP: Workshop on Simple and Efficient Natural Language Processing, pages 41–47
Online, November 20, 2020. ©2020 Association for Computational Linguistics

Method	Training	Storage	Estimation
Re-train	$O(|D|^2)$	$O(|\theta||D|)$	$O(F|D|)$
Hara+	$O(|D|)$	$O(|\theta|T)$	$O(F|D| + (F+F')TB)$
Koh+	$O(|D|)$	$O(|\theta|)$	$O(F|D| + (F+F')rtb)$
Ours	$O(|D|)$	$O(|\theta|)$	$O(F|D|)$

Table 1: Comparison of computational complexity for estimating the influence of all instance on another instance, with Hara et al. (2019) and Koh and Liang (2017), where $|\theta|$ is the number of parameters, F is a forward/backward computation, F' is a double backward computation, T is the training steps, B is a training minibatch size, b is a minibatch size for stabilizing approximation, rt are the hyper-parameters; typically $rt \approx |D|$. See the references in detail.

prediction on another instance z_{target}. The instance of interest z_{target} is typically an instance in a test or validation dataset.

2.2 Related Methods

Computing the influence in Equation (1) by retraining two models for each instance is computationally expensive, and several estimation methods are proposed. Koh and Liang (2017) proposed an estimation method that assumed a strongly convex loss function and a global optimal solution[1]. While the method is used even with neural models (Koh and Liang, 2017; Han et al., 2020), which do not satisfy the assumption, it still requires high computational cost. Hara et al. (2019) proposed a method without these restrictions; however, it consumes large disk storage and computation time that depend on the number of optimization steps. Our proposed method is much more efficient, as shown in Table 1. For example, in a case where Koh and Liang (2017)'s method took 10 minutes to estimate the influences of 10,000 training instances on another instance with BERT (Han et al., 2020), our method only required 35 seconds[2]. This efficiency will expand the scope of applications of computing influence. For example, it would enable real-time interpretation of model predictions for users of the machine learning models.

---

[1] Strictly speaking, Koh and Liang (2017) studied a similar but different value from I in Equation (1). Briefly, the formulation in Koh and Liang (2017) considers convex models with the optimal parameters for $f_{D \setminus \{z_i\}}$ and f_D. The definition in Hara et al. (2019) did not have such conditions and treated the broader problem. We follow Hara et al. (2019); therefore, the definition in Equation (1) allows any f_D and $f_{D \setminus \{z_i\}}$, as long as they have the same initial parameters and optimization procedures using the same mini-batches except for z_i.

[2] For the details, see Appendix B.

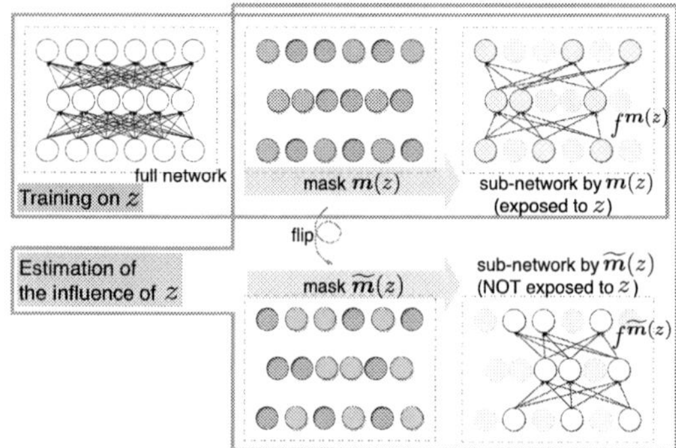

Figure 1: Dropout generates a sub-network for each training instance z, and updates its parameters (red; top) only. By contrast, the (blue; bottom) sub-network is not influenced by z. Our estimation uses the difference between the two sub-networks.

3 Proposed Method

3.1 Background: Dropout

Dropout (Hinton et al., 2012; Srivastava et al., 2014) is a popular regularization methods for deep neural networks. During training, d-dimensional random mask vector m, where d refers to the number of parameters of a layer, is sampled, and a neural network model f is transformed into a variant f^m with a parameter set multiplied with m each update[3]. The elements of mask $m \in \{0, \frac{1}{p}\}^d$ are randomly sampled as follows: $m_j := m'_j/p$, $m'_j \sim$ Bernoulli(p). Parameters masked (multiplied) with 0 are disabled in an update step like pruning. Thus, dropout randomly selects various sub-networks f^m to be updated at every step. During inference at test time, dropout is not applied. One interpretation of dropout is that it trains numerous sub-networks and uses them as ensemble (Hinton et al., 2012; Srivastava et al., 2014; Bachman et al., 2014; Baldi and Sadowski, 2014; Bul et al., 2016). In this work, $p = 0.5$; approximately half of the parameters are zero-masked.

3.2 Proposed Method: Turn-over Dropout

In the standard dropout method, dropout masks are sampled independently at every update. In our proposed method, however, we use *instance-specific dropout masks* $m(z)$, which are also random vectors but *deterministically* generated and

---

[3] Typically, dropout is applied to the layers of the neural network rather than its parameter matrices. In this case, each instance in a minibatch drops different column-wise parameters of matrices at once.

tied with each instance z. Thus, when the network is trained with an instance z, only a deterministic subset of its parameters is updated, as shown in Figure 1. In other words, the sub-network $f^{m(z)}$ is updated; however the corresponding counterpart of the network $f^{\widetilde{m}(z)}$ is not at all affected by z, where $\widetilde{m}(z)$ is the *flipped* mask of $m(z)$, i.e., $\widetilde{m}(z) := \frac{1}{p} - m(z)$. Both sub-networks, $f^{m(z)}$ and $f^{\widetilde{m}(z)}$, can be used by applying the individual masks to f. These sub-networks are analogously comprehended as two different networks trained on a dataset with or without an instance, respectively, f_D and $f_{D \setminus \{z_i\}}$[4]. From this analogy, the influence of a training instance can be evaluated by considering these two sub-networks. The influence $I(z_{\text{target}}, z_i; D) = L(f_{D \setminus \{z_i\}}, z_{\text{target}}) - L(f_D, z_{\text{target}})$ is estimated as

$$\hat{I}(z_{\text{target}}, z_i; D)$$
$$:= L(f_D^{\widetilde{m}(z_i)}, z_{\text{target}}) - L(f_D^{m(z_i)}, z_{\text{target}}), \quad (2)$$

which corresponds to the gain when using $f_D^{m(z_i)}$, instead of $f_D^{\widetilde{m}(z_i)}$ for a prediction on z_{target}. We call this estimation method *turn-over dropout*. Its summarized advantages are as follows:

- **Lower computation time**: The method only requires running forward procedure two times.

- **No snapshot or re-training**: A single model can be used for all training instances.

- **Easy to implement**: The model modification and estimation procedure are very simple.

3.3 Memory-efficient Instance-specific Masks

One may think that using instance-specific masks require a large space, depending on the dataset size and the number of parameters to be masked. However, this cost is drastically reduced to a constant $O(1)$, using a trick. As the masks are not updated, we do not have to save them directly. Instead, we can deterministically generate the random masks with a fixed random seed number anytime. Thus, models can avoid storing masks and generate masks when using them. We call this trick as *volatile mask generation*[5].

---

[4] In this paper, we associate $f^{m(z)}$ and $f^{\widetilde{m}(z)}$ with f_D and $f_{D \setminus \{z_i\}}$, respectively. However, while f_D does not focus on any instance in D so much, its substitute $f^{m(z)}$ may be a little biased to some characteristic of z. For ignoring bias, we can use f_D itself (i.e., full network) instead of $f^{m(z)}$, while the representation powers of f_D and $f_{D \setminus \{z_i\}}$ are different. We tested the alternative but did not find large improvements. Further exploration is an interesting future work.

[5] The volatile mask generation method solved storage and memory issues in our experiments. However, the memory

4 Experiments

The computational efficiency of our method is discussed in Section 2. Moreover, we answer a question: even if it is efficient, does it work well on applications? To demonstrate the applicability, we conducted experiments using different models and datasets.

Setup First, we used the Stanford Sentiment TreeBank (SST-2) (Socher et al., 2013) binary sentiment classification task. Five thousand instances were sampled from the training set, and 872 instances in the development set were used. We trained BERT-base classifiers (Wolf et al., 2019) with the adapter modules (Houlsby et al., 2019), which froze the pre-trained BERT parameters but newly trained branch networks in addition to the output layers. We applied the turn-over dropout on the adapter modules and output layers.

In addition, we used the CIFAR-10 (Krizhevsky, 2009) 10-class image classification task, with the 50,000 training instances and 10,000 validation instances. We trained the VGGNet19 classifier (Simonyan and Zisserman, 2015) with the turn-over dropout.

Models were trained with the cross-entropy loss. Further details of the setup are shown in Appendix A.

4.1 Side Effect on Model Performance

Note that turn-over dropout is not for improving the accuracy of models. It gives the models the method of efficiently estimating the influence of each training instance. A possible side effect is a deterioration of accuracy due to introducing instance-specific dropout with $p = 0.5$[6]. Thus, we first explored the change of classification accuracy when using the turn-over dropout.

For BERT with the adapter modules on SST-2, if we use a small dataset (N=5,000), the accuracy slightly decreased from the baseline model, from 90.0% to 88.3%. If we use a larger dataset (N=20,000), the change is negligible; 90.5% and 90.2%. Thus, in a case with large datasets, where

---

issue could occur even with the method, depending on implementations. For such a particular case and another solution for it, see Appendix C in detail.

[6] Dropout with $p = 0.5$ is often used in various neural networks, especially on linear layers of them, and improves the accuracy. However, dropout on all layers could damage. It is also unclear how dropout with "static" masks effect because the idea is novel.

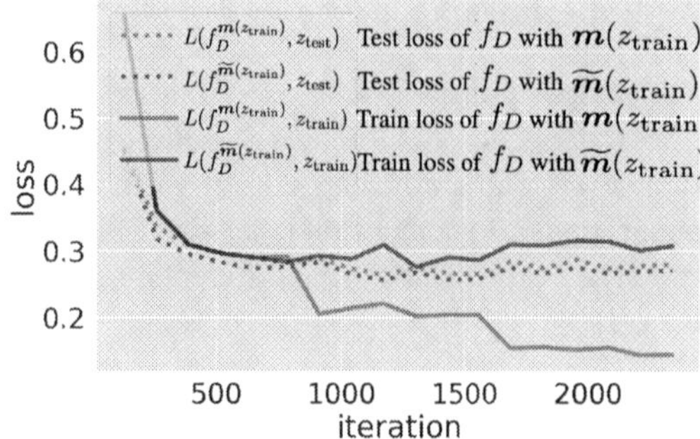

Figure 2: Loss curves of BERT on SST-2.

Test input: if s ##te ##ven so ##der ##berg ##h ' s ` solar ##is '
is a failure it is a glorious failure .
(if steven soderbergh ' s ` solaris ' is a failure it is a glorious failure .)
[positive → negative]
Influential: un ##fo ##cus ##ed , ex ##c ##ru ##ciating ##ly te ##dious
(unfocused . excruciatingly tedious)

Figure 3: A misclassified text in the test set and the text with the highest influence with the error label in the training set for BERT on SST-2.

Test input:
- why do some people assume they know who the ask ##er is , based on the question he asks ? from reading back the answers that i get on my questions , i am now officially a m ##us ##lim - ch ##rist ##ian - b ##udd ##his ##t , a straight ... it ok with you that i still don ' t have an identity - crisis ?
[Society & Culture → Business & Finance]
Influentials:
- is ch ##rist ##mas eve in the evening or is it just the day before ch ##rist ##mas ? my sister thinks that ch ##rist ##mas eve ...
- how i can be ch ##rist ##ain ? i want to be real ch ##rist ##ain , how i can be ch ##rist ##ain ask ch ##rist into ...

Figure 4: A misclassified text in the test set and the texts with the highest influence with the error label in the training set for BERT on Yahoo Answers.

we typically want to use turn-over dropout for efficiency, applying the turn-over dropout does not decrease the validation accuracy compared with the baseline. However, when we use turn-over dropout on all layers of BERT *without* the adapter modules using makes training unstable. Furthermore the same is true for VGGNet on CIFAR-10. Instead, we first applied the turn-over dropout only for all layers after the 11th layer, although this means early layers can learn all instances in the training dataset and make the turn-over dropout leaky[7]. We found that VGGNet with turn-over dropout can overfit more than the baseline does; their accuracies are 86.2% and 92.0%, respectively. If we add regularization using the original dropout, the accuracy is recovered to 91.3%. Thus, in some cases, we have to care about the decrease of model performances when using turn-over dropout. While we experimented with the successful architectures only, exploring the side effect in various architectures and its remedy is important future work.

4.2 Sanity Check: Learning Curves

We first observed an interesting property of the turn-over dropout from the loss curves during training, as shown in Figure 2. The solid red line of training loss using $m(z_{\text{train}})$, $L(f_D^{m(z_{\text{train}})}, z_{\text{train}})$, showed a typical tendency of training loss. However, the solid blue line of training loss using $\widetilde{m}(z_{\text{train}})$, $L(f_D^{\widetilde{m}(z_{\text{train}})}, z_{\text{train}})$, indicated loss values close to the test losses (in dotted lines), without overfitting. This fact agrees with the idea behind the turn-over dropout; the sub-network $f^{\widetilde{m}(z_{\text{train}})}$ us-

ing the flipped mask does not learn each training instance z_{train}.

4.3 Interpretation of Error of Predictions

Neural network models are notorious for their black-box prediction, which harms the trust and usability (Ribeiro et al., 2016). The influence estimation can mitigate this problem by suggesting possible reasons for a wrong model prediction by identifying influential training instances.

To verify this benefit, we collected the misclassified instances of the validation or test set and searched for the training instances that most influenced the wrong predictions. Figure 3 indicates a text example from the results. Rare words of named entities were divided into many subwords (Schuster and Nakajima, 2012; Sennrich et al., 2016; Wu et al., 2016) and requiring more complex processing. A guess is that BERT might fail to understand the input due to the cluttered subwords, and predict a wrong label, which depended on a training instance similarly with many subwords. Additionally, we conducted the same experiment on Yahoo Answers 10-label question classification dataset (Zhang et al., 2015)[8], which is more complex than sentiment analysis. Figure 4 shows the results on Yahoo Answers. The misclassified text shares the phrase "ch ##rist" with the two influen-

---

[7] Yuki M. Asano (2020) demonstrated that early layers of CNN contained limited information about the statistics of images, and such low-level statistics can be learned even through a single image. Based on the finding, we assumed that early layers did not fit each instance so much, and the effect of leakage was small.

[8] We used 5,000 training instances as well as SST-2.

Figure 5: Misclassified images in the validation set (upper row) and images with the highest influence in the training set (lower row) for VGGNet on CIFAR-10.

	Accuracy (%)	Loss
1% Random Removal	76.8 ± 1.1	0.521 ± 0.030
No Cleansing	77.0 ± 0.9	0.536 ± 0.063
1% Cleansing	**78.3 ± 0.2**	**0.484 ± 0.008**

Table 2: The results of data cleansing. Loss is the cross entropy loss. The averages and standard deviations from four difference runs are shown.

tial instances. Such a low-level cue is not critical in the test. However, it seemed that the model focused on the phrase and predicted the label of training instances containing the phrase.

In addition, more intuitively, image results are shown in Figure 5. The two leftmost instances with the "bird" label were wrongly predicted as "airplane." The training instances of airplane with the highest influence on the error predictions are shown in the row below. The corresponding images had similar visual features, such as shape, layout, or color, which probably led to the wrong predictions.

4.4 Data Cleansing

Another possible application of the influence estimation is to eliminate harmful instances from the training dataset. If the mean influence of a training instance on unseen instances is negative, the instance can be harmful for generalization. We experimented with data cleansing in a case of domain shift, where the training dataset is of SST-2 (movie review); however, the validation and test dataset are of the 'electronics' subset in Multi-Domain Sentiment Dataset (Blitzer et al., 2007) (Elec). We split the Elec dataset into 200 instances for validation and 1,800 instances for the test. Note that we do not use Elec dataset as a training dataset for studying only the effect of data cleansing.

We finetuned BERT models (with turn-over dropout) on SST-2 dataset and calculated the mean influences considering Elec's validation set. Af-

ter that, we re-trained models without turn-over dropout on datasets that removed training instances with 1% of the most negative influences. Finally, the model performances on Elec's test dataset are compared, as shown in Table 2. The models trained on the cleansed datasets achieved better accuracy and lower loss than those trained on the original dataset. This result demonstrated that our estimation of the influence could also be used for data cleansing.

5 Conclusion

This paper proposed a method that required a low computational cost for estimating the influence of a training instance. The method alters dropout with instance-specific masks and, for estimation, uses sub-networks that are not trained with each instance. The experiments demonstrated that this method could be applied even for complex models.

Acknowledgments

We appreciate the helpful comments from the anonymous reviewers. We thank Sho Takase, Hiroshi Noji, Hitomi Yanaka, Koki Washio, Saku Sugawara, Benjamin Heinzerling, and Kazuaki Hanawa for constructive comments. This work was supported by JSPS KAKENHI Grant Number JP19H04162.

References

Philip Bachman, Ouais Alsharif, and Doina Precup. 2014. Learning with pseudo-ensembles. In *Advances in Neural Information Processing Systems 27*, pages 3365–3373.

Pierre Baldi and Peter Sadowski. 2014. The dropout learning algorithm. *Artificial Intelligence*, 210(C):78–122.

John Blitzer, Mark Dredze, and Fernando Pereira. 2007. Biographies, Bollywood, boom-boxes and blenders: Domain adaptation for sentiment classification. In *Proceedings of the 45th Annual Meeting of the Association of Computational Linguistics*, pages 440–447, Prague, Czech Republic. Association for Computational Linguistics.

Samuel Rota Bul, Lorenzo Porzi, and Peter Kontschieder. 2016. Dropout distillation. In *Proceedings of The 33rd International Conference on Machine Learning*, volume 48, pages 99–107.

R Dennis Cook. 1977. Detection of influential observation in linear regression. *Technometrics*, pages 15–18.

Jacob Devlin, Ming-Wei Chang, Kenton Lee, and Kristina Toutanova. 2019. BERT: Pre-training of deep bidirectional transformers for language understanding. In *Proceedings of the 2019 Conference of the North American Chapter of the Association for Computational Linguistics: Human Language Technologies, Volume 1 (Long and Short Papers)*, pages 4171–4186.

Xiaochuang Han, Byron C. Wallace, and Yulia Tsvetkov. 2020. Explaining black box predictions and unveiling data artifacts through influence functions. In *Proceedings of the 2020 Annual Conference of the Association for Computational Linguistics (to appear)*.

Satoshi Hara, Atsushi Nitanda, and Takanori Maehara. 2019. Data cleansing for models trained with sgd. In *Advances in Neural Information Processing Systems 32*, pages 4215–4224.

Geoffrey E. Hinton, Nitish Srivastava, Alex Krizhevsky, Ilya Sutskever, and Ruslan R. Salakhutdinov. 2012. Improving neural networks by preventing co-adaptation of feature detectors. *CoRR*, abs/1207.0580.

Neil Houlsby, Andrei Giurgiu, Stanislaw Jastrzebski, Bruna Morrone, Quentin De Laroussilhe, Andrea Gesmundo, Mona Attariyan, and Sylvain Gelly. 2019. Parameter-efficient transfer learning for NLP. In *Proceedings of the 36th International Conference on Machine Learning*, volume 97 of *Proceedings of Machine Learning Research*, pages 2790–2799, Long Beach, California, USA. PMLR.

Pang Wei Koh and Percy Liang. 2017. Understanding black-box predictions via influence functions. In *Proceedings of the 34th International Conference on Machine Learning*, pages 1885–1894.

Alex Krizhevsky. 2009. Learning multiple layers of features from tiny images. Technical report.

Peng Qi, Yuhao Zhang, Yuhui Zhang, Jason Bolton, and Christopher D. Manning. 2020. Stanza: A Python natural language processing toolkit for many human languages. In *Proceedings of the 58th Annual Meeting of the Association for Computational Linguistics: System Demonstrations*.

Marco Ribeiro, Sameer Singh, and Carlos Guestrin. 2016. "why should I trust you?": Explaining the predictions of any classifier. In *Proceedings of the 2016 Conference of the North American Chapter of the Association for Computational Linguistics: Demonstrations*, pages 97–101, San Diego, California. Association for Computational Linguistics.

Mike Schuster and Kaisuke Nakajima. 2012. Japanese and korean voice search. In *International Conference on Acoustics, Speech and Signal Processing*, pages 5149–5152.

Rico Sennrich, Barry Haddow, and Alexandra Birch. 2016. Neural machine translation of rare words with subword units. In *Proceedings of the 54th Annual Meeting of the Association for Computational Linguistics (Volume 1: Long Papers)*, pages 1715–1725, Berlin, Germany. Association for Computational Linguistics.

Karen Simonyan and Andrew Zisserman. 2015. Very deep convolutional networks for large-scale image recognition. In *International Conference on Learning Representations*.

Richard Socher, Alex Perelygin, Jean Wu, Jason Chuang, Christopher D. Manning, Andrew Ng, and Christopher Potts. 2013. Recursive deep models for semantic compositionality over a sentiment treebank. In *Proceedings of the 2013 Conference on Empirical Methods in Natural Language Processing*, pages 1631–1642.

Nitish Srivastava, Geoffrey Hinton, Alex Krizhevsky, Ilya Sutskever, and Ruslan Salakhutdinov. 2014. Dropout: A simple way to prevent neural networks from overfitting. *Journal of Machine Learning Research*, 15:1929–1958.

Adina Williams, Nikita Nangia, and Samuel Bowman. 2018. A broad-coverage challenge corpus for sentence understanding through inference. In *Proceedings of the 2018 Conference of the North American Chapter of the Association for Computational Linguistics: Human Language Technologies, Volume 1 (Long Papers)*, pages 1112–1122, New Orleans, Louisiana. Association for Computational Linguistics.

Thomas Wolf, Lysandre Debut, Victor Sanh, Julien Chaumond, Clement Delangue, Anthony Moi, Pierric Cistac, Tim Rault, R'emi Louf, Morgan Funtowicz, and Jamie Brew. 2019. Huggingface's transformers: State-of-the-art natural language processing. *arXiv*, abs/1910.03771.

Yonghui Wu, Mike Schuster, Zhifeng Chen, Quoc V. Le, Mohammad Norouzi, Wolfgang Macherey, Maxim Krikun, Yuan Cao, Qin Gao, Klaus Macherey, Jeff Klingner, Apurva Shah, Melvin Johnson, Xiaobing Liu, Lukasz Kaiser, Stephan Gouws, Yoshikiyo Kato, Taku Kudo, Hideto Kazawa, Keith Stevens, George Kurian, Nishant Patil, Wei Wang, Cliff Young, Jason Smith, Jason Riesa, Alex Rudnick, Oriol Vinyals, Greg Corrado, Macduff Hughes, and Jeffrey Dean. 2016. Google's neural machine translation system: Bridging the gap between human and machine translation. *CoRR*, abs/1609.08144.

Andrea Vedaldi Yuki M. Asano, Christian Rupprecht. 2020. A critical analysis of self-supervision, or what we can learn from a single image. In *International Conference on Learning Representations (ICLR)*.

Xiang Zhang, Junbo Zhao, and Yann LeCun. 2015. Character-level convolutional networks for text classification. In C. Cortes, N. D. Lawrence, D. D. Lee,

M. Sugiyama, and R. Garnett, editors, *Advances in Neural Information Processing Systems 28*, pages 649–657. Curran Associates, Inc.

Xuezhou Zhang, Xiaojin Zhu, and Stephen Wright. 2018. Training set debugging using trusted items. In *AAAI Conference on Artificial Intelligence*.

Efficient Inference For Neural Machine Translation

Yi-Te Hsu[1][*]   **Sarthak Garg**[2]   **Yi-Hsiu Liao**[2]   **Ilya Chatsviorkin**[2]

[1]Johns Hopkins University
[2]Apple Inc.

`yhsu16@jhu.edu, {sarthak_garg, yihsiu_liao, ilych}@apple.com`

Abstract

Large Transformer models have achieved state-of-the-art results in neural machine translation and have become standard in the field. In this work, we look for the optimal combination of known techniques to optimize inference speed without sacrificing translation quality. We conduct an empirical study that stacks various approaches and demonstrates that combination of replacing decoder self-attention with simplified recurrent units, adopting a deep encoder and a shallow decoder architecture and multi-head attention pruning can achieve up to 109% and 84% speedup on CPU and GPU respectively and reduce the number of parameters by 25% while maintaining the same translation quality in terms of BLEU.

1 Introduction and Related Work

Transformer models (Vaswani et al., 2017) have outperformed previously used RNN models and traditional statistical MT techniques. This improvement, though, comes at the cost of higher computation complexity. The decoder computation often remains the bottleneck due to its autoregressive nature, large depth and self-attention structure.

There has been a recent trend towards making the models larger and ensembling multiple models to achieve the best possible translation quality (Lepikhin et al., 2020; Huang et al., 2019). Leading solutions on common benchmarks (Zhu et al., 2020; Brown et al., 2020) usually use an ensemble of Transformer big models, which combined can have more than 1 billion parameters.

Previous works suggest replacing the expensive self-attention layer in the decoder with simpler alternatives like the Average Attention Network (AAN) (Zhang et al., 2018), Simple Recurrent Unit (SRU) (Lei et al., 2018) and Simpler Simple Recurrent Unit (SSRU) (Kim et al., 2019). AAN is a simpler version of the self-attention layer which places equal attention weights on all previously decoded words instead of dynamically computing them. SRU and SSRU are lightweight recurrent networks, with SSRU consisting of only 2 matrix multiplications per decoded token.

Because of the autoregressive property of the decoder in a standard Transformer model, reducing computation cost in the decoder is much more important than in the encoder. Recent publications (Miceli Barone et al., 2017; Wang et al., 2019a; Kasai et al., 2020) thus suggest that a deep encoder, shallow decoder architecture can speed up inference while maintaining a similar BLEU score.

Another line of research focuses on model pruning techniques to make NMT models smaller and more efficient. In this paper, we only explore structured pruning methods, in which smaller components of the network are pruned away. Applications of structured pruning to NMT include works by Voita et al. (2019) and Michel et al. (2019) which show that most of the attention heads in the network learn redundant information and can be pruned. Michel et al. (2019) proposed the idea of pruning heads by head importance scoring. Voita et al. (2019) uses a relaxation of L_0 regularization (Louizos et al., 2018) to prune the attention heads.

All of the above mentioned methods use the vanilla Transformer architecture as their baseline, so it is not clear if these approaches can give complimentary results when combined together. In this work, we explore and benchmark, combining all of the above techniques, with the goal of maximizing inference speed without hurting translation quality.

After carefully stacking the approaches, our proposed architecture is able to achieve a significant speed improvement of 84% on GPU and 109% on CPU architectures without any degradation of translation quality in terms of BLEU.

---

[*] Work done during internship at Apple Inc.

Proceedings of SustaiNLP: Workshop on Simple and Efficient Natural Language Processing, pages 48–53
Online, November 20, 2020. ©2020 Association for Computational Linguistics

2 Efficient Inference for Neural Machine Translation

This section presents the proposed efficient inference architecture for neural machine translation. First, we outline the overall procedure of building an efficient inference architecture. Then, we detail each step in the process.

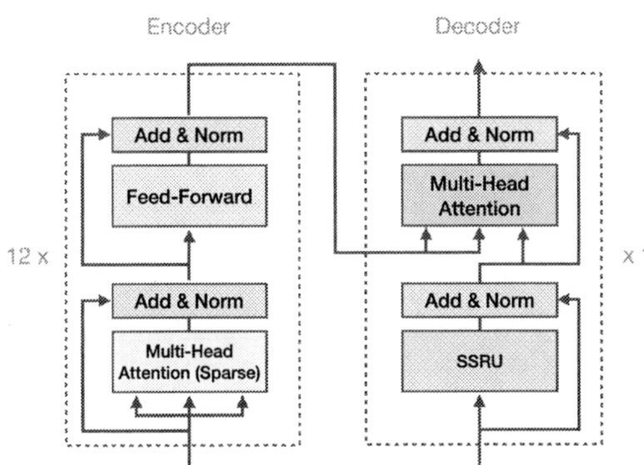

Figure 1: Efficient Transformer Architecture

First, we use sequence-level knowledge distillation (Kim and Rush, 2016) to transfer knowledge from a strong teacher model to a smaller student model. This approach allows the student model to learn from a simpler target distribution and therefore enables us to use a simpler architecture.

Then, to simplify the decoder of the student model, the self-attention mechanism is replaced by lightweight recurrent units (Kim et al., 2019), and the feed-forward network is removed. To further reduce the decoder computation, we adopt the deep encoder, shallow decoder architecture (Kasai et al., 2020). Lastly, we prune redundant attention heads through L_0 regularization (Voita et al., 2019). Each architecture modification is performed by retraining the student model. Figure 1 shows the proposed efficient Transformer architecture.

2.1 Teacher-student Training

We follow the procedure described in Kim et al. (2019), to train an ensemble of 8 Transformer-big models, 4 forward, 4 reverse direction, as the first round of teacher models (T). Without the help of extra monolingual corpora, we apply multi-agent dual learning (MADL) (Wang et al., 2019b) to train another 8 Transformer big teacher models (T-MADL) by re-decoded bitext with ensemble teacher models (T) in both directions. Then we use noisy backward-forward translation (Edunov et al., 2018) with the

T-MADL model to, again, re-decode the original bitext, but with more variance on the source side. Finally, we use the above generated synthetic data along with the original bitext to train our student model.

We use interpolated sequence-level knowledge distillation (Kim and Rush, 2016) in most of the described re-decoding runs except the noisy backward-forward translation where sampling is used in the reverse direction. More details about model training and architecture can be found in Kim et al. (2019).

2.2 Replacing Self-attention with Lightweight Recurrent Units

Inspired by Kim et al. (2019), we replace the decoder self-attention with an RNN, reducing its time complexity from $O(N^2)$ to $O(N)$, where N is the length of the output sentence. We compare replacing self-attention with two lightweight layers: SSRU and AAN, in Section 3.1. The SSRU layer is as follows:

$$
\begin{aligned}
f_t &= \sigma(W_t x_t + b_f) \\
c_t &= f_t \odot c_{t-1} + (1 - f_t) \odot W x_t \\
o_t &= ReLU(c_t)
\end{aligned}
\quad (1)
$$

where the $\odot$ is element-wise multiplication. x_t, o_t, f_t and c_t are the input, output, forget-gate and cell-state, respectively. We optimized the SSRU by combining the two matrix multiplications, $W_t x_t$ and $W x_t$, into one. We find this simple trick can improve speed by 6% on GPU.

For AAN, we found that removing the gating layer does not degrade the translation quality while reducing the computation. In our experiments, we use the following implementation of AAN (without a gating layer):

$$
o_t = FFN(\frac{1}{t}\sum_{k=1}^{t} \mathbf{x}_k) \quad (2)
$$

where $FFN(\cdot)$ is a position-wise two-layer feed-forward network. t, o_t and x_k denote the current position, output at position t and input at position k respectively.

2.3 Removing the Feed-forward Layer

Each decoder layer consists of a lightweight recurrent unit, followed by an encoder-decoder multi-head attention component and a pointwise feed-forward layer. The feed-forward sub-layer is responsible for 33% of parameters within the 6-layer decoder; however, we found that it can be removed entirely from the decoder without hurting the translation quality with our implementation of SSRU (Section 3.1).

2.4 Deep Encoder, Shallow Decoder

In order to further reduce the decoder computation, we decrease the number of decoder layers. In line with the work done by Kasai et al. (2020), to maintain the same model capacity, we increase the number of encoder layers. We explore the speed-accuracy trade-off while varying the depth of both components in Section 3.2, and find that using 12 encoder layers and 1 decoder layer gives a significant speedup without losing translation quality.

2.5 Pruning Attention Heads

Adopting a deep encoder, shallow decoder architecture achieves a good speed-quality tradeoff; however, it increases the number of parameters in the encoder. To further improve efficiency and reduce parameters, we apply multi-head attention pruning proposed by Voita et al. (2019) to our architecture. The output of each head h_i across all attention layers is multiplied by a learnable gate g_i, before it is passed to subsequent layers of the network. To switch off less informative heads (i.e. $g_i = 0$), we applied L_0 regularization to the gates. L_0 norm is the number of non-zero gates across the model. However, because of the non-differentiable property of the L_0 norm, a differentiable approximation is used. Each gate g_i, is modeled as a random variable sampled from a Hard Concrete Distribution (Louizos et al., 2018) parameterized by ϕ_i, and takes values in the range $[0, 1]$. We then minimize the differentiable approximation of L_0 regularization loss, L_c:

$$L_c(\phi) = \sum_{i=1}^{h}(1 - P(g_i = 0|\phi_i)), \qquad (3)$$

where h denotes the total number of heads, ϕ is the set of gate parameters, and $P(g_i = 0|\phi_i)$ is computed according to the Hard Concrete Distribution.

The model is initially trained with the standard cross entropy loss $L_{x_{ent}}$ and then fine-tuned with the additional regularization loss as follows:

$$L(\theta, \phi) = L_{xent}(\theta, \phi) + \lambda L_c(\phi), \qquad (4)$$

where θ denotes the set of original model parameters, and λ is a hyperparameter which controls how aggressively the attention heads are pruned. During inference time, all heads h_j, where $P(g_j = 0|\phi_j) = 1$ are completely removed from the network. Our experiments in Section 3.3 show that we can effectively prune out a large portion of redundant self-attention heads from the deep-encoder.

3 Experiments

We use the Transformer base model (Vaswani et al., 2017) trained on teacher decoded data as our baseline. All the described methods are stacked on top of this baseline model. Following Kim et al. (2019), we use 4 million bitext from the WMT'14 English-German news translation task. All sentences are encoded with 32K subword units using Sentence-Piece (Kudo and Richardson, 2018). We report BLEU on the newstest2014 in all the experiments and use newstest2015 for the final evaluation in Section 3.4

All experiments are implemented in fairseq (Ott et al., 2019). The configuration of teacher-student training follows the settings in Kim et al. (2019). We use an effective batch size of 458k words and 16 GPUs for training. Adam optimizer is applied with $\beta = (0.9, 0.98)$. We use label smoothing with $\varepsilon = 0.1$, inverse square root learning rate schedule with 2500 warmup steps and peak learning rate of 0.0007. The models are trained with 50k updates except for the models with pruning, where additional fine-tuning with 100-150k updates is applied. We use a beam size of 5 during inference. We evaluate the inference speed with batch size of 128 sentences on GPU, batch size 1 on CPU and report speed in words per second (wps), averaged over 10 decoding runs.

Hardware: We evaluate our performance on 1 GPU (NVIDIA Tesla V100-SXM2-32GB) and 1 core CPU (Intel Xeon E5-2640 v4 @ 2.40GHz)

3.1 Replacing Self-Attention with RNN

From Table 1, we can observe that replacing the self-attention with lightweight recurrent units gives significant speed improvements (18-25%) without any impact on BLEU score.

Removing the feed-forward network in the decoder leads to an additional 10-13% speedup for both AAN and SSRU, but results in 0.9 BLEU degradation for AAN. Therefore, we use SSRU as our main architecture in further experiments.

	BLEU	wps	speedup
Baseline	28.9	4510	-
AAN	28.9	5323	18%
SSRU	28.7	5629	25%
AAN w/o ffn	28.0	5915	31%
SSRU w/o ffn	28.5	6079	35%

Table 1: Results of replacing self-attention with lightweight recurrent units and removing the feed-forward network (ffn) in the decoder. Decoding on a GPU with batch-size 128.

	attention heads (enc/enc-dec/dec)	BLEU
Baseline	96/8/8	29.2
+ pruned	22/7/8	29.0
SSRU w/o ffn	96/8/-	28.9
+ pruned	18/8/-	28.6

Table 2: Head pruning through L_0 regularization on the $12 - 1$ layer (encoder-decoder) structure. The (enc/enc-dec/dec) refers to the total number of attention heads in encoder self-attention, encoder-decoder attention and decoder self-attention respectively.

3.2 Number of Layers

We evaluate different combinations of depths in the encoder and decoder. In the decoder, the self-attention mechanism is replaced by the SSRU, and the feed-forward network is removed.

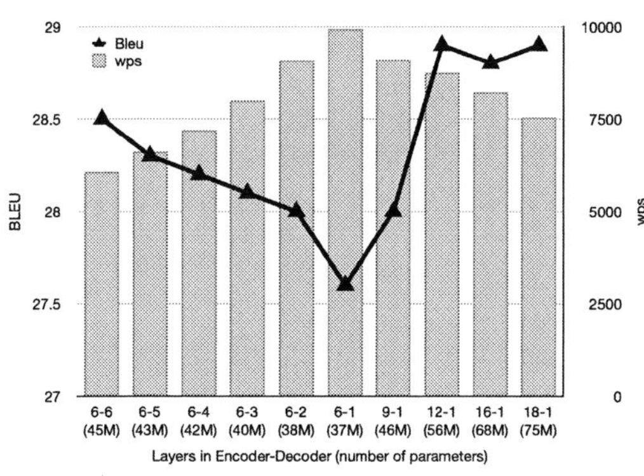

Figure 2: Translation quality – inference speed trade-off over different number of encoder – decoder layers.

From Figure 2, removing one decoder layer at a time from the baseline model increases wps by 10% at a cost of BLEU score degradation since model capacity goes down. As we increase the number of encoder layers to 12 or more, we observe up to 45% speedup, better BLEU score but higher number of parameters than the original 6-6 structure.

3.3 Pruning Attention Heads

Pruning allows us to remove up to 75% of attention heads with slight BLEU degradation. We observe from the remaining heads that for the pruned baseline (22/7/8) model, the self-attention heads are more important in the deeper layers rather than the lower layers. On the other hand, in our best configuration (SSRU 18/8/-), there is no clear pattern of remaining heads.

3.4 Combined Results

We combine all of the methods and evaluate our model on the newstest2015 testset.

	BLEU	speedup GPU/CPU	#params
Baseline	31.1	-	61M
SSRU	31.1	14/12%	57M
+ Remove ffn	31.0	28/49%	45M
+ 12-1	31.5	82/103%	56M
+ Prune heads	31.4	84/109%	46M

Table 3: Decoding on a GPU with batch-size 128, and a single CPU core with batch-size 1. [12-1] refers to the number of layers in the encoder and the decoder.

Table 3 shows that by using all of the techniques in combination, the model achieves 84% and 109% speed improvement on GPU and CPU, respectively compared to the baseline model (Transformer-base). There are only 25% heads remain in the deep-encoder after pruning and the total number of parameters is 25% fewer.

4 Conclusion

In this paper we explored the combination of techniques aimed at improving inference speed which lead to the discovery of a very efficient architecture. The best architecture has a deep 12-layer encoder, and a shallow decoder with only one single lightweight recurrent unit layer and one encoder-decoder attention mechanism. 75% of the encoder heads were pruned giving rise to a model with 25% fewer parameters than the baseline Transformer. In terms of inference speed, the proposed architecture is 84% faster on a GPU, and 109% faster on a CPU.

Acknowledgments

We would like to thank Andrew Finch, Stephan Peitz, Udhay Nallasamy, Matthias Paulik and Russ Webb for their helpful comments and reviews. Many thanks to the rest of the Machine Translation Team for interesting discussions and support.

References

Tom B Brown, Benjamin Mann, Nick Ryder, Melanie Subbiah, Jared Kaplan, Prafulla Dhariwal, Arvind Neelakantan, Pranav Shyam, Girish Sastry, Amanda Askell, et al. 2020. Language models are few-shot learners. *arXiv preprint arXiv:2005.14165*.

Sergey Edunov, Myle Ott, Michael Auli, and David Grangier. 2018. Understanding back-translation at scale. In *Proceedings of the 2018 Conference on Empirical Methods in Natural Language Processing*, page 489–500, Brussels, Belgium.

Yanping Huang, Youlong Cheng, Ankur Bapna, Orhan Firat, Dehao Chen, Mia Chen, HyoukJoong Lee, Jiquan Ngiam, Quoc V Le, Yonghui Wu, and Zhifeng Chen. 2019. Gpipe: Efficient training of giant neural networks using pipeline parallelism. In *Advances in Neural Information Processing Systems 32*, pages 103–112, Vancouver, Canada.

Jungo Kasai, Nikolaos Pappas, Hao Peng, James Cross, and Noah A Smith. 2020. Deep encoder, shallow decoder: Reevaluating the speed-quality tradeoff in machine translation. *arXiv preprint arXiv:2006.10369*.

Yoon Kim and Alexander M. Rush. 2016. Sequence-level knowledge distillation. In *Proceedings of the 2016 Conference on Empirical Methods in Natural Language Processing*, pages 1317–1327, Austin, Texas. Association for Computational Linguistics.

Young Jin Kim, Marcin Junczys-Dowmunt, Hany Hassan, Alham Fikri Aji, Kenneth Heafield, Roman Grundkiewicz, and Nikolay Bogoychev. 2019. From research to production and back: Ludicrously fast neural machine translation. In *Proceedings of the 3rd Workshop on Neural Generation and Translation*, pages 280–288, Hong Kong. Association for Computational Linguistics.

Taku Kudo and John Richardson. 2018. SentencePiece: A simple and language independent subword tokenizer and detokenizer for neural text processing. In *Proceedings of the 2018 Conference on Empirical Methods in Natural Language Processing: System Demonstrations*, pages 66–71, Brussels, Belgium.

Tao Lei, Yu Zhang, Sida I. Wang, Hui Dai, and Yoav Artzi. 2018. Simple recurrent units for highly parallelizable recurrence. In *Proceedings of the 2018 Conference on Empirical Methods in Natural Language Processing*, pages 4470–4481, Brussels, Belgium.

Dmitry Lepikhin, HyoukJoong Lee, Yuanzhong Xu, Dehao Chen, Orhan Firat, Yanping Huang, Maxim Krikun, Noam Shazeer, and Zhifeng Chen. 2020. Gshard: Scaling giant models with conditional computation and automatic sharding. *arXiv preprint arXiv:2006.16668*.

Christos Louizos, Max Welling, and Diederik P. Kingma. 2018. Learning sparse neural networks through l_0 regularization. In *International Conference on Learning Representations*, Vancouver, Canada.

Antonio Valerio Miceli Barone, Jindřich Helcl, Rico Sennrich, Barry Haddow, and Alexandra Birch. 2017. Deep architectures for neural machine translation. In *Proceedings of the Second Conference on Machine Translation*, pages 99–107, Copenhagen, Denmark. Association for Computational Linguistics.

Paul Michel, Omer Levy, and Graham Neubig. 2019. Are sixteen heads really better than one? In *Advances in Neural Information Processing Systems 32*, pages 14014–14024. Vancouver, Canada.

Myle Ott, Sergey Edunov, Alexei Baevski, Angela Fan, Sam Gross, Nathan Ng, David Grangier, and Michael Auli. 2019. fairseq: A fast, extensible toolkit for sequence modeling. In *Proceedings of Annual Conference of the North American Chapter of the Association for Computational Linguistics: Human Language Technologies: Demonstrations*, Minneapolis, USA.

Ashish Vaswani, Noam Shazeer, Niki Parmar, Jakob Uszkoreit, Llion Jones, Aidan N. Gomez, Łukasz Kaiser, and Illia Polosukhin. 2017. Attention is all you need. In *Proceedings of the 31st International Conference on Neural Information Processing Systems*, page 6000–6010, Red Hook, NY, USA. Curran Associates Inc.

Elena Voita, David Talbot, Fedor Moiseev, Rico Sennrich, and Ivan Titov. 2019. Analyzing multi-head self-attention: Specialized heads do the heavy lifting, the rest can be pruned. In *Proceedings of the 57th Annual Meeting of the Association for Computational Linguistics*, pages 5797–5808, Florence, Italy. Association for Computational Linguistics.

Qiang Wang, Bei Li, Tong Xiao, Jingbo Zhu, Changliang Li, Derek F. Wong, and Lidia S. Chao. 2019a. Learning deep transformer models for machine translation. In *Proceedings of the 57th Annual Meeting of the Association for Computational Linguistics*, pages 1810–1822, Florence, Italy. Association for Computational Linguistics.

Yiren Wang, Yingce Xia, Tianyu He, Fei Tian, Tao Qin, ChengXiang Zhai, and Tie-Yan Liu. 2019b. Multi-agent dual learning. In *International Conference on Learning Representations*, New Orleans, Louisiana, United States.

Biao Zhang, Deyi Xiong, and Jinsong Su. 2018. Accelerating neural transformer via an average attention network. In *Proceedings of the 56th Annual Meeting of the Association for Computational Linguistics*, Melbourne, Australia. Association for Computational Linguistics.

Jinhua Zhu, Yingce Xia, Lijun Wu, Di He, Tao Qin, Wengang Zhou, Houqiang Li, and Tieyan Liu. 2020. Incorporating bert into neural machine translation. In *International Conference on Learning Representations*, Addis Ababa, Ethiopia.

Sparse Optimization for Unsupervised Extractive Summarization of Long Documents with the Frank-Wolfe Algorithm

Alicia Y. Tsai
University of California, Berkeley
aliciatsai@berkeley.edu

Laurent El Ghaoui
University of California, Berkeley
elghaoui@berkeley.edu

Abstract

We address the problem of unsupervised extractive document summarization, especially for long documents. We model the unsupervised problem as a sparse auto-regression one and approximate the resulting combinatorial problem via a convex, norm-constrained problem. We solve it using a dedicated Frank-Wolfe algorithm. To generate a summary with k sentences, the algorithm only needs to execute $\approx k$ iterations, making it very efficient. We explain how to avoid explicit calculation of the full gradient and how to include sentence embedding information. We evaluate our approach against two other unsupervised methods using both lexical (standard) ROUGE scores, as well as semantic (embedding-based) ones. Our method achieves better results with both datasets and works especially well when combined with embeddings for highly paraphrased summaries.

1 Introduction

With the overwhelming increase of digital information, automatic text summarization has become important for many applications such as financial reviews, medical articles, etc. Manually summarizing this amount of information takes a considerable amount of time and effort. This has motivated the study of efficient and reliable automatic text summarization methods. The task of automatic summarization is the process of generating a condensed version of a text that best describes the original one (Hahn and Mani, 2000; Luhn, 1958). The two mainstream approaches in the field of automatic summarization are *extractive* and *abstractive*.

Extractive approaches generate summaries by selecting a subset of informative words, phrases, or sentences directly from the source text. In contrast, abstractive approaches use linguistic methods to decompose and build a semantic representation of the text and use natural language generation techniques to generate a summary (Chopra et al., 2016; Nallapati et al., 2016; Zeng et al., 2016; Rush et al., 2015). In recent years, neural network architectures have made abstractive summarization popular. However, abstractive approaches are generally harder to develop as they require high performing natural language generation techniques, which is also an active research field. Besides these two categories, mixed strategies that combine both extractive and abstractive approaches have also been proposed in recent literature (Peng et al., 2019; Cao et al., 2018; See et al., 2017). Previous work in extractive approaches to summarization include statistical (Saggion and Poibeau, 2012; Das and Martins, 2007; Goldstein et al., 1999; Kupiec et al., 1995; Paice, 1990), graph-based and optimization-based ones. The graph-based approaches treat text as a network instead of as a simple bag of words and use graph-based ranking methods to generate a summary (Erkan and Radev, 2011; Ouyang et al., 2009; Mihalcea and Tarau, 2004). Optimization-based methods use techniques such as sparse optimization (Yao et al., 2015; Elhamifar and Vidal, 2013), integer linear programming (ILP) (Qian and Liu, 2013; Berg-Kirkpatrick et al., 2011; Woodsend and Lapata, 2011; Gillick and Favre, 2009) and constraint optimization (Durrett et al., 2016; McDonald, 2007) to reconstruct the summary.

In this work, we focus on extractive summarization for long documents. Performing automatic text summarization for long documents is especially challenging as obtaining high quality human summaries for long documents is often quite costly and time consuming. Recent works on extractive summarization have been focusing on neural network architectures (Nallapati et al., 2017; Cheng and Lapata, 2016). Although these methods are successful in generating summaries for short documents, they often have difficulties with long input

Proceedings of SustaiNLP: Workshop on Simple and Efficient Natural Language Processing, pages 54–62
Online, November 20, 2020. ©2020 Association for Computational Linguistics

sequences (Shao et al., 2017).

Most recent works have started to investigate neural extractive summarization methods for long documents (Xiao and Carenini, 2019; Wang et al., 2017). However, these methods are supervised and require high quality training data in order to train the neural network models. This creates challenges for domains that do not have massive training datasets. Kedzie et al. (2018) compared recent neural extractive summarization models across different domains including news, personal stories, and medical articles. They found that many sophisticated neural extractive summarizers do not have better performance than those consisting of simpler models, and that word embedding averaging performs equally or better than RNNs or CNNs for sentence embedding. This suggests that a simpler model combined with pre-trained word embeddings show promise for summarizing long documents in domains that have few or no training data.

In this work, we propose an unsupervised method for extracting long documents based on a sparse optimization framework and solve it using a dedicated Frank-Wolfe algorithm, which can be combined with pre-trained word embeddings to construct a distributive input representation. Our work is based on the previous work of Cheng et al. (2018) but designed specifically for the summarization task. The proposed framework is an unsupervised model that is efficient and does not require a training corpora, as typical supervised solutions would require. We test our method on two datasets that contain long documents, 2019 FINANCIAL OUTLOOKS and CLASSICAL LITERATURE, and compare it against two baselines: sparse subspace clustering (SSC) and TextRank. The experimental results show that our method gives a higher ROUGE score than our baseline for both datasets. In particular, when combined with sentence embedding, our method gives a higher semantic ROUGE score when evaluated on paraphrased summaries. Moreover, we show that our method is computationally more efficient compared to others.

2 Methodologies

Notation We denote $X_{(i)}$ and $X^{(i)}$ as the i-th row and i-th column of a matrix X respectively. The matrix X_t denotes the value of X at iteration t while $[X_t]_{(i)}$ and $[X_t]^{(i)}$ denotes the i-th row and i-th column of X_t. The sum $\sum_{i=1}^{n} \|X_{(i)}\|_2$ is the L_2

norm group LASSO constraint. The norm $\| \cdot \|_F$ is the Forbenium norm.

2.1 Sparse auto-regressive problem

Extractive summarization aims at finding a minimal set of representative sentences of the original document that effectively summarizes the entire document. Let $A \in \mathbb{R}^{d \times n}$ be the data matrix that represents the document where each column of A represents a sentence in the source document. Here, d is the number of features for each sentence, and n is the number of sentences in the source document. The source document A is written as

$$A \triangleq \begin{bmatrix} a_1 & a_2 \cdots & a_n \end{bmatrix}$$

where the column vector a_i is a sentence in the source document. Finding the set of representative sentences assumes that the source document A can be approximated by a sparse combination of sentences in the document:

$$A \approx a_1 x_1^T + a_2 x_2^T + \cdots + a_n x_n^T$$

The column vector x_i is a decision variable to be learned. Our goal is to select k sentences whose corresponding decision variable x_i is non-zero. If we write it in a matrix form with x_i^T being the row of the matrix variable X, we can formulate the above problem as an auto-regressive problem of the form:

$$\begin{aligned}
\min_{X} \quad & \|AX - A\|_F^2 \\
\text{s.t.} \quad & \|v\|_0 \leq k \\
& v_i = \|X_{(i)}\|_2, \quad \forall i \in [n] \\
& X \geq 0
\end{aligned} \quad (1)$$

where X is row-sparse. Here, $X_{(i)}$ represents the i-th row of the matrix variable X, v_i is its norm, and the constraint is written in terms of the L_0-norm (cardinality, or number of non-zero entries) of v, effectively forcing at least $n - k$ entire rows of X to be zero, thereby singling out a short list of at most k sentences that well represent the whole data set.

The above problem is non-convex and hard to solve but can be well approximated by the so-called L_1-norm heuristic, leading to a convex approximation:

$$\begin{aligned}
\min_{X} \quad & \|AX - A\|_F^2 \\
\text{s.t.} \quad & \|v\|_1 \leq \beta \\
& v_i = \|X_{(i)}\|_2, \quad \forall i \in [n] \\
& X \geq 0
\end{aligned} \quad (2)$$

where β is a hyper-parameter and indirectly controls the row-sparsity (number of non-zero rows). Note that the model simply uses the L_1-norm of vector v in (1) to approximate the cardinality constraint on v. If X^* is the solution of problem (2), then columns in the data matrix $A^{(j)}$ that correspond to the non-zero rows of X^*, $X_{(j)} \neq 0$, are the selected sentences.

2.2 Frank-Wolfe unsupervised extractive summarization

The Frank-Wolfe (FW) or conditional gradient algorithm is an iterative first-order optimization algorithm for constrained convex optimization (Frank and Wolfe, 1956). Although the algorithm was introduced over half a century ago, it has experienced a revival in recent years due to its projection-free iterations and broad applications in machine learning (Jaggi, 2013).

The FW algorithm solves a general constrained optimization problem of the form $\min_{x \in \mathcal{D}} f(x)$, where the convex function f is differentiable and L-Lipschitz and the domain $\mathcal{D}$ is a convex compact set. At each iteration, the FW algorithm requires solving a linear approximation to the objective function over the domain, often referred to as a *linear minimization oracle* (LMO), and then updates the solution accordingly. At each iteration, we first calculate the gradient, solve the LMO problem to find a descent direction, calculate the step size by line search or by $\frac{2}{t+2}$, and update the estimate. Algorithm 1 summarizes the FW process.

Algorithm 1 Frank-Wolfe algorithm

1: Let $t \leftarrow 0$ and $x_0 \in \mathcal{D}$
2: **for** $t = 0, 1, \ldots,$ **do**
3:      $s_t = \arg\min_{s \in \mathcal{D}} \langle s, \nabla f(x_t) \rangle$
4:      Set step size $r_t \leftarrow \frac{2}{t+2}$ or
5:      $r_t \leftarrow \arg\min_{r \in [0,1]} f(x_t + r(s_t - x_t))$
6:      Update $x_{t+1} = x_t + r_t(s_t - x_t)$
7: **return** x_t

Unlike other descent methods for constrained optimization that require a projection step at each iteration, the FW algorithm is a projection-free algorithm and only needs to solve the LMO. Applying the FW algorithm to our sparse constrained optimization problem (2) results in an unsupervised method for extractive summarization. Algorithm 1 is written in terms of vector variable x; however, it

is straightforward to extend it to the matrix variable X. The algorithm starts with $X_0 \leftarrow 0$, meaning no sentence is selected at first. Then the algorithm greedily selects one sentence at each iteration. The algorithm terminates once k rows of X_t are non-zero (dense) or when the algorithm converges to a row-sparse solution with $k^* < k$ non-zero rows. The complete algorithm of Frank-Wolfe unsupervised extractive summarization is outlined in algorithm 2. Next, we explain the details of the algorithm and provide an efficient gradient calculation scheme.

Linear minimization oracle The algorithm requires solving the LMO at each iteration. The solution of the LMO S_t specifies the direction of descent at each step.

$$S_t = \arg\min_{S \in \mathcal{D}} \langle S, \nabla f(X_t) \rangle$$

Because of the group LASSO constraint in (2), the solution matrix S_t is a rank-1 matrix. The non-zero row of S_t is chosen based on the maximum L_2 norm of the gradient's rows:

$$j = \arg\max_i = \| [\nabla f(X_t)]_{(i)} \|_2$$

We denote the non-zero row of S_t at row j as $[S_t]_{(j)}$. The magnitude of $[S_t]_{(j)}$ is β and the direction is chosen to minimize the inner product:

$$[S_t]_{(j)} = -\beta \frac{[\nabla f(X_t)]_{(j)}}{\| [\nabla f(X_t)]_{(j)} \|_2}$$

The algorithm produces sparse and low-rank iterates since at most one extra row of X becomes non-zero in each step by the addition of $r_t S_t$.

Efficient gradient calculation The algorithm requires calculating the gradient at each iteration. The gradient of the objective function in (2) is:

$$\nabla f(X) = 2(A^T A X - A^T A) = 2(KX - K)$$

The matrix $K = A^T A$ can be calculated once and used throughout the algorithm. Explicitly calculating the gradient is expensive due to the matrix-matrix product (naively $\mathcal{O}(n^3)$). However, the structure of the problem allows us to efficiently calculate KX at each iteration. From line 6 in Algorithm 1, we know that X_t is a weighted average of X_{t-1} and a rank-1 matrix S_{t-1}:

$$X_t = (1 - r_{t-1})X_{t-1} + r_{t-1}S_{t-1}$$

This suggests that $(KX)_t$ is a weighted average of $(KX)_{t-1}$ and $KS_{t-1} = K^{(j)}[S_{t-1}]_{(j)}$. $K^{(j)}$ is the j-th column corresponding to the j-th non-zero row of S_{t-1}. Since $(KX)_{t-1}$ is known at iteration t, we are only required to calculate $K^{(j)}[S_{t-1}]_{(j)}$, which is extremely fast (in $\mathcal{O}(n)$).

Stopping criteria The algorithm terminates once k rows of X_t are non-zero (dense) or when X_t converges to a row-sparse solution such that $-\langle \nabla f(X_t), S_t - X_t \rangle < \epsilon$. Once the algorithm terminates, it returns the k sentences that correspond to the non-zero rows of X_t by **GetSummary**(X_t, k).

Sentence similarity measure We note that the gradient of (2) depends only on the kernel (or, "Gram") matrix $K = A^T A$ and not on A. This matrix is akin to a similarity matrix, with K_{ij} measuring the similarity between sentences i and j. If the matrix A is normalized, K_{ij}'s are cosine similarities. As a result, we may replace the matrix K with any matrix $\Phi(A)$ that offers a good similarity measure between sentences. This allow us to incorporate various sentence scoring functions $\Phi(\cdot)$. In this paper, we experimented with two such similarity measures: 1) TF-IDF-like, and 2) sentence embedding.

For TF-IDF-like similarity measure, we use Okapi BM25 (Robertson and Zaragoza, 2009) to construct the kernel matrix K. BM25 and its variants represent the state-of-the-art TF-IDF-like sentence scoring functions. Similarly, any sentence embedding technique can be used to embed the document matrix A in a much lower dimensional space; that is, we can set $K_{ij} = \phi(a_i)^T \phi(a_j)$, with $\phi(a)$ the (low-dimensional) vector representing the sentence a. In this work, we use a simple yet effective sentence embedding method called smooth inverse frequency (SIF) (Arora et al., 2017) to measure the sentence similarities. In Arora et al. (2017), the authors show that SIF, a simple weighted average of word vectors modified by SVD, outperforms complex methods such as RNNs and LSTMs. More sophisticated sentence embedding techniques such as neural architectures can also be used here; however, once should also consider the cost of computing the kernel matrix K with such a technique.

In the following, the acronyms FWSum-BM25 and FWSum-SIF are used to refer to the corresponding Frank-Wolfe unsupervised extractive summarization method used in conjunction with the BM25 and SIF similarity kernels.

3 Experiments

3.1 Datasets

Dernoncourt et al. (2018) surveyed the current large-scale dataset for summarization. Most of them are relatively short; usually less than 2 pages. To experiment on long documents, we used the recently open-sourced 2019 FINANCIAL OUT-LOOKS and CLASSICAL LITERATURE dataset[1], which contain much longer documents than those surveyed in Dernoncourt et al. (2018).

2019 FINANCIAL OUTLOOKS This corpus contains 10 publicly available reports on finance from a number of large financial institutions. Each report ranges from 10 to 144 pages, with a median length of 33 pages. There are no Gold summaries *per se* since the data is not annotated by a human. Hence, we chose to define the gold summaries as the collection of sentences or parts of sentences that appear in bold in the content, or any sentences that are highlighted as an insert within the content. This is a reasonable heuristic as these parts are generally prepared by the authors to highlight the takeaway of the content.

CLASSICAL LITERATURE The corpus contains summaries of books that have been summarized by human writers. The corpus contains 11 English-language classical books ranging from 53 to 1139 pages, with a median length of 198 pages. The Gold summaries for each chapter of the book are retrieved from WikiSummary [2].

3.2 Baselines

We compared our method with two other unsupervised extractive approaches; one uses a sparse optimization-based method and the other uses a graph-based method.

Sparse subspace clustering (SSC) Sparse subspace clustering (SSC) solves a sparse optimization program on the auto-regressive problem similar to (1), called the *self-expressiveness property* of the data (Elhamifar and Vidal, 2013). This property assumes that each data point can be efficiently reconstructed by a combination of other points in the data and that there exists a sparse representation

---

[1] https://github.com/SumUpAnalytics/goldsum

[2] http://wikisum.com/w/Main_Page

Algorithm 2 Frank-Wolfe unsupervised extractive summarization

---

1: **input** β, k, ϵ
2: **initialize** $X_0, (KX)_0, r_0, t \leftarrow 0, 0, 0, 1$
3: **compute** $K = A^T A$ or $\Phi(A)$
4: **for** $t = 1, 2, \ldots$ **do**
5: $\quad (KX)_t = (1 - r_{t-1})(KX)_{t-1} + r_{t-1}K^{(j)}[S_{t-1}]_{(j)}$
6: $\quad \nabla f(X_t) = 2\big((KX)_t - K\big)$
7: $\quad j = \arg\max_j \left\| [\nabla f(X_t)]_{(j)} \right\|_2$
8: $\quad S_t = 0$
9: $\quad [S_t]_{(j)} = -\beta \dfrac{[\nabla f(X_t)]_{(j)}}{\left\| [\nabla f(X_t)]_{(j)} \right\|_2}$
10: $\quad r_t = \frac{2}{t+2}$ or $\arg\min_{r \in [0,1]} f(X_t + r(S_t - X_t))$
11: $\quad X_{t+1} = X_t + r_t(S_t - X_t)$
12: $\quad$ **if NumSent**$(X_{t+1}) = k$ or $-\langle \nabla f(X_t), S_t - X_t \rangle < \epsilon$ **then**
13: $\quad\quad$ **break** $\qquad\qquad\qquad \triangleright k$ rows are non-zero or X_t converges
14: $\quad t = t + 1$
15: **return GetSummary**(X_{t+1}, k)

---

of the data point. The authors consider a convex relaxation as we did in (2) since solving the original sparse optimization is in general NP-hard. SSC uses the Alternating Direction Method of Multipliers (ADMM) for solving the sparse optimization problem. In our work, we employ the Frank-Wolfe algorithm on the problem, which is more efficient compared to SSC. Subsequent work tried to speed up SSC (You et al., 2016) but with an expense of removing the group LASSO constraint that is crucial for our summarization problem. In our work, we are able to preserve the group LASSO constraint and obtain a faster run-time. In our experiment, we used the implementation of Elhamifar and Vidal (2013), which can be found on their website[3].

TextRank TextRank (Mihalcea and Tarau, 2004) is a commonly used graph-based unsupervised extractive summarization method. It is also very efficient when extracting summaries from a long document. TextRank employs the similar idea of PageRank where vertices in the graph are sentences in the document and edges between two sentences are measured as a function of their content overlap.

3.3 Lexical and semantic ROUGE scores

We evaluate the systems using the ROUGE-1, ROUGE-2, and ROUGE-L (Lin, 2004) so as to account for different summary lengths. The raw

ROUGE score only measures the lexical overlaps between the generated summaries and the reference summaries. We refer to the raw ROUGE score defined in Lin (2004) as the *lexical ROUGE* and used the implementation of the Python `rouge` library[4]. When summarizing a long document, humans tend to paraphrase the source document in order to condense and synthesize the information. However, the lexical ROUGE scores are unable to measure the quality of paraphrasing. To address this shortcoming of lexical ROUGE when the summaries are paraphrased, word embedding ROUGE scores (Ng and Abrecht, 2015) are also used to evaluate the quality of the generated summaries. The word embedding ROUGE scores are more capable of measuring semantic similarity of the words instead of only lexical overlaps. Ng and Abrecht (2015) showed that the embedding ROUGE achieved better correlations with human assessments compared to lexical ROUGE when measured with the Spearman and Kendall rank coefficients on the TAC AESOP summarization dataset. We refer to the word embedding ROUGE scores as the *semantic ROUGE* in our evaluation.

4 Results and Analysis

In our experiment, we set the number of selected sentences k to be the same as the length of reference summary for all methods. The performance of

---

[3] http://www.ccs.neu.edu/home/eelhami/codes.htm

[4] https://pypi.org/project/rouge/

Lexical ROUGE		SSC	TextRank	FWSum-BM25	FWSum-SIF
FINANCIAL OUTLOOK	ROUGE-L F1	11.88	14.43	13.92	**14.99**
	ROUGE-2 F1	2.15	3.76	**5.17**	3.05
	ROUGE-1 F1	14.6	19.94	19.9	18
CLASSICAL LITERATURE	ROUGE-L F1	7.48	16.27	**18.7**	13.18
	ROUGE-2 F1	0.38	2.54	**3.23**	1.25
	ROUGE-1 F1	9.97	19.61	**20.2**	16.58
Semantic ROUGE		SSC	TextRank	FWSum-BM25	FWSum-SIF
FINANCIAL OUTLOOK	ROUGE-L F1	30.01	26.2	22.97	**34.56**
	ROUGE-2 F1	55.56	61.43	**61.82**	58.92
	ROUGE-1 F1	43.4	48.28	**49.97**	47.73
CLASSICAL LITERATURE	ROUGE-L F1	31.92	39.15	39.1	**46.6**
	ROUGE-2 F1	47.73	53.35	54.1	**60.53**
	ROUGE-1 F1	38.72	44.15	42.43	**48.18**

Table 1: Lexical and semantic ROUGE performance for FINANCIAL OUTLOOK and CLASSICAL LITERATURE data. Results that are statistically better are bold faced and results that are statistically indistinguishable are colored as gray. An additional experimental results can be found in appendix A.

all methods on FINANCIAL OUTLOOK and CLASSICAL LITERATURE are shown in Table 1. As shown in the table, FWSum-BM25 has a similar performance with TextRank although slightly better. This may be explained by the sentence scoring functions used by TextRank and FWSum-BM25. TextRank uses lexical overlaps between two sentences while FWSum-BM25 uses the TF-IDF-like scoring function, which are similar in nature.

FWSum-BW25 performs especially well when evaluated with lexical ROUGE, highlighting its capabilities of capturing lexical information (measured by unigram and bigram). When evaluated on the FINANCIAL OUTLOOK data, FWSum-BW25 and TextRank generally outperform FWSum-SIF, with FWSum-BM25 being the best performing method. Presumably, this is due to the fact that the Gold summaries of the FINANCIAL OUTLOOK data are taken directly from the source document without much paraphrasing, favoring sentence scoring functions that directly measure the content overlaps.

However, when evaluated by the semantic ROUGE on the CLASSICAL LITERATURE data, FWSum-SIF start to show promises. The Gold summaries of the CLASSICAL LITERATURE data are written by human writers and are highly paraphrased and condensed. As a result, semantic ROUGE is a better measurement for this dataset. As shown in the table, FWSum-SIF starts to outperform other methods by a significant amount. The improvement over the other methods suggests that using embedding in the sentence scoring function allows for comparisons based on the semantics of words sequences.

This results show that different sentence scoring functions may be used based on the nature of the summary. For summaries that are mostly taken from the source document without much paraphrasing, a lexical overlap or TF-IDF-like kernel matrix may be used. For summaries that are highly paraphrased, an embedding-like kernel matrix may be more suitable. Our method is able to work with both.

Computational complexity Our method requires an up-front cost of calculating the kernel matrix K. Each subsequent iteration requires mostly the LMO and gradient calculation as detailed in section 2. By exploiting the structure of the problem, we are able to avoid explicitly calculating the full gradient. Furthermore, due to the greedy nature of the algorithm, it terminates when k sentences are selected or the solution converges with $k^* < k$ sentences. This means that the algorithm only needs to execute $\approx k$ iterations; each iteration has a cost linear in problem size. Figure 1 compares the algorithm run-time of our method (FWSum-BM25), TextRank and SSC. As shown in the figure, our method is the most efficient among the three, showing its potential for summarizing long documents.

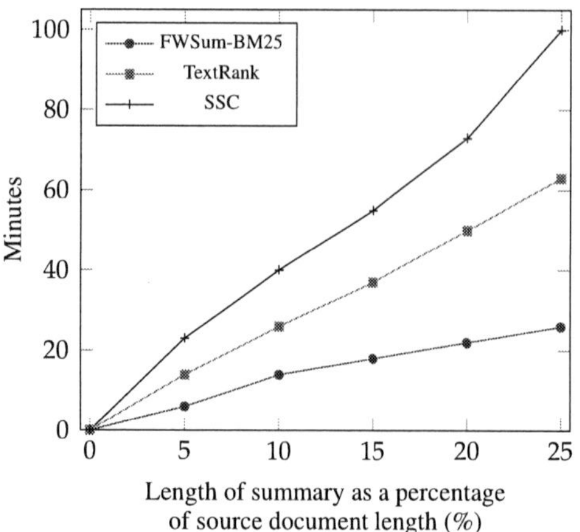

Figure 1: Algorithm run-time for FWSum-BM25, TextRank and SSC on the FINANACIAL OUTLOOK data. The x-axis shows the length of the generated summary (*i.e.* k) as a percentage of the source document length (number of sentences in the source document).

5   Conclusion

Unsupervised document summarization has been a challenging task, especially on long documents. In this work, we propose an efficient unsupervised extractive summarization model that is suitable for long documents by employing a dedicated Frank-Wolfe algorithm. Our method allows one to incorporate sentence embedding or any sentence scoring functions that is best suited for the dataset or the application. We evaluate our method and compare it with two other unsupervised extractive summarization methods on two datasets that are much longer than other summarization corpora used in the past. We evaluate the methods on both lexical and semantic ROUGE in order to overcome the shortcoming of lexical ROUGE and to provide a better assessment of the quality of the summaries. We observed that our methods (both FWSum-BM25 and FWSum-SIF) achieve the best results for both datasets and that FWSum-SIF works especially well with summaries that are paraphrased. Our results also motivate the exploration of different kernel functions or embedding methods, which is left as a future work.

Acknowledgments

The authors would like to thank Richard Liou, Tanya Roosta, and Gary Cheng for their constructive discussions on drafts of this paper and SumUp Analytics for providing the dataset.

References

Sanjeev Arora, Yingyu Liang, and Tengyu Ma. 2017. A simple but tough-to-beat baseline for sentence embeddings.

Taylor Berg-Kirkpatrick, Dan Gillick, and Dan Klein. 2011. Jointly learning to extract and compress. In *Proceedings of the 49th Annual Meeting of the Association for Computational Linguistics: Human Language Technologies - Volume 1*, HLT '11, pages 481–490, Stroudsburg, PA, USA. Association for Computational Linguistics.

Ziqiang Cao, Wenjie Li, Sujian Li, and Furu Wei. 2018. Retrieve, rerank and rewrite: Soft template based neural summarization. In *Proceedings of the 56th Annual Meeting of the Association for Computational Linguistics (Volume 1: Long Papers)*, pages 152–161, Melbourne, Australia. Association for Computational Linguistics.

Gary Cheng, Armin Askari, Laurent El Ghaoui, and Kannan Ramchandran. 2018. Frank-wolfe algorithm for exemplar selection. *CoRR*, abs/1811.02702.

Jianpeng Cheng and Mirella Lapata. 2016. Neural Summarization by Extracting Sentences and Words. In *Proceedings of the 54th Annual Meeting of the Association for Computational Linguistics (Volume 1: Long Papers)*, pages 484–494, Berlin, Germany. Association for Computational Linguistics.

Sumit Chopra, Michael Auli, and Alexander M. Rush. 2016. Abstractive sentence summarization with attentive recurrent neural networks. In *Proceedings of the 2016 Conference of the North American Chapter of the Association for Computational Linguistics: Human Language Technologies*, pages 93–98, San Diego, California. Association for Computational Linguistics.

Dipanjan Das and André F. T. Martins. 2007. A survey on automatic text summarization.

Franck Dernoncourt, Mohammad Ghassemi, and Walter Chang. 2018. A Repository of Corpora for Summarization. In *Proceedings of the Eleventh International Conference on Language Resources and Evaluation (LREC 2018)*, Miyazaki, Japan. European Language Resources Association (ELRA).

Greg Durrett, Taylor Berg-Kirkpatrick, and Dan Klein. 2016. Learning-based single-document summarization with compression and anaphoricity constraints. *CoRR*, abs/1603.08887.

Ehsan Elhamifar and Rene Vidal. 2013. Sparse Subspace Clustering: Algorithm, Theory, and Applications. *arXiv:1203.1005 [cs, math, stat]*. ArXiv: 1203.1005.

Günes Erkan and Dragomir R. Radev. 2011. Lexrank: Graph-based lexical centrality as salience in text summarization. *CoRR*, abs/1109.2128.

Marguerite Frank and Philip Wolfe. 1956. An algorithm for quadratic programming. *Naval Research Logistics Quarterly*, 3(1-2):95–110.

Dan Gillick and Benoit Favre. 2009. A scalable global model for summarization. In *Proceedings of the Workshop on Integer Linear Programming for Natural Language Processing*, pages 10–18, Boulder, Colorado. Association for Computational Linguistics.

Jade Goldstein, Mark Kantrowitz, Vibhu Mittal, and Jaime Carbonell. 1999. Summarizing text documents: Sentence selection and evaluation metrics. In *Proceedings of the 22Nd Annual International ACM SIGIR Conference on Research and Development in Information Retrieval*, SIGIR '99, pages 121–128, New York, NY, USA. ACM.

Udo Hahn and Inderjeet Mani. 2000. The challenges of automatic summarization. *Computer*, 33(11):29–36.

Martin Jaggi. 2013. Revisiting frank-wolfe: Projection-free sparse convex optimization. In *ICML (1)*, pages 427–435.

Chris Kedzie, Kathleen McKeown, and Hal Daumé III. 2018. Content Selection in Deep Learning Models of Summarization. In *Proceedings of the 2018 Conference on Empirical Methods in Natural Language Processing*, pages 1818–1828, Brussels, Belgium. Association for Computational Linguistics.

Julian Kupiec, Jan Pedersen, and Francine Chen. 1995. A trainable document summarizer. In *Proceedings of the 18th Annual International ACM SIGIR Conference on Research and Development in Information Retrieval*, SIGIR '95, pages 68–73, New York, NY, USA. ACM.

Chin-Yew Lin. 2004. Rouge: A package for automatic evaluation of summaries. In *Text Summarization Branches Out: Proceedings of the ACL-04 Workshop*, pages 74–81, Barcelona, Spain. Association for Computational Linguistics.

H. P. Luhn. 1958. The automatic creation of literature abstracts. *IBM J. Res. Dev.*, 2(2):159–165.

Ryan McDonald. 2007. A study of global inference algorithms in multi-document summarization. In *Proceedings of the 29th European Conference on IR Research*, ECIR'07, pages 557–564, Berlin, Heidelberg. Springer-Verlag.

Rada Mihalcea and Paul Tarau. 2004. TextRank: Bringing order into text. In *Proceedings of the 2004 Conference on Empirical Methods in Natural Language Processing*, pages 404–411, Barcelona, Spain. Association for Computational Linguistics.

Ramesh Nallapati, Bing Xiang, and Bowen Zhou. 2016. Sequence-to-sequence rnns for text summarization. *CoRR*, abs/1602.06023.

Ramesh Nallapati, Feifei Zhai, and Bowen Zhou. 2017. SummaRuNNer: a recurrent neural network based sequence model for extractive summarization of documents. In *Proceedings of the Thirty-First AAAI Conference on Artificial Intelligence*, AAAI'17, pages 3075–3081, San Francisco, California, USA. AAAI Press.

Jun-Ping Ng and Viktoria Abrecht. 2015. Better summarization evaluation with word embeddings for ROUGE. In *Proceedings of the 2015 Conference on Empirical Methods in Natural Language Processing*, pages 1925–1930, Lisbon, Portugal. Association for Computational Linguistics.

You Ouyang, Wenjie Li, Furu Wei, and Qin Lu. 2009. Learning similarity functions in graph-based document summarization. In *Computer Processing of Oriental Languages. Language Technology for the Knowledge-based Economy*, pages 189–200, Berlin, Heidelberg. Springer Berlin Heidelberg.

C. D. Paice. 1990. Constructing literature abstracts by computer: Techniques and prospects. *Inf. Process. Manage.*, 26(1):171–186.

Hao Peng, Ankur P. Parikh, Manaal Faruqui, Bhuwan Dhingra, and Dipanjan Das. 2019. Text generation with exemplar-based adaptive decoding. *CoRR*, abs/1904.04428.

Xian Qian and Yang Liu. 2013. Fast joint compression and summarization via graph cuts. In *Proceedings of the 2013 Conference on Empirical Methods in Natural Language Processing*, pages 1492–1502, Seattle, Washington, USA. Association for Computational Linguistics.

Stephen Robertson and Hugo Zaragoza. 2009. The probabilistic relevance framework: Bm25 and beyond. *Found. Trends Inf. Retr.*, 3(4):333–389.

Alexander M. Rush, Sumit Chopra, and Jason Weston. 2015. A neural attention model for abstractive sentence summarization. In *Proceedings of the 2015 Conference on Empirical Methods in Natural Language Processing*, pages 379–389, Lisbon, Portugal. Association for Computational Linguistics.

Horacio Saggion and Thierry Poibeau. 2012. Automatic Text Summarization: Past, Present and Future. In R. Yangarber T. Poibeau; H. Saggion. J. Piskorski, editor, *Multi-source, Multilingual Information Extraction and Summarization*, Theory and Applications of Natural Language Processing, pages 3–13. Springer.

Abigail See, Peter J. Liu, and Christopher D. Manning. 2017. Get to the point: Summarization with pointer-generator networks. In *Proceedings of the 55th Annual Meeting of the Association for Computational*

Linguistics (Volume 1: Long Papers), pages 1073–1083, Vancouver, Canada. Association for Computational Linguistics.

Louis Shao, Stephan Gouws, Denny Britz, Anna Goldie, Brian Strope, and Ray Kurzweil. 2017. Generating High-Quality and Informative Conversation Responses with Sequence-to-Sequence Models. *arXiv:1701.03185 [cs]*. ArXiv: 1701.03185.

Shuai Wang, Xiang Zhao, Bo Li, Bin Ge, and Daquan Tang. 2017. Integrating Extractive and Abstractive Models for Long Text Summarization. In *2017 IEEE International Congress on Big Data (BigData Congress)*, pages 305–312.

Kristian Woodsend and Mirella Lapata. 2011. Learning to simplify sentences with quasi-synchronous grammar and integer programming. In *Proceedings of the 2011 Conference on Empirical Methods in Natural Language Processing*, pages 409–420, Edinburgh, Scotland, UK. Association for Computational Linguistics.

Wen Xiao and Giuseppe Carenini. 2019. Extractive Summarization of Long Documents by Combining Global and Local Context. *arXiv:1909.08089 [cs]*. ArXiv: 1909.08089.

Jin-ge Yao, Xiaojun Wan, and Jianguo Xiao. 2015. Compressive document summarization via sparse optimization. In *Proceedings of the 24th International Conference on Artificial Intelligence*, IJCAI'15, pages 1376–1382. AAAI Press.

Chong You, Daniel P. Robinson, and Rene Vidal. 2016. Scalable Sparse Subspace Clustering by Orthogonal Matching Pursuit. *arXiv:1507.01238 [cs, stat]*. ArXiv: 1507.01238.

Wenyuan Zeng, Wenjie Luo, Sanja Fidler, and Raquel Urtasun. 2016. Efficient summarization with read-again and copy mechanism. *CoRR*, abs/1611.03382.

Don't Read Too Much Into It:
Adaptive Computation for Open-Domain Question Answering

Yuxiang Wu   Pasquale Minervini   Pontus Stenetorp   Sebastian Riedel
University College London
{yuxiang.wu,p.minervini,p.stenetorp,s.riedel}@cs.ucl.ac.uk

Abstract

Most approaches to Open-Domain Question Answering consist of a light-weight retriever that selects a set of candidate passages, and a computationally expensive reader that examines the passages to identify the correct answer. Previous works have shown that as the number of retrieved passages increases, so does the performance of the reader. However, they assume all retrieved passages are of equal importance and allocate the same amount of computation to them, leading to a substantial increase in computational cost. To reduce this cost, we propose the use of *adaptive computation* to control the computational budget allocated for the passages to be read. We first introduce a technique operating on individual passages in isolation which relies on anytime prediction and a per-layer estimation of an early exit probability. We then introduce SKY-LINEBUILDER, an approach for dynamically deciding on which passage to allocate computation at each step, based on a resource allocation policy trained via reinforcement learning. Our results on SQuAD-Open show that adaptive computation with global prioritisation improves over several strong static and adaptive methods, leading to a 4.3x reduction in computation while retaining 95% performance of the full model.

1 Introduction

Open-Domain Question Answering (ODQA) requires a system to answer questions using a large collection of documents as the information source. In contrast to context-based machine comprehension, where models are to extract answers from single paragraphs or documents, it poses a fundamental technical challenge in *machine reading at scale* (Chen et al., 2017) .

Most ODQA systems consist of two-stage pipelines, where *1)* a context retriever such as BM25 (Robertson, 2004) or DPR (Karpukhin et al., 2020) first selects a small subset of passages that are likely to contain the answer to the question, and *2)* a machine reader such as BERT (Devlin et al., 2019) then examines the retrieved contexts to extract the answer. This two-stage process leads to a computational trade-off that is indicated in Fig. 1. We can run computationally expensive deep networks on a large number of passages to increase the probability that we find the right answer ("All Layers, All Passages"), or cut the number of passages and layers to reduce the computational footprint at the possible cost of missing an answer ("6 Layers, Top-2 Passages").

We hypothesise that a better accuracy-efficiency trade-off can be found if the computational budget is not allocated statically, but based on the complexity of each passage, see "Adaptive Computation" in Fig. 1. If a passage is likely to contain the answer, allocate more computation. If it isn't, allocate less. The idea of conditioning neural network computation based on inputs has been pursued in previous work on *Adaptive Computation* (Bengio et al., 2015; Graves, 2016; Elbayad et al., 2020), however how to apply this idea to ODQA is still an open research question.

In this work, we introduce two adaptive computation methods for ODQA: TOWERBUILDER and SKYLINEBUILDER. TOWERBUILDER builds a *tower*, a composition of transformer layers on a single passage, until an early stopping condition is met—we find that this method already helps reducing the computational cost required for reading the retrieved passages. Then, for coordinating the construction of multiple towers in parallel, we introduce a global method, SKYLINEBUILDER, that incrementally builds multiple towers one layer at a time and learns a policy to decide which tower to extend one more layer next. Rather than building single transformer towers in isolation, it constructs

63

Proceedings of SustaiNLP: Workshop on Simple and Efficient Natural Language Processing, pages 63–72
Online, November 20, 2020. ©2020 Association for Computational Linguistics

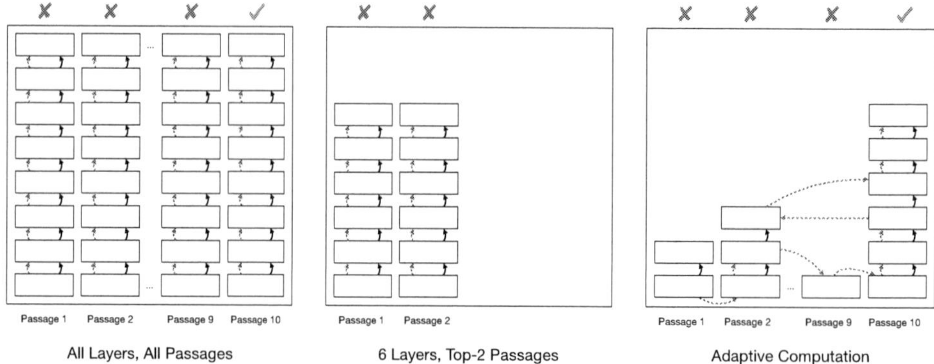

Figure 1: Static and adaptive computation for Open-Domain QA. Each block represents one layer of transformer computation on a passage. The solid arrows show how activations flow, and the dashed arrows indicate the order of computation. Only passage 10 contains the actual answer. Using all layers on all passages can find the answer, while processing only the top 2 retrieved passages with 6 layers is unable to find it. Adaptive computation can find the right passage, and allocates most computation budget to reading it.

a *skyline* of towers with different heights, based on which passages seem most promising to process further.

Our experiments on the SQuAD-Open dataset show that our methods are very effective at reducing the computational footprint of ODQA models. In particular, we find that SKYLINEBUILDER retains 95% of the accuracy of a 24-layer model using only 5.6 layers on average. In comparison, an adaptation of the method proposed by Schwartz et al. (2020) requires 9 layers for achieving the same results. Improvements are even more substantial for smaller number of layers—for example, with an average of 3 layers SKYLINEBUILDER reaches 89% of the full performance, whereas the approach of Schwartz et al. (2020) yields 57% and a model trained to use exactly 3 layers reaches 65%. Finally, SKYLINEBUILDER retains nearly the same accuracy at full layer count.

To summarise, we make the following contributions: *1)* we are the first to explore adaptive computation for ODQA by proposing two models: TOWERBUILDER and SKYLINEBUILDER; *2)* we experimentally show that both methods can be used for adaptively allocating computational resources so to retain the predictive accuracy with a significantly lower cost, and that coordinating the building of multiple towers via a learned policy yields more accurate results; *3)* when compared to their non-adaptive counterparts, our proposed methods can reduce the amount of computation by as much as 4.3 times.

2 Background

We first give an overview of ODQA and the relevant work in adaptive computation.

2.1 Open Domain Question Answering

In ODQA we are given a natural language query $\mathbf{q}$ and a large number of passages C—for example, all paragraphs in Wikipedia. The goal is to use C to produce the answer $\mathbf{y}$. In extractive ODQA this answer corresponds to a span in one of the documents of C. The corpus C can be very large, and a common approach to reduce computational costs is to first determine a smaller document set $D_{\mathbf{q}} \subseteq C$ by retrieving the most relevant n passages using an information retrieval module. Then we run a neural reader model on this subset. In most works, the reader model extracts answers by applying a per-passage reader to each input passage $\mathbf{x}_1, \ldots, \mathbf{x}_n \in D_{\mathbf{q}}$ and then apply some form of aggregation function on the per-passage answers to produce a final answer. Note that the passage reader can either produce an answer span as output, or NoAnswer in case the passage does not contain an answer for the given question.

2.2 Transformers for ODQA

Most current ODQA models rely on transformer-based architectures (Vaswani et al., 2017), usually pre-trained, to implement the PReader passage reader interface. In such models, an input passage is processed via a sequence of transformer layers; in the following, we denote the i-th transformer layer in the sequence as TransformerLayer$_i$. Let

$\mathbf{h}_i$ be the input to the i-th transformer layer and $\mathbf{h}_{i+1} = \text{TransformerLayer}_i(\mathbf{h}_i)$ its output. We set $\mathbf{h}_1 = \mathbf{x}$ to be the input passage. In standard non-adaptive Transformer-based models, we incrementally build a *tower*—a composition of Transformer layers—until we reach some pre-defined height n and use an output layer to produces the final output, $\mathbf{y} = \text{OutputLayer}(\mathbf{h}_n)$. In this work, due to efficiency reasons, we restrict ourselves to pre-trained ALBERT (Lan et al., 2020) models. One critical property of these models is parameter tying across layers: $\text{TransformerLayer}_i(\mathbf{h}) = \text{TransformerLayer}_j(\mathbf{h})$ for any i, j.

2.3 Adaptive Computation

Our goal is to early-exit the iterative layer-by-layer process in order to save computation. We assume this can be happening adaptively, based on the input, since some passages might require less computation to produce an answer than others. Schwartz et al. (2020) show how this can be achieved for classification tasks. They first require internal layers to be able to produce outputs too, yielding an *anytime* algorithm. [1] This can be achieved with a suitable training objective. Next, for each candidate layer i, they calculate the exit probability given its hidden state $\mathbf{h}_i$, and use them for taking an early-exit decision: if the highest exit probability is above a global threshold τ, they return $\text{OutputLayer}(\mathbf{h}_i)$ otherwise they continue with the following layers.

The output layer probabilities are not calibrated for exit decisions, and hence Schwartz et al. (2020) tune them on an held-out validation set via temperature calibration (Guo et al., 2017; Desai and Durrett, 2020), where a temperature T is tuned to adapt the softmax output probabilities at each layer.

3 Adaptive Computation in ODQA

Our goal is to incrementally build up towers of transformer layers for all passages in $D_\mathbf{q}$ in a way that minimises unnecessary computation. Our algorithms maintain a state, or *skyline*, $S = (H, A)$, consisting of current tower heights $H = (h_1, \ldots, h_n)$, indicating how many layers have been processed for each of the n towers, and the last representations $A = (\mathbf{a}_1, \ldots, \mathbf{a}_n)$ computed for each of the towers. We want to build up the

skyline so that we reach an accurate solution fast and then stop processing.

3.1 Early Exit with Local Exit Probabilities

Our first proposal is to extend the method from Schwartz et al. (2020) in order to build up the skyline S. In particular, we will process each passage $\mathbf{x}_i \in D_\mathbf{q}$ in isolation, building up height h_i and representation $\mathbf{a}_i$ until an *exit probability* reaches a threshold. For Schwartz et al. (2020) the exit probability is set to be the probability of the most likely class. While ODQA is not a classification problem per se, it requires solving one as a sub-step, either explicitly or implicitly: deciding whether a passage contains the answer. In turn, our first method TOWERBUILDER, uses the probability $1 - \text{HasAnswer}(\mathbf{a}_i)$ of the passage not containing the answer to calculate the exit probability at such given layer. In practice the probability $\text{HasAnswer}(\mathbf{a}_i)$ is calculated as the Sigmoid output of an MLP applied the representation of the CLS token in $\mathbf{a}_i$. Moreover, models are trained to produce HasAnswer probabilities for each layer using a per-layer loss. Following Schwartz et al. (2020), we also conduct temperature calibration for the HasAnswer modules using the development set.

When building up the towers, TOWERBUILDER produces early exit decisions for each tower in isolation. Once all towers have been processed, the method selects the highest m towers in the final S^* to produce the final answer, where m is a hyperparameter. Since some of the selected towers in S^* may not have full height, we will need to continue unrolling them to full height to produce an answer. We will call this the LastLayer strategy. Alternatively, we can return the solution at the current height, provided that we use an anytime model not just for HasAnswer predictions but also for answer extraction. We will refer to this strategy as AnyLayer. By default we use LastLayer but we will conduct ablation study of these two approaches in Section 5.3.

3.2 Global Scheduling

We can apply TOWERBUILDER independently to each passage $\mathbf{x}_i \in D_\mathbf{q}$. However, if we have already found an answer after building up one tower for a passage $\mathbf{x}_i$, we can avoid reading other passages. Generally, we imagine that towers that are more likely to produce the answers should be processed first and get more layers allocated to. To

---

[1] In practice, Schwartz et al. (2020) choose a subset of layers to be candidate output layers, so strictly speaking we cannot exit any time, but only when a candidate layer is reached.

assess if one tower is more likely to contain an answer, we need to compare them and decide which tower has highest *priority*. This type of strategy cannot be followed when processing passages in isolation, and hence we consider a global multi-passage view.

A simple approach for operating on multiple passages is to re-use information provided to the TOWERBUILDER method and select the next tower to extend using the HasAnswer probabilities. In particular, we can choose the next tower to build up as $j = \arg\max_i \text{HasAnswer}(\mathbf{a}_i)$, and then set $\mathbf{a}_j \leftarrow \text{TransformerLayer}(\mathbf{a}_j)$ and $h_j \leftarrow h_j + 1$ in the state S. To efficiently implement this strategy we use a priority queue. Every time a tower is expanded, its HasAnswer probability is re-calculated and used in a priority queue we choose the next tower from. Once we reach the limit of our computation budget, we can stop the reading process and return the results of the highest m towers S^* as inputs to its Output phase. The two aforementioned answer extraction methods (i.e., AnyLayer and LastLayer) also apply to this method.

3.3 Learning a Global Scheduler

Using HasAnswer probabilities to prioritise towers is a sensible first step, but not necessarily optimal. First, while the probabilities are calibrated, they are tuned for optimising the negative log-likelihood, not the actual performance of the method. Second, the HasAnswer probability might not capture everything we need to know about the towers in order to make decisions. For example, it might be important to understand what the rank of the tower's passage is in the retrieval result, as higher ranked passages might be more fruitful to expand. Finally, the HasAnswer probabilities are not learnt with the global competition of priorities across all towers, so they are not optimal for comparing priorities between towers that have different heights.

To overcome the above issues, we frame the tower selection process as a reinforcement learning (RL) problem: we consider each tower $i \in \{1, \ldots, n\}$ as a candidate action, and learn a policy $\pi(i|S)$ that determines which tower to expand next based on the current skyline. We present the corresponding details below.

3.3.1 Policy

Our policy calculates $\pi(i|S)$ using a priority vector $\mathbf{p}(S) \in \mathbb{R}^n$. The priority $p_i(S)$ of each tower i is calculated using a linear combination of the HasAnswer probability of that tower and the output of a multi-layer perceptron MLP_θ. The perceptron is parametrised by θ and uses a feature representation $\mathbf{f}_i(S)$ of tower i in state S as input. Concretely, we have:

$$p_i(S) = \alpha \text{HasAnswer}(\mathbf{a}_i) + \text{MLP}_\theta(\mathbf{f}_i(S))$$

where α is a learnable mixture weight. As feature representation we use $\mathbf{f}_i(S) = [\text{HeightEmb}(h_i), \text{IndexEmb}(i), \text{HasAnswer}(\mathbf{a}_i)]$ where the tower height h_i and index i are represented using embedding matrices $\text{HeightEmb} \in \mathbb{R}^{l \times d}$ and $\text{IndexEmb} \in \mathbb{R}^{n \times d}$ respectively. When a tower is currently empty, an initial priority p_i^0 will be provided: it can either be a fixed value or a learnable parameter, and its impact is analysed in Section 5.2. Given the above priority vector, the policy simply maps per tower priorities to the probability simplex:

$$\pi(i|S) = \text{Softmax}_i(\mathbf{p}(S)).$$

The parameters (α, θ) introduced by this policy do not introduce much computational overhead: with embedding size $d = 8$ and using 32-dimensional hidden representations in the MLP, this model only introduces 1,039 new parameters, a small amount compared to ALBERT ($\approx$ 18M).

3.3.2 Training

While executing a policy, the scheduler needs to make discrete decisions as which tower to pursue. These discrete decisions mean we cannot simply frame learning as optimising a differentiable loss function. Instead we use the REINFORCE algorithm (Williams, 1992) for training our policy, by maximising the expected cumulative reward. For us, this reward is defined as follows. Let $\mathbf{i}_1^m = i_1, \ldots, i_m$ and $\mathbf{S}_1^m = S_1, \ldots, S_m$ be a trajectory of (tower selection) actions and states, respectively. We then set the cumulative reward to $R(\mathbf{i}_t^m, \mathbf{S}_t^m) = r(i_t, S_t) + \gamma R(\mathbf{i}_{t+1}^m, \mathbf{S}_{t+1}^m)$ where $r(i_t, S_t)$ is a immediate per-step reward we describe below, and γ is a discounting factor.

We define an immediate per-step reward $r(i, S)$ of choosing tower i in state S as $r(i, S) = r - c$ where $r = 1$ if the selected tower contains an answer and $r = 0$ otherwise. $c \in \mathbb{R}_+$ is a penalty cost of taking a step. In our experiments, we set $c = 0.1$.

4   Related Work

Adaptive Computation   One strategy to reduce a model's complexity consists in dynamically deciding which layers to execute during inference (Bengio et al., 2015; Graves, 2016). *Universal transformers* (Dehghani et al., 2019) can learn after how many layers to emit an output conditioned on the input. Elbayad et al. (2020) generalise universal transformers by also learning which layer to execute at each step. Schwartz et al. (2020); Liu et al. (2020) propose methods that can adaptively decide when to early stop the computation in sentence classification tasks. To the best of our knowledge, previous work has focused adaptive computation for a single input. We are the first to learn how to prioritise computation across instances in the context of ODQA.

Smaller Networks   Another strategy consists in training smaller and more efficient models. In *layer-wise dropout* (Liu et al., 2018), during training, layers are randomly removed, making the model robust to layer removal operations. This idea was expanded Fan et al. (2020) to modern Transformer-based models. Other methods include *Distillation* (Hinton et al., 2015) of a teacher model into a student model, *Pruning* of architectures after training (LeCun et al., 1989) and *Quantisation* of the parameter space (Wróbel et al., 2018; Shen et al., 2019; Zafrir et al., 2019). These methods are not adaptive, but could be used in concert with the methods proposed here.

Open Domain Question Answering   Most modern ODQA systems adopt a two-stage approach that consists of a retriever and a reader, such as DrQA (Chen et al., 2017), HardEM (Min et al., 2019), BERTserini (Yang et al., 2019), Multi-passage BERT (Wang et al., 2019), and PathRetriever (Asai et al., 2020). As observed by Chen et al. (2017); Yang et al. (2019); Karpukhin et al. (2020); Wang et al. (2019), the accuracy of such two-stage models increases with more passages retrieved. But it remains a challenge to efficiently read a large number of passages as the reader models are usually quite computationally costly.

5   Experiments

Dataset   SQuAD-Open (Chen et al., 2017) is a popular open-domain question answering dataset based on SQuAD. We partition the dataset into four subsets: training set, two development sets

SQuAD-Open	train	dev_0	dev_1	test
Size	78,839	4,379	4,379	10,570
Hits@30	71.2%	72.7%	72.1%	77.9%

Table 1: Dataset sizes and retriever performances.

(dev_0 and dev_1), and test set, and their details are summarised in Table 1.

Experimental Setup   We follow the preprocessing approached proposed by Wang et al. (2019) and split passages into 100-word long chunks with 50-word long strides. We use a BM25 retriever to retrieve the top n passages for each question as inputs to the reader and the Wikipedia dump provided by Chen et al. (2017) as source corpus. Following Wang et al. (2019), we set $n = 5$ for training and $n = 30$ for test evaluations. Table 1 shows the Hits@30 results of our BM25 retriever on the dataset and they are comparable with previous works (Yang et al., 2019; Wang et al., 2019).

Reader Model   For all our experiments, we fine-tune a pre-trained ALBERT model (Lan et al., 2020), consisting of 24 transformer layers and cross-layer parameter sharing. We do *not* use global normalisation (Clark and Gardner, 2018) in our implementation, but our full system (without adaptive computation) achieves an EM score of 52.6 and is comparable to Multi-passage BERT (Wang et al., 2019) which uses global normalisation.

Training Pipeline   The anytime reader models are first trained on training set and validated on dev_0. Then we conduct temperature calibration on dev_0. For SKYLINEBUILDER, the scheduler model is trained on dev_0 with the calibrated anytime model, and validated with dev_1.

Baselines   Following Schwartz et al. (2020), we use three types of baselines: *1*) the *standard baseline* that reads all passages and outputs predictions at the final layer, *2*) the *efficient baseline* that always exits at a given intermediate layer for all passages, and is optimised to do so, *3*) the *top-k baseline* that only reads the k top ranked passages and predicts the answer at their final layers.

Evaluation protocol   Our goal is to assess the computational efficiency of a given method in terms of accuracy vs. computational budget used. We follow Fan et al. (2020) and consider the computation of one layer as a unit of computational

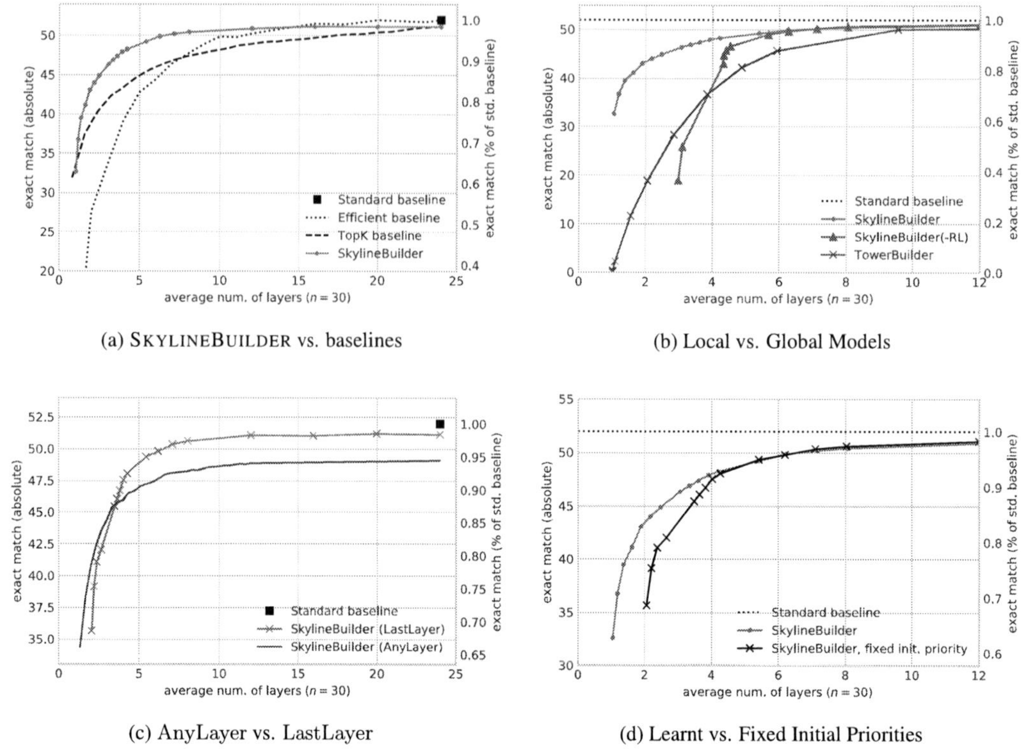

(a) SKYLINEBUILDER vs. baselines   (b) Local vs. Global Models

(c) AnyLayer vs. LastLayer   (d) Learnt vs. Fixed Initial Priorities

Figure 2: Evaluation results on the SQuAD-Open test set with 30 passages.

cost. In particular, we will assess how many layers, on average, each method builds up for each passage. Similarly to Schwartz et al. (2020), we show the accuracy-efficiency trade-off for different strategies by showing the computation cost on the x-axis, and the Exact Match (EM) [2] score on the y-axis.

5.1 Static vs. Adaptive Computation

We first investigate how adaptive computation compares to the static baselines. We will focus on a single adaptive method, SKYLINEBUILDER, and assess different adaptive variants later.

Fig. 2a shows the accuracy of SKYLINEB-UILDER at different budgets when compared to the standard, efficient, and top-k baselines. We note that it reaches the similar results of the static baselines with much fewer layers. In particular, it yields substantially higher performance than static methods when the computational budget is smaller than ten layers. For example, when given four layers on average, SKYLINEBUILDER achieves EM

---

[2]The evaluation script can be found at this address: https://github.com/facebookresearch/DrQA.

Method	Avg. #layers	Reduction
Standard baseline	24	1.0x
Efficient baseline	9.5	2.5x
Top-k baseline	14.4	1.7x
TOWERBUILDER	9.0	2.7x
SKYLINEBUILDER(-RL)	6.1	3.9x
SKYLINEBUILDER	**5.6**	**4.3x**

Table 2: Reduction in layer computations while achieving 95% of the accuracy of the standard baseline.

score 48.0, significantly outperforming EM score 44.2 of the top-k baseline.

In Table 2 we consider a setting where SKYLINEBUILDER and the static baseline reach comparable (95%) performance of the full 24-layer model. We see that simply reducing the number of passages to process is giving a poor accuracy-efficiency trade-off, requiring 14.4 layers (or 18 passages) to achieve this accuracy. The efficient baseline fares better with 9.5 layers, but it is still outperformed by SKYLINEBUILDER, that only needs 5.6 layers on average to reach the desired accuracy.

	$\mathrm{Var}(h)$	Avg(rank)	Flips	$h_+ - h_-$	HAP	Exact Match
Efficient Baselines	0.00	14.50	-	0.00	6.1%	23.47
TOWERBUILDER	11.05	13.38	-	3.68	22.0%	17.10
SKYLINEBUILDER(-RL)	7.46	13.06	13.37	3.46	27.4%	27.95
SKYLINEBUILDER	12.71	8.78	6.48	5.99	40.5%	**33.60**

Table 3: Quantitative analysis on SQuAD Open dev_1 set with top 30 passages and two layers of computation per passage on average.

5.2 Local vs. Global Models

What is the impact of globally selecting which towers to extend, rather than taking early-exit decisions on a per-tower basis? To answer this question, we consider two global methods: SKYLINEBUILDER and SKYLINEBUILDER(-RL), the method in Section 3.2 that uses HasAnswer probabilities as priorities without any RL-based selection policy. We compare both to the local method TOWERBUILDER.

Fig. 2b shows that, while for very low budgets TOWERBUILDER outperforms SKYLINEBUILDER(-RL), with a budget larger than 4 layers it is not the case anymore. This may be due to a tendency of SKYLINEBUILDER(-RL) spending an initial computation budget on exploring many towers—in Fig. 3 we show examples of this behaviour. It is also shown that SKYLINEBUILDER considerably outperforms both TOWERBUILDER and SKYLINEBUILDER(-RL). Along with the results in Table 2, the comparisons above indicate that *1)* global scheduling across multiple towers is crucial for improving efficiency, and *2)* optimising the adaptive policy with RL manage to exploit global features for tower selection, leading to further improvements.

5.3 Ablation Studies

Any Layer vs. Last Layer Model   For comparing the LastLayer and the AnyLayer strategies introduced in Section 3.1, we show the behaviour of these methods for the SKYLINEBUILDER scheduling algorithm in Fig. 2c. Using an anytime answer extraction model has a negative effect on accuracy. We see this clearly at 24 layers where AnyLayer lags substantially behind the standard baseline while LastLayer almost reaches it. We see this gap across the whole budget spectrum, leading to less accurate results except for very small budgets.

Learning Initial Priorities   SKYLINEBUILDER uses a learnt initial priority for each tower. This not only enables it learn which towers to process first at the beginning, but also how long to wait until other towers are visited. Fig. 2d shows the benefit gained from adopting this strategy: without training the initialisation priorities, SKYLINEBUILDER spend more computation on passages that are likely not needed. Once an average of 4 layers have been added, the benefit disappears as SKYLINEBUILDER with learnt initial priorities will try to visit more candidates itself.

5.4 Quantitative Analysis

This section aims at understanding where and how our adaptive strategies behave differently, and what contributes to the gain in the accuracy-efficiency trade-off. We propose the following quantitative metrics: *1)* $\mathrm{Var}(h)$: variance of the heights of the towers. *2)* Avg(rank): average rank of the tower when the method chooses which tower to build on. *3)* Flips: how often does the strategy switch between towers, measuring the exploration-exploitation trade-off of a method. *4)* $h_+ - h_-$: h_+ (resp. h_-) is the average height of towers with (resp. without) an answer. Their difference measures the difference in amount of computation between passages with the answer and the ones without an answer. *5)* HasAnswer Precision (HAP): how often a tower selection action selects a tower whose passage contains the answer.

We analyse our proposed methods along with static baselines on the SQuAD development set; results are outlined in Table 3. Overall, the higher the HasAnswer Precision, the more accurate the method. This finding matches with our intuition that, if a tower selection strategy can focus its computation on passages that contain the answer, it yields more accurate results with smaller computation budgets.

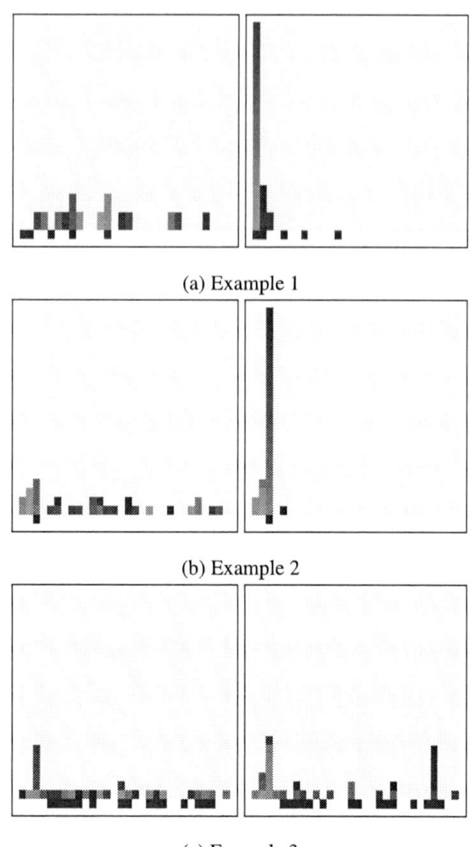

(a) Example 1

(b) Example 2

(c) Example 3

Figure 3: Examples of the skylines built by SKYLINEBUILDER(-RL) (left) and SKYLINEB-UILDER (right), with two layers per passage on average. The green blocks indicate towers that contain the answer.

Comparing SKYLINEBUILDER(-RL) and SKY-LINEBUILDER gives more insights regarding what the RL training scheme learns. SKYLINEBUILDER learns a policy with the highest Var(h), the lowest Avg(rank), and the lowest number of tower flips, suggesting that *1)* it focuses on a few towers rather than distributing its computation over all passages, *2)* it is more likely to select top-ranked passages, and *3)* it switches less between towers, and tends to build one tower before switching to another. SKY-LINEBUILDER also yields the highest HasAnswer Precision and $h_+ - h_-$, meaning that tends to prioritise the passages containing the answer.

5.5 Qualitative Analysis and Visualisation

Here we analyse how different methods build the skyline. Fig. 3 shows some examples of skylines built by SKYLINEBUILDER(-RL) and SKYLINEB-

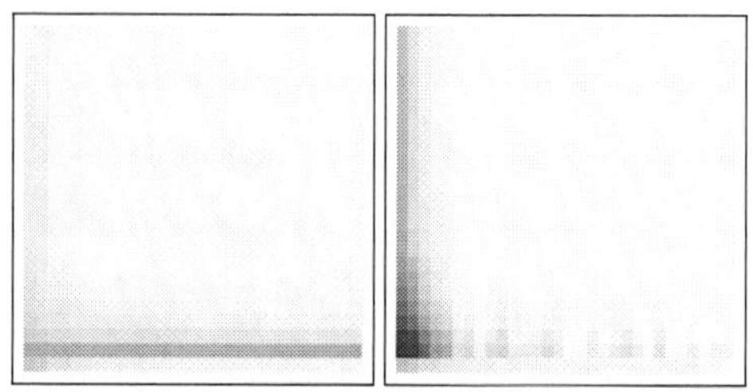

Figure 4: Heatmap of the tower selections by SKYLINEBUILDER(-RL) (left) and SKYLINEB-UILDER (right). The colour gradient of the blues blocks reflects their selection frequencies.

UILDER. The towers are ordered by the rank of their associated passages in the retrieval results from left to right, and are built bottom-up. The colour gradient of the blues blocks reflects the order in which the layers are built: darker cells correspond to layers created later in the process.

In Fig. 3a and Fig. 3b we can see that SKY-LINEBUILDER tends to focus on one or two towers, whereas SKYLINEBUILDER(-RL) has a more even distribution of computation across different towers. In Fig. 3b, even when only one tower contains the answer, SKYLINEBUILDER manages to locate it and build a full-height tower on it.

Fig. 3c shows a case where none of the top 4 passages contains the answer. SKYLINEBUILDER goes over these irrelevant towers quickly and start exploring later towers, until it reaches the tower with rank 27 and becomes confident enough to keep building on it. These examples shows how SKYLINEBUILDER learns an efficient scheduling algorithm to locate passages containing the answer with very limited budgets.

To understand how our proposed methods work at macro level, we use heat-maps (Fig. 4) for showing how frequently each block is selected. The green row at the bottom indicates the frequency of each passage containing the answer. SKYLINEBUILDER(-RL) explores all passages quite evenly, whereas SKYLINEBUILDER learns to prioritise top-ranked towers. This preference is reasonable because, as shown by the green row at the bottom, top-ranked towers are more likely to contain the answer. Also note that SKYLINEB-UILDER does not naively process towers from left to right like the top-k baseline does, but instead it learns a trade-off between *exploration and exploitation*, leading to the significant improvement over the top-k baseline shown in Fig. 2a.

Models	Num. layers	EM
DistilBERT (Sanh et al., 2019)	6	40.5
SKYLINEBUILDER	1.6	41.1
SKYLINEBUILDER	3	46.4
SKYLINEBUILDER	6	**49.7**

Table 4: Comparing adaptive computation with distillation on SQuAD-Open test set.

5.6 Adaptive Computation vs. Distillation

Distillation is another orthogonal approach to reduce computational cost. We compare our adaptive computation method SKYLINEBUILDER with a static DistilBERT (Sanh et al., 2019) baseline, and the results are shown in Table 4. Our method significantly outperforms DistilBERT while computing much fewer layers.

6 Discussions and Future Works

In this paper, we focus on reducing the number of layers and operations of ODQA models, but the actual latency improvement also depends on the hardware specifications. On GPUs we cannot expect a reduction in the number of operations to translate 1:1 to lower execution times, since they are highly optimised for parallelism. [3] We leave the parallelism enhancements of SKYLINEBUILDER for future work.

We also notice that the distillation technique is complementary to the adaptive computation methods. It will be interesting to integrate these two approaches to achieve further computation reduction for ODQA models.

7 Conclusions

In this work we show that adaptive computation can lead to substantial efficiency improvements for ODQA. In particular, we find that it is important to allocate budget dynamically across a large number of passages and prioritise different passages according to various features such as the probability that the passage has an answer. Our best results emerge when we learn prioritisation policies using reinforcement learning that can switch between exploration and exploitation. On our benchmark, our method achieves 95% of the accuracy of a 24-layer model while only needing 5.6 layers on average.

---

[3] When evaluated on an NVIDIA TITAN X GPU, our proposed SKYLINEBUILDER achieves approximately 2.6x latency reduction while retaining 95% of the performance.

Acknowledgements

This research was supported by the European Union's Horizon 2020 research and innovation programme under grant agreement no. 875160.

References

Akari Asai, Kazuma Hashimoto, Hannaneh Hajishirzi, Richard Socher, and Caiming Xiong. 2020. Learning to retrieve reasoning paths over wikipedia graph for question answering. In *ICLR*. OpenReview.net.

Emmanuel Bengio, Pierre-Luc Bacon, Joelle Pineau, and Doina Precup. 2015. Conditional computation in neural networks for faster models. *CoRR*, abs/1511.06297.

Danqi Chen, Adam Fisch, Jason Weston, and Antoine Bordes. 2017. Reading wikipedia to answer open-domain questions. In *ACL (1)*, pages 1870–1879. Association for Computational Linguistics.

Christopher Clark and Matt Gardner. 2018. Simple and effective multi-paragraph reading comprehension. In *ACL (1)*, pages 845–855. Association for Computational Linguistics.

Mostafa Dehghani, Stephan Gouws, Oriol Vinyals, Jakob Uszkoreit, and Lukasz Kaiser. 2019. Universal transformers. In *ICLR (Poster)*. OpenReview.net.

Shrey Desai and Greg Durrett. 2020. Calibration of pre-trained transformers. *CoRR*, abs/2003.07892.

Jacob Devlin, Ming-Wei Chang, Kenton Lee, and Kristina Toutanova. 2019. BERT: pre-training of deep bidirectional transformers for language understanding. In *NAACL-HLT (1)*, pages 4171–4186. Association for Computational Linguistics.

Maha Elbayad, Jiatao Gu, Edouard Grave, and Michael Auli. 2020. Depth-adaptive transformer. In *ICLR*. OpenReview.net.

Angela Fan, Edouard Grave, and Armand Joulin. 2020. Reducing transformer depth on demand with structured dropout. In *ICLR*. OpenReview.net.

Alex Graves. 2016. Adaptive computation time for recurrent neural networks. *CoRR*, abs/1603.08983.

Chuan Guo, Geoff Pleiss, Yu Sun, and Kilian Q. Weinberger. 2017. On calibration of modern neural networks. In *ICML*, volume 70 of *Proceedings of Machine Learning Research*, pages 1321–1330. PMLR.

Geoffrey E. Hinton, Oriol Vinyals, and Jeffrey Dean. 2015. Distilling the knowledge in a neural network. *CoRR*, abs/1503.02531.

Vladimir Karpukhin, Barlas Oguz, Sewon Min, Ledell Wu, Sergey Edunov, Danqi Chen, and Wen-tau Yih. 2020. Dense passage retrieval for open-domain question answering. *CoRR*, abs/2004.04906.

Zhenzhong Lan, Mingda Chen, Sebastian Goodman, Kevin Gimpel, Piyush Sharma, and Radu Soricut. 2020. ALBERT: A lite BERT for self-supervised learning of language representations. In *ICLR*. OpenReview.net.

Yann LeCun, John S. Denker, and Sara A. Solla. 1989. Optimal brain damage. In *NIPS*, pages 598–605. Morgan Kaufmann.

Liyuan Liu, Xiang Ren, Jingbo Shang, Xiaotao Gu, Jian Peng, and Jiawei Han. 2018. Efficient contextualized representation: Language model pruning for sequence labeling. In *EMNLP*, pages 1215–1225. Association for Computational Linguistics.

Weijie Liu, Peng Zhou, Zhiruo Wang, Zhe Zhao, Haotang Deng, and Qi Ju. 2020. Fastbert: a self-distilling BERT with adaptive inference time. In *ACL*, pages 6035–6044. Association for Computational Linguistics.

Sewon Min, Danqi Chen, Hannaneh Hajishirzi, and Luke Zettlemoyer. 2019. A discrete hard EM approach for weakly supervised question answering. In *EMNLP/IJCNLP (1)*, pages 2851–2864. Association for Computational Linguistics.

Stephen Robertson. 2004. Understanding inverse document frequency: on theoretical arguments for IDF. *Journal of Documentation*, 60(5):503–520.

Victor Sanh, Lysandre Debut, Julien Chaumond, and Thomas Wolf. 2019. Distilbert, a distilled version of BERT: smaller, faster, cheaper and lighter. *CoRR*, abs/1910.01108.

Roy Schwartz, Gabriel Stanovsky, Swabha Swayamdipta, Jesse Dodge, and Noah A. Smith. 2020. The right tool for the job: Matching model and instance complexities. In *ACL*, pages 6640–6651. Association for Computational Linguistics.

Sheng Shen, Zhen Dong, Jiayu Ye, Linjian Ma, Zhewei Yao, Amir Gholami, Michael W. Mahoney, and Kurt Keutzer. 2019. Q-BERT: hessian based ultra low precision quantization of BERT. *CoRR*, abs/1909.05840.

Ashish Vaswani, Noam Shazeer, Niki Parmar, Jakob Uszkoreit, Llion Jones, Aidan N. Gomez, Lukasz Kaiser, and Illia Polosukhin. 2017. Attention is all you need. In *NIPS*, pages 5998–6008.

Zhiguo Wang, Patrick Ng, Xiaofei Ma, Ramesh Nallapati, and Bing Xiang. 2019. Multi-passage BERT: A globally normalized BERT model for open-domain question answering. In *EMNLP/IJCNLP (1)*, pages 5877–5881. Association for Computational Linguistics.

R. J. Williams. 1992. Simple statistical gradient-following algorithms for connectionist reinforcement learning. *Machine Learning*, 8:229–256.

Krzysztof Wróbel, Marcin Pietron, Maciej Wielgosz, Michal Karwatowski, and Kazimierz Wiatr. 2018. Convolutional neural network compression for natural language processing. *CoRR*, abs/1805.10796.

Wei Yang, Yuqing Xie, Aileen Lin, Xingyu Li, Luchen Tan, Kun Xiong, Ming Li, and Jimmy Lin. 2019. End-to-end open-domain question answering with bertserini. In *NAACL-HLT (Demonstrations)*, pages 72–77. Association for Computational Linguistics.

Ofir Zafrir, Guy Boudoukh, Peter Izsak, and Moshe Wasserblat. 2019. Q8BERT: quantized 8bit BERT. *CoRR*, abs/1910.06188.

A Two-stage Model for Slot Filling in Low-resource Settings: Domain-agnostic Non-slot Reduction and Pretrained Contextual Embeddings

Cennet Oguz, Ngoc Thang Vu

Institute for Natural Language Processing (IMS), University of Stuttgart

`cennet.oguz|thang.vu@ims.uni-stuttgart.de`

Abstract

Learning-based slot filling - a key component of spoken language understanding systems - typically requires a large amount of in-domain hand-labeled data for training. In this paper, we propose a novel two-stage model architecture that can be trained with only a few in-domain hand-labeled examples. The first step is designed to remove non-slot tokens (i.e., *O* labeled tokens), as they introduce noise in the input of slot filling models. This step is domain-agnostic and therefore, can be trained by exploiting out-of-domain data. The second step identifies slot names only for slot tokens by using state-of-the-art pretrained contextual embeddings such as ELMO and BERT. We show that our approach outperforms other state-of-art systems on the SNIPS benchmark dataset.

1 Introduction

Slot filling models, which predict task-specific names (e.g. artist, time) for these slots from user utterances, are a key component of spoken language understanding (SLU) systems. Deep learning approaches (Mesnil et al., 2013; Hakkani-Tür et al., 2016; Zhang and Wang, 2016; Zhu and Yu, 2018; Chen et al., 2013; Gupta et al., 2018; Bapna et al., 2017a) for SLU involve training on a large amount of annotated training data. Likewise, multi-domain studies (Hakkani-Tür et al., 2016; Liu and Lane, 2017) that rely on deep learning methods require a large amount of data for each domain. However, slot filling is a very challenging task if only a few labeled samples are available. Therefore, this paper proposes methods to address the low-resource domain issue of slot filling.

We aim at improving performance of the slot filling task in different low-resource scenarios by exploring the effective usage of a few in-domain samples with two different scenarios: (1) if data from other domains is not possible but a few samples are available in the current domain (2) if data from other domains are available and a few samples are accessible in the current domain. We exploit domain-agnostic syntactic similarities (e.g., the main verb of a sentence cannot be a slot) to learn the conceptual differences between slot and non-slot tokens in order to dismiss non-slot tokens from the input space. Therefore, using labeled data (SLOT and O labels) across domains can improve the non-slot token reduction step in the target domain and thereby the slot name prediction step. Therefore, we propose a novel two-stage model that first reduces this noise by adding a non-slot detection step and then predicts slot names. The identified non-slots are then removed from the input space of the name prediction step. Our modeling approach is inspired by (Zhai et al., 2017; Dauphin et al., 2013; Shah et al., 2019).

We suggest using a few annotated samples as training input instead of slot descriptions and slot names as in zero-shot learning studies (Bapna et al., 2017a; Lee and Jha, 2019; Shah et al., 2019). This is for two reasons: (1) The creation of slot descriptions needs qualified linguistic expertise and is thus expensive. (2) The relationship between slot names and the corresponding tokens is not constant. To give an example, the relationship between the '*genre*' slot name and '*drama*' token is hypernymic whereas the relationship between the '*artist*' slot name and '*Tarkan*' token is instance based. Hence, it may not be valid to learn only one function to represent the different relationships between names and tokens.

As a classification algorithm, we employ Rocchio classification method (Rocchio, 1971) for labeling the tokens with their domain specific name labels after reducing the non-slot tokens from the input. Rocchio classifier is a very simple classification method that separates the inputs into centroids

Proceedings of SustaiNLP: Workshop on Simple and Efficient Natural Language Processing, pages 73–82

Online, November 20, 2020. ©2020 Association for Computational Linguistics

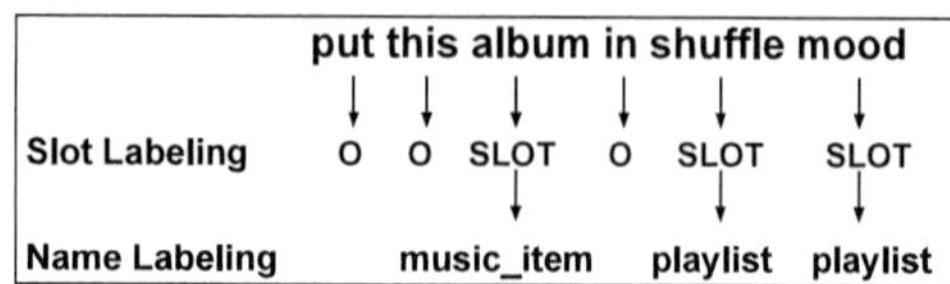

Figure 1: An example for the two-stage modeling approach for an example utterance from SNIPS.

computed as the center of mass of all vectors in the class, i.e., builds a prototype vector for each class. Decision process is simply made based on distance metrics. Because of the availability of only a small amount of data in the current domain and the semantically rich and robust presentation in contextual pretrained embeddings, we argue that Rocchio classifier is sufficient for our task. Furthermore by using this simple classification method, we show the effectiveness of the non-slot noise reduction step from the input.

2   Problem Statement

2.1   Problem Definition

We partition the slot filling task in two consecutive sub-tasks which are called *Slot Labeling* and *Name Labeling*. The *Slot Labeling* task requires to predict for each token in a sentence one of classes $S = \{O, SLOT\}$ where $SLOT$ corresponds to slots whereas O represents non-slot tokens. The *Name Labeling* task requires to predict one label from a predefined name label set $N = \{...\}$ for a set of candidate slots. This implies that candidate slots have already been identified as $SLOT$ by *Slot Labeling* task as shown in Figure 1.

While S is shared across domains, N is domain-specific. Therefore, training data can be shared across domains for the *Slot Labeling* task, but not for the *Name Labeling* task. Thus, we run into the limited data problem for *Name Labeling*.

2.2   Evaluation

We state the evaluation of the proposed systems by computing the average of the precision and recall, i.e, F1 score, over the results of *Name Labeling* task, although the system consists of two consecutive models. In order to understand the overall performance, the average F1 scores of 7 domains are computed. Additionally, the evaluation values represent the average F1 over three random data splits.

3   Model Architecture

We define our consecutive model structure as follows: given an utterance with T tokens, first we employ *Slot Labeling* model in order to identify $SLOT$ tokens while eliminating the non-slot tokens of input utterance. Consecutively, we predict the slot name of the $SLOT$ tokens which are received from the *Slot Labeling* model. The Figure 3 illustrates the overview of the consecutive model architecture with its inputs and outputs while showing the usage of contextualized word embeddings in order to represent input tokens.

3.1   Inputs

The contextualized word representation methods, e.g., ELMo (Peters et al., 2018) and BERT (Devlin et al., 2019), use a pre-trained network over the sentence in order to produce unique embeddings based-on the current context, instead of using a single, fixed vector per word like in Word2Vec (Mikolov et al., 2013) or GloVe (Pennington et al., 2014). The pre-trained models, usually an LSTM (Hochreiter and Schmidhuber, 1997) or a Transformer (Vaswani et al., 2017) can be trained for token-level classification tasks, e.g., named entity recognition, part-of-speech, or sentence-level classifications, e.g., text classification, sentiment analysis. At the same time, they can leverage the the language modeling (Peters et al., 2018; Devlin et al., 2019) by fine-tuning (Howard and Ruder, 2018) the trained objectives on domain-specific dataset as well as they can be used as feature-based models (Peters et al., 2018; Tenney et al., 2019; Brunner et al., 2020) for the down-stream tasks. In this study, we employ feature-based BERT and ELMo for the slot-filling task in low-resource domain.

BERT uses a bidirectional transformer model which is trained on a masked language modeling task. It uses WordPiece embeddings (Wu et al., 2016) which means each word of an input represented with its sub-tokens. Thus, we use the first sub-token for representing the word as it turns out in (Devlin et al., 2019). Additionally, BERT consists of multiple successive layers, i.e., 24 layers because of preferred *BERT-large-cased model*, and each layer represents different linguistic notions of syntax or semantics (Clark et al., 2019). In order to find the focused layers on local context (Tenney et al., 2019) in these linguistic notions, the attention visualization tool (Vig, 2019) is used on randomly

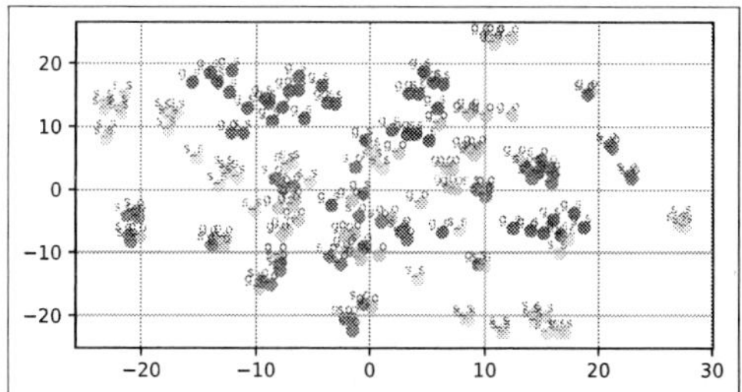

Figure 2: Two dimensional representation of ELMo vectors of randomly selected slot and non-slot token in two example domains in SNIPS dataset: GetWeather and SearchScreeningE. s_o (red) = vectors of non-slot tokens of SearchScreeningE.; s_s (green) = slot tokens of SearchScreeningE.; g_o (blue) = non-slot tokens of GetWeather; g_s (purple) = slot tokens of GetWeather.

selected samples. We select *10th*, *11th*, *12th*, and *13th* layers and concatenate hidden states of these layers in order to represent the corresponding word.

ELMo concatenates the output of two LSTM independently trained on the bidirectional language modeling task and return the hidden states for the given input sequence.

The proposed consecutive approach uses two different label sets S and N, i.e., as explained in Section 2.1, which share the same sequences per domains. We operate the contextual embeddings on given utterance with the input sequence to assign the contextual embeddings to their corresponding input tokens.

3.2 Slot Labeling

Figure 2 shows the domain-agnostic pattern between non-slot token vectors of *GetWeather* and *SearchScreeningE.*, non-slot tokens (g_o) from *GetWeather*, and non-slot tokens (s_o) from *SearchScreeningE.* show higher similarity than slot tokens from both. The *Slot Labeling* step aims to make efficient use of the existing slot labeled dataset from current and different domains in order to exploit that domain-agnostic semantic frames for the current domain. Therefore, we employ two different *Slot Labeling* models separately according to data availability. Thus, we define two common scenarios to cope with: (1) the absence of data from different domains whereas the occurrence of few labeled samples in the current domain (2) available data from different domains as well as the presence of few labeled samples in the current domain. For the first scenario, we apply Rocchio Slot Labeling

whereas Neural Slot Labeling is employed as the solution of the second one.

Rocchio Slot Labeling: It is proposed for utilizing a few available labeled samples from the current domain and show the performance of non-slot reduction without any additional samples from different domain on slot and name labeling. Utilizing only a few samples to build classification model for slot labeling, we apply a Rocchio classifier that assigns to observations the label of the class of training samples whose centroid is closest to the observation.

$$\hat{y} = \arg\min_{Y_s \in S} \|\mu_s - v_i\|, \mu_s = \frac{1}{|X|} \sum_{v_i \in X} v_i \quad (1)$$

where $X = \{v_1, v_2, ..., v_n\}$, v_i represents a slot value. Thus, the Rocchio classifier is trained to map the given slot value to the slot label by using the centroid (μ_s) of the prototypes (X) of the corresponding slot label.

Neural Slot Labeling: We use this with the purpose of using available labeled data from different domains in addition to a few labeled samples of the current domain. The availability of large amount of labeled data from different domain make use of complex architecture such as neural networks. Thus, for ELMo embeddings we use the token classification model proposed by (Peters et al., 2018) whereas for BERT embeddings we implement the token classification model proposed by (Devlin et al., 2019). Thus, for the given $X = \{w_1, w_2, ..., w_T\}$ in order to predict $Y_s = (y_1, y_2, ..., y_T)$ where T is the token number of the given input and $y_i \in S$,

ELMo embeddings are used with an LSTM+CRF which is trained by maximizing the conditional log-likelihood,

$$\hat{Y}_s = \arg\max \sum_{i=1}^{T} \ln p(y_i|w_i, X) \quad (2)$$

BERT embeddings are used with a Linear layer and a following softmax function,

$$\hat{Y}_s = \arg\max \sum_{i=1}^{T} softmax(W * w_i) \quad (3)$$

The aim of the Neural Slot model is efficiently leveraging domain agnostic features of different task-oriented domains with the networks. Because the existence of available data lets us train the networks in order to find slot/non-slot tokens.

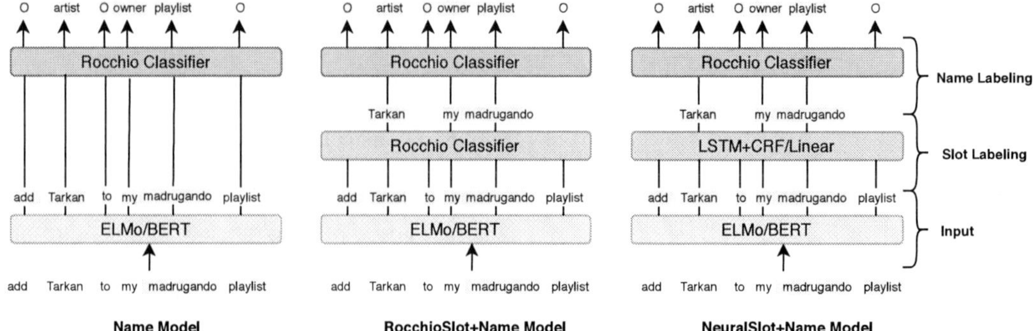

Figure 3: The overview of proposed model variations with input and output shown for an example utterance from SNIPS. *Name Model* represents the baseline without *Slot Labeling* stage and uses only a few samples from the current domain. *RocchioSlot+Name Model* employs Rocchio classifier for *Slot Labeling* stage with a few SLOT/O labeled samples from the current domain in order to reduce the non-slot tokens and then uses the same samples with Name labels to train *Name Model*. *NeuralSlot+Name Model* utilizes the out-domain SLOT/O labeled samples together with a few current domain SLOT/O labeled samples in order to train *Neural Slot Labeling* whereas it uses only the current domain samples with *Name* labels for Rocchio *Name Model*.

3.3 Name Labeling

We assume, only a few samples for the current domain is available for training a model. Thus, the absence of a huge amount of labeled data for the current domain makes it impossible for the use of neural networks. Therefore, we utilize Rocchio classifier as presented in equation 1 to map the given slot value to the name label by using the centroid of the prototypes of the corresponding name label.

4 Dataset and Experimental Setup

4.1 Resources

We utilize the SNIPS dataset (Coucke et al., 2018) as a base dataset in our experiment. SNIPS is a SLU dataset of crowd-sourced user utterances with 39 slots and 7 intents. We split SNIPS with the purpose of creating a single-domain dataset.

We create *Prototype-* and *Test*-data in order to train the models and evaluate their performance on each domain. Four *Prototype* groups are generated from SNIPS in order to investigate the performance when the number of samples increases. To accomplish this, we randomly select 10 slot samples embedded in their input sequences (complete sentences) per label in SNIPS. With the initial sample of 10 slots per label, we increment the previous set by 5 randomly-selected slot samples up to 2 times, resulting in 10, 15, and 20 sub-sample groups (10-Prototype $\subset$ 15-Prototype $\subset$ 20-Prototype). Se-

lected slot phases represent one sample in the label space even if the token number is greater then 1. For example, *Wind of Change* consists of three tokens, however, these three tokens represents one sample. *Test* data consists of 1000 randomly selected sentences. *Prototype* and *Test* include two annotation sets, *Name* and *Slot*.

Name Set: Provides annotation for the sentences with labels such as *artist, object_name* and *O* tags for the input sequences.

Slot Set: We convert the labels in the *Name Set* to *SLOT* tags while keeping the *O* tags the same.

Auxiliary Slot Set: We utilize the slot filling dataset of different domains in order to reduce non-slot tokens by exploiting syntactic similarities between domains. For example, the verb of a sentences does not represent a slot in any domain. Therefore, instead of trying to leverage the semantic similarity between the slot tokens in different domains, we use non-slot token similarity to reduce them from the input space. We obtain this dataset with the same process that converting *Name Set* to *Slot Set*.

4.1.1 Proposed Systems

4.2 Experimental Setup

We design our experimental settings to investigate the following research questions. The first question focuses on exploring the impact of existing annotated data from different domains on the performance of the slot/non-slot classification step.

Table 1: Name F1 scores. The results of previous studies, the baseline Name and proposed RocchioSlot+Name and NeuralSlot+Name models in different sample size. The values represent the average F1 over 3 data splits. 'Domain Avg.' represents the average values across sample sizes.

	Previous Systems			BERT Name			ELMo Name			BERT RocchioSlot+Name			ELMo RocchioSlot+Name			BERT NeuralSlot+Name			ELMo NeuralSlot+Name		
Data	CT	ZAT	CDS	10	15	20	10	15	20	10	15	20	10	15	20	10	15	20	10	15	20
AddToPlaylist	74	73	**76**	45	46	47	45	46	48	62	62	63	57	59	63	66	67	67	63	65	67
PlayMusic	56	56	58	56	56	55	59	59	59	70	70	72	65	66	66	72	73	74	72	73	**74**
BookRestaurant	63	63	63	55	56	56	58	59	59	63	64	65	64	65	66	67	68	69	70	71	**73**
GetWeather	72	71	**77**	46	47	46	49	49	49	66	66	66	64	66	67	75	75	75	73	75	76
RateBook	82	83	82	73	74	73	64	65	66	90	92	92	81	82	82	95	96	**97**	89	91	92
SearchCreativeW.	62	63	65	45	46	46	45	44	44	79	81	81	81	82	82	80	87	**89**	83	84	86
SearchScreeningE.	64	64	67	38	40	40	61	61	60	50	55	55	69	71	72	65	64	65	78	78	**81**
Domain Avg.	68.2	68.0	70.1	51.1	52.1	51.8	54.4	54.7	55.0	68.5	70.0	70.5	68.7	70.1	71.1	74.2	75.7	76.5	75.4	76.7	**78.4**

Table 2: F1 scores for BERT slot/non-slot classification.

	Rocchio Slot			Neural Slot		
Domain	10	15	20	10	15	20
AddToPlaylist	93.3	93.3	93.7	97.3	98.2	97.5
PlayMusic	93.7	94.5	94.4	98.1	98.8	98.8
BookRestaurant	92.2	92.1	91.8	98.5	99.0	99.2
GetWeather	94.3	94.3	94.2	98.9	99.0	98.8
RateBook	94.7	96.5	96.0	98.7	98.6	98.7
SearchCreativeW.	96.4	96.4	96.3	96.4	97.4	98.4
SearchScreeningE.	90.7	91.8	91.7	99.1	99.1	99.1

Table 3: F1 scores for ELMo slot/non-slot classification.

	Rocchio Slot			Neural Slot		
Domain	10	15	20	10	15	20
AddToPlaylist	91.1	91.6	91.7	94.8	95.7	96.6
PlayMusic	91.1	91.1	90.9	97.1	97.2	97.9
BookRestaurant	88.5	87.7	87.9	96.6	98.2	98.5
GetWeather	92.7	92.8	93.0	98.0	98.7	98.7
RateBook	93.1	93.4	93.5	96.8	97.4	97.8
SearchCreativeW.	96.8	96.4	96.4	97.2	97.7	98.0
SearchScreeningE.	90.7	91.1	91.3	97.8	98.0	98.4

We assume that we have sufficient training data for different domains but not for a target domain. The second question aims at exploring the effectiveness of exploiting *Prototypes* with respect to example sizes. The third question focuses on the comparison between the two contextual embeddings, ELMO and BERT.

4.2.1 Baseline

Name Model: In order to examine the effect of low-resource domain in slot tagging, we train the *Name Labeling* by using *Prototype Name Set*. Then, we test the model with *Test Name Set* that includes 1000 samples with corresponding *Name* labels N. We use contextual embeddings, either ELMO or BERT, as input representation, resulting in two main baseline models without using the non-slot reduction step. We employ *Name Model* to show to performance of a few samples.

RocchioSlot+Name Model: We use *Prototype Slot Set* to make use of Rocchio Slot Labeling whereas we utilize *Prototype Name Set* to train Name Model. Here, we aim to understand the efficiency of non-slot reduction with only a few current domain samples. The *Slot Set* from *Prototype* that includes only a few samples with the corresponding *Slot* labels S is used to train the *Rocchio Slot Labeling* model. This trained Rocchio Slot Labeling (*RocchioSlot*) model then reduces the non-slot tokens from the input of the *Name Labeling* model. The *Name Labeling* model then predicts the token labels N.

NeuralSlot+Name Model: The process of using this model is identical to *RocchioSlot+Name Model*. The only difference is that we add *Slot Sets* from other domains - *Auxiliary Slot Set*- and train the *Neural Slot Labeling* model in order to analyze the impact of out-domain samples on the performance of non-slot reduction and *Name Model* . An example of this would be the usage of annotated "AddToPlaylist" and "GetWeather" domains data converting the labels to *SLOT* labels for "PlayMusic" in order to train the *Neural Slot Labeling* model.

5 Results

Non-slot/slot Classification Results Table 2 and 3 show the results from the *Rocchio Slot Labeling* and *Neural Slot Labeling* models for both BERT and ELMo. According to the overall results, we strongly claim that *SLOT* label for a token is a domain-agnostic feature. Moreover, BERT embeddings show better performance then ELMo on *Slot Labeling* task in both model setups.

Two-stage Slot Name Labeling Results Table 1 shows that the proposed models outperforms the baseline across domains and sample sizes. It is apparent that the increase of samples sizes largely improves F1 score per domain. As can be seen in *Domain Avg.*, our non-slot reduction models *RocchioSlot+Name* and *NeuralSlot+Name* outperform the baseline *Name Model* with $> 20\%$. In addition, by comparing *NeuralSlot+Name* and *RocchioSlot+Name*, we see that *NeuralSlot+Name* model results in an $> 6\%$ percent increase in the average performance.

Impact of Different Contextualized Embeddings ELMo and BERT have comparable performance, with ELMo slightly better on most tasks, e.g., as expected after the study of (Tenney et al., 2019), but the Transformer scoring higher on *RateBook* and *SearchCreativeW.* consistently with all the models.

Comparisons with State-of-art Systems We compared our systems with the three following studies: (1) Zero-shot Adaptive Transfer (ZAT) (Lee and Jha, 2019) that used condition slot filling on slot descriptions with hierarchical six LSTM and CRF layers; (2) Concept Tagger (CT) (Bapna et al., 2017b) by exploiting multi-task bidirectional stacked LSTM ; (3) Cross Domain Slot filling study (CDS) (Shah et al., 2019) that used a conditional sequence tagging model by utilizing BiGRU-BiLSTM model. The results of previous studies are taken from (Shah et al., 2019)). Table 1 demonstrates that even though the previous systems use a large amount of data with the neural networks, *RocchioSlot+Name* outperforms the best performance of previous system (CDS) with up to 1% with 20 training examples, whereas the *NeuralSlot+Name* model outperforms them with up to 8.3% improvement.

6 Qualitative Analysis

We analyzed the results on individual slots by comparing them according to contextualized embeddings and proposed models. We observed that BERT shows consistent lower results for the tokens like city, state from *BookResteurant*, and *location_name*, *object_location_type* from *SearchScreeningE* whereas it outperforms ELMo for proper name detection like *object_name* from *RateBook* and *SearchCreativeW.* domains.

The wrong predictions of Name Labeling, e.g., false-positive rates of names (e.g., object_select, cuisine, spatial_relation) for O label, draw the attention. An extreme difference between low precision and relatively high recall is observed. However, the precision results are drastically improved when RocchioSlot+ and NeuralSlot+Name models are employed. For example, *RateBook* domain's slot *object_select* has 0.41 precision with Name Model whereas the precision of it is 0.69 and 0.93 with RocchioSlot+ and NeuralSlot+Name models respectively.

On the other hand, when the *timeRange* label of *GetWeather* is reviewed, RocchioSlot+Name as well as Name Model failed. Due to leak of non-slot tokens, *timeRange* values labeled as 'O'. RocchioSlot fails for labeling the values (e.g., eleven months from now) of *timeRange* with *S*, because it is a clustering-based method and is not able to capture the sequential dependencies. NeuralSlot+Name models, however, shows significant increases. The comparison of the results from both models indicates that the wrong predictions of the 'O' label drastically reduced with NeuralSlot+Name model.

Similar proper nouns, e.g., *album* and *track*, in the same domain denote the weakness of the proposed systems. NeuralSlot+Name model is not able to distinguish similar proper nouns. For example, the highest false-negative rate for *album* is *track* while it is *album* for *track*.

7 Related Work

7.1 Low-resource Domain in NLP

Typically in NLP, the domain is meant to refer to some coherent type of dataset that related to the underlying linguistic distribution (Ramponi and Plank, 2020). When the linguistic distribution between target and source domain differ, the performance drops on the target domain. Therefore, hand-labeled samples are needed for many NLP applications even though they are expensive to create and often not available for low-resource languages or domains. Many studies have recently been proposed to tackle the low-resource issue by using different approaches such as transfer learning for domain adaptation (Daume III and Marcu, 2006; Pan and Yang, 2009), and multi-task learning (Peng and Dredze, 2017a). Here, we review the slot filling like sequence labeling studies such as part-of-speech tagging (POS) and named entity recognition (NER) within domain adaptation and multi-task learning.

The domain adaptation approach is used to transfer the domain-general feature space from source tasks as "prior knowledge" to the target task in order to overcome the hand-labeled data scarcity (Blitzer et al., 2006; Daume III and Marcu, 2006; Ramponi and Plank, 2020). For POS tagging, Jiang and Zhai (2007) propose a supervised instance weighting technique with or without labeled instances in target domain, whereas Kann et al. (2018) use character-level and subword-level supervision. However, Han and Eisenstein (2019) demonstrate unsupervised multi-task learning with the domain-adaptive fine-tuning method by utilizing contextualized word embeddings for the new domains. Similarly, NER is a sequence labeling task that is often addressed by domain adaptation and multi-task learning because of the low-resource domain. But, most of the NER tasks consist of different label spaces. Jia et al. (2019) use cross-domain language modeling for performing cross-task knowledge transfer by extracting knowledge of domain differences from raw text, while Peng and Dredze (2017b) utilize multi-task learning approach for shared representations in multiple tasks simultaneously to have better generalize for domain adaptation.

As examined here, most existing work in NLP considers the low-resource issue as a problem of shared feature spaces. The main consideration is always augmenting the most similar feature intersection of source and target domains and use this feature space to improve the low-resource target domain (Daumé III, 2009; Ruder and Plank, 2017; Ramponi and Plank, 2020).

7.2 Low-resource Domain in Slot Filling

In a broader sense, two ways of training model have often been applied to slot filling in low-resource domain scenario: (1) use a multi-task learning method (Jaech et al., 2016a; Bingel and Søgaard, 2017) (2) train a model that performs well across domains using domain adaptation or transfer learning techniques e.g., based on external memory (Peng and Yao, 2015), ranking loss (Vu et al., 2016), encoder (Kurata et al., 2016), attention (Zhu and Yu, 2017), multi-task modeling (Jaech et al., 2016b), adversarial training (Kim et al., 2017), pointer networks (Zhai et al., 2017) have recently been proposed. These methods, however, still require a substantial amount of data for adaptation. Additionally, Louvan and Magnini (2018) propose to joint learning

with NER as an auxiliary task through a multi-task learning setup and show improvement in slot filling with low-resource scenarios.

Another direction relies on zero-shot learning approaches, i.e., learning method with label descriptions or label names, which have recently been popular in slot filling task. Zero-shot learning (Socher et al., 2013) is a classification setup in learning systems, where the model predict samples from classes that were not seen during training at test time. Zero-shot slot filling, i,e., either relies on slot names or slot descriptions, has been influenced the studies of the domain scaling problem for slots prediction. (Bapna et al., 2017b) leverage the encoding of the slot names and descriptions within a multi-task deep learned slot filling model, to align slots across domains with shared feature extraction. Likewise, (Lee and Jha, 2019) propose a zero-shot adaptive transfer method for slot tagging that utilizes the slot description for transferring reusable concepts across domains for eliminating the need of labeled examples for transferring reusable concepts whereas (Shah et al., 2019) add the a target domain samples to slot descriptions for conveying the domain-agnostic concepts between the intents.

8   Conclusion and Future Work

We propose a novel two-stage model for slot filling in low-resource domains. Our results demonstrate the importance of non-slot token reduction on slot filling with resource constraints by using a simple classification method. Furthermore, the benefit of employing slot filling data from other different domains for non-slot reduction is demonstrated. In addition, increasing sample sizes for the *Prototypes* shows significant improvements. Base on our findings, future usage of multi-domain or limited data could be effective in improving slot filling methods from a non-slot reduction perspective. Additionally, the outcomes of the multi-domain data usage in our study contributes a new perspective in supervised domain adaptation and generalization studies.

References

Ankur Bapna, Gokhan Tür, Dilek Hakkani-Tür, and Larry Heck. 2017a. Sequential dialogue context modeling for spoken language understanding. In *Proceedings of the 18th Annual SIGdial Meeting on Discourse and Dialogue*, pages 103–114.

Ankur Bapna, Gokhan Tür, Dilek Hakkani-Tür, and Larry Heck. 2017b. Towards zero-shot frame semantic parsing for domain scaling. *Proc. Interspeech 2017*, pages 2476–2480.

Joachim Bingel and Anders Søgaard. 2017. Identifying beneficial task relations for multi-task learning in deep neural networks. In *Proceedings of the 15th Conference of the European Chapter of the Association for Computational Linguistics: Volume 2, Short Papers*, pages 164–169, Valencia, Spain. Association for Computational Linguistics.

John Blitzer, Ryan McDonald, and Fernando Pereira. 2006. Domain adaptation with structural correspondence learning. In *Proceedings of the 2006 conference on empirical methods in natural language processing*, pages 120–128. Association for Computational Linguistics.

Gino Brunner, Yang Liu, Damian Pascual Ortiz, Oliver Richter, Massimiliano Ciaramita, and Roger Wattenhofer. 2020. On identifiability in transformers.

Yun-Nung Chen, William Yang Wang, and Alexander I Rudnicky. 2013. Unsupervised induction and filling of semantic slots for spoken dialogue systems using frame-semantic parsing. In *2013 IEEE Workshop on Automatic Speech Recognition and Understanding*, pages 120–125. IEEE.

Kevin Clark, Urvashi Khandelwal, Omer Levy, and Christopher D Manning. 2019. What does bert look at? an analysis of bert's attention. In *Proceedings of the 2019 ACL Workshop BlackboxNLP: Analyzing and Interpreting Neural Networks for NLP*, pages 276–286.

Alice Coucke, Alaa Saade, Adrien Ball, Théodore Bluche, Alexandre Caulier, David Leroy, Clément Doumouro, Thibault Gisselbrecht, Francesco Caltagirone, Thibaut Lavril, et al. 2018. Snips voice platform: an embedded spoken language understanding system for private-by-design voice interfaces. *arXiv preprint arXiv:1805.10190*.

Hal Daumé III. 2009. Frustratingly easy domain adaptation. *arXiv preprint arXiv:0907.1815*.

Hal Daume III and Daniel Marcu. 2006. Domain adaptation for statistical classifiers. *Journal of artificial Intelligence research*, 26:101–126.

Yann N Dauphin, Gokhan Tur, Dilek Hakkani-Tur, and Larry Heck. 2013. Zero-shot learning for semantic utterance classification. *arXiv preprint arXiv:1401.0509*.

Jacob Devlin, Ming-Wei Chang, Kenton Lee, and Kristina Toutanova. 2019. Bert: Pre-training of deep bidirectional transformers for language understanding. In *Proceedings of the 2019 Conference of the North American Chapter of the Association for Computational Linguistics: Human Language Technologies, Volume 1 (Long and Short Papers)*, pages 4171–4186.

Raghav Gupta, Abhinav Rastogi, and Dilek Hakkani-Tür. 2018. An efficient approach to encoding context for spoken language understanding. *Proc. Interspeech 2018*, pages 3469–3473.

Dilek Hakkani-Tür, Gökhan Tür, Asli Celikyilmaz, Yun-Nung Chen, Jianfeng Gao, Li Deng, and Ye-Yi Wang. 2016. Multi-domain joint semantic frame parsing using bi-directional rnn-lstm. In *Interspeech*, pages 715–719.

Xiaochuang Han and Jacob Eisenstein. 2019. Unsupervised domain adaptation of contextualized embeddings for sequence labeling. In *Proceedings of the 2019 Conference on Empirical Methods in Natural Language Processing and the 9th International Joint Conference on Natural Language Processing (EMNLP-IJCNLP)*, pages 4229–4239.

Sepp Hochreiter and Jürgen Schmidhuber. 1997. Long short-term memory. *Neural computation*, 9(8):1735–1780.

Jeremy Howard and Sebastian Ruder. 2018. Universal language model fine-tuning for text classification. In *Proceedings of the 56th Annual Meeting of the Association for Computational Linguistics (Volume 1: Long Papers)*, pages 328–339.

Aaron Jaech, Larry Heck, and Mari Ostendorf. 2016a. Domain adaptation of recurrent neural networks for natural language understanding. *Interspeech 2016*, pages 690–694.

Aaron Jaech, Larry Heck, and Mari Ostendorf. 2016b. Domain adaptation of recurrent neural networks for natural language understanding. *arXiv preprint arXiv:1604.00117*.

Chen Jia, Xiaobo Liang, and Yue Zhang. 2019. Cross-domain NER using cross-domain language modeling. In *Proceedings of the 57th Annual Meeting of the Association for Computational Linguistics*, pages 2464–2474, Florence, Italy. Association for Computational Linguistics.

Jing Jiang and ChengXiang Zhai. 2007. Instance weighting for domain adaptation in NLP. In *Proceedings of the 45th Annual Meeting of the Association of Computational Linguistics*, pages 264–271, Prague, Czech Republic. Association for Computational Linguistics.

Katharina Kann, Johannes Bjerva, Isabelle Augenstein, Barbara Plank, and Anders Søgaard. 2018. Character-level supervision for low-resource pos tagging. In *Proceedings of the Workshop on Deep Learning Approaches for Low-Resource NLP*, pages 1–11.

Young-Bum Kim, Karl Stratos, and Dongchan Kim. 2017. Adversarial adaptation of synthetic or stale data. In *Proceedings of the 55th Annual Meeting of the Association for Computational Linguistics (Volume 1: Long Papers)*, pages 1297–1307.

Gakuto Kurata, Bing Xiang, Bowen Zhou, and Mo Yu. 2016. Leveraging sentence-level information with encoder lstm for semantic slot filling. In *Proceedings of the 2016 Conference on Empirical Methods in Natural Language Processing*, pages 2077–2083.

Sungjin Lee and Rahul Jha. 2019. Zero-shot adaptive transfer for conversational language understanding. In *Proceedings of the AAAI Conference on Artificial Intelligence*, volume 33, pages 6642–6649.

Bing Liu and Ian Lane. 2017. Multi-domain adversarial learning for slot filling in spoken language understanding. *arXiv preprint arXiv:1711.11310*.

Samuel Louvan and Bernardo Magnini. 2018. Exploring named entity recognition as an auxiliary task for slot filling in conversational language understanding. In *Proceedings of the 2018 EMNLP Workshop SCAI: The 2nd International Workshop on Search-Oriented Conversational AI*, pages 74–80.

Grégoire Mesnil, Xiaodong He, Li Deng, and Yoshua Bengio. 2013. Investigation of recurrent-neural-network architectures and learning methods for spoken language understanding. In *Interspeech*, pages 3771–3775.

Tomas Mikolov, Ilya Sutskever, Kai Chen, Greg S Corrado, and Jeff Dean. 2013. Distributed representations of words and phrases and their compositionality. In *Advances in neural information processing systems*, pages 3111–3119.

Sinno Jialin Pan and Qiang Yang. 2009. A survey on transfer learning. *IEEE Transactions on knowledge and data engineering*, 22(10):1345–1359.

Baolin Peng and Kaisheng Yao. 2015. Recurrent neural networks with external memory for language understanding. *arXiv preprint arXiv:1506.00195*.

Nanyun Peng and Mark Dredze. 2017a. Multi-task domain adaptation for sequence tagging. In *Proceedings of the 2nd Workshop on Representation Learning for NLP*, pages 91–100.

Nanyun Peng and Mark Dredze. 2017b. Multi-task domain adaptation for sequence tagging. In *Proceedings of the 2nd Workshop on Representation Learning for NLP*, pages 91–100, Vancouver, Canada. Association for Computational Linguistics.

Jeffrey Pennington, Richard Socher, and Christopher D Manning. 2014. Glove: Global vectors for word representation. In *Proceedings of the 2014 conference on empirical methods in natural language processing (EMNLP)*, pages 1532–1543.

Matthew Peters, Mark Neumann, Mohit Iyyer, Matt Gardner, Christopher Clark, Kenton Lee, and Luke Zettlemoyer. 2018. Deep contextualized word representations. In *Proceedings of the 2018 Conference of the North American Chapter of the Association for Computational Linguistics: Human Language Technologies, Volume 1 (Long Papers)*, pages 2227–2237.

Alan Ramponi and Barbara Plank. 2020. Neural unsupervised domain adaptation in nlp—a survey. *arXiv preprint arXiv:2006.00632*.

Joseph Rocchio. 1971. Relevance feedback in information retrieval. *The Smart retrieval system-experiments in automatic document processing*, pages 313–323.

Sebastian Ruder and Barbara Plank. 2017. Learning to select data for transfer learning with bayesian optimization. In *Proceedings of the 2017 Conference on Empirical Methods in Natural Language Processing*, pages 372–382.

Darsh J Shah, Raghav Gupta, Amir A Fayazi, and Dilek Hakkani-Tur. 2019. Robust zero-shot cross-domain slot filling with example values. *arXiv preprint arXiv:1906.06870*.

Richard Socher, Milind Ganjoo, Christopher D Manning, and Andrew Ng. 2013. Zero-shot learning through cross-modal transfer. In *Advances in neural information processing systems*, pages 935–943.

Ian Tenney, Patrick Xia, Berlin Chen, Alex Wang, Adam Poliak, R Thomas McCoy, Najoung Kim, Benjamin Van Durme, Samuel R Bowman, Dipanjan Das, et al. 2019. What do you learn from context? probing for sentence structure in contextualized word representations. *arXiv preprint arXiv:1905.06316*.

Ashish Vaswani, Noam Shazeer, Niki Parmar, Jakob Uszkoreit, Llion Jones, Aidan N Gomez, Lukasz Kaiser, and Illia Polosukhin. 2017. Attention is all you need. In *Advances in neural information processing systems*, pages 5998–6008.

Jesse Vig. 2019. A multiscale visualization of attention in the transformer model. In *Proceedings of the 57th Annual Meeting of the Association for Computational Linguistics: System Demonstrations*, pages 37–42.

Ngoc Thang Vu, Pankaj Gupta, Heike Adel, and Hinrich Schütze. 2016. Bi-directional recurrent neural network with ranking loss for spoken language understanding. In *2016 IEEE International Conference on Acoustics, Speech and Signal Processing (ICASSP)*, pages 6060–6064. IEEE.

Yonghui Wu, Mike Schuster, Zhifeng Chen, Quoc V Le, Mohammad Norouzi, Wolfgang Macherey, Maxim Krikun, Yuan Cao, Qin Gao, Klaus Macherey, et al. 2016. Google's neural machine translation system: Bridging the gap between human and machine translation. *arXiv preprint arXiv:1609.08144*.

Feifei Zhai, Saloni Potdar, Bing Xiang, and Bowen Zhou. 2017. Neural models for sequence chunking. In *Thirty-First AAAI Conference on Artificial Intelligence*.

Xiaodong Zhang and Houfeng Wang. 2016. A joint model of intent determination and slot filling for spoken language understanding. In *IJCAI*, volume 16, pages 2993–2999.

Su Zhu and Kai Yu. 2017. Encoder-decoder with focus-mechanism for sequence labelling based spoken language understanding. In *2017 IEEE International Conference on Acoustics, Speech and Signal Processing (ICASSP)*, pages 5675–5679. IEEE.

Su Zhu and Kai Yu. 2018. Concept transfer learning for adaptive language understanding. In *Proceedings of the 19th Annual SIGdial Meeting on Discourse and Dialogue*, pages 391–399.

Early Exiting BERT for Efficient Document Ranking

Ji Xin,[1,2] **Rodrigo Nogueira,**[1] **Yaoliang Yu,**[1,2] and **Jimmy Lin**[1,2]

[1] David R. Cheriton School of Computer Science, University of Waterloo
[2] Vector Institute for Artificial Intelligence

Abstract

Pre-trained language models such as BERT have shown their effectiveness in various tasks. Despite their power, they are known to be computationally intensive, which hinders real-world applications. In this paper, we introduce early exiting BERT for document ranking. With a slight modification, BERT becomes a model with multiple output paths, and each inference sample can exit early from these paths. In this way, computation can be effectively allocated among samples, and overall system latency is significantly reduced while the original quality is maintained. Our experiments on two document ranking datasets demonstrate up to $2.5\times$ inference speedup with minimal quality degradation. The source code of our implementation can be found at `https://github.com/castorini/earlyexiting-monobert`.

1 Introduction

Large scale pre-trained language models such as ELMo (Peters et al., 2018), GPT (Radford et al., 2019), BERT (Devlin et al., 2019), RoBERTa (Liu et al., 2019), and ALBERT (Lan et al., 2019) have brought impressive improvements to natural language processing (NLP) and information retrieval (IR) applications. However, these large-scale models bring to our community not only exciting results, but also concerns about intensive computation demands and high inference latency, especially in real-world deployments.

In this paper, we study how to accelerate inference of BERT-based IR models. We follow the framework of MonoBERT (Nogueira and Cho, 2019), which performs binary classification on query–document pairs into relevant/non-relevant. To accelerate inference for BERT, we employ the idea of *early exiting* as in DeeBERT (Xin et al., 2020). In DeeBERT, extra classification layers

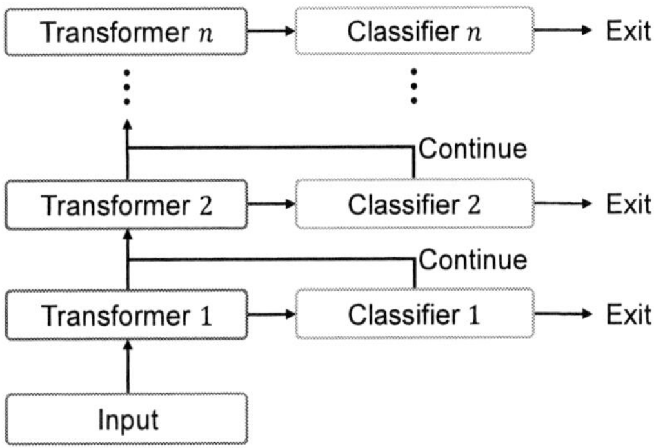

Figure 1: Overview of early exiting BERT for document ranking. Blue blocks are transformer layers and orange blocks are classifiers.

are attached to transformer layers of a pre-trained BERT model (Figure 1). The model is then fine-tuned on the downstream training dataset. At inference time, a sample is sequentially processed by transformer layers and classifiers. If a classifier is confident of its prediction, it returns the result and inference ends early; otherwise, the next transformer layer proceeds with the computation. Different from DeeBERT, which treats all classes equally, we use *asymmetric* early exiting for document ranking: the exiting threshold for positive predictions is higher than for negative ones, since the two classes in document ranking are intrinsically different, and it is natural to allocate more computational resources for positive samples.

We conduct experiments on BERT$_{\text{BASE}}$ with two document ranking datasets, MS MARCO passage (Bajaj et al., 2016) and ASNQ (Garg et al., 2019). We compare against Cascade Transformer (Soldaini and Moschitti, 2020), a recently proposed technique to accelerate inference in BERT-based document ranking. Results show that our method can reduce inference latency by up to $2.5\times$ with minimal effectiveness degradation.

Proceedings of SustaiNLP: Workshop on Simple and Efficient Natural Language Processing, pages 83–88
Online, November 20, 2020. ©2020 Association for Computational Linguistics

2 Related Work

Neural document ranking models have brought significant improvements to IR tasks. Throughout this paper, we refer to candidates to be retrieved as *documents*, although they may actually be passages, answers to a question, etc. Representative neural ranking models include DRMM (Guo et al., 2016), DUET (Mitra et al., 2017), KNRM (Xiong et al., 2017), Co-PACRR (Hui et al., 2018) — just to name a few. In recent years, large-scale pre-trained language models, especially those based on the transformer architecture (Vaswani et al., 2017), have been applied to IR tasks and have pushed the state of the art even further (Nogueira and Cho, 2019; Dai and Callan, 2019; Yilmaz et al., 2019; Li et al., 2020).

The idea of early exiting for neural networks originates from BranchyNet (Teerapittayanon et al., 2017), and is also applied to NLP tasks in several papers (Xin et al., 2020; Schwartz et al., 2020; Liu et al., 2020; Zhou et al., 2020). Our work differs from them by using an early exiting strategy that specializes for document ranking. Another related work that focuses on retrieval is Cascade Transformer (Soldaini and Moschitti, 2020), where a fixed proportion of samples are dropped after each layer. In contrast, our work drops samples based on their scores, and empirically we are able to achieve higher inference speedups.

3 Early Exiting for Document Ranking

The task of concern is *document re-ranking*, i.e., to rank among a small candidate document set, which is generated by a "bag of words" IR technique such as BM25. We assume in this paper that the candidate set is provided as input.

3.1 MonoBERT

We first briefly describe MonoBERT (Nogueira and Cho, 2019), the neural ranking model on which our early exiting model is built.

The input to MonoBERT is a query–document pair, which is organized as one input sequence in the following format:

$$[\text{CLS}] \ Q \ [\text{SEP}] \ D \ [\text{SEP}]$$

Here, Q and D are the query and the document, and [CLS] and [SEP] are special tokens for marking the beginning of input and separating the query and document sequences. Details can be found in the BERT paper (Devlin et al., 2019).

The task of MonoBERT is binary classification: it produces a probability distribution over two classes, relevant and non-relevant.

MonoBERT is initialized with a pre-trained BERT model (or other models with a similar architecture such as RoBERTa). A classifier, which is typically a single-layer fully-connected network, is attached to the last transformer layer of the BERT model; concretely, the classifier takes as input the last layer hidden state corresponding to the [CLS] token, and outputs the binary prediction. For fine-tuning, the model is updated with binary label supervision. For inference, a query–document pair's relevance score is the predicted probability of the document being relevant, and this score is used for subsequent re-ranking of the candidates.

3.2 Fine-Tuning Early Exiting MonoBERT

Our model, early exiting MonoBERT, is a multi-output variant of BERT which enables early exiting. Similar to MonoBERT, we start with a pre-trained $\text{BERT}_{\text{BASE}}$ model with n transformer layers and attach n classifiers to it (Figure 1).

Our fine-tuning method is different from Dee-BERT (Xin et al., 2020), where a two-stage finc-tuning method is employed. Instead, we fine-tune the model by simply minimizing the sum of loss functions of all classifiers. The rationale is that with abundant training data, as in our case, this simple fine-tuning method yields comparable or even better results and is also faster. The loss function of the ith classifier is

$$L_i(x, y; \theta) = H(y, f_i(x; \theta)), \qquad (1)$$

where x is the input query–document pair, y the binary label of whether the pair is relevant, θ the collection of all parameters, H the cross-entropy loss function, and f_i the binary probability distribution returned by the ith classifier. The network is fine-tuned with the following objective:

$$\min_{\theta} \sum_{(x,y)\in\mathcal{D}} \sum_i L_i(x, y; \theta), \qquad (2)$$

where $\mathcal{D}$ is the fine-tuning dataset.

3.3 Asymmetric Early Exiting

After the multi-output model is fine-tuned, it is used for inference with early exiting. When an inference sample is fed into the model, it is processed sequentially by each transformer layer and classifier. If the ith layer classifier is confident of

---

Algorithm 1: Asymmetric Early Exiting

> **for** $i = 1$ to n **do**
> $prob_i = f_i(x; \theta)$
>   **if** $prob_i^{\mathrm{pos}} > \tau_p$ **or** $prob_i^{\mathrm{neg}} > \tau_n$ **then**
>   **return** $prob_i^{\mathrm{pos}}$
>   **end if**
> **end for**
> **return** $prob_n^{\mathrm{pos}}$

---

the prediction $f_i(x; \theta)$, early exiting is performed and subsequent transformer layers are skipped. We define the *confidence* of $f_i(x; \theta)$ as the higher probability of the two classes. Finally, documents are ranked with respect to their predicted probability of the positive class (relevant).

In previous early exiting BERT for NLP papers, *symmetric* early exiting is used, i.e., if the model's confidence exceeds a threshold, the sample exits. The early exiting algorithm is therefore symmetric with respect to all classes. In the case of early exiting for document ranking, however, there are two fundamental differences from NLP applications. Firstly, the two classes (relevant and non-relevant) are clearly not symmetric: we only care about relevant documents, and the more relevant they are, the more computation resources should be allocated to them. Secondly, for positive samples, confidence is not only the criterion for early exiting, but also the score for subsequent re-ranking.

To bridge the differences mentioned above, we propose to use *asymmetric* early exiting for document ranking. Concretely, we define two thresholds for confidence, τ_p and τ_n, for positive (relevant) and negative (non-relevant) predictions, respectively. We will show by experiments that we should choose a higher positive confidence threshold than the negative one, i.e., if a document is likely to be non-relevant, then we can stop its inference earlier, but if it is expected to be relevant, we should be prudent and use more layers to obtain accurate scores. Details are shown in Algorithm 1.

4 Experimental Setup

We apply early exiting on $\mathrm{BERT_{BASE}}$ and conduct experiments on two datasets for document ranking, MS MARCO passage (Bajaj et al., 2016) and ASNQ (Garg et al., 2019).

Model and Implementation. We start from a pre-trained $\mathrm{BERT_{BASE}}$ model. The implementation

is adapted from the HuggingFace Transformers Library (Wolf et al., 2019). We fine-tune the model on 4 NVIDIA Tesla V100 GPUs, with a batch size of 60. For other hyperparameters such as learning rate and maximum sequence length, we follow MonoBERT (Nogueira and Cho, 2019) for MS MARCO passage and Cascade Transformer (Soldaini and Moschitti, 2020) for ASNQ.

Dataset Details. MS MARCO passage provides a small version of the training set,[1] from which we build our training set by selecting tuples with *unique* pairs of query–relevant document, yielding a dataset of 832k query–document pairs, half relevant and half non-relevant. We fine-tune the model for 4 epochs. Its development set has 6.9k queries, and for each query there are 1k candidate documents, among which there is approximately 1 relevant document.

ASNQ's training set[2] has 20M query–document pairs. Similar to MS MARCO passage, we select only unique pairs of query–relevant document, and then complement the dataset with the same amount of query–non-relevant document pairs to yield a training set of 114k pairs. We fine-tune for 2 epochs. Its development set has 1.3k queries, and each query has, on average, 400 candidate documents and 3 relevant ones.

5 Experimental Results

We show the trade-offs between model quality and computation of early exiting in Tables 1 and 2 for MS MARCO passage and ANSQ, respectively. Different trade-offs are achieved by setting various negative confidence threshold τ_n, while τ_p is always set to 1; we will provide detailed analyses of these thresholds later. Inference efficiency is quantified by the average exit layer of inference samples; this metric is, according to our experiments, proportional to actual wall-clock runtime, while being invariant across multiple runs.

We can see that in both datasets, early exiting is able to accelerate inference by $\sim 2.5\times$ while maintaining the original model effectiveness. It is worth noting that in Cascade Transformer (CT) (Soldaini and Moschitti, 2020), only a part of the development set is used for evaluation, and therefore the scores are not directly comparable. However, in

---

[1] https://msmarco.blob.core.windows.net/msmarcoranking/triples.train.small.tar.gz

[2] https://github.com/alexa/wqa_tanda

Method	MRR @10	τ_n	Speedup
MB	0.347		1.0×
	0.343	1.00	1.0×
	0.343 (−0%)	0.95	2.6×
	0.340 (−1%)	0.90	2.9×
eeMB	0.336 (−2%)	0.85	3.2×
	0.327 (−5%)	0.80	3.5×
	0.312 (−9%)	0.75	3.9×
	0.290 (−15%)	0.70	4.3×

Table 1: MS MARCO passage development set results. MB: MonoBERT; eeMB: early exiting MonoBERT.

Method	nDCG @10	MRR	τ_n	Speedup
	0.661	0.654		1.0×
CT	0.653	0.653		1.6×
	0.650	0.648		1.8×
	0.650	0.645		2.0×
	0.650	0.633	1.00	1.0×
	0.650	0.633	0.99	2.5×
eeMB	0.648	0.632	0.95	3.2×
	0.646	0.632	0.90	3.6×
	0.638	0.627	0.80	4.1×

Table 2: ASNQ development set results. CT: Cascade Transformer; eeMB: early exiting MonoBERT. Absolute values of scores of CT and eeMB are not directly comparable due to dataset differences.

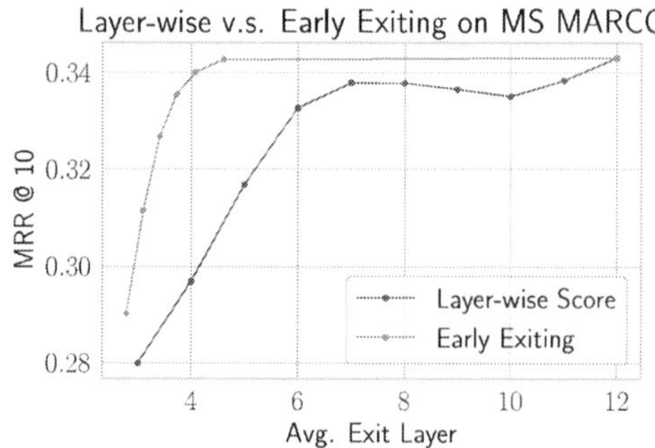

Figure 2: Comparison between layer-wise scores and early exiting trade-offs, on the MS MARCO passage development set.

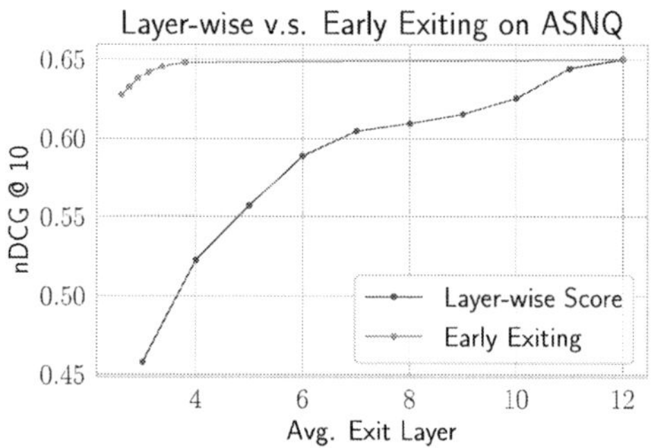

Figure 3: Comparison between layer-wise scores and early exiting trade-offs, on the ASNQ development set.

terms of *relative* performance, our model appears to achieve a bit higher inference speedup with a comparable score degradation.

We also compare confidence-based early exiting trade-offs with *layer-wise scores* of the model in Figures 2 and 3. The layer-wise score of the ith layer is obtained by forcing all inference samples to exit through the classifier at the ith layer. It provide a series of baselines: if we want to save 50% inference computation for a 12-layer model, a straightforward way is to use the 6th layer's classifier for all samples. The first two layers are omitted from the layer-wise score curves since their scores are too low to be useful. The figures show that the early exiting idea significantly outperforms the naïve baselines.

To analyze the effect of different confidence thresholds, we plot in Figure 4 the comparison of confidence thresholds τ_p and τ_n using the MS MARCO passage dataset. Results from ASNQ are very similar and therefore omitted. Each curve corresponds to one τ_p value, and points within a curve are plotted by choosing different τ_n values.[3]

We notice that the trade-off performance is monotonic with respect to the positive confidence threshold: the higher τ_p is, the better the trade-offs are. We speculate the reason is that while smaller τ_p improves efficiency by allowing more samples to exit earlier, the quality of predictions from earlier layers of relevant samples degrades drastically. Considering the fact that relevant samples constitute only a tiny fraction of all candidates in both datasets, setting $\tau_p = 1$, i.e., using as many transformer layers as we can on positive samples, is the optimal choice. It is worth noting that for other datasets with higher relevant candidate proportions, the optimal τ_p may be smaller than 1.

Within one curve (a fixed τ_p), τ_n controls the

---

[3]Points on each curve, from left to right, correspond to τ_n values in Table 1, from bottom to top.

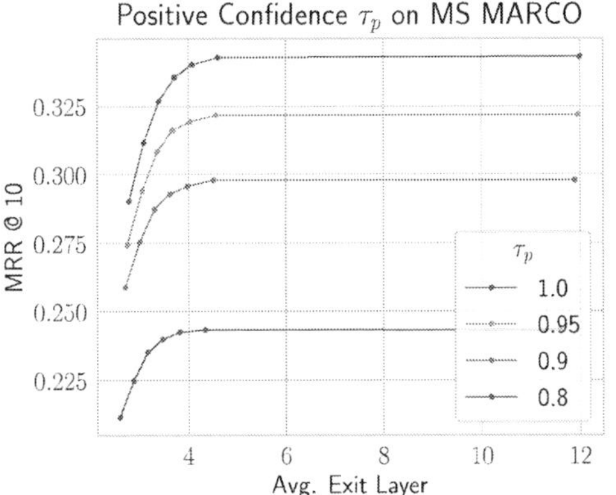

Figure 4: Comparison between different values of τ_p (curves) and τ_n (points on a curve).

trade-offs between efficiency and quality: lower τ_n allows more negative samples to exit earlier, thus improving efficiency with relatively small quality degradation. Such asymmetry demonstrates the necessity of using two confidence thresholds instead of one: while we can safely perform early exiting on negative samples and save computation, we should allocate far more resources to positive samples for the most accurate predictions.

6 Conclusion

We propose asymmetric early exiting BERT for document ranking, an effective method to improve model efficiency in IR tasks. Computation resources are allocated to samples according to their needs. Experiments show that our method is able to achieve different quality–latency trade-offs by setting different thresholds, and also improves model efficiency over baselines.

Acknowledgments

This research was supported in part by the Canada First Research Excellence Fund and the Natural Sciences and Engineering Research Council (NSERC) of Canada.

References

Payal Bajaj, Daniel Campos, Nick Craswell, Li Deng, Jianfeng Gao, Xiaodong Liu, Rangan Majumder, Andrew McNamara, Bhaskar Mitra, Tri Nguyen, et al. 2016. MS MARCO: A human generated machine reading comprehension dataset. *arXiv preprint arXiv:1611.09268.*

Zhuyun Dai and Jamie Callan. 2019. Deeper text understanding for IR with contextual neural language modeling. In *Proceedings of SIGIR*, pages 985–988.

Jacob Devlin, Ming-Wei Chang, Kenton Lee, and Kristina Toutanova. 2019. BERT: Pre-training of deep bidirectional transformers for language understanding. In *Proceedings of NAACL*, pages 4171–4186.

Siddhant Garg, Thuy Vu, and Alessandro Moschitti. 2019. Tanda: Transfer and adapt pre-trained transformer models for answer sentence selection. *arXiv preprint arXiv:1911.04118.*

Jiafeng Guo, Yixing Fan, Qingyao Ai, and W. Bruce Croft. 2016. A deep relevance matching model for ad-hoc retrieval. In *Proceedings of CIKM*, pages 55–64.

Kai Hui, Andrew Yates, Klaus Berberich, and Gerard De Melo. 2018. Co-PACRR: A context-aware neural IR model for ad-hoc retrieval. In *Proceedings of WSDM*, pages 279–287.

Zhenzhong Lan, Mingda Chen, Sebastian Goodman, Kevin Gimpel, Piyush Sharma, and Radu Soricut. 2019. ALBERT: A lite BERT for self-supervised learning of language representations. *arXiv preprint arXiv:1909.11942.*

Canjia Li, Andrew Yates, Sean MacAvaney, Ben He, and Yingfei Sun. 2020. PARADE: Passage representation aggregation for document reranking. *arXiv preprint arXiv:2008.09093.*

Weijie Liu, Peng Zhou, Zhiruo Wang, Zhe Zhao, Haotang Deng, and Qi Ju. 2020. FastBERT: a self-distilling BERT with adaptive inference time. In *Proceedings of ACL*, pages 6035–6044.

Yinhan Liu, Myle Ott, Naman Goyal, Jingfei Du, Mandar Joshi, Danqi Chen, Omer Levy, Mike Lewis, Luke Zettlemoyer, and Veselin Stoyanov. 2019. RoBERTa: A robustly optimized BERT pretraining approach. *arXiv preprint arXiv:1907.11692.*

Bhaskar Mitra, Fernando Diaz, and Nick Craswell. 2017. Learning to match using local and distributed representations of text for web search. In *Proceedings of WWW*, pages 1291–1299.

Rodrigo Nogueira and Kyunghyun Cho. 2019. Passage re-ranking with BERT. *arXiv preprint arXiv:1901.04085.*

Matthew Peters, Mark Neumann, Mohit Iyyer, Matt Gardner, Christopher Clark, Kenton Lee, and Luke Zettlemoyer. 2018. Deep contextualized word representations. In *Proceedings of NAACL*, pages 2227–2237.

Alec Radford, Jeffrey Wu, Rewon Child, David Luan, Dario Amodei, and Ilya Sutskever. 2019. Language models are unsupervised multitask learners. *OpenAI Blog.*

Roy Schwartz, Gabriel Stanovsky, Swabha Swayamdipta, Jesse Dodge, and Noah A. Smith. 2020. The right tool for the job: Matching model and instance complexities. In *Proceedings of ACL*, pages 6640–6651.

Luca Soldaini and Alessandro Moschitti. 2020. The Cascade Transformer: An application for efficient answer sentence selection. In *Proceedings of ACL*, pages 5697–5708.

Surat Teerapittayanon, Bradley McDanel, and Hsiang-Tsung Kung. 2017. BranchyNet: Fast inference via early exiting from deep neural networks. *arXiv preprint arXiv:1709.01686.*

Ashish Vaswani, Noam Shazeer, Niki Parmar, Jakob Uszkoreit, Llion Jones, Aidan N. Gomez, Łukasz Kaiser, and Illia Polosukhin. 2017. Attention is all you need. In *Proceedings of NeurIPS*, pages 5998–6008.

Thomas Wolf, Lysandre Debut, Victor Sanh, Julien Chaumond, Clement Delangue, Anthony Moi, Pierric Cistac, Tim Rault, R'emi Louf, Morgan Funtowicz, and Jamie Brew. 2019. HuggingFace's Transformers: State-of-the-art natural language processing. *arXiv preprint arXiv:1910.03771.*

Ji Xin, Raphael Tang, Jaejun Lee, Yaoliang Yu, and Jimmy Lin. 2020. DeeBERT: Dynamic early exiting for accelerating BERT inference. In *Proceedings of ACL*, pages 2246–2251.

Chenyan Xiong, Zhuyun Dai, Jamie Callan, Zhiyuan Liu, and Russell Power. 2017. End-to-end neural ad-hoc ranking with kernel pooling. In *Proceedings of SIGIR*, pages 55–64.

Zeynep Akkalyoncu Yilmaz, Wei Yang, Haotian Zhang, and Jimmy Lin. 2019. Cross-domain modeling of sentence-level evidence for document retrieval. In *Proceedings of EMNLP*, pages 3481–3487.

Wangchunshu Zhou, Canwen Xu, Tao Ge, Julian McAuley, Ke Xu, and Furu Wei. 2020. BERT loses patience: Fast and robust inference with early exit. *arXiv preprint arXiv:2006.04152.*

Keyphrase Generation with GANs in Low-Resources Scenarios

Giuseppe Lancioni   Saida S.Mohamed   Beatrice Portelli
Giuseppe Serra   Carlo Tasso

AILAB, UniUd - University of Udine, Italy
{lancioni.giuseppe,mahmoud.saidasaadmohamed,
portelli.beatrice}@spes.uniud.it
{giuseppe.serra, carlo.tasso}@uniud.it

Abstract

Keyphrase Generation is the task of predicting Keyphrases (KPs), short phrases that summarize the semantic meaning of a given document. Several past studies provided diverse approaches to generate Keyphrases for an input document. However, all of these approaches still need to be trained on very large datasets. In this paper, we introduce BeGan-KP, a new conditional GAN model to address the problem of Keyphrase Generation in a low-resource scenario. Our main contribution relies in the Discriminator's architecture: a new BERT-based module which is able to distinguish between the generated and human-curated KPs reliably. Its characteristics allow us to use it in a low-resource scenario, where only a small amount of training data are available, obtaining an efficient Generator. The resulting architecture achieves, on five public datasets, competitive results with respect to the state-of-the-art approaches, using less than 1% of the training data.

1   Introduction

A Keyphrase (KP) is a piece of text that conveys the main semantic meaning of a document. KPs can be either present (or extractive) or absent (or abstractive): present KPs are exact substrings of the document while absent KPs are not. Their automatic prediction is an important challenge for the community research as KPs are a key component for a wide range of applications such as text summarization (Zhang et al., 2004), opinion mining (Berend, 2011), document clustering (Hammouda et al., 2005), information retrieval (Jones and Staveley, 1999) and text categorization (Hulth and Megyesi, 2006).

Historically, the first approaches focused on simply extracting substrings of the text to be used as keyphrases candidates (Ye and Wang, 2018; Luan et al., 2017; Zhang et al., 2016).

Recently, the research community has focused on the broader task of Keyphrase Generation (Meng et al., 2017; Chen et al., 2018, 2019a). Keyphrase Generation aims to *produce* a set of phrases that summarize the essential information in a given text, as opposed to simply *look for them* in the text. This allows for greater flexibility.

Several approaches introduced generative models based on the Encoder-Decoder architecture (Meng et al., 2017; Chen et al., 2018). This architecture works by compressing the contents of the input (e.g. the text document) into a hidden representation using an Encoder module. The same representation is then decompressed using the Decoder module, which returns the desired output (e.g. a sequence of KPs). The modules are trained jointly to learn the best intermediate representation to perform this mapping.

More recently, an approach based on GAN (Generative Adversarial Networks (Goodfellow et al., 2014)) architecture has been proposed to address the task (Swaminathan et al., 2019). Although all these solutions achieved interesting results, they require a very large amount of data in order to be trained.

Our aim is to improve training efficiency, so that a model can be trained using only small subsets of the data. We focus our research in the generation of present KPs and we propose a new conditional GAN architecture for Keyphrase Generation that can be trained with a relatively small set of samples. The key component of our solution is the Discriminator: a model based on BERT that is able to distinguish between human and machine-generated Keyphrases leveraging on the language modelling information obtained from finetuning in a low-resource scenario. A Reinforcement Learning (RL) strategy is then used to train the Generator, with rewards evaluated by the Discriminator. This encourages the model to generate more accurate

Proceedings of SustaiNLP: Workshop on Simple and Efficient Natural Language Processing, pages 89–96
Online, November 20, 2020. ©2020 Association for Computational Linguistics

and relevant KPs.

Thanks to the characteristics of our architecture, we are able to use only a small subset of the available data, using less than 1% of them to train our system. Compared to all the previous approaches that needed to be fully trained on large set of training samples, our architecture greatly reduces required resources, while still providing competitive results in the generation of present KPs.

2 Related Work

2.1 Keyphrase Extraction

Extractive methods aim at identifying Keyphrases in the span of the source text. Most of the algorithms in this field adopt a two steps pipeline to extract KPs. First, given a document, a list of candidates phrases is selected using heuristic methods (Wang et al., 2016; Le et al., 2016). Secondly, all candidates are scored against the document. The first step has a considerable impact on the ability of the whole model to correctly identify all KPs, so selecting a sufficiently high number of candidates is of utmost importance. The second step can be done either in a supervised or unsupervised manner (Mihalcea and Tarau, 2004; Witten et al., 1999; Nguyen and Kan, 2007). The top-scoring candidates are returned as KPs. Two interesting strategies that differ from the common pipeline approach have been proposed by Tomokiyo and Hurst (2003) and Zhang et al. (2016). The first method employs two statistical language-based models to extract Keyphrases. The latter introduces a model based on joint layer recurrent neural network to extract Keyphrases from tweets.

2.2 Keyphrase Generation

Recently, research has focused on the introduction of methods of text generation to predict Keyphrases. Most of these approaches rely on Encoder-Decoder framework in which the source text is first mapped to an encoded representation, and then decoded to the target text, that is the Keyphrases to predict.

Meng et al. (2017) proposed CopyRNN, a RNN-based generative model for KP Generation, which is an Encoder-Decoder model with copy mechanism. Chen et al. (2018) proposed CorrRNN model which is a sequence-to-sequence architecture for Keyphrase Generation that captures the correlations among Keyphrases. TG-Net model was introduced by Chen et al. (2019b) for improving automatic Keyphrase Generation using the information contained in the title of the document. Chen et al. (2019a) proposed an integrated approach for Keyphrase Generation which is a multitask learning framework that jointly learns an extractive model and a generative model.

Two recurrent generative based models, CatSeq and CatSeqD, were proposed by Yuan et al. (2018). One of their main characteristics is the ability to determine the appropriate number of Keyphrases for each input document. CatSeq is based on an Encoder-Decoder mechanism, which is used to identify relevant components of the source text (abstracts) and generate KPs (sequence-to-concatenated sequences) (Yuan et al., 2018; Chan et al., 2019). It employed the sequence-to-sequence framework combined with an attention mechanism and pointer softmax mechanisms in the Decoder. CatSeqD introduces the following techniques: orthogonal regularization, which prevents the model from predicting the same word after generating the constant KP separator; semantic coverage, which encodes again the decoded sequences and uses it as a representation of the target phrases. These representations are employed as further input during a self-supervised training phase with the aim of improve the semantic content of the predictions.

Chan et al. (2019) subsequently proposed a Reinforcement Learning approach with adaptive rewards to improve catSeq, CatSeqD, CorrRNN and TG-Net generative models, leading to a new version for each of them. These versions are called, respectively, catSeq-2RF1, catSeqD-2RF1, catSeqCorr-2RF1 and catSeqTG-2RF1.

Recently, (Swaminathan et al., 2019) proposed a GAN model conditioned on scientific articles for KP Generation. The author uses a catSeq model to implement the Generator, conditioning it on abstracts of scientific articles. The Discriminator is based on a hierarchical attention mechanism consisting of two GRU layers. The two layers model the relationship between the document and each generated KP to assess whether the KP is synthetic or human in origin.

To the best of our knowledge, no attempts have been made of either extracting or generating KPs in a low-resources scenario, in which only a small amount of the available data samples is used during training. Our proposed architecture, based on a Discriminator that relies on a language model, requires less than 1% of the available training data to achieve good results.

3 The proposed Approach

To generate present KPs in a low-resource scenario we propose an approach based on the GAN Framework that we call BeGan-KP. It mainly consists of three components: (1) a conditioned Generator model that produces a set of KPs, (2) a novel Bert Discriminator model that checks if the KPs are fake (generated) or real (human-curated), and (3) the Reinforcement Learning (RL) module that is involved in the training process of the system as a whole (see Figure 1).

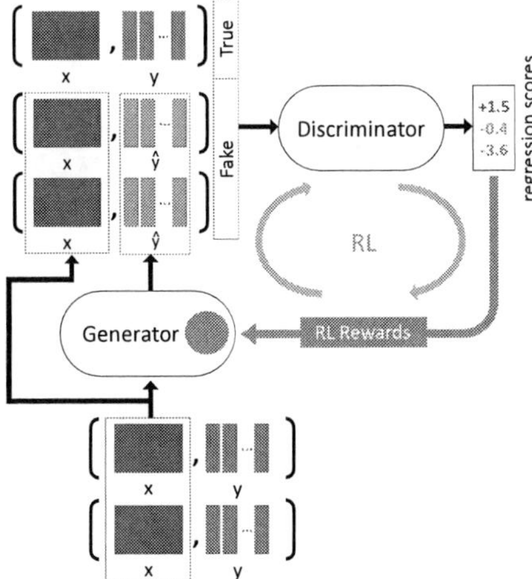

Figure 1: Schema of BeGan-KP.

3.1 Notations and Problem Definition

The samples available to train the system are pairs $(\mathbf{x}, \mathbf{y})$, where $\mathbf{x}$ is a document and $\mathbf{y} = (\mathbf{y}^1, \mathbf{y}^2, \ldots, \mathbf{y}^M)$ is the set of M Keyphrases (True KPs) associated to $\mathbf{x}$. Note that both $\mathbf{x}$ and $\mathbf{y}^i$ are sequences of words:

$$\mathbf{x} = x_1, x_2, \ldots, x_L$$

$$\mathbf{y}^i = y_1^i, y_2^i, \ldots, y_{K_i}^i$$

where L and K_i are the number of words of $\mathbf{x}$ and of its i-th KP respectively.

The Generator takes as input $\mathbf{x}$ and outputs $\hat{\mathbf{y}} = (\hat{\mathbf{y}}^1, \hat{\mathbf{y}}^2, \ldots, \hat{\mathbf{y}}^J)$, that is the set of the J predicted KPs for $\mathbf{x}$ (Fake KPs).

The objective is to generate Fake KPs that match exactly the True KPs: $\hat{\mathbf{y}} \equiv \mathbf{y}$.

3.2 Generator

The Generator G takes as input the document $\mathbf{x}$ and generates as output the sequence of $\hat{\mathbf{y}}$ (Fake KPs).

Following the work of Swaminathan et al. (2019) we use the catSeq model as Generator. It consists in an Encoder-Decoder model in which the Encoder is a bidirectional Gated Recurrent Unit (GRU) and the Decoder is a forward GRU. It is based on Copy-RNN by Meng et al. (2017).

We choose this component because it embeds some interesting features. It exploits the copying mechanism (Gu et al., 2016) to deal with long-tail words. These are words which are removed from the vocabulary due to their low frequency but are often topic-specific and therefore good candidates to be KPs. It also introduces the capability of predicting a variable number of Keyphrases for different documents. Furthermore it employs a beam-search strategy during the decoding step, meaning that at each time step the model decodes not just one word (greedy-search) but the top k most probable words. This allows generating more consistent sequences of words.

3.3 Discriminator

The Discriminator D receives as input the document $\mathbf{x}$ and a set of Keyphrases. These might be either the True KPs $\mathbf{y}$ or the Fake KPs $\hat{\mathbf{y}}$. Its task is to judge whether the KPs are True or Fake.

We introduce a novel Discriminator based on the language model BERT (Devlin et al., 2018). Differently from the previous literature, our idea is to exploit the strength of the language model characteristics to classify the quality of the input pair $(\mathbf{x}, \mathbf{y})$. This judgement is given as a *regression score*, which is lower for Fake KPs and higher for True KPs. In this way the regression score can be easily interpreted as the *reward* in the Reinforcement Learning module, giving to the system an inherent clarity. Moreover, different BERT-based models and reward configurations have been tested at an early stage, and the choice of a regression model provided the best results.

The language modelling component is able to achieve a better comprehension of the relationship of the two input sequences, while the robust pretraining allows us to use it efficiently even in a low-resource scenario.

In particular, the Discriminator model consists of four subcomponents (see Figure 2) :

- **Input preparation**. The input pairs $(\mathbf{x}, \mathbf{y})$ are tokenized and the tokens are concatenated to be compliant with the general pattern `[CLS]<x>[SEP]<y1><;>...<;><yn>[SEP]`.

`[CLS]` and `[SEP]` are special tokens which signal the start of the input and the end of text sequence respectively, `<x>` is the sequence of tokens for the document $\mathbf{x}$, `<yi>` is the sequence of tokens for the KP $\mathbf{y}^i$. Different KPs are separated by semicolon `<;>`. Note that the `[SEP]` token in the center is used to split the input sequence into document and KPs.

- **BERT modelling**. The input sequence is processed by a pretrained BERT model. It performs a word embedding of all the tokens and then passes them through 12 Encoder blocks. As it is basically a positional language model, it returns the last hidden states for each of the initial tokens.

- **Output aggregation**. Each of the outputs of the preceding step can be seen as an highly abstract embedding of the corresponding token. We aggregate the output of all the hidden states and evaluate their mean to obtain an embedding for the whole input sequence $E = E(\mathbf{x}, \mathbf{y})$. Note that in this way E is not generated using only the output obtained from the `[CLS]` token, but making use of the representations of all the tokens instead. Based on our preliminary experiments as well as literature references (Devlin et al., 2018), this value is considered to represent a better summary of the semantic content of the input.

- **Regression**. E is processed by the regression layer, a fully connected linear classifier, and a regression score is calculated. This is trained to be high for True KPs (human-curated) and low for Fake KPs (artificially generated), and is used as the reward in Reinforcement Learning.

The overall output of the Discriminator is therefore a regression score relative to the combination of input document and the related KPs.

3.4 Reinforcement Learning

To overcome the problem of non differentiability of the output layer of our architecture we extend the Reinforcement Learning strategy proposed by Yu et al. (2016) in the domain of KP Generation. In particular, we consider the Generator G as an agent whose action a at time step t is to generate a *word* y_t, which is part of the set of predicted KPs $\hat{\mathbf{y}}$ for the document $\mathbf{x}$. In this scenario the Discriminator

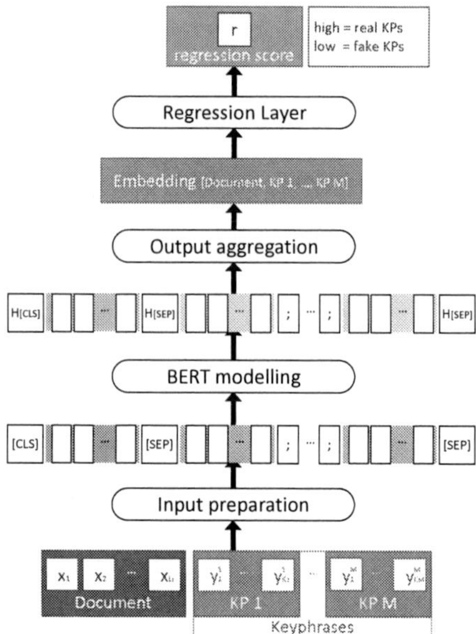

Figure 2: Schema of the Discriminator and its four processing phases.

D plays the role of the environment that evaluates the actions made by G and gives back a reward. Agent G acts following a policy

$$\pi = \pi(y_t | s_t, \mathbf{x}, \theta) \tag{1}$$

that is a function representing the probability distribution of y_t given the current state $s_t = (y_1, \ldots, y_{t-1})$, the sequence of words so far generated. The policy function is differentiable with respect to the set of parameters θ of G. Once the agent G generates the predictions, the environment D gives back a reward

$$r_t = f(y_1, \ldots, y_t | \mathbf{x}) \tag{2}$$

and moves to the state s_{t+1}. The reward is a quality measure of the action made by the agent G, and depends on the words generated up to the current time step (subset of $\hat{\mathbf{y}}$) given the input document $\mathbf{x}$. The agent G acts to maximize the reward, that is to maximize a differentiable optimization function $J(\theta)$ that gives a measure of the performance of G. According to the policy gradient theorem and the REINFORCE algorithm (Williams, 1992) the gradient of $J(\theta)$ can be expressed as:

$$\nabla J(\theta) = \mathbb{E}_\pi \left[\sum_t r_t \nabla log(\pi(y_t | s_t, \mathbf{x}, \theta)) \right] \tag{3}$$

where the sum extends to all the time steps needed to generate the complete sequence $\mathbf{y}$.

The expectation $\mathbb{E}_\pi$ in Equation 3 can be approximated using a complete sequence $\hat{\mathbf{y}}$. In order to calculate the cumulative rewards of Equation 2 we use the regression score of a complete sequence of generated KPs: $r = D(\hat{\mathbf{y}})$.

Considering that maximizing the optimization function $J(\theta)$ is equivalent to minimizing its additive inverse, we can define the loss function of G as $L(\theta) = -J(\theta)$ and an estimator of its gradient as:

$$\nabla L(\theta) \approx -\sum_t (r - b)\nabla log(\pi(y_t|s_t, \mathbf{x}, \theta)) \quad (4)$$

where the regularization term b is introduced to reduce the variance of the above $\nabla L(\theta)$ estimator. It is essentially the cumulative reward $r = D(\bar{\mathbf{y}})$ where $\bar{\mathbf{y}}$ is a greedy decoded predicted sequence. The aim is to promote rewards that show effective improvements over greedy sequences (Rennie et al., 2017).

3.5 GAN Training

The first step is to train a first version G_0 of the Generator using the Maximum Likelihood Estimation (MLE). G_0 is then used to generate the Fake KPs $\hat{\mathbf{y}}$. $\hat{\mathbf{y}}$ and the ground truth $\mathbf{y}$ are used to train the first version of the Discriminator D_0 with Mean Squared Error (MSE) loss:

$$MSE(x, \hat{x}) = \frac{1}{N}\sum_{i=0}^{N}(x_i - \hat{x}_i)^2 \quad (5)$$

Starting from Generator G_1 training is performed using RL, so the loss is given by $L(\theta)$ as shown in Section 3.4. The training of the Discriminator remains the same. After each training iteration (G_j, D_j), predictions are tested to evaluate the scores $F1@M$ and $F1@5$.

4 Experiments and Evaluation

4.1 Datasets and Metrics

We compare our solution with state-of-the-art approaches on five datasets which are commonly used in literature:

KP20K (Meng et al., 2017) It consists of 567,830 titles and abstracts from computer science papers. The usual split is performed using 20,000 samples for testing, another 20,000 for validation, while the remaining 527,830 samples are used for training. In our low-resource scenario we only use 2,000 out of the >500,000 training samples.

INSPEC (Hulth, 2003) The complete dataset is composed of 2,000 abstracts from Computers and Control, and Information Technology disciplines. A subset of 500 samples is used for testing.

KRAPIVIN (Krapivin et al., 2009) The original released dataset is composed by 500 complete articles belonging to the domain of computer science. For KP Generation purposes only titles and abstract are used. The first 400 samples in alphabetical order are selected for testing.

NUS (Nguyen and Kan, 2007) A set of 211 scientific publications, all used for testing.

SEMEVAL2010 (Kim et al., 2010) 288 conference and workshop papers from the ACL Computer Library. 100 used for testing.

A brief report of main statistics of the test sets used is given in Table 1.

All datasets are preprocessed following Chan et al. (2019): duplicate papers are removed from KP20K, and for each document the list of KPs is sorted in order of appearance in the document. Digits in the input texts are replaced with the special token `<digit>`.

Results are evaluated using $F1$ score. In particular $F1@5$ and $F1@M$ are employed: the first is calculated considering only the top 5 high scoring KPs, the second is computed taking into account all the predictions.

All sample documents are annotated with human curated KPs. Of the above mentioned datasets, only KP20K is used for training; all the others are used only for testing and evaluation. Note that the strength of the language model of our Discriminator allows us to use only a small subset of the data samples during training: the whole architecture has been trained with a subset of 2,000 samples instead of the >500,000 used by the other state-of-the-art approaches.

4.2 Implementation Details

The initial MLE model G_0 is trained with a batch size of 12 and Adam optimizer (Kingma and Ba,

	KP20K		INSPEC		KRAPIVIN		NUS		SEMEVAL2010	
	#	%	#	%	#	%	#	%	#	%
Present KPs	66,267	62.91	3,602	73.59	1,297	55.57	1,191	52.26	612	42.41
Absent KPs	39,076	37.09	1,293	26.41	1,037	44.43	1,088	47.74	831	57.59
Total KPs	105,343	100.00	4,895	100.00	2,334	100.00	2,279	100.00	1,443	100.00
Test samples	20,000		500		400		211		100	

Table 1: Statistics on test samples for the five datasets.

Model	KP20K		INSPEC		KRAPIVIN		NUS		SEMEVAL2010	
	$F1@M$	$F1@5$	$F1@M$	$F1@5$	$F1@M$	$F1@5$	$F1@M$	$F1@5$	$F1@M$	$F1@5$
catSeqD (Yuan et al., 2018)	-	**0.348**	-	0.276	-	**0.325**	-	0.374	-	**0.327**
catSeqCorr-2RF1 (Chan et al., 2019)	0.382	0.308	0.291	0.240	0.369	0.286	0.414	0.349	0.322	0.278
catSeqTG-2RF1 (Chan et al., 2019)	**0.386**	0.321	0.301	0.253	0.369	0.300	**0.433**	**0.375**	**0.329**	0.287
GAN (Swaminathan et al., 2019)	0.381	0.300	0.297	0.248	**0.370**	0.286	0.430	0.368	-	-
BeGan-KP (our approach)	0.318	0.309	**0.383**	**0.356**	0.332	0.317	0.388	0.366	**0.329**	0.319

Table 2: Results of present keyphrases for five datasets. Our approach is BeGan-KP.

2015); during RL training, batch size is 32. The Discriminator is trained with a batch size of 3 and AdamW optimizer (Loshchilov and Hutter, 2017). The pretrained BERT model is the base uncased version, with 12 layers, 12 attention heads, and hidden size of 768. The maximum input length after tokenization is fixed to 384 tokens. We use the implementation provided in the python library transformers by huggingface (Wolf et al., 2019)[1].

Training and experiments have been executed on a PC with a GeForce RTX 2080 GPU, 11GB.

4.3 Experimental Results

Our proposed solution BeGan-KP, trained on 2,000 samples, has then been compared with the following state-of-the-art approaches: catSeqD (Yuan et al., 2018); catSeqCorr-2RF1 and catSeqTG-2RF1 (Chan et al., 2019), and GAN (Swaminathan et al., 2019). The results of our tests are shown in Table 2.

First, we can note that BeGan-KP achieves results competitive with the best performing techniques, even using a limited set of samples (all the other approaches were trained on the whole KP20K).

Looking at the results in detail, we obtain by far the best performance for INSPEC both in $F1@5$ and $F1@M$.

Our approach has other good results in $F1@5$ metrics, specifically in KRAPIVIN and SEMEVAL2010 where our values are only slightly lower than the best. Since $F1@5$ is calculated considering the 5 predictions with the highest score, we

can say that our model is capable of producing high quality Keyphrases reliably, and of outperforming or at least matching other best-performing models in this specific task. This confirms the strength and consistency of our architecture.

In addition, we obtain the best $F1@M$ score for SEMEVAL2010. Note that SEMEVAL2010 is a demanding test dataset as it is the smallest of the five, and the gross amount of KPs to predict is the lowest (612 present KPs out of a total of 1,443), leading to a great variance in the output.

Finally, consider that in Equation 3 the expectation of the policy function is evaluated using only one complete sequence $\hat{y}$, inducing a high variance in the ∇J. This is a general issue of Reinforcement Learning applied to GANs for text generation and generally leads to unstable training process and slow convergence (Yu et al., 2016). Thanks to the capability of the language model embedded in our architecture, in our experiments the training process shows a quick convergence in terms of number of training iterations. In fact, the reported results have been achieved at the second iteration (G_2 generator).

5 Conclusion

In this paper we introduced an approach to the task of present Keyphrase Generation in a low-resources scenario, BeGan-KP. It is based on the GAN framework with a novel Bert based Discriminator model, trained by mean of the Reinforcement Learning paradigm. It has been tested on five public datasets showing performances competitive with state-of-the-art approaches while using less than 1% of the available training data, achieving a great training efficiency.

References

Gábor Berend. 2011. Opinion Expression Mining by Exploiting Keyphrase Extraction. In *IJCNLP*.

Hou Pong Chan, Wang Chen, Lu Wang, and Irwin King. 2019. Neural Keyphrase Generation via Reinforcement Learning with Adaptive Rewards. In *ACL*.

Jun Chen, Xiaoming Zhang, Yu Wu, Zhao Yan, and Zhoujun Li. 2018. Keyphrase Generation with Correlation Constraints. In *EMNLP*.

Wang Chen, Hou Pong Chan, Piji Li, Lidong Bing, and Irwin King. 2019a. An Integrated Approach for Keyphrase Generation via Exploring the Power of Retrieval and Extraction. In *NAACL-HLT*.

Wang Chen, Yifan Gao, Jiani Zhang, Irwin King, and Michael R. Lyu. 2019b. Title-Guided Encoding for Keyphrase Generation. In *AAAI*.

Jacob Devlin, Ming-Wei Chang, Kenton Lee, and Kristina Toutanova. 2018. BERT: Pre-training of Deep Bidirectional Transformers for Language Understanding. In *NAACL-HLT*.

Ian Goodfellow, Jean Pouget-Abadie, Mehdi Mirza, Bing Xu, David Warde-Farley, Sherjil Ozair, Aaron Courville, and Yoshua Bengio. 2014. Generative Adversarial Nets. In *Advances in Neural Information Processing Systems*. Curran Associates, Inc.

Jiatao Gu, Zhengdong Lu, Hang Li, and Victor O. K. Li. 2016. Incorporating Copying Mechanism in Sequence-to-Sequence Learning. In *ACL*.

Khaled M. Hammouda, Diego N. Matute, and Mohamed S. Kamel. 2005. CorePhrase: Keyphrase Extraction for Document Clustering. In *MLDM*.

Anette Hulth. 2003. Improved Automatic Keyword Extraction Given More Linguistic Knowledge. In *EMNLP*.

Anette Hulth and Beáta Megyesi. 2006. A Study on Automatically Extracted Keywords in Text Categorization. In *ACL*.

Steve Jones and Mark S. Staveley. 1999. Phrasier: A System for Interactive Document Retrieval Using Keyphrases. In *SIGIR*.

Su Nam Kim, Olena Medelyan, Min-Yen Kan, and Timothy Baldwin. 2010. SemEval-2010 Task 5 : Automatic Keyphrase Extraction from Scientific Articles. In *Workshop on Semantic Evaluation*.

Diederik P. Kingma and Jimmy Ba. 2015. Adam: A Method for Stochastic Optimization. In *ICLR*.

Mikalai Krapivin, Aliaksandr Autaeu, and Maurizio Marchese. 2009. Large Dataset for Keyphrases Extraction. Technical Report DISI-09-055, University of Trento.

Tho Thi Ngoc Le, Minh Le Nguyen, and Akira Shimazu. 2016. Unsupervised Keyphrase Extraction: Introducing New Kinds of Words to Keyphrases. In *Advances in Artificial Intelligence*.

Ilya Loshchilov and Frank Hutter. 2017. Fixing Weight Decay Regularization in Adam. *ICLR*.

Yi Luan, Mari Ostendorf, and Hannaneh Hajishirzi. 2017. Scientific Information Extraction with Semi-supervised Neural Tagging. In *EMNLP*.

Rui Meng, Sanqiang Zhao, Shuguang Han, Daqing He, Peter Brusilovsky, and Yu Chi. 2017. Deep Keyphrase Generation. In *ACL*.

Rada Mihalcea and Paul Tarau. 2004. TextRank: Bringing Order into Text. In *EMNLP*.

Thuy Dung Nguyen and Min-Yen Kan. 2007. Keyphrase Extraction in Scientific Publications. In *ICADL*.

Steven J. Rennie, Etienne Marcheret, Youssef Mroueh, Jerret Ross, and Vaibhava Goel. 2017. Self-Critical Sequence Training for Image Captioning. In *CVPR*.

Avinash Swaminathan, Raj Kuwar Gupta, Haimin Zhang, Debanjan Mahata, Rakesh Gosangi, and Rajiv Ratn Shah. 2019. Keyphrase Generation for Scientific Articles using GANs. In *AAAI*.

Takashi Tomokiyo and Matthew Hurst. 2003. A language model approach to keyphrase extraction. In *ACL workshop on Multiword expressions*.

Minmei Wang, Bo Zhao, and Yihua Huang. 2016. PTR: Phrase-Based Topical Ranking for Automatic Keyphrase Extraction in Scientific Publications. In *ICONIP*.

Ronald J. Williams. 1992. Simple Statistical Gradient-Following Algorithms for Connectionist Reinforcement Learning. *Machine Learning*.

Ian H. Witten, Gordon W. Paynter, Eibe Frank, Carl Gutwin, and Craig G. Nevill-Manning. 1999. KEA: Practical Automatic Keyphrase Extraction. In *ACM*.

Thomas Wolf, Lysandre Debut, Victor Sanh, Julien Chaumond, Clement Delangue, Anthony Moi, Pierric Cistac, Tim Rault, R'emi Louf, Morgan Funtowicz, and Jamie Brew. 2019. HuggingFace's Transformers: State-of-the-art Natural Language Processing. *ArXiv:abs/1910.03771*.

Hai Ye and Lu Wang. 2018. Semi-Supervised Learning for Neural Keyphrase Generation. In *EMNLP*.

Lantao Yu, Weinan Zhang, Jun Wang, and Yong Yu. 2016. SeqGAN: Sequence Generative Adversarial Nets with Policy Gradient. In *AAAI*.

Xingdi Yuan, Tong Wang, Rui Meng, Khushboo
Thaker, Daqing He, and Adam Trischler. 2018. Gen-
erating Diverse Numbers of Diverse Keyphrases.
ArXiv:abs/1810.05241.

Qi Zhang, Yang Wang, Yeyun Gong, and Xuanjing
Huang. 2016. Keyphrase Extraction Using Deep Recurrent Neural Networks on Twitter. In *EMNLP*.

Yongzheng Zhang, A. Nur Zincir-Heywood, and Evan-
gelos E. Milios. 2004. World Wide Web site summarization. *Web Intelligence and Agent Systems*.

Quasi-Multitask Learning:
an Efficient Surrogate for Constructing Model Ensembles

Norbert Kis-Szabó[1] and Gábor Berend[1,2]

[1]Institute of Informatics, University of Szeged
[2]SZTE-MTA Research Group on Artificial Intelligence
{ksznorbi,berendg}@inf.u-szeged.hu

Abstract

We propose the technique of quasi-multitask learning (Q-MTL), a simple and easy to implement modification of standard multitask learning, in which the tasks to be modeled are identical. With this easy modification of a standard neural classifier we can get benefits similar to an ensemble of classifiers with a fraction of the resources required. We illustrate it through a series of sequence labeling experiments over a diverse set of languages, that applying Q-MTL consistently increases the generalization ability of the applied models. The proposed architecture can be regarded as a new regularization technique that encourages the model to develop an internal representation of the problem at hand which is beneficial to multiple output units of the classifier at the same time. Our experiments corroborate that by relying on the proposed algorithm, we can approximate the quality of an ensemble of classifiers at a fraction of computational resources required. Additionally, our results suggest that Q-MTL handles the presence of noisy training labels better than ensembles.

1 Introduction

Ensemble methods are frequently used in machine learning applications due to their tendency of increasing model performance. While the increase in the prediction performance is undoubtedly an important aspect when we train a model, it should not be forgotten that the increased performance of ensembling comes at the price of training multiple models for solving the same task.

The question that we tackle in this paper is the following: *Can we enjoy the benefits of ensemble learning, while avoiding its overhead for training models from scratch multiple times?* This question is highly relevant these days, since state-of-the-art neural models tend to be extremely resource-intensive on their own (Strubell et al., 2019), pro-

hibiting their inclusion in a traditional ensemble setting.

Our proposed architecture simultaneously offers the benefit of ensemble learning, while avoiding its drawback of training multiple models. The method introduced here employs a special form of multitask learning (MTL). Caruana (Caruana, 1997) argues in his seminal work that MTL can be a useful source of introducing inductive bias into machine learning models. Standard MTL have been shown to be fruitfully applicable in solving a series of NLP tasks: Collobert and Weston (2008); Plank et al. (2016); Rei (2017); Kiperwasser and Ballesteros (2018); Sanh et al. (2018), *inter alia*. We introduce quasi-multitask learning (Q-MTL), where the goal is to simultaneously learn multiple neural models that solve *identical tasks*, while relying on a *shared representation* layer.

Besides the considerable speedup that comes with the proposed technique, we additionally argue that by applying multiple output units on top of a shared parameter set is beneficial, as we can avoid converging to such degenerate internal representations that are highly tailored for a particular classification model. In that sense, Q-MTL can also be viewed as an implicit regularizer.

Our experiments with Q-MTL illustrate that the presence of multiple classifier layers for the same task affect each other positively – similar to ensemble learning – without the additional overhead of actually training multiple models.

A similar technique have already been derived from MTL called Pseudo-Task Augmentation (Meyerson and Miikkulainen, 2018), which builds on the idea of common representation, but the management of these tasks differs. We conducted experiments comparing the two methods for a greater comprehension of the differences.

Proceedings of SustaiNLP: Workshop on Simple and Efficient Natural Language Processing, pages 97–106
Online, November 20, 2020. ©2020 Association for Computational Linguistics

2 Applied models

We release all our source code used for our experiments at `https://github.com/N0rbi/Quasi-Multitask-Learning/`. Our models are based on the sequence classification framework from Plank et al. (2016) implemented in DyNet (Neubig et al., 2017). Figure 1 provides a visual summary of the different architectures we implemented. Figure 1b highlights that Q-MTL has the benefit of training multiple classification models over the same internal representation, as opposed to traditional ensemble model, which requires the training of multiple LSTM parameters as well (cf. Figure 1c).

2.1 Baseline architecture

Our baseline classifier is a bidirectional LSTM (Hochreiter and Schmidhuber, 1997) incorporating character and word level embeddings. We first compute the input embedding for the network at position i as

$$\mathbf{e_i} = \mathbf{w_i} \oplus \overrightarrow{\mathbf{c_i}} \oplus \overleftarrow{\mathbf{c_i}},$$

where $\oplus$ is the concatenation operator, $\mathbf{w_i}$ denotes the word embedding, $\overrightarrow{\mathbf{c_i}}$ and $\overleftarrow{\mathbf{c_i}}$ refers to the left-to-right and right-to-left character-based embeddings, respectively. We subsequently feed $\mathbf{e_i}$ into a bi-LSTM, which determines a hidden representation $\mathbf{h_i} \in \mathbb{R}^m$ for every token position as $\mathbf{h_i} = \overrightarrow{\mathbf{h_i}} \oplus \overleftarrow{\mathbf{h_i}}$, i.e., the concatenation of the hidden states of the two LSTMs processing the input from its beginning to the end, and in reverse direction.

The final output of the network for token position i gets computed as

$$\mathbf{y_i} = softmax(ReLU(\mathbf{h_i}V + \mathbf{b_V})W + \mathbf{b_W}) \quad (1)$$

with $V \in \mathbb{R}^{h \times m}$ and $\mathbf{b_V} \in \mathbb{R}^m$ denoting the weight matrix and the bias of a regular perceptron layer with m outputs, whereas $W \in \mathbb{R}^{m \times c}$ and $\mathbf{b_W} \in \mathbb{R}^c$ are the parameters of the neuron performing classification over the c target classes.

2.2 Q-MTL architecture

The Q-MTL network behaves similarly to the model introduced in Section 2.1, with the notable exception that it trains k distinct classification models, all of which operate over the same hidden representation as input obtained from a single bi-LSTM unit.

More concretely, we replace the single prediction of the standard single task learning (STL)

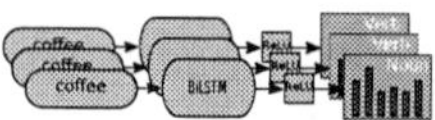

(a) Sequence of single task learners (STLs)

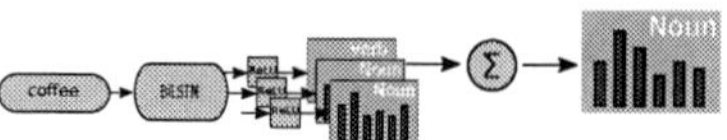

(b) Quasi-Multitask Learning (Q-MTL)

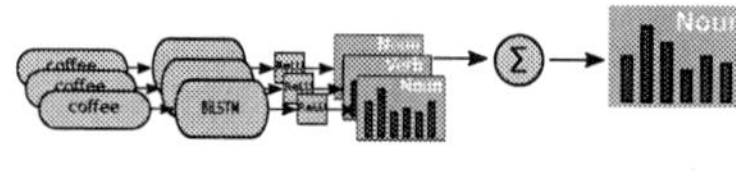

(c) Ensemble

Figure 1: A schematic illustration of the different architectures employed in our experiments. Quasi-Multitask Learning (Q-MTL) averages the predictions of multiple classification units similar to ensembling without the computational bottleneck of adjusting the parameters of multiple LSTM cells.

model from Eq. 1 by a series of predictions for Q-MTL according to

$$\mathbf{y_{i,j}} = softmax(ReLU(\mathbf{h_i}V^{(j)} + \mathbf{b_V^{(j)}})W^{(j)} + \mathbf{b_W^{(j)}}), \quad (2)$$

with $j \in \{1, \ldots, k\}$. As argued before, this approach behaves efficiently from a computational point of view, as it relies on a shared representation $\mathbf{h_i}$ for all the k classification units.

The loss of the network for token position i and gold standard class label $\mathbf{y_i^*}$ can be conveniently generalized as

$$l_{Q-MTL}(i) = \sum_{j=1}^{k} CE(\mathbf{y_i^*}, \mathbf{y_{i,j}}),$$

where CE denotes categorical cross entropy loss and k is the number of (identical) tasks in the Q-MTL model, with the special case of $k = 1$ resulting in standard STL.

Losses from the different outputs can be efficiently aggregated for backpropagation, hence the shared LSTM cell benefit from multiple error signals without the actual need of going through multiple individual forward and backward passes.

Q-MTL outputs k predictions by all of its prediction units, however, we can as well derive a combined prediction from the distinct outputs of

Q-MTL according to

$$\frac{1}{k}\sum_{j=1}^{k} softmax(ReLU(\mathbf{h_i}V^{(j)}+\mathbf{b_V^{(j)}})W^{(j)}+\mathbf{b_W^{(j)}}),$$
(3)

which is a weighted average according to the predicted probabilities of the distinct models. As introducing averaging at the model-level would eliminate diversity of the individual classifiers (Lee et al., 2015), this kind of averaging took place in a post-hoc manner, only when making predictions.

2.3 Traditional ensemble model

As an additional model, we also employ a traditional ensemble of k independently trained STL models. We define the prediction of the ensemble model by averaging the predictions of k independent models as

$$\frac{1}{k}\sum_{j=1}^{k} softmax(ReLU(\mathbf{h_i^{(j)}}V^{(j)}+\mathbf{b_V^{(j)}})W^{(j)}+\mathbf{b_W^{(j)}}).$$
(4)

The distinctive difference between Eq. 4 and the Q-MTL model formulation in Eq. 3 is that ensembling relies on the hidden representations originating from k independently trained LSTM models as denoted by the superscripts of the hidden states in $\mathbf{h_i^{(j)}}$. Such an ensemble necessarily requires approximately k-times as much computational resources compared to Q-MTL, due to the LSTM models being trained in total isolation. For the above reason, ensembling is a strictly more expensive form of training a model, therefore we regard its performance as a glass ceiling for Q-MTL.

3 Experiments

Our model uses character embeddings of 100 dimensions and the word representations get initialized by the 64-dimensional pre-trained polyglot word embeddings (Al-Rfou et al., 2013) as suggested by Plank and Agić (2018). We use the bi-LSTM introduced in the previous section. We refer to the hidden representation of the LSTM for readability as $\mathbf{h_i} \in \mathbb{R}^{200}$ which stands for the concatenation of $\overrightarrow{\mathbf{h_i}}, \overleftarrow{\mathbf{h_i}} \in \mathbb{R}^{100}$. Instead of directly applying a fully-connected layer to perform classification based on $\mathbf{h_i}$, we first transform $\mathbf{h_i}$ by an intermediate perceptron unit with ReLU activation – as shown in 2. The perceptron transforms $\mathbf{h_i}$ into 20 dimensions, that is, we have $V \in \mathbb{R}^{20\times200}$. Our motivation with the extra non-linearity introduced

by ReLU is to encourage an increased diversity in the behavior of the different output units.

Upon training the LSTMs, we used the default architectural settings employed by Plank et al. (2016), i.e., we relied on a word dropout rate of 0.25 (Kiperwasser and Goldberg, 2016) and an additive Gaussian noise (with $\sigma = 0.2$) over the input embeddings. We trained all our models for 20 epochs using stochastic gradient descent with a batch size of 1. First, we assess the quality of Q-MTL towards POS tagging, then we evaluate it on named entity recognition as well.

When comparing the performance of different approaches, Q-MTL models are compared against the average performance of k STL models, where k denotes the number of task in the case of Q-MTL. The k STL models are also used to derive a single prediction by the ensemble model.

3.1 POS tagging experiments

We set our POS tagging related experiments on 10 treebanks from the Universal Dependencies dataset v2.2 (Nivre et al., 2018), namely the Greek-GDT (el), English-LinES (en), Basque-BDT (eu), Finnish-FTB (fi), Croatian-SET (hr), Hungarian-Szeged (hu), Indonesian-GSD (id), Dutch-Alpino (nl), Tamil-TTB (ta) and Turkish-IMST (tr) treebanks. These treebanks not only cover a typologically diverse set of languages, but they also vary substantially in the number of available training sequences between 400 (for Tamil) and 14980 (for Finnish).

3.1.1 Experiments with the number of tasks

We first investigate how changing the value of k, i.e., the number of simultaneously learned tasks, affects the performance of Q-MTL. We experimented with $k \in \{1, 10, 30\}$. Based on the results in Table 1, we set the number of tasks to be employed as $k = 10$ for all upcoming experiments. In order to choose k without overfitting to the training data, this experiment was conducted on the development set.

3.1.2 Comparing Q-MTL with STL

Following the recommendation in Dodge et al. (2019), we report learning curves over the development set as a function of the number epochs in Figure 2 As a general observation, we can see that Q-MTL tends to perform consistently better than STL models right from the beginning of training.

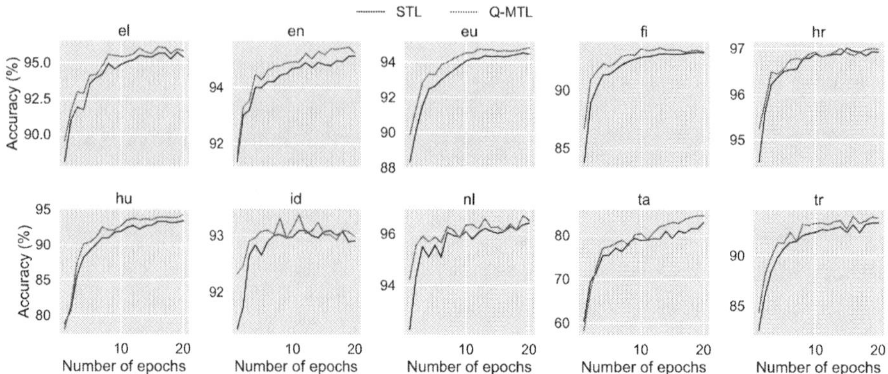

Figure 2: The accuracy of the different model types over the training epochs on the dev set.

Table 1: Results of Q-MTL on the dev sets for varying number of tasks employed (k).

k	el	en	eu	fi	hr	hu	id	nl	ta	tr	Avg.
1	95.61	94.99	94.49	93.19	96.84	93.95	93.05	96.05	82.74	93.61	93.45
10	95.84	**95.23**	**94.81**	**93.30**	**96.99**	**94.25**	92.98	**96.53**	**84.48**	**93.78**	**93.82**
30	**95.86**	95.21	94.59	93.09	96.93	93.79	**93.25**	96.27	83.85	93.46	93.63

Directly comparing the classifiers One benefit of Q-MTL is that it learns k different classification models during training with only a marginal computational overhead compared to training a STL baseline, since all the tasks share a common internal representation. As discussed earlier, we can combine the predictions from the k classifiers from Q-MTL according to Eq. 2. It is also possible, however, to use the k distinct predictions of Q-MTL. In what follows next, we compare the performance of the k STL models we train to the k classifiers that are incorporated within a Q-MTL model.

Upon comparing the performance of a Q-MTL classifier with a STL model, we made it sure that the overlapping parameters (matrices V and W) were initialized with the same values and that they receive the training instances in the exact same order. This way the performance achieved by the ith output of Q-MTL is directly comparable with the ith STL baseline. Comparison of the results of the individual outputs of Q-MTL and their corresponding STL counterpart are included in Figure 3.

Training Q-MTL models with k tasks simultaneously is not only faster than training k distinct STL models separately, but the individual Q-MTL models typically outperform their baseline counterparts evaluated against both the development and the test data.

The regularizing effect of Q-MTL We have argued earlier that Q-MTL has an implicit regularizing effect. Among most recent techniques, such as dropout (Srivastava et al., 2014), weight decay (Krogh and Hertz, 1992) is one of the most typical form of regularization for fostering the generalization capability of the learned models. When employing weight decay, we add an extra term penalizing the magnitude of the values learned by our model, which results in an overall shrinkage in the values of the model parameters.

Figure 4 illustrates that the effects of employing Q-MTL is similar to applying weight decay, as the Frobenius norm of the parameter matrices from the classifiers of Q-MTL are substantially smaller than those of the STL classifiers. This observation holds for both the of parameter sets V and W. Recall that the initial values for these matrices were identical for both Q-MTL and STL.

3.1.3 Comparison to an ensemble of classifiers

We next compared the Q-MTL technique with ensemble learning. Our comparison additionally assesses the sensitivity of the different approaches towards the presence of noisily labeled tokens during training. To do so, we conducted multiple experiments for each language, for which we randomly replaced the true class label of a token by some pre-

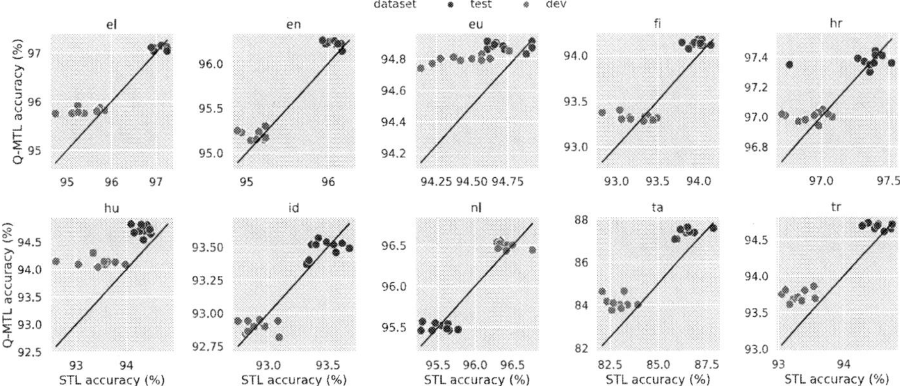

Figure 3: Scatter plot comparing the accuracy of the individual classifiers from Q-MTL ($k = 10$) and their corresponding STL counterpart. Each model that is above the diagonal line performs better after training in the Q-MTL setting.

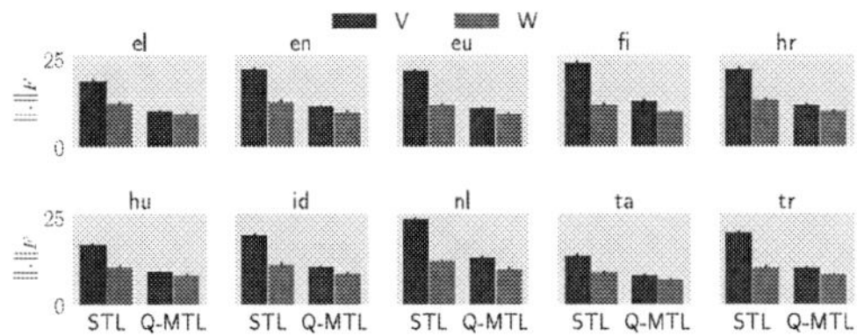

Figure 4: The average Frobenius norms of the learned parameter matrices V and W for the different approaches and treebanks.

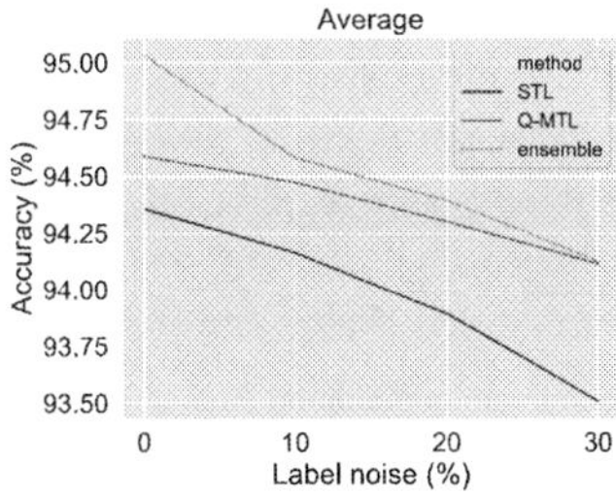

Figure 5: Model performances averaged over the 10 treebanks, when a varying amount of noisy training samples are introduced during training.

defined probability $p \in \{0, 0.1, 0.2, 0.3\}$. During the random replacement of the class labels, we ensured that the same tokens got randomly relabeled by the same label for the different approaches.

Figure 5 contains the performance of the three different models in conjunction with the different amounts of noisy labels introduced to the training set. We can observe from Figure 5 that Q-MTL outperforms STL irrespective to the amount of noisy tokens being present encountered during training.

Figure 5 further reveals that the performances of the ensemble models – which are based on the predictions of the STL classifiers – are dominantly better than the average performance of the individual STL models. When mislabeled tokens are not present in the training data at all, ensemble also has a slight advantage over Q-MTL, however, this advantage of the ensembling model gradually fades out as the proportion of noisy training labels increases. Indeed, for the case when 30% of the training labels are randomly replaced, the performance of Q-MTL reaches that of the ensemble model. The proposed approach has the additional benefit over the ensemble model that it requires a fraction of computational resources as we will demonstrate it in Section 3.1.5.

3.1.4 Comparison to Pseudo-Task Augmentation

Pseudo-Task Augmentation (PTA) architecture (Meyerson and Miikkulainen, 2018) introduces a similar architecture to Q-MTL for leveraging a better representation of the task by fitting multiple outputs to the same task. PTA makes a series of predictions according to

$$\mathbf{y_{i,j}} = softmax(\mathbf{h_i}W^{(j)} + \mathbf{b_W^{(j)}}). \qquad (5)$$

PTA introduces two special subroutines, named as *DecInit* and *DecUpdate*. These subroutines introduce various heuristics with the goal of encouraging the different decoders to behave differently.

DecInit *DecInit* gets called right before the start of the training and can contain any of the following three methods. PTA-I means that the weight of the

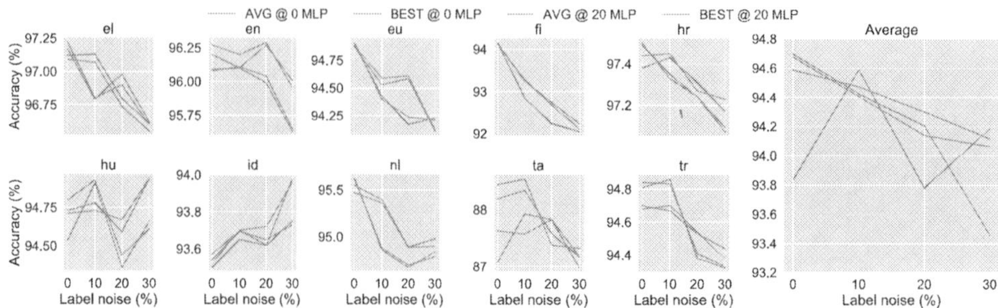

Figure 6: PTA and Q-MTL compared in an analogue manner. The model with the highest dev score (BEST) is compared to model averaging (AVG) and MLP (20 MLP) compared to linear classifier (0 MLP). From PTA (BEST @ 0 MLP) to Q-MTL (AVG @ 20 MLP) we can see all combinations of these parameters.

tasks get different random initialization. PTA-F, which freezes all k tasks except for the first one. Finally, PTA-D adds dropout independently to the tasks.

DecUpdate *DecUpdate* introduces the so-called *meta-iteration* into the learning process. A *meta-iteration* is invoked after M^{th} gradient update. The methods used in *DecUpdate* all require a ranking of the tasks based on their dev dataset performance. This makes performing an evaluation step necessary at the beginning of each *meta-iteration*. The goal of the ranking is to identify the best task (BT) with the highest dev set performance.

PTA introduces three methods for the *DecUpdate* as well. PTA-P perturbs the weight matrix of the tasks excluding the BT. Hyperturb (PTA-H) modifies the tasks in the same manner, but instead of adding noise to the weight matrices, noise gets added to the hyperparameters of the tasks (in our case it is the dropout probability preceding the softmax layers). The remaining method is called greedy (PTA-G), which takes the parameters of BT and replaces the actual parameters for all the remaining $k - 1$ decoders besides BT.

The most similar PTA method to Q-MTL is PTA-I, with the main difference that Q-MTL uses an extra transformation and a ReLU non-linearity over the hidden representation of the LSTM (cf. Eq. 2 and Eq. 5 for Q-MTL and PTA-I, respectively).

Another key difference is that PTA uses model selection ($BEST$), whereas Q-MTL relies on model averaging (AVG). This means that PTA makes prediction for test instances during inference based on the model which achieves best performing dev set accuracy at the end of the training phase. Q-MTL, on the other hand, aggregates all the models according to Eq. 3.

Figure 6 shows the effects of the different combinations of inference strategies (BEST/AVG) and the usage of a Multi-Layered Perceptron (MLP) in the model ($0MLP/20MLP$). In these experiments the 0 MLP means we do not add the extra layer before the output. Note, that the AVG inference strategy used in conjunction with the $0MLP$ architecture is essentially equivalent to the PTA-I architecture.

Figure 6 demonstrates that the Q-MTL model with its MLP layer can facilitate the use of model averaging shown in Eq. 3 as it outperforms the Q-MTL using model selection ($BEST$ @ 20 MLP). On the other hand it is indeed discouraged to use the AVG model when no MLP is applied, as $BEST$ often outperforms AVG in case of 0 MLP. Interestingly, when the train set contains high label noise, the later observation seems to pivot towards the ensemble of linear classifiers. Additionally, we can see that the MLP layer improves the tolerance of the models to the increasing label noise, as it outperforms 7 out of 10 treebanks the model not employing extra ReLU non-linearity.

As an interesting note, the Q-MTL has an improved performance for Indonesian as the amount of noisy training labels increases. A possible explanation for this is that corrupting the class labels of the training data can be viewed as an alternative form of label smoothing (Szegedy et al., 2016), which is known to increase the generalization ability of neural models.

After the detailed differentiation between PTA-I and Q-MTL we also compare Q-MTL to the more complex PTA variants that were introduced in Meyerson and Miikkulainen (2018). We conducted these experiments for English only because of the computational overhead introduced by the meta-

Table 2: Comparison of Q-MTL to the different types of PTA. This table shows the performance (%) of Q-MTL and the different PTA models on the en POS tagging dataset.

Q-MTL	PTA-I	PTA-GP	PTA-P	PTA-D	PTA-GD	PTA-HGD	PTA-F	PTA-FP
96.27	96.17	96.04	96.16	96.22	96.22	96.1	80.87	80.85

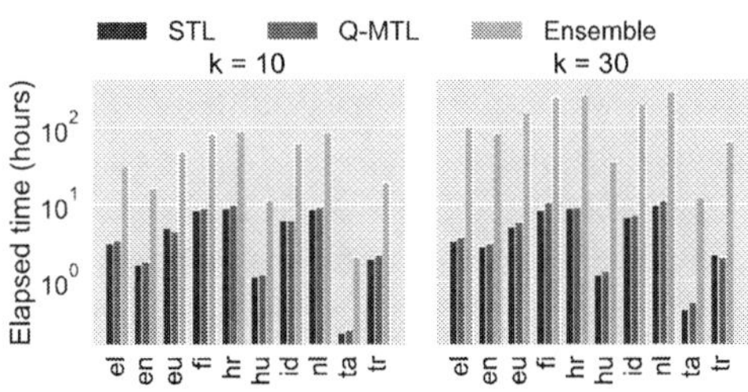

Figure 7: Training times of the different approaches for the different languages.

iterations being part of the PTA approach. In cases when there are more than one letter after the prefix of the keyword, it refers to a combination of multiple approaches (eg. PTA-HGD: hyperturb, greedy, dropout).

Table 2 shows that while most PTA architectures slightly underperform the Q-MTL, two variants of PTA – namely freeze (F) and freeze combined with perturb (FP) – had a substantially inferior performance.

These experiments have also shown that the meta-iterations of PTA are responsible for the non-gradient based updates create a considerable computational overhead – as noted above – compared to the traditional SGD without external heuristics. We used $M = 100$ for our POS tagging classifiers. This means, that 100 training samples are followed by an evaluation on the dev set, making the training phase 5 and a half hours on average for the different PTA models, while our method took slightly less than 2 hours to finish training. We do not report the performance of all eight methods due to the limitation by this training time overhead.

3.1.5 Comparison of training times

One of the main benefits of Q-MTL resides in its training efficiency compared to traditional ensemble models as also demonstrated by Figure 7, which includes the training times for the different approaches. We plot the training times on the logarithmic scale for better readability for both $k = 10$ and $k = 30$. We can see that the training times for

STL and Q-MTL practically concur, whereas the overall costs of ensembling exceeds the training time of STL and Q-MTL models by a factor of k.

The training times reported in Figure 7 were obtained without GPU acceleration – on an Intel Xeon E7-4820 CPU – in order to simulate a setting with limited computational resources. We also repeated training on a TITAN Xp GPU. The GPU-based training was 3 to 10 times quicker depending on the languages, but the relative performance between the different approaches remained the same, i.e., STL and Q-MTL training times did not differ substantially, whereas the ensemble model took k-times as much time to be created.

This training overhead is due to the number of excess parameters in the ensemble and Q-MTL models. Given we have a $k = 5$ English model, the ensemble has 5 times the parameter numbers of STL while the Q-MTL has only 1.003 times the number of STL parameters.

3.2 Evaluation on Named Entity Recognition

We also conducted experiments on the CoNLL 2002/2003 shared task data on named entity recognition (NER) in English, Spanish and Dutch (Tjong Kim Sang, 2002; Tjong Kim Sang and De Meulder, 2003). For these experiments, we report performance in terms of overall F1 scores calculated by the official scorer of the shared task. We trained models with $k = 10$ and compared the average performance of the individual STL models to the performance of the Q-MTL and ensemble models.

Table 3a shows the results for NER over the different languages, corroborating our previous observation that Q-MTL is capable of closing the gap between the performance of STL models and the much more resource-intensive ensemble model derived from k independent models.

In our POS tagging experiment, we trained models on treebanks of radically differing sizes, whereas during our NER experiments, we had access to training data sets of comparable sizes (ranging between 218K and 273K tokens). In order to simulate the effects of having access to limited training data on NER as well, we artificially relied on only 10% of the available training sets.

These results for the limited training data setting are included in Table 3b, from which we can see that Q-MTL manages to preserve more of its original performance, i.e., 87.5% on average as opposed to the ensemble and STL models, which preserved

Table 3: F1 performance scores for the NER experiments.

(a) 100% training data used

	Avg. STL	Q-MTL	Ensemble
en	86.68	86.88	**87.86**
es	82.28	82.35	**83.76**
nl	81.84	83.15	**83.61**
Avg.	83.60	84.13	**85.07**

(b) 10% training data used

	Avg. STL	Q-MTL	Ensemble
en	77.54	**80.24**	78.52
es	70.71	71.57	**72.56**
nl	68.47	69.16	**70.33**
Avg.	72.42	73.66	**73.80**

only 86.7% and 86.4% of their original F-scores.

4 Related work

Caruana (1997) showed that neural networks can be trained for multiple tasks, leveraging cross domain information. More recently, Søgaard and Goldberg (2016); Sanh et al. (2018) argues that solving low-level NLP tasks can improve the performance of high level tasks. Additionally, Plank et al. (2016); Bingel and Søgaard (2017) show that better performing models can be trained by introducing multiple auxiliary tasks. Rei (2017) proposes an auxiliary task for NLP sequence labeling tasks, where the auxiliary tasks is to predict the previous and next word in the sequence. Our results complement these findings by showing that this generalization property holds even if the tasks are the same.

Meyerson and Miikkulainen (2018) introduced Pseudo-Task Augmentation a similar architecture that aims to build a robust internal representation from multiple classifier units optimized for the same task in the same network. Section 3.1.4 describes the similarities and differences to our method. PTA architecture is evaluated on multitask as well, while our work only considers single tasks at the moment.

Ruder and Plank (2018) has shown that self-learning and tri-training can be adapted to deep neural nets in the semi-supervised regime. Their tri-training architecture resembles our approach in that they were utilizing multiple classifier units that

were built on top of a common representation layer for providing labels to previously unlabeled data.

Cross-view training (CVT) (Clark et al., 2018) resembles Q-MTL in that it also employs a shared bi-LSTM layer used by multiple output layers. The main difference between CVT and Q-MTL is that we are utilizing an bi-LSTM to solve the same task multiple times in a supervised setting, whereas Clark et al. used it to solve different tasks in a semi-supervised scenario.

A series of studies have made use of ensemble learning in the context of deep learning (Hansen and Salamon, 1990; Krogh and Vedelsby, 1995; Lee et al., 2015; Huang et al., 2017). Our proposed model is also related to the line of research on mixture of experts proposed by Jacobs et al. (1991), which has already been applied successfully in NLP before (Le et al., 2016). The main difference in our proposed architecture is that the internal LSTM representation is shared across the classifiers, hence a more efficient training could be achieved as opposed to training multiple independent expert models as it was done in Shazeer et al. (2017).

Model distillation (Hinton et al., 2015) is an alternative approach for making computationally demanding models more effective during inference, however, the approach still requires training of a "cumbersome" model first.

5 Conclusions

We proposed quasi-multitask learning (Q-MTL), which can be viewed as an efficiently trainable alternative of traditional ensembles. We additionally demonstrated that it acts as an implicit form of regularization as well. In our experiments, Q-MTL consistently outperformed the single task learning (STL) baseline for both POS tagging and NER. We have also illustrated that Q-MTL generalizes better on smaller and noisy datasets compared to both STL and ensemble models.

The computational overhead for the additional classification units in Q-MTL is infinitesimal due to the effective aggregation of the losses and the shared recurrent unit between the identical tasks. Although we evaluated Q-MTL over an LSTM, the idea can be applied for more resource-heavy architectures, like transformer (Vaswani et al., 2017) based models where training an ensemble would be too expensive. This is the future direction of our research.

Acknowledgements

This research was supported by the European Union and co-funded by the European Social Fund through the project "Integrated program for training new generation of scientists in the fields of computer science" (EFOP-3.6.3-VEKOP-16-2017-0002) and by the National Research, Development and Innovation Office of Hungary through the Artificial Intelligence National Excellence Program (2018-1.2.1-NKP-2018-00008).

References

Rami Al-Rfou, Bryan Perozzi, and Steven Skiena. 2013. Polyglot: Distributed word representations for multilingual nlp. In *Proceedings of the Seventeenth Conference on Computational Natural Language Learning*, pages 183–192. Association for Computational Linguistics.

Joachim Bingel and Anders Søgaard. 2017. Identifying beneficial task relations for multi-task learning in deep neural networks. In *Proceedings of the 15th Conference of the European Chapter of the Association for Computational Linguistics: Volume 2, Short Papers*, pages 164–169. Association for Computational Linguistics.

Rich Caruana. 1997. Multitask learning. *Machine Learning*, 28(1):41–75.

Kevin Clark, Minh-Thang Luong, Christopher D. Manning, and Quoc Le. 2018. Semi-supervised sequence modeling with cross-view training. In *Proceedings of the 2018 Conference on Empirical Methods in Natural Language Processing*, pages 1914–1925. Association for Computational Linguistics.

Ronan Collobert and Jason Weston. 2008. A unified architecture for natural language processing: Deep neural networks with multitask learning. In *Proceedings of the 25th International Conference on Machine Learning*, ICML '08, pages 160–167, New York, NY, USA. ACM.

Jesse Dodge, Suchin Gururangan, Dallas Card, Roy Schwartz, and Noah A. Smith. 2019. Show your work: Improved reporting of experimental results. *CoRR*, abs/1909.03004.

Lars Kai Hansen and Peter Salamon. 1990. Neural network ensembles. *IEEE Transactions on Pattern Analysis & Machine Intelligence*, (10):993–1001.

Geoffrey Hinton, Oriol Vinyals, and Jeffrey Dean. 2015. Distilling the knowledge in a neural network. In *NIPS Deep Learning and Representation Learning Workshop*.

Sepp Hochreiter and Jürgen Schmidhuber. 1997. Long short-term memory. *Neural computation*, 9:1735–80.

Gao Huang, Yixuan Li, Geoff Pleiss, Zhuang Liu, John E. Hopcroft, and Kilian Q. Weinberger. 2017. Snapshot ensembles: Train 1, get M for free. *CoRR*, abs/1704.00109.

Robert A. Jacobs, Michael I. Jordan, Steven J. Nowlan, and Geoffrey E. Hinton. 1991. Adaptive mixtures of local experts. *Neural Comput.*, 3(1):79–87.

Eliyahu Kiperwasser and Miguel Ballesteros. 2018. Scheduled multi-task learning: From syntax to translation. *Transactions of the Association for Computational Linguistics*, 6:225–240.

Eliyahu Kiperwasser and Yoav Goldberg. 2016. Simple and accurate dependency parsing using bidirectional lstm feature representations. *Transactions of the Association for Computational Linguistics*, 4:313–327.

Anders Krogh and John A. Hertz. 1992. A simple weight decay can improve generalization. In J. E. Moody, S. J. Hanson, and R. P. Lippmann, editors, *Advances in Neural Information Processing Systems 4*, pages 950–957. Morgan-Kaufmann.

Anders Krogh and Jesper Vedelsby. 1995. Neural network ensembles, cross validation, and active learning. In *Advances in neural information processing systems*, pages 231–238.

Phong Le, Marc Dymetman, and Jean-Michel Renders. 2016. Lstm-based mixture-of-experts for knowledge-aware dialogues. In *Proceedings of the 1st Workshop on Representation Learning for NLP*, pages 94–99. Association for Computational Linguistics.

Stefan Lee, Senthil Purushwalkam, Michael Cogswell, David J. Crandall, and Dhruv Batra. 2015. Why M heads are better than one: Training a diverse ensemble of deep networks. *CoRR*, abs/1511.06314.

Elliot Meyerson and Risto Miikkulainen. 2018. Pseudo-task augmentation: From deep multitask learning to intratask sharing—and back.

Graham Neubig, Chris Dyer, Yoav Goldberg, Austin Matthews, Waleed Ammar, Antonios Anastasopoulos, Miguel Ballesteros, David Chiang, Daniel Clothiaux, Trevor Cohn, Kevin Duh, Manaal Faruqui, Cynthia Gan, Dan Garrette, Yangfeng Ji, Lingpeng Kong, Adhiguna Kuncoro, Gaurav Kumar, Chaitanya Malaviya, Paul Michel, Yusuke Oda, Matthew Richardson, Naomi Saphra, Swabha Swayamdipta, and Pengcheng Yin. 2017. Dynet: The dynamic neural network toolkit. *arXiv preprint arXiv:1701.03980*.

Joakim Nivre, Mitchell Abrams, and et al. 2018. Universal dependencies 2.2. LINDAT/CLARIN digital library at the Institute of Formal and Applied Linguistics (ÚFAL), Faculty of Mathematics and Physics, Charles University.

Barbara Plank and Željko Agić. 2018. Distant supervision from disparate sources for low-resource part-of-speech tagging. In *Proceedings of the 2018 Conference on Empirical Methods in Natural Language Processing*, pages 614–620. Association for Computational Linguistics.

Barbara Plank, Anders Søgaard, and Yoav Goldberg. 2016. Multilingual part-of-speech tagging with bidirectional long short-term memory models and auxiliary loss. In *Proceedings of the 54th Annual Meeting of the Association for Computational Linguistics (Volume 2: Short Papers)*, pages 412–418. Association for Computational Linguistics.

Marek Rei. 2017. Semi-supervised multitask learning for sequence labeling. In *Proceedings of the 55th Annual Meeting of the Association for Computational Linguistics (Volume 1: Long Papers)*, pages 2121–2130. Association for Computational Linguistics.

Sebastian Ruder and Barbara Plank. 2018. Strong baselines for neural semi-supervised learning under domain shift. In *Proceedings of the 56th Annual Meeting of the Association for Computational Linguistics (Volume 1: Long Papers)*, pages 1044–1054. Association for Computational Linguistics.

Victor Sanh, Thomas Wolf, and Sebastian Ruder. 2018. A hierarchical multi-task approach for learning embeddings from semantic tasks.

Noam Shazeer, Azalia Mirhoseini, Krzysztof Maziarz, Andy Davis, Quoc Le, Geoffrey Hinton, and Jeff Dean. 2017. Outrageously large neural networks: The sparsely-gated mixture-of-experts layer.

Anders Søgaard and Yoav Goldberg. 2016. Deep multi-task learning with low level tasks supervised at lower layers. In *Proceedings of the 54th Annual Meeting of the Association for Computational Linguistics (Volume 2: Short Papers)*, pages 231–235. Association for Computational Linguistics.

Nitish Srivastava, Geoffrey Hinton, Alex Krizhevsky, Ilya Sutskever, and Ruslan Salakhutdinov. 2014. Dropout: A simple way to prevent neural networks from overfitting. *Journal of Machine Learning Research*, 15:1929–1958.

Emma Strubell, Ananya Ganesh, and Andrew McCallum. 2019. Energy and policy considerations for deep learning in NLP. In *Proceedings of the 57th Annual Meeting of the Association for Computational Linguistics*, pages 3645–3650, Florence, Italy. Association for Computational Linguistics.

Christian Szegedy, Vincent Vanhoucke, Sergey Ioffe, Jonathon Shlens, and Zbigniew Wojna. 2016. Rethinking the inception architecture for computer vision. In *CVPR*, pages 2818–2826. IEEE Computer Society.

Erik F. Tjong Kim Sang. 2002. Introduction to the CoNLL-2002 shared task: Language-independent named entity recognition. In *Proceedings of CoNLL-2002*, pages 155–158. Taipei, Taiwan.

Erik F. Tjong Kim Sang and Fien De Meulder. 2003. Introduction to the CoNLL-2003 shared task: Language-independent named entity recognition. In *Proceedings of the Seventh Conference on Natural Language Learning at HLT-NAACL 2003 - Volume 4*, CONLL '03, pages 142–147, Stroudsburg, PA, USA. Association for Computational Linguistics.

Ashish Vaswani, Noam Shazeer, Niki Parmar, Jakob Uszkoreit, Llion Jones, Aidan N. Gomez, Lukasz Kaiser, and Illia Polosukhin. 2017. Attention is all you need. *CoRR*, abs/1706.03762.

A Little Bit Is Worse Than None: Ranking with Limited Training Data

Xinyu Zhang,[1] **Andrew Yates,**[2] and **Jimmy Lin**[1]

[1] David R. Cheriton School of Computer Science, University of Waterloo
[2] Max Planck Institute for Informatics

Abstract

Researchers have proposed simple yet effective techniques for the retrieval problem based on using BERT as a relevance classifier to rerank initial candidates from keyword search. In this work, we tackle the challenge of fine-tuning these models for specific domains in a data and computationally efficient manner. Typically, researchers fine-tune models using corpus-specific labeled data from sources such as TREC. We first answer the question: How much data of this type do we need? Recognizing that the most computationally efficient training is no training, we explore zero-shot ranking using BERT models that have already been fine-tuned with the large MS MARCO passage retrieval dataset. We arrive at the surprising and novel finding that "some" labeled in-domain data can be worse than none at all.

1 Introduction

Given a corpus C comprised of an arbitrary number of texts, the goal of the retrieval task is to generate a ranked list of k results for a user query q that maximizes some metric of interest. Texts can differ in length: if the corpus is comprised of paragraph-length segments, the task is referred to as *passage retrieval*. Otherwise, information retrieval (IR) researchers use the term *document retrieval.*

BERT (Devlin et al., 2019) has been successfully applied to the passage retrieval task by using it as a relevance classifier that reranks an initial list of candidate results (Nogueira and Cho, 2019), which are retrieved using bag-of-words queries and efficient exact-match scoring techniques such as BM25. As passages are usually shorter than the 512 token input length limit of BERT, this solution is straightforward. Even in cases where the candidate text exceeds this length limitation, Dai and Callan (2019) showed that simply taking the best-scoring passage from a longer document as a proxy

for the document score is an effective technique. In keeping with the theme of this workshop, these are simple yet effective approaches to tackling the retrieval problem.

Building on these two previous innovations, our work tackles the problem of training ranking models for specific domains (corpora) in a data and computationally efficient manner. While the most straightforward solution would be to gather relevance judgments on the target corpus, this is a non-trivial task. Such IR test collections are usually produced via efforts like the Text Retrieval Conferences (TRECs) organized by the U.S. National Institute for Standards and Technology. These collections are the result of community-wide efforts and beyond the capabilities of individual research teams. We consider the question of how much training data are needed to fine-tune an effective ranking model. Does adapting a BERT-based ranker to a new domain require TREC-like levels of effort?

The most data and computationally efficient training procedure is, of course, no training at all— that is, zero-shot learning. Given the appeal of skipping the fine-tuning process altogether, we also explore how a zero-shot approach compares to fine-tuning on the target domain. There exists publicly available BERT models that have already been fine-tuned with existing labeled data, for example, in the "model zoo" of HuggingFace's Transformer library (Wolf et al., 2019). We explore using these directly on our target corpora, and arrive at the interesting finding that a bit of labeled in-domain data can be worse than having none at all. In other words, if we don't have sufficient in-domain training data, it's better to simply adopt a zero-shot ranking approach using an already fine-tuned model: for this task, "few shot" is worse than "zero shot"! The primary contribution of this paper is an explication of this surprising finding that, to our knowledge, has not been reported in the literature.

Proceedings of SustaiNLP: Workshop on Simple and Efficient Natural Language Processing, pages 107–112
Online, November 20, 2020. ©2020 Association for Computational Linguistics

2   Related Work

While BERT's pretraining has reduced the burden of applying the model to downstream tasks, BERT's maximum input length of 512 tokens presents a challenge for document retrieval. This length limitation prevents the straightforward application of BERT to documents in typical corpora used for retrieval tasks, which are frequently longer. The obvious solution is to split documents into smaller passages, but this immediately raises the question of how to construct "passage-level" relevance labels from document-level labels. Dai and Callan (2019) proposed the simple strategy of giving all passages the same label as the document (at training time) and aggregating passage scores (at inference time). Their most effective approach, BERT–MaxP, uses the maximum passage score as the document score at inference (ranking) time.

Alternatively, this obstacle can be entirely avoided with a zero-shot approach: the model is fine-tuned on a passage retrieval dataset and then directly applied to the target corpus (Yilmaz et al., 2019; Nogueira et al., 2020). For example, Yilmaz et al. (2019) found that when BERT was fine-tuned on a combination of (out-of-domain) datasets, the model exhibited state-of-the-art effectiveness (at the time) on Robust04. Nogueira et al. (2020) confirmed this finding and further improved zero-shot effectiveness on Robust04 by fine-tuning T5 (Raffel et al., 2020) on the MS MARCO passage dataset (Bajaj et al., 2018). Cohen et al. (2018) investigated the use of adversarial regularization to prevent pre-BERT neural models from learning representations closely tied to a specific domain. They found that training on a dataset fused from multiple domains was effective and can be further improved using adversarial regularization.

In a supervised setting with transformers, fine-tuning on a related "intermediate" dataset before fine-tuning on the target dataset can be beneficial. Phang et al. (2018) was the first to show this for natural language inference tasks, and the evidence is consistent for retrieval tasks. Dai and Callan (2019) showed that fine-tuning BERT on Bing search logs before fine-tuning on a TREC dataset improved BERT–MaxP's effectiveness. Similarly, Li et al. (2020) found that BERT–MaxP also benefits from intermediate fine-tuning on MS MARCO.

As expected, we encounter diminishing returns in effectiveness improvements as the amount of labeled training data increases; that is, increasing amounts of data are needed to obtain further improvements. Nogueira et al. (2020) demonstrated this on the MS MARCO passage ranking dataset. However, to the best of our knowledge, no previous work has investigated the effect of training data size for traditional TREC-style datasets on BERT-based models, which are smaller than MS MARCO by orders of magnitude.

Beyond ranking tasks, methods for tackling the limited labeled data issue using transfer learning have also been investigated. Rietzler et al. (2019) conducted supervised learning on the source dataset and unsupervised learning on the target dataset. Ma et al. (2019) employed adversarial learning to generate pseudo-labels for target datasets. Interestingly, both papers reported that directly transferring knowledge learned from a supervised out-of-domain dataset or unsupervised in-domain dataset to a target domain consistently underperforms supervised in-domain training without the intervention of special techniques (e.g., adversarial regularization).

3   Methodology

In order to analyze the impact of fine-tuning a BERT ranking model with limited training data, we sample standard benchmark datasets to simulate having less data available. Rather than proposing a new model, we use the BERT–MaxP model (Dai and Callan, 2019) due to its simplicity and demonstrated effectiveness on several datasets.

To simulate the impact of having limited data, we prepare six different datasets that comprise relevance judgments sampled from the full dataset at a sampling rate $r \in \{0.1, 0.3, 0.5, 0.7, 0.9, 1.0\}$. The setting $r = 1.0$ is equivalent to using the full dataset. Specifically, given a dataset with N queries and M relevance judgements, the r-sampled dataset contains roughly $r \times N$ queries and exactly $r \times M$ judgements. That is, queries (along with all their associated judgments) are dropped with a higher priority. This is accomplished by randomly dropping a query until doing so would result in fewer than $r \times M$ judgments. When this condition is reached, we loop over the remaining queries, randomly removing one judgment per query until there are exactly $r \times M$ judgments remaining. When we split our datasets into training, validation, and test folds for experiments, sampling is applied to only training and validation; we always calculate evaluation metrics using all available judgments.

r	No. of judgements	No. of queries	No. avg. docs per query
(a) Robust04			
0.1	31,141	25	1,245
0.3	93,423	79	1,182
0.5	155,705	125	1,245
0.7	217,987	175	1,245
0.9	280,269	229	1,223
1.0	311,410	249	1,250
(b) GOV2			
0.1	13,535	20	676
0.3	40,605	51	796
0.5	67,676	83	815
0.7	94,746	114	831
0.9	121,816	140	870
1.0	135,352	149	908

Table 1: Robust04 (1a) and GOV2 (1b) statistics, where r is the sampling rate and $r = 1.0$ corresponds to the full dataset.

4 Experiments

4.1 Datasets

We conduct experiments on two standard TREC benchmarks from different domains, namely the Robust04[1] and GOV2[2] collections. Robust04 is a collection of newswire documents, whereas GOV2 contains crawled websites under the .gov domain. Summary statistics are shown in Table 1. On both datasets, we consider only keyword queries.

On Robust04, we use 5-fold cross-validation with three folds for training, one for validation, and the other for evaluation, matching the splits in (Yang et al., 2019). On GOV2, we randomly split the queries into three groups and run 3-fold cross-validation with one fold for training, one for validation, and the final for evaluation.

4.2 Experimental setup

Following previous work, we initialize BERT–MaxP with the BERT-Base model (Dai and Callan, 2019; Li et al., 2020). For experiments involving MS MARCO fine-tuning prior to fine-tuning on the target domain (i.e., using MS MARCO as an intermediate dataset), we initialize BERT–MaxP with

the BERT-Base checkpoint released by Nogueira and Cho (2019).[3] To obtain candidate documents to rerank, we use Anerini's implementation of BM25 with its default parameters ($k_1 = 0.9$, $b = 0.4$) as the first-stage ranker (Yang et al., 2017). BERT–MaxP reranks the top 100 candidate documents at test time and uses the top 1000 during training.

For both datasets, we split documents into a maximum of 30 overlapping passages. Each passage contains 150 tokens and we use a stride of 75 tokens. Following the original work,[4] passages after the first are randomly selected with probability 0.1 during training.

All experiments use pairwise hinge loss over 36 epochs, where one epoch contains 256 batches. Each batch consists of 16 training pairs. We use the Adam optimizer (Kingma and Ba, 2014) with $lr = 10^{-3}$ for non-BERT parameters and $lr = 10^{-5}$ for BERT parameters; other parameters are $\beta_1 = 0.9, \beta_2 = 0.999$, and $\epsilon = 10^{-7}$. The validation set is used to determine the best model for evaluation. We implement our experiments in Capreolus (Yates et al., 2020), a toolkit for ad hoc retrieval with neural models. Our models are trained with Tensorflow 2.3. We perform the Robust04 and GOV2 experiments on TPU v2-8 and NVIDIA Quadro RTX 8000, respectively.

We only report effectiveness in terms of nDCG@20 due to space limitations, but we observed similar trends for mAP and P@20. When experimenting with different sampling rates, we run each model configuration five times and report the median nDCG@20. Our code and experimental outputs are available on GitHub.[5]

5 Results and Discussion

In this section, we investigate BERT–MaxP's effectiveness on the Robust04 and GOV2 datasets when trained with limited data. Figure 1 shows the model's effectiveness as the amount of training data increases both with and without first fine-tuning on the intermediate MS MARCO dataset. We also include BM25 (our first-stage retrieval), the unsupervised BM25+RM3 query expansion approach, and a zero-shot model in which BERT–MaxP is fine-tuned only on MS MARCO. These correspond

[1] https://trec.nist.gov/data/robust/04.guidelines.html

[2] http://ir.dcs.gla.ac.uk/test_collections/gov2-summary.htm

[3] https://github.com/nyu-dl/dl4marco-bert

[4] https://github.com/AdeDZY/SIGIR19-BERT-IR/blob/master/run_qe_classifier.py#L468-L471

[5] https://github.com/crystina-z/a-little-bit-is-worse-than-none

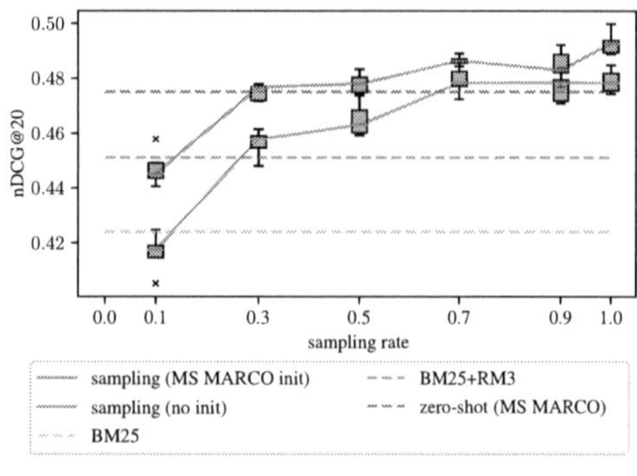

(a) Robust04

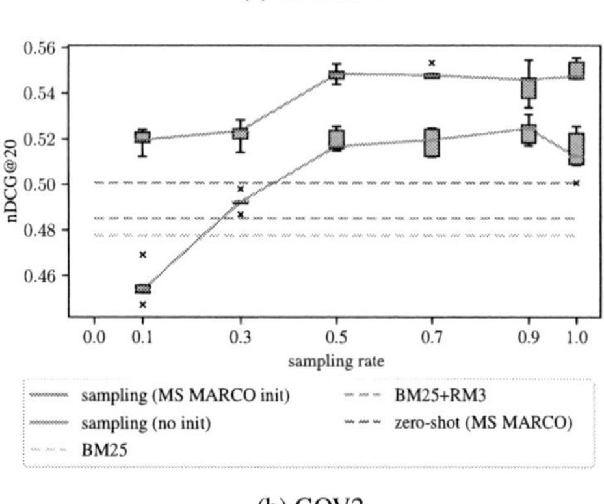

(b) GOV2

Figure 1: nDCG@20 on Robust04 (1a) and GOV2 (1b) fine-tuned on r-sampled judgements. The box plot shows the distribution of the five runs while the lines connect the median values for each condition. The × symbol indicates outliers.

to horizontal dotted lines in the plots. Corresponding numerical values can be found in Table 2.

Impact of dataset size. As expected, we observe in Figure 1 that effectiveness generally increases as the amount of training data grows (i.e., as the sampling rate increases) on both collections regardless of whether the model is first fine-tuned on MS MARCO. The increase in effectiveness is most obvious when the amount of data is small, e.g., from $r = 0.1$ to 0.3.

Effectiveness appears to plateau at $r = 0.7$, which is surprising given that both corpora contain relatively small numbers of examples when compared to the sizes of datasets typically used in deep learning today. Effectiveness even drops slightly when the full GOV2 dataset is used (when not using MS MARCO). This suggests that the amount of relevance judgments available in both corpora is sufficient for fine-tuning the BERT–MaxP model.

	Robust04		GOV2	
BM25	0.4240		0.4774	
BM25RM3	0.4510		0.4851	
Zero shot	0.4751		0.5007	
	w/ MS	w/o MS	w/ MS	w/o MS
Dai and Callan (2019)	–	0.469	–	–
Li et al. (2020)	0.4931	–	0.560	–
$r = 0.1$	0.4451	0.4173	0.5197	0.4538
$r = 0.3$	0.4767	0.4578	0.5236	0.4923
$r = 0.5$	0.4781	0.4630	0.5484	0.5168
$r = 0.7$	0.4865	0.4784	0.5479	0.5196
$r = 0.9$	0.4830	0.4785	0.5459	0.5247
$r = 1.0$	0.4927	0.4929	0.5475	0.5123

Table 2: Tabular presentation of median nDCG@20 scores from Figure 1, compared to previously reported scores. Columns "w/ MS" and "w/o MS" indicate training with and without intermediate MS MARCO fine-tuning, respectively.

Zero-shot effectiveness. Surprisingly, fine-tuning BERT with in-domain data is sometimes *worse* than zero shot, i.e., worse than not using in-domain data. From Figure 1, we see that this occurs up to $r = 0.3$ on both Robust04 and GOV2 when no intermediate dataset is used. On Robust04, this also occurs at $r = 0.1$ even when the model is initialized with the MS MARCO checkpoint. At a sampling rate of $r = 0.3$, fine-tuning on in-domain data directly (without MS MARCO) barely beats the traditional BM25+RM3 approach, which does not involve any neural network. When using intermediate data, however, the models are able to beat this non-neural baseline more easily.

Note that zero-shot BERT is more effective than BM25+RM3, which confirms that all these observed effectiveness differences are the result of different fine-tuning procedures using in-domain data (i.e., Robust04 or GOV2). Interestingly, even using all available data for Robust04, the model only modestly improves over the zero-shot baseline. This finding is consistent with the recent work of Nogueira et al. (2020), who eschew in-domain training data completely in the context of ranking with sequence-to-sequence models.

Computational efficiency. Although competitive (and in some cases, even better) effectiveness results can be obtained without using all available judgments (i.e., with $r < 1.0$), these settings do not appear to be more computationally efficient; the total training time remains roughly the same. In other words, it is not the case that we regularly reach peak validation effectiveness earlier when fine-tuning with fewer judgments.

110

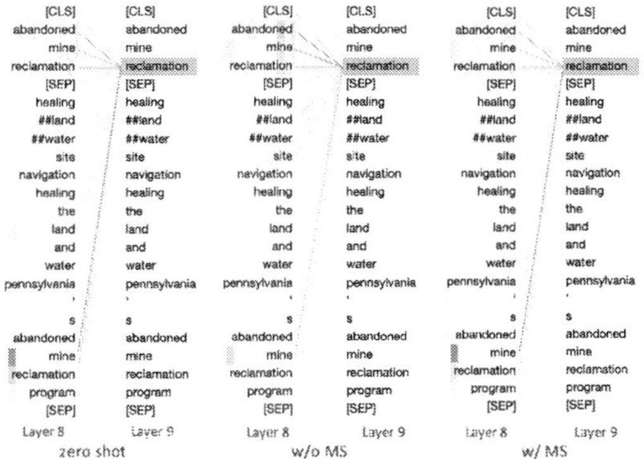

Figure 2: Attention visualization from three BERT models, where "w/o MS" and "w/ MS" indicate without and with MS MARCO fine-tuning, respectively. Colors refer to different attention heads. Deeper colors indicate stronger attention. All attention connections are from layer 8 to layer 9.

Attention visualizations. To investigate how MS MARCO increases effectiveness in other domains, we visualize attention from three models using the BertViz toolkit (Vig, 2019): a zero-shot model, a model fine-tuned on GOV2 directly, and a model fine-tuned on GOV2 after first fine-tuning on MS MARCO. Figure 2 compares the attention that the query term "reclamation" received in each model when predicting the relevance between the query *"abandoned mine reclamation"* and the text *"healinglandwater site navigation healing the land and water pennsylvania's abandoned mine reclamation program"*. Both the query and the text snippet are from GOV2. The attention map visualizes interactions from layer 8 to layer 9 in the models.

From Figure 2, it can be observed that the model with prior MS MARCO fine-tuning (right) captures a similar pattern as the zero-shot model (left), where "reclamation" receives the strongest signal from "mine", its bigram complement. However, this particular relation is more weakly captured by the model without prior fine-tuning (middle). This suggests that one way in which fine-tuning on a large intermediate dataset could help is by providing a more accurate basis for determining the relationships between terms for retrieval tasks, which might be hard to learn with only a small amount of (target domain) training data. While this particular attention analysis is anecdotal, we do observe many similar instances. Nevertheless, how to precisely determine what a BERT model learns from fine-tuning remains an open question.

6   Conclusions

This paper shows that, on two TREC collections from different domains, the effectiveness of a fine-tuned BERT–MaxP model plateaus as the amount of available judgements increases. This suggests that the current sizes of TREC test collections are sufficient for training with current BERT architectures for document retrieval. We find that performing zero-shot learning by adapting a model trained on a different domain provides a strong baseline and can even be a substitute for in-domain fine-tuning under data-poor conditions. Whether these results are due to limitations with existing datasets (e.g., their annotation schemes), ranking models (e.g., their inability to extract more signal), or the training procedure (e.g., hyperparameter settings to properly mix out-of-domain and in-domain data) remains an interesting open-research question.

Our findings present interesting guidance to practitioners: before embarking on any annotation effort in a document ranking task, it would be wise to first carefully plan out the amount of resources that are available. Our experimental results show that a bit of data can be worse than none!

Acknowledgments

This research was supported in part by the Canada First Research Excellence Fund and the Natural Sciences and Engineering Research Council (NSERC) of Canada. In addition, we would like to thank Google Cloud and TensorFlow Research Cloud for credits to support this work.

References

Payal Bajaj, Daniel Campos, Nick Craswell, Li Deng, Jianfeng Gao, Xiaodong Liu, Rangan Majumder, Andrew McNamara, Bhaskar Mitra, Tri Nguyen, Mir Rosenberg, Xia Song, Alina Stoica, Saurabh Tiwary, and Tong Wang. 2018. MS MARCO: A Human Generated MAchine Reading COmprehension Dataset. *arXiv preprint arXiv:1611.09268v3*.

Daniel Cohen, Bhaskar Mitra, Katja Hofmann, and W. Bruce Croft. 2018. Cross domain regularization for neural ranking models using adversarial learning. In *Proceedings of the 41st International ACM SIGIR Conference on Research and Development in Information Retrieval*, pages 1025–1028.

Zhuyun Dai and Jamie Callan. 2019. Deeper text understanding for IR with contextual neural language modeling. In *Proceedings of the 42nd Annual International ACM SIGIR Conference on Research and*

Development in Information Retrieval (SIGIR 2019), pages 985–988.

Jacob Devlin, Ming-Wei Chang, Kenton Lee, and Kristina Toutanova. 2019. BERT: Pre-training of deep bidirectional transformers for language understanding. In *Proceedings of the 2019 Conference of the North American Chapter of the Association for Computational Linguistics: Human Language Technologies, Volume 1 (Long and Short Papers)*, pages 4171–4186.

Diederik P. Kingma and Jimmy Ba. 2014. Adam: A method for stochastic optimization. *arXiv preprint arXiv:1412.6980*.

Canjia Li, Andrew Yates, Sean MacAvaney, Ben He, and Yingfei Sun. 2020. PARADE: Passage representation aggregation for document reranking. *arXiv preprint arXiv:2008.09093*.

Xiaofei Ma, Peng Xu, Zhiguo Wang, Ramesh Nallapati, and Bing Xiang. 2019. Domain adaptation with bert-based domain classification and data selection. In *Proceedings of the 2nd Workshop on Deep Learning Approaches for Low-Resource NLP (DeepLo 2019)*, pages 76–83.

Rodrigo Nogueira and Kyunghyun Cho. 2019. Passage re-ranking with BERT. *arXiv preprint arXiv:1901.04085*.

Rodrigo Nogueira, Zhiying Jiang, Ronak Pradeep, and Jimmy Lin. 2020. Document ranking with a pretrained sequence-to-sequence model. In *Findings of EMNLP*.

Jason Phang, Thibault Févry, and Samuel R. Bowman. 2018. Sentence encoders on STILTs: Supplementary Training on Intermediate Labeled-data Tasks. *arXiv preprint arXiv:1811.01088*.

Colin Raffel, Noam Shazeer, Adam Roberts, Katherine Lee, Sharan Narang, Michael Matena, Yanqi Zhou, Wei Li, and Peter J. Liu. 2020. Exploring the limits of transfer learning with a unified text-to-text transformer. *Journal of Machine Learning Research*, 21(140):1–67.

Alexander Rietzler, Sebastian Stabinger, Paul Opitz, and Stefan Engl. 2019. Adapt or get left behind: Domain adaptation through BERT language model finetuning for aspect-target sentiment classification. *arXiv preprint arXiv:1908.11860*.

Jesse Vig. 2019. A multiscale visualization of attention in the transformer model. *arXiv preprint arXiv:1906.05714*.

Thomas Wolf, Lysandre Debut, Victor Sanh, Julien Chaumond, Clement Delangue, Anthony Moi, Pierric Cistac, Tim Rault, Rémi Louf, Morgan Funtowicz, Joe Davison, Sam Shleifer, Patrick von Platen, Clara Ma, Yacine Jernite, Julien Plu, Canwen Xu, Teven Le Scao, Sylvain Gugger, Mariama Drame, Quentin Lhoest, and Alexander M. Rush. 2019. HuggingFace's Transformers: State-of-the-art natural language processing. *arXiv preprint arXiv:1910.03771*.

Peilin Yang, Hui Fang, and Jimmy Lin. 2017. Anserini: enabling the use of Lucene for information retrieval research. In *Proceedings of the 40th Annual International ACM SIGIR Conference on Research and Development in Information Retrieval (SIGIR 2017)*, pages 1253–1256.

Wei Yang, Kuang Lu, Peilin Yang, and Jimmy Lin. 2019. Critically examining the neural hype weak baselines and the additivity of effectiveness gains from neural ranking models. In *Proceedings of the 42nd International ACM SIGIR Conference on Research and Development in Information Retrieval*, pages 1129–1132.

Andrew Yates, Kevin Martin Jose, Xinyu Zhang, and Jimmy Lin. 2020. Flexible IR pipelines with Capreolus. In *Proceedings of the 29th International Conference on Information and Knowledge Management (CIKM 2020)*.

Zeynep Akkalyoncu Yilmaz, Wei Yang, Haotian Zhang, and Jimmy Lin. 2019. Cross-domain modeling of sentence-level evidence for document retrieval. In *Proceedings of the 2019 Conference on Empirical Methods in Natural Language Processing and the 9th International Joint Conference on Natural Language Processing (EMNLP-IJCNLP)*, pages 3481–3487.

Predictive Model Selection for Transfer Learning in Sequence Labeling Tasks

Parul Awasthy[†], **Bishwaranjan Bhattacharjee**[†], **John R Kender**[†§] and **Radu Florian**[†]

[†] IBM Research AI
Yorktown Heights, NY 10598
USA

[§] Columbia University
NY 10027
USA

`awasthyp,bhatta,raduf@us.ibm.com`   `jrk@cs.columbia.edu`

Abstract

Transfer learning is a popular technique to learn a task using less training data and fewer compute resources. However, selecting the correct source model for transfer learning is a challenging task. We demonstrate a novel predictive method that determines which existing source model would minimize error for transfer learning to a given target. This technique does not require learning for prediction, and avoids computational costs of trial-and-error.

We have evaluated this technique on nine datasets across diverse domains, including newswire, user forums, air flight booking, cybersecurity news, etc. We show that it performs better than existing techniques such as fine-tuning over vanilla BERT, or curriculum learning over the largest dataset on top of BERT, resulting in average F_1 score gains in excess of 3%. Moreover, our technique consistently selects the best model using fewer tries.

1 Introduction

When deploying deep learning in real-life scenarios, training data is often sparse. Transfer learning improves learning of such target tasks by leveraging knowledge from a source task, as shown in Figure 1. The improvement in learning could be measured by either improvement in accuracy (for example, F_1 score), or reduction in the time taken to learn the task.

With the increased popularity of the large transformer-based models Devlin et al. (2019), transfer learning in the form of fine-tuning a base model is ubiquitous in NLP. However, the performance of the learned target model depends critically on the chosen source model. Simply selecting the largest dataset can lead to sub-optimal performance, and trying all sources is computationally expensive.

We demonstrate a prediction technique for the sequence labelling task, which given a target model,

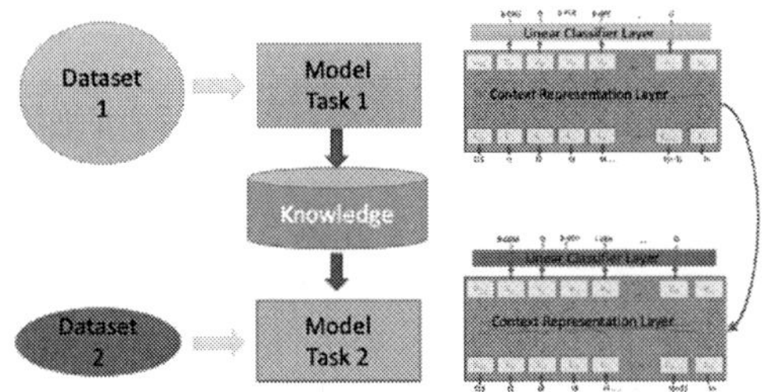

Figure 1: Transfer Learning Methodology. The rightmost column of the figure shows the architecture of a Sequence Labelling Model. Transfer learning reuses the context representation layer of Model 1 to fine-tune a new representation layer for Model 2.

selects the "best" source model from among a set of available source models, according to a novel and inexpensive metric. Then, only that single selected (trained) source model is further fine-tuned on the target dataset. We show that our selection technique is effective at selecting the source model that most improves F_1 score, over nine different tasks, with no additional training. Further, our technique results in an average gain of over 3% in F_1 over selecting a base model randomly, and over 4% in F_1 over training a model without transfer learning from any source model.

In the rest of the paper, we chronicle prior work in the area of transfer learning, describe the sequence labeling task, and follow with the description of our predictive model selection methodology.

2 Prior Work

The transfer learning literature spans different topics and strategies such as few-shot learning (Socher et al., 2013), domain adaptation (Patricia and Caputo, 2014), weight synthesis (Sussillo and Abbott, 2017), and multitask learning (Jiang, 2009; Nguyen et al., 2016; Torrey and Shavlik, 2009). Some works propose novel combinations of these approaches, in order to improve transfer performance

Proceedings of SustaiNLP: Workshop on Simple and Efficient Natural Language Processing, pages 113–118
Online, November 20, 2020. ©2020 Association for Computational Linguistics

Figure 2: Example of Span Similarity (SS) and Weighted Span Similarity (WSS). Top line: input sentence. Next line: ground truth labeling. Last two lines: labelings due to two different transfer learning sources. Rightmost columns: metric values * 100, showing the "goodness" of each source as SrcF1. Note that SrcF1 * SS = WSS.

under conditions of domain transfer with limited or incomplete annotations (Luo et al., 2017).

Some prior research on optimizing source selection has focused on instance transfer techniques, like Zhou et al. (2016) and Lin et al. (2013), which select a subset of examples from a source for transfer learning. Other approaches, like Schultz et al. (2018), propose methods to select the right set of source domain datasets for a task such as sentiment classification. Yet another approach, Afridi et al. (2018), which is more popular in computer vision research, selects sub-models of the source model and re-trains only on those.

Alternatively, Bhattacharjee et al. (2020) focuses on predicting the best source model, in the domains of computer vision and of semantic relations, by measuring the similarity between the source and target datasets, using a mix of metrics like KL divergence and source dataset size. In NLP, this approach works for sentence-level classification tasks such as sentiment classification. But it does not adapt well for sequence labelling tasks, where labels span across tokens rather than sentences, and where the similarity of the label spaces need to be accounted for. Additionally, their approach requires either the entire source dataset or its feature vector representation to be available. In contrast, the method we demonstrate here only needs the source model itself.

3   Task Definition

A sequence labelling task assigns a label to each member of a sequence of observed values. An example is Named Entity Recognition (NER), which identifies in unstructured text all contiguous typed references to task-specific real-world entities, such as persons, organizations, facilities, locations, etc. An example is shown in Figure 2.

We formally define the Transfer Learning task for this paper as follows: given a set $\mathcal{M}$ of N source models trained for sequence labelling, $\mathcal{M} = \{M_1, M_2, \ldots, M_N\}$, and one target set t, the task

is to find the best source model M_k, which when used as a base model for transfer learning, would result in a model with highest performance.

We use F_1 as the metric to measure performance, and compute relative gain in F_1 to measure the improvement in performance.

4   Predictive Model Selection

To select the best transfer learning base model, our method compares the target and source using a novel similarity metric. Instead of comparing the source and target datasets, our method compares the target test-set with the output of the source model on the target test-set. This comparison takes label weights into account.

To compare a target with each of the source models, we decode the target test-set through the source model. We call this output $\hat{y}$, and the original target annotation y. We next compare y and $\hat{y}$ using the metrics described. The source model with the highest metric score is chosen as the best source model.

4.1   Metrics

For predicting which model would be the best for a target dataset, we have experimented with two measures, called Span Similarity and Weighted Span Similarity, described here.

For Named Entity Recognition, an extracted span is customarily considered correct if the offset of the span matches that of the reference span, and the type of the span matches that of the reference span. In this work, however, we ignore the types of the spans. We therefore define *Span Similarity (SS)* based on the score computed between gold (y) and system output ($\hat{y}$) using only the offsets.

$$ SS = \frac{2 * TP}{2 * TP + FP + FN} \tag{1} $$

where TP = number of true positives, FP = number of false positives, and FN = number of false negatives, as decided by the above selection criteria. This is basically the Sorensen-Dice coefficient.

Dataset	Description	Label-Set Size	Source Size	Source F_1	Target Size	Target F_1
7 Categories (Coucke et al., 2017)	7 similar workspaces	71	2802	96.46	468	86.49
Alchemy1	News	47	2100	86.68	431	62.93
Alchemy2	News	54	7994	87.19	799	64.83
ATIS (Dahl et al., 1994)	Airline Travel	121	5873	96.91	647	92.84
CoNLL (Sang and De Meulder, 2003)	News	9	18467	96.81	1847	91.49
Klue Forum (Florian et al., 2004)	User Forum part of Klue	1050	19323	84.14	1933	75.28
Klue News (Florian et al., 2004)	Large News part of Klue	1050	14586	87.31	1514	82.95
TAC (LDC, 2019)	News	13	9639	79.76	1082	75.5
Cybersecurity	Cybersecurity articles	85	55386	83.14	2405	73.7

Table 1: Details of all datasets. Dataset size is in number of sentences. F_1 values are scores * 100. Each target dataset is down-sampled from its source dataset, allowing a full comparison matrix of sources versus targets.

To account for the "goodness" of the source model, we weight Span Similarity by the F_1 score of the source model on the source test-set, $F_1(s)$. This we call the *Weighted Span Similarity (WSS)*.

$$WSS = F_1(s) * SS \qquad (2)$$

We select the source model with the highest WSS score to be the best base model for transfer learning.

4.2 Transfer Learning

The architecture of a typical transformer-based Named Entity Recognition model is shown in Figure 1. The model can be divided into two parts, the context representation encoding layer (e.g., a BERT model), and the classifier layer (e.g, a linear classifier).

Once the source model with the highest WSS is selected, we use it as the base for transfer learning. To capture the knowledge of the source model, we use the context representation layer of the source model, but replace its classifier layer with a new classifier mapped to the target model space. We then fine-tune this new model on the target dataset.

5 Experimental Evaluation

5.1 Datasets and Source Models

We test our method on the various datasets shown in Table 1, all comprising of named entity annotated data, with different number of types as described in the lined citations. Alchemy1 and Alchemy2 are newswire datasets labeled internally with 47 and 54 types (person, organization, company, etc), respectively. Cybersecurity, the other dataset that is not cited, is a dataset of cybersecurity related articles (descriptions of virus attacks, etc.), labeled internally.

For each of the datasets, we sample a small percentage (5–20%) of examples in order to create our target sets. We use the full dataset as a source, and the small sampled sets as target sets. We train NER models using the method described in Devlin et al. (2019) on full source datasets, using the setup described in Section 5.4.

5.2 Generating Ground Truth

To test our method, we need to determine which source is truly the best for a given target. We proceed as follows.

We formally denote the N source datasets as $S = \{s_1, s_2, \ldots, s_N\}$, and the N target datasets as $\mathcal{T} = \{t_1, t_2, \ldots, t_N\}$.

To set up the evaluation of our method, we first train NER models on all source datasets, to get a set of source models $M = \{M_1, M_2, \ldots, M_N\}$. Each one of these is comprised of a context layer and a classifier layer.

Next, to get the absolute ground truth model for a given target dataset t_k, we train a model G_k for t_k without any transfer learning.

Lastly, we train a suite of ground truth transfer models for each dataset t_k. We fine-tune each of the source models $M_i, i \neq k$, by retaining its context layer but adapting its classifier layer. This gives for each t_k a suite of ground truth transfer models, $\mathcal{G}_k = \{G_{k,i}, i \neq k\}$, where $G_{k,i}$ is the ground truth transfer model for t_k using source M_i.

For each of the models in M_k we then compute the relative gain in F_1 in the usual way:

$$RGF_1(k, i) = (F_1(k, i) - F_1(k))/F_1(k) \qquad (3)$$

where $F_1(k, i)$ returns the F_1 score of the model $G_{k,i}$, and where $F_1(k)$ does the same for G_k. Therefore, the best ground truth transfer model for t_k is defined to be: $G_k^* = \underset{i}{argmax}\ RGF_1(k, i)$

5.3 Baselines

We compare our method to the following baselines:

Target	SS Predict Correct	WSS Predict Correct	Largest Source $(F_1 - B_1)/B_1$	Random Selection $(F_1 - B_2)/B_2$	Cosine Similarity $(F_1 - B_3)/B_3$	KL Divergence $(F_1 - B_4)/B_4$	Target Only $(F_1 - B_5)/B_5$
Alchemy1	Yes	**Yes**	25.66	15.95	0	5.45	23.17
Alchemy2	Yes	**Yes**	4.08	4.09	4.42	4.09	11.23
Atis	Yes	**Yes**	1.12	0.93	0.43	1.12	0.4
Klue Forum	Yes	**Yes**	0	2.24	3.26	2.33	3.13
Klue News	Yes	**Yes**	0	1.99	3.32	2.08	2.78
CoNLL	No	**Yes**	1.57	1.33	0	1.85	1.05
Cyber	No	**Yes**	0.48	0.93	0	0.48	1.75
7 Categories	No	No	-2.48	1.15	-0.93	-2.48	-0.68
TAC	No	No	-3.11	2.25	0	-2.68	0.83
$\overline{RGF_1}$			3.04	3.43	1.17	1.36	4.85

Table 2: Results, showing values * 100. $\overline{RGF_1}$ = Average Relative Gain using our method. $B_1 = F_1$ when source is largest training set. $B_2 = \overline{F_1}$, average of randomly picked source models. $B_3 = F_1$ when source is model with max cosine. $B_4 = F_1$ when source is model with lowest D_{KL}. $B_5 = F_1$ when model learnt only on target data.

1. Largest Source: This method picks the source with the largest dataset size as the best base model.

2. Random Selection: This method picks a source at random as the best base model.

3. Cosine Similarity: Cosine similarity has been frequently used in distributional semantics (Mikolov et al., 2013; Peterson, 2009; Wagstaff et al., 2001). We compute the cosine similarity between a target model G_k and each of the source models M_i (see Section 5.2), by decoding the t_k test-set with both target and source models, and using the outputs of their respective context representation layers, called A and B, to compute:

$$CosSim(A, B) = \frac{\Sigma_i A_i \times B_i}{\sqrt{\Sigma_i A_i^2} \times \sqrt{\Sigma_i B_i^2}} \quad (4)$$

We do this for all $M_i, i \neq k$, and choose the M_i with highest cosine similarity with the test-set t_k.

4. KL Divergence: Bhattacharjee et al. (2020) use KL divergence as selection metric in their method. To compute the KL Divergence between the source dataset s_i and the target dataset t_k, we decode both datasets with M_i, and compare their context representation layers, called P and Q, to compute:

$$D_{KL}(P, Q) = \sum_i P(i) \log \frac{P(i)}{Q(i)} \quad (5)$$

5. Target-only Model: We also compare our method with models trained directly with vanilla BERT over the target test-set, i.e., over t_k as described in Section 5.2.

5.4 Experimental Setup Details

The models are built using the HuggingFace Py-Torch implementation of Transformers Wolf et al. (2019). Our model uses *bert-base-cased* with the standard hyperparameters. We train the source and target models for 20 epochs, with a learning rate of 5e-5 and a batch of 32. We use K80 gpus to train our models.

6 Results and Discussion

6.1 Accuracy and Time Cost

Table 2 shows a summary of the F_1 gains by using our method to predict the best source model, compared to other baseline selection methods. Our SS method is able to predict the correct source model 5 out of 9 times, and our WSS method can predict the correct source model 7 out of 9 times. This is significantly better than any other baseline.

In terms of accuracy, our WSS method outperforms the baselines, as follows: largest source, 6 out of 9 times, with average gain of 3.04%; random selection, 9 out of 9 times, with average gain of 3.43%; cosine similarity, 4 out of 9 times, with average gain of 1.17%; KL divergence, 7 out of 9 times, with average gain of 1.36%; and no NER transfer learning, 8 out of 9 times, with average gain of 4.85%.

We note that some of our performance improvements can be attributed to a fundamental difference between our method and other baseline methods like Cosine Similarity, KL divergence, etc. Whereas other methods compare similarity of the input text space, our method computes similarity within the label space, taking advantage of learned contextual relationships.

Our method consistently works across diverse domains, and is able to correctly predict models particularly for news, forum, airline travel, and cybersecurity domains. None of the baselines work as well across these domains.

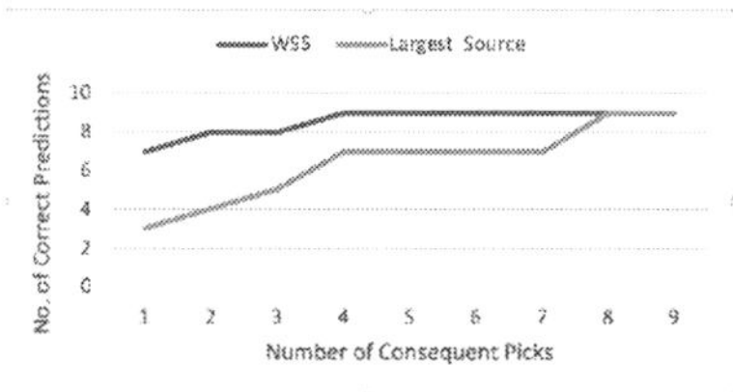

Figure 3: Number of correctly selected best models versus number of attempts. Our method in one try does as well as the largest source baseline does after four.

Our method also saves substantially on computational time and resources, as it finds the best source model with fewer tries, as shown in Figure 3. In most cases, our method is able to predict the best model on the first try, whereas the largest source baseline needs four tries. With the experimental setup described in section 5.4 it takes on average 1.5 hours to train a target model, as compared to the 6 hours it takes the largest source baseline to produce the best model. This is a compute cost saving of 75%.

6.2 Potential Application to Computer Vision

The problem of finding both a span boundary and a label is not limited to sequence labelling in NLP. Object Detection (Szegedy et al., 2013) in vision research, has similar requirements: one is expected to label objects in an image and to mark the bounding box of the objects individually. Figure 4 shows an example where the task is to detect cookies and mark the bounding boxes around them. Moreover, both Object Detection and Sequence Labelling have similar measures of accuracy.

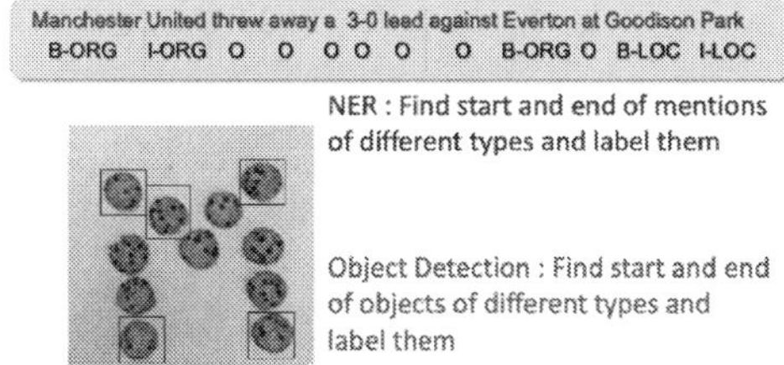

Figure 4: Similarity between Mention Detection in NLP and Object Detection in Vision.

It would be interesting to expand the method proposed in this paper to determine which source object detection base model would be a good fit for a given target data set from a collection of source object detection models. We plan to explore this in future.

7 Conclusion

In this paper we present a simple and effective method to predict the best source model for transfer learning in a sequence labelling task, NER. We show our method outperforms popular baselines such as the selection of the largest source, by an average relative 3 F_1 points. And, it is more than average relative 4 F_1 points better than a method that does not use NER transfer learning. Moreover, our method consistently selects the best model with fewer tries, saving computational cycles by roughly 75%.

8 Acknowledgments and Disclaimer

This material is based upon work supported by the Defense Advanced Research Projects Agency (DARPA) under Contract No. FA8750-19-C-1001.

Any opinions, findings and conclusions or recommendations expressed in this material are those of the authors and do not necessarily reflect the views of the Defense Advanced Research Projects Agency (DARPA).

References

Muhammad Jamal Afridi, Arun Ross, and Erik M Shapiro. 2018. On automated source selection for transfer learning in convolutional neural networks. *Pattern recognition*, 73:65–75.

Bishwaranjan Bhattacharjee, John R Kender, Matthew Hill, Parijat Dube, Siyu Huo, Michael R Glass, Brian Belgodere, Sharath Pankanti, Noel Codella, and Patrick Watson. 2020. P2l: Predicting transfer learning for images and semantic relations. In *Proceedings of the IEEE/CVF Conference on Computer Vision and Pattern Recognition Workshops*, pages 760–761.

Alice Coucke, Adrien Ball, ClÃ©ment Delpuech, ClÃ©ment Doumouro, Sylvain Raybaud, Thibault Gisselbrecht, and Joseph Dureau. 2017. Benchmarking natural language understanding systems: Google, facebook, microsoft, amazon, and snips.

Deborah A Dahl, Madeleine Bates, Michael K Brown, William M Fisher, Kate Hunicke-Smith, David S Pallett, Christine Pao, Alexander Rudnicky, and Elizabeth Shriberg. 1994. Expanding the scope of the atis task: The atis-3 corpus. In *HUMAN LANGUAGE TECHNOLOGY: Proceedings of a Workshop held at Plainsboro, New Jersey, March 8-11, 1994*.

Jacob Devlin, Ming-Wei Chang, Kenton Lee, and Kristina Toutanova. 2019. BERT: Pre-training of deep bidirectional transformers for language understanding. In *NAACL-HLT*.

Radu Florian, Hany Hassan, Abraham Ittycheriah, Hongyan Jing, Nanda Kambhatla, Xiaoqiang Luo, H Nicolov, and Salim Roukos. 2004. A statistical model for multilingual entity detection and tracking. Technical report, IBM Thomas J. Watson Research Center, Yorktown Heights, NY.

J Jiang. 2009. Multi-task transfer learning for weakly supervised relation extraction. In *4th International Joint Conference on Natural Language Processing. Association for Computational Linguistics*.

LDC. 2019. Tac kbp entity discovery and linking - comprehensive training and evaluation data 2014-2015.

Di Lin, Xing An, and Jian Zhang. 2013. Double-bootstrapping source data selection for instance-based transfer learning. *Pattern Recognition Letters*, 34:1279–1285.

Z Luo, Y Zou, J Hoffman, and L Fei-Fei. 2017. efficient learning of transferable representations across domains and tasks. In *Conference on Neural Information Processing Systems (NIPS)*.

Tomas Mikolov, Ilya Sutskever, Kai Chen, Greg S Corrado, and Jeff Dean. 2013. Distributed representations of words and phrases and their compositionality. In *Advances in neural information processing systems*, pages 3111–3119.

T.H Nguyen, L Fu, K Cho, and R Grishman. 2016. Two-stage approach for extending event detection to new types via neural networks. In *ACL Representation Learning for NLP Workshop*.

N Patricia and B Caputo. 2014. Learning to learn, from transfer learning to domain adaptation: A unifying perspective. In *Conference on Computer Vision and Pattern Recognition (CVPR)*.

Leif E Peterson. 2009. K-nearest neighbor. *Scholarpedia*, 4(2):1883.

Erik F Sang and Fien De Meulder. 2003. Introduction to the conll-2003 shared task: Language-independent named entity recognition. *arXiv preprint cs/0306050*.

Lex Razoux Schultz, Marco Loog, and Peyman Mohajerin Esfahani. 2018. Distance based source domain selection for sentiment classification. *arXiv preprint arXiv:1808.09271*.

R Socher, M Ganjoo, H Sridhar, O Bastani, D Manning, C, and A.Y Ng. 2013. Zero-shot learning through cross-modal transfer. pages 935–943.

D Sussillo and L Abbott. 2017. Transferring learning from external to internal weights in echo-state networks with sparse connectivity. In *PLoS ONE*.

Christian Szegedy, Alexander Toshev, and Dumitru Erhan. 2013. Deep neural networks for object detection. In *Advances in neural information processing systems*, pages 2553–2561.

L. Torrey and J. Shavlik. 2009. Transfer learning. In *Handbook of Research on Machine Learning Applications*.

Kiri Wagstaff, Claire Cardie, Seth Rogers, Stefan Schrödl, et al. 2001. Constrained k-means clustering with background knowledge. In *Icml*, volume 1, pages 577–584.

Thomas Wolf, Lysandre Debut, Victor Sanh, Julien Chaumond, Clement Delangue, Anthony Moi, Pierric Cistac, Tim Rault, Rémi Louf, Morgan Funtowicz, and Jamie Brew. 2019. Huggingface's transformers: State-of-the-art natural language processing. *ArXiv*, abs/1910.03771.

Shuang Zhou, Gijs Schoenmakers, Evgueni Smirnov, Ralf Peeters, Kurt Driessens, and Siqi Chen. 2016. Largest source subset selection for instance transfer. In *Asian Conference on Machine Learning*, pages 423–438.

Load What You Need: Smaller Versions of Multilingual BERT

Amine Abdaoui
Geotrend / Toulouse
amine@geotrend.fr

Camille Pradel
Geotrend / Toulouse
camille@geotrend.fr

Grégoire Sigel
Geotrend / Toulouse
gregoire@geotrend.fr

Abstract

Pre-trained Transformer-based models are achieving state-of-the-art results on a variety of Natural Language Processing data sets. However, the size of these models is often a drawback for their deployment in real production applications. In the case of multilingual models, most of the parameters are located in the embeddings layer. Therefore, reducing the vocabulary size should have an important impact on the total number of parameters. In this paper, we propose to generate smaller models that handle fewer number of languages according to the targeted corpora. We present an evaluation of smaller versions of multilingual BERT on the XNLI data set, but we believe that this method may be applied to other multilingual transformers. The obtained results confirm that we can generate smaller models that keep comparable results, while reducing up to 45% of the total number of parameters. We compared our models with DistilmBERT (a distilled version of multilingual BERT) and showed that unlike language reduction, distillation induced a 1.7% to 6% drop in the overall accuracy on the XNLI data set. The presented models and code are publicly available.

1 Introduction

While transformer based models are getting larger, there is a growing difficulty to meet production requirements when deploying them. Reducing the size of these models is therefore an important step towards a democratization of transformers in real industrial environments. In addition to the model architecture, the vocabulary size may have a huge impact on the total number of parameters. However, in the case of multilingual transformers, we need to increase the model vocabulary as we include more languages. For instance, the cased version of multilingual BERT (mBERT) has a vocabulary of 119k entries, while the english version (BERT$_{\text{BASE}}$) has

only a 30k tokens vocabulary (Devlin et al., 2018). Therefore, even if both models share the same architecture, mBERT has 178 million parameters, while BERT$_{\text{BASE}}$ has only 110 million. As a matter of fact, mBERT allocates more than 51% of its parameters to the embeddings layer.

Still, reducing the vocabulary size may induce an important drop of the model performance on downstream tasks. Indeed, Conneau et al. (2020) obtained more than 3% improvement in overall accuracy on XNLI by increasing the vocab size from 128k to 512k. Here, we propose to reduce the vocabulary size by reducing the number of languages the model handles. Indeed, most of multilingual transformers have been learned on more than 100 languages. However, in several real world applications, we need to handle a lower number of languages. In this paper, we suggest to extract smaller multilingual transformers that handle fewer languages. Here, we evaluate smaller versions of mBERT on the XNLI data set (Conneau et al., 2018), but we believe that this method may be applied to other multilingual transformers and other NLP tasks.

We compared our models with the original mBERT and the hugging face multilingual DistilBERT (DistilmBERT) (Sanh et al., 2019). To our knowledge this is the first detailed evaluation of DistilmBERT on the XNLI data set. The obtained results confirm that unlike DistilmBERT, our strategy reduces the model size without decreasing the average accuracy. The aim of this work is to draw the attention of the community on this simple yet efficient way of reducing the size of multilingual transformers.

2 Related work

Several methods have recently emerged to compress transformer models.

119

Proceedings of SustaiNLP: Workshop on Simple and Efficient Natural Language Processing, pages 119–123
Online, November 20, 2020. ©2020 Association for Computational Linguistics

A family of approaches focuses on quantizing model weights, i.e. reducing the memory footprint of a model by representing its weights by lower-precision values. This method, especially effective when used with specific hardware, has been recently applied by Shen et al. (2020) to the transformer architecture.

Knowledge distillation (Buciluǎ et al., 2006; Hinton et al., 2015) consists in transferring knowledge learned by a large teacher network to a smaller student. Works from this area aim at building models with simpler architectures than the original ones while mocking their behaviour. Knowledge distillation has been applied to reduce the number of layers of BERT models (Sun et al., 2019; Tang et al., 2019). Not limited to architecture simplification, Zhao et al. (2019) performs a model distillation by simultaneously training the teacher and student models in order to reduce the vocabulary size and the embeddings size.

Regarding multilingual transformers, Tsai et al. (2019) evaluated distilled versions of BERT and mBERT for POS tagging and Morphology tasks. Their version of mBERT is 6 times smaller and 27 times faster but induces an average F1 drop of 1.6% and 5.4% in the two evaluated tasks. Furthermore, the learnt model is not publicly available on the internet. In this paper, we compare our models with the widely used DistilmBERT (Sanh et al., 2019), a distilled version of mBERT that reduces its size by 21%.

Finally, fewer methods have tried to reduce the number of parameters located in the embeddings. Unlike Mehta et al. (2020), our method do not require to train the model from scratch.

3   Methods

In order to generate smaller versions of mBERT, we have (i) identified the vocabulary of each language, and then (ii) rebuilt the embedding layer to generate the corresponding models.

3.1   Selecting Language Vocabularies

As for the original mBERT, we started from the entire Wikipedia dump of each language[1]. In our case, we selected the 15 languages covered by the XNLI data set (Conneau et al., 2018). The recommended mBERT cased tokenizer has been used to tokenize the data. The frequency of each entry of

---

[1] https://lindat.mff.cuni.cz/repository/xmlui/handle/11234/1-2735

Language	#Selected tokens	Proportion of original tokens
English (en)	28458	23.8%
French (fr)	24482	20.5%
Spanish (es)	26346	22.0%
German (de)	26031	21.8%
Greek (el)	11616	9.7%
Bulgarian (bg)	12121	10.1%
Russian (ru)	14270	11.9%
Turkish (tr)	19086	16.0%
Arabic (ar)	7292	6.1%
Vietnamese (vi)	17512	14.6%
Thai (th)	8493	7.1%
Chinese (zh)	12928	10.8%
Hindi (hi)	5664	4.7%
Swahili (sw)	16619	13.9%
Urdu (ur)	8656	7.2%
Union (15 langs)	**71577**	**60%**

Table 1:   The number of selected tokens for each language and the proportion it covers in the original mBERT vocabulary.

the original mBERT vocabulary has been computed for each language. Manual evaluation of the tokens distributions over the different data sets allowed us to chose an appropriate frequency threshold. For each language, tokens appearing in at least 0.05% of its paragraphs (lines) were selected in its vocabulary. Table 1 presents the number of selected tokens for each language and their proportions in the original mBERT vocabulary. As expected, the number of selected tokens for the 15 languages (union) is not equal to the sum of selected tokens in each language. Indeed, several languages should share a certain number of tokens (proper nouns, punctuation signs, numbers, etc.).

3.2   Generating Smaller Models

Once the tokens selected for each targeted language, we extracted their corresponding embeddings to generate smaller models. Except the embeddings selection and re-arranging, no other modification has been applied to the model parameters. We generated 30 models covering the 15 XNLI languages in different ways:

- One multilingual model covering all the 15 languages (mBERT$_{15langs}$).

- 14 bilingual models combining english with another language from the remaining ones (mBERT$_{en-xx}$);

- 15 monolingual models (mBERT$_{xx}$);

All these models have been uploaded to the transformers hub to facilitate their use by the NLP community[2]. They can be easily fine-tuned on downstream tasks as conducted in the following section. The data and code are also available on github to allow users to generate other configurations of multilingual transformers[3].

4 Results and Discussion

In this section, we present the results of the original mBERT, its available distilled version (DistilmBERT) and our extracted mBERT versions on the XNLI data set. We also discuss the obtained results and show a few limitations of the proposed method.

4.1 Results

The above cited models have been evaluated for Cross-lingual Natural Language Inference. We used the XNLI data set which is an extension of the MultiNLI corpus (Williams et al., 2018) to 15 languages. The original english development and test sets have been manually translated to the remaining 14 languages. Furthermore, the XNLI data set comes with other configurations where the items have been automatically translated. In this paper, we used all the proposed configurations:

- *Cross-lingual Transfer*: Cross-lingual transfer from an english training set;

- *Translate Train*: Translate the english training set in order to learn the models on the same language of the test data;

- *Translate Train-all*: Translate the english training set and learn the models on all languages;

- *Translate Test*: Translate each test set to english and learn on the english training data.

Table 2 presents the obtained accuracies as well as the number of parameters of each model. All the results presented here may be reproduced using the shared models and the evaluation scripts available in the *transformers* library (Wolf et al., 2019).

---

[2] https://huggingface.co/Geotrend
[3] https://github.com/Geotrend-research/smaller-transformers

4.2 Discussion

Overall, our extracted versions of mBERT give similar results to those of the original model while being between 21% and 45% smaller in size. Regarding disilmBERT, the results show an average drop of 1.7% to 6.1% in terms of accuracy while being 25% smaller than the original mBERT. The drop in DistilmBERT's accuracy is much higher in the case of *Cross-lingual Transfer* from english to other languages (6.1%). On the contrary, our extracted versions seem to be resilient over all configurations.

The average accuracy of mBERT$_{15langs}$ is always very close to the one obtained by the original mBERT except for the *Translate Train-all* configuration. In this case, the accuracy of mBERT$_{15langs}$ is higher by 1.1%. Conneau et al. (2020) reported similar observations showing that the average accuracy decreases when the number of languages goes from 15 to 100. However, the authors kept the same vocabulary size in both experiments (150k tokens). Therefore, the per-language vocabulary should be lower in the 100-languages model than in the one handling only 15 languages. In our experiments, the vocabulary size of mBERT$_{15langs}$ is 40% smaller than the one of mBERT since we were trying to select tokens that are frequent only in these languages. Another important difference is that we are starting from models that were already trained on more than 100 languages and just fine-tuning them on less languages. Here the obtained results may suggest that starting from a certain point, keeping tokens that are very rare (or non-existent) in some languages may harm the fine-tuning of multilingual transformers on these specific languages even if we increase the vocabulary capacity.

Bilingual models (mBERT$_{en-xx}$) have been evaluated for *Cross-lingual Transfer* from the original english training set to the human translated test sets. They obtained a similar average accuracy to the one obtained by mBERT. All the presented models show better accuracies when evaluated on languages that are somewhat similar to english such as: french (fr), spanish (es) and german (de).

Finally, monolingual models (mBERT$_{xx}$) have been evaluated when the training and test sets are in the same language (*Translate Train* and *Translate Test*). Their average accuracies are lower but very close to ones obtained by mBERT. The difference is so small (less than 0.2%) that we avoid making interpretations here.

Models	#params	en	fr	es	de	el	bg	ru	tr	ar	vi	th	zh	hi	sw	ur	avg
Fine-tune multilingual model on English training set (Cross-lingual Transfer)																	
mBERT	178 M	82.1	73.8	73.9	70.3	**66.7**	67.8	68.4	60.4	64.5	70.7	53.0	68.2	**59.5**	**50.3**	57.0	65.8
DistilmBERT	135 M	78.5	70.2	70.1	65.3	60.4	63.1	63.9	55.8	58.6	57.4	37.2	64.2	51.6	46.7	53.3	59.7
mBERT$_{15langs}$	141 M	**82.2**	**74.1**	73.7	70.2	66.3	**68.1**	68.7	**61.1**	64.9	70.6	53.1	**68.8**	58.9	49.0	57.1	65.8
mBERT$_{en-xx}$	108-113 M	**82.2**	73.8	**75.0**	**71.6**	65.3	**68.1**	**69.1**	60.1	**65.0**	**70.9**	**53.2**	68.2	**59.5**	49.1	**57.9**	**65.9**
Fine-tune multilingual model on each training set (TRANSLATE-TRAIN)																	
mBERT	178 M	82.1	77.2	78.1	**77.1**	**74.5**	75.2	**74.2**	71.5	70.6	**75.3**	64.9	76.2	66.5	**66.8**	61.6	72.8
DistilmBERT	135 M	78.5	74.6	75.6	72.9	71.0	70.9	70.4	68.1	66.0	71.1	60.5	72.7	63.1	62.0	60.3	69.2
mBERT$_{15langs}$	141 M	**82.2**	**77.8**	**78.5**	76.5	74.1	**76.1**	73.6	**71.8**	**71.5**	75.2	**65.2**	75.6	**67.1**	65.7	**62.4**	**72.9**
mBERT$_{xx}$	90-108 M	81.6	**77.8**	77.1	76.0	74.3	75.0	**74.2**	71.4	71.4	75.1	64.9	**77.0**	67.0	64.3	61.6	72.6
Fine-tune multilingual models on all training sets (TRANSLATE-TRAIN-ALL)																	
mBERT	178 M	81.3	77.5	78.0	75.6	75.0	75.7	74.2	**72.9**	72.0	75.5	66.4	76.3	68.9	66.7	65.2	73.4
DistilmBERT	135 M	79.9	75.6	76.6	75.0	73.2	74.1	72.4	70.8	70.3	73.7	62.7	74.5	65.6	66.5	64.1	71.7
mBERT$_{15langs}$	141 M	**82.7**	**78.2**	**79.1**	**77.8**	**76.1**	**77.6**	**75.5**	**72.9**	**72.9**	**76.4**	**66.9**	**77.9**	**70.2**	**67.1**	**66.1**	**74.5**
Translate everything to English and use English-only model (TRANSLATE-TEST))																	
mBERT	178 M	82.1	74.9	**76.6**	73.7	74.2	**76.7**	**71.3**	70.8	70.4	68.4	**66.6**	**70.9**	65.8	61.9	**63.0**	**71.2**
DistilmBERT	135 M	78.5	72.9	73.9	72.4	72.3	73.4	69.4	69.1	69.1	67.5	65.7	69.0	65.1	61.7	62.2	69.5
mBERT$_{15langs}$	141 M	**82.2**	**75.3**	76.3	**74.5**	**74.6**	75.8	70.9	70.6	**71.3**	68.6	**66.6**	70.8	**65.8**	62.0	61.9	71.1
mBERT$_{en}$	108 M	**82.2**	74.4	76.4	73.8	74.2	75.9	71.1	**71.1**	70.5	**69.1**	65.9	70.2	65.7	**62.1**	62.3	71.0

Table 2: Results on the XNLI data set of mBERT, its distilled version (DistilmBERT) and our extracted smaller versions mBERT$_{15langs}$, mBERT$_{en-xx}$ and mBERT$_{xx}$. We also report the number of parameters of each model.

4.3 Limitations

In this work, we were interested in reducing the number of parameters of multilingual transformer models, which leads to smaller models that require less memory. We believe that memory limits are crucial especially when deploying transformers on public cloud platforms. Moreover, smaller models are loaded faster than larger ones which may also improve the speed of deployed applications. However, the proposed method does not improve the inference speed since the model architecture has not changed. Whereas distillation allows to build smaller models that usually run faster. For example, DistilmBERT reduces the number of layers by a factor of 2 (from 12 to 6 layers), which also reduces the number of operations executed either during training or inference.

Table 3 presents the model size, the allocated memory, the loading time and the inference time for all the evaluated versions of mBERT. All these measurements have been computed on a Google Cloud *n1-standard-1*[4] machine (1 vCPU, 3.75 GB). As expected, our extracted models allow to reduce the first three measurements but without changing the inference time. Whereas ditilmBERT, in addition to reducing the size, the memory and the loading time, also enhances the inference speed by a factor of 2. Our experiments confirm that reduc-

[4]https://cloud.google.com/compute/
docs/machine-types#n1_machine_type

Model	Size (MB)	Memory (MB)	Loading (sec)	Inference (sec)
mBERT	714	1401	4.18	0.24
DistilmBERT	542	1070	3.08	**0.12**
mBERT$_{15langs}$	564	1098	3.14	0.24
mBERT$_{en_xx}$	445	860	2.76	0.24
mBERT$_{xx}$	**393**	**760**	**2.45**	0.24

Table 3: The model size, the allocated memory, the loading time and the inference time for all the evaluated versions of mBERT. We present the average measurements for bilingual and monolingual models. The loading times were computed 10 times for each model, while the inference times were averaged over 100 items from the XNLI data set (batch size = 1).

ing the number of embeddings and therefore the cost of the lookup operation has almost no impact on the inference time.

That being said, we can still apply language reduction to distilled transformers to take advantage of both methods and make our models even smaller.

5 Conclusion

Multilingual transformers have several advantages such as their capacity to do zero shot cross-lingual transfer. Therefore, most of multilingual transformers have been learnt to handle an important number of languages (around 100 languages). However, handling more languages requires to increase the vocabulary capacity and therefore the model size.

In this paper, we evaluated a simple method to break multilingual transformers into smaller models according to the targeted languages. We evaluated smaller versions of mBERT on the XNLI data set and showed that they reduced the number of parameters without decreasing the average accuracy.

As a future work, it would be interesting to evaluate this method on more models and tasks. Indeed, we are planning to reduce more recent multilingual transformers that showed better results than mBERT such as XLM-R (Conneau et al., 2020). We hope that these models will facilitate the deployment of multilingual transformers in real world applications.

References

Cristian Buciluǎ, Rich Caruana, and Alexandru Niculescu-Mizil. 2006. Model compression. In *Proceedings of the 12th ACM SIGKDD international conference on Knowledge discovery and data mining*, pages 535–541.

Alexis Conneau, Kartikay Khandelwal, Naman Goyal, Vishrav Chaudhary, Guillaume Wenzek, Francisco Guzmán, Edouard Grave, Myle Ott, Luke Zettlemoyer, and Veselin Stoyanov. 2020. Unsupervised cross-lingual representation learning at scale. In *Proceedings of the 58th Annual Meeting of the Association for Computational Linguistics*, page 8440–8451.

Alexis Conneau, Ruty Rinott, Guillaume Lample, Adina Williams, Samuel R. Bowman, Holger Schwenk, and Veselin Stoyanov. 2018. Xnli: Evaluating cross-lingual sentence representations. In *Proceedings of the 2018 Conference on Empirical Methods in Natural Language Processing*. Association for Computational Linguistics.

Jacob Devlin, Ming-Wei Chang, Kenton Lee, and Kristina Toutanova. 2018. Bert: Pre-training of deep bidirectional transformers for language understanding. *arXiv preprint arXiv:1810.04805*.

Geoffrey Hinton, Oriol Vinyals, and Jeff Dean. 2015. Distilling the knowledge in a neural network. *arXiv preprint arXiv:1503.02531*.

Sachin Mehta, Rik Koncel-Kedziorski, Mohammad Rastegari, and Hannaneh Hajishirzi. 2020. Define: Deep factorized input token embeddings for neural sequence modeling. In *Proceedings of the 2020 International Conference on Learning Representations*.

Victor Sanh, Lysandre Debut, Julien Chaumond, and Thomas Wolf. 2019. Distilbert, a distilled version of bert: smaller, faster, cheaper and lighter. *arXiv preprint arXiv:1910.01108*.

Sheng Shen, Zhen Dong, Jiayu Ye, Linjian Ma, Zhewei Yao, Amir Gholami, Michael W Mahoney, and Kurt Keutzer. 2020. Q-bert: Hessian based ultra low precision quantization of bert. In *AAAI*, pages 8815–8821.

Siqi Sun, Yu Cheng, Zhe Gan, and Jingjing Liu. 2019. Patient knowledge distillation for bert model compression. *arXiv preprint arXiv:1908.09355*.

Raphael Tang, Yao Lu, Linqing Liu, Lili Mou, Olga Vechtomova, and Jimmy Lin. 2019. Distilling task-specific knowledge from bert into simple neural networks. *arXiv preprint arXiv:1903.12136*.

Henry Tsai, Jason Riesa, Melvin Johnson, Naveen Arivazhagan, Xin Li, and Amelia Archer. 2019. Small and practical bert models for sequence labeling. *arXiv preprint arXiv:1909.00100*.

Adina Williams, Nikita Nangia, and Samuel Bowman. 2018. A broad-coverage challenge corpus for sentence understanding through inference. In *Proceedings of the 2018 Conference of the North American Chapter of the Association for Computational Linguistics: Human Language Technologies, Volume 1 (Long Papers)*, pages 1112–1122. Association for Computational Linguistics.

Thomas Wolf, Lysandre Debut, Victor Sanh, Julien Chaumond, Clement Delangue, Anthony Moi, Pierric Cistac, Tim Rault, Rémi Louf, Morgan Funtowicz, Joe Davison, Sam Shleifer, Patrick von Platen, Clara Ma, Yacine Jernite, Julien Plu, Canwen Xu, Teven Le Scao, Sylvain Gugger, Mariama Drame, Quentin Lhoest, and Alexander M. Rush. 2019. Huggingface's transformers: State-of-the-art natural language processing. *ArXiv*, abs/1910.03771.

Sanqiang Zhao, Raghav Gupta, Yang Song, and Denny Zhou. 2019. Extreme language model compression with optimal subwords and shared projections. *arXiv preprint arXiv:1909.11687*.

SqueezeBERT: What can computer vision teach NLP about efficient neural networks?

Forrest N. Iandola
forresti@berkeley.edu

Albert E. Shaw
ashaw596@gmail.com

Ravi Krishna
UC Berkeley EECS
ravi.krishna@berkeley.edu

Kurt W. Keutzer
UC Berkeley EECS
keutzer@berkeley.edu

Abstract

Humans read and write hundreds of billions of messages every day. Further, due to the availability of large datasets, large computing systems, and better neural network models, natural language processing (NLP) technology has made significant strides in understanding, proofreading, and organizing these messages. Thus, there is a significant opportunity to deploy NLP in myriad applications to help web users, social networks, and businesses. Toward this end, we consider smartphones and other mobile devices as crucial platforms for deploying NLP models at scale. However, today's highly-accurate NLP neural network models such as BERT and RoBERTa are extremely computationally expensive, with BERT-base taking 1.7 seconds to classify a text snippet on a Pixel 3 smartphone. To begin to address this problem, we draw inspiration from the computer vision community, where work such as MobileNet has demonstrated that grouped convolutions (e.g., depthwise convolutions) can enable speedups without sacrificing accuracy. We demonstrate how to replace several operations in self-attention layers with grouped convolutions and use this technique in a novel network architecture called Squeeze-BERT, which runs 4.3x faster than BERT-base on the Pixel 3 while achieving competitive accuracy on the GLUE test set.

A PyTorch-based implementation of Squeeze-BERT is available as part of the Hugging Face Transformers library: https://huggingface.co/squeezebert

1 Introduction and Motivation

The human race writes over 300 billion messages per day (Sayce, 2019; Schultz, 2019; Al-Heeti, 2018; Templatify, 2017). Out of these, more than half of the world's emails are read on mobile devices, and nearly half of Facebook users exclusively access Facebook from a mobile device (Lovely Mobile News, 2017; Donnelly, 2018). Natural language processing (NLP) technology has the potential to aid these users and communities in several ways. When a person writes a message, NLP models can help with spelling and grammar checking as well as sentence completion. When content is added to a social network, NLP can facilitate content moderation before it appears in other users' news feeds. When a person consumes messages, NLP models can help classify messages into folders, compose news feeds, prioritize messages, and identify duplicates.

In recent years, the development and adoption of Attention Neural Networks have led to dramatic improvements in almost every area of NLP. In 2017, Vaswani *et al.* proposed the multi-head self-attention module, which demonstrated superior accuracy to recurrent neural networks on English-German machine language translation (Vaswani et al., 2017).[1] These modules have since been adopted by GPT (Radford et al., 2018) and BERT (Devlin et al., 2019) for sentence classification, and by GPT-2 (Radford et al., 2019) and CTRL (Keskar et al., 2019) for sentence completion and generation. Recent works such as ELEC-TRA (Clark et al., 2020) and RoBERTa (Liu et al., 2019) have shown that larger datasets and more sophisticated training regimes can further improve the accuracy of self-attention networks.

Considering the enormity of the textual data created by humans on mobile devices, a natural approach is to deploy the NLP models directly onto mobile devices, embedding them in the apps used to read, write, and share text. Unfortunately, highly-accurate NLP models are computationally expensive, making mobile deployment impractical. For example, we observe that running the BERT-base

---

[1] Neural networks that use the self-attention modules of Vaswani *et al.* are sometimes called "Transformers," but in the interest of clarity, we call them "self-attention networks."

Proceedings of SustaiNLP: Workshop on Simple and Efficient Natural Language Processing, pages 124–135
Online, November 20, 2020. ©2020 Association for Computational Linguistics

network on a Google Pixel 3 smartphone approximately 1.7 seconds to classify a single text data sample.[2] Much of the research on efficient self-attention networks for NLP has just emerged in the past year. However, starting with SqueezeNet (Iandola et al., 2016b), the mobile computer vision (CV) community has spent the last four years optimizing neural networks for mobile devices. Intuitively, it seems like there must be opportunities to apply the lessons learned from the rich literature of mobile CV research to accelerate mobile NLP. In the following, we review what has already been applied and propose two additional techniques from CV that we will leverage to accelerate NLP models.

1.1 What has CV research already taught NLP research about efficient networks?

In recent months, novel self-attention networks have been developed with the goal of achieving faster inference. At present, the MobileBERT network defines the state-of-the-art in low-latency text classification for mobile devices (Sun et al., 2020). MobileBERT takes approximately 0.6 seconds to classify a text sequence on a Google Pixel 3 smartphone while achieving higher accuracy on the GLUE benchmark, which consists of 9 natural language understanding (NLU) datasets (Wang et al., 2018), than other efficient networks such as Distil-BERT (Sanh et al., 2019), PKD (Sun et al., 2019a), and several others (Lan et al., 2019; Turc et al., 2019; Jiao et al., 2019; Xu et al., 2020). To achieve this, MobileBERT introduced two concepts into their NLP self-attention network that are already in widespread use in CV neural networks:

1. **Bottleneck layers.** In ResNet (He et al., 2016), the 3x3 convolutions are computationally expensive, so a 1x1 "bottleneck" convolution is employed to reduce the number of channels input to each 3x3 convolution layer. Similarly, MobileBERT adopts bottleneck layers that reduce the number of channels before each self-attention layer, reducing the computational cost of the self-attention layers.

2. **High-information flow residual connections.** In BERT-base, the residual connections serve as links between the low-channel-count (768 channels) layers. The high-channel-count (3072 channels) layers in BERT-base do not have residual connections. However, the ResNet and Residual-SqueezeNet (Iandola et al., 2016b) CV networks connect the high-channel-count layers with residuals, enabling higher information flow through the network. Similar to these CV networks, MobileBERT adds residual connections between the high-channel-count layers.

1.2 What else can CV research teach NLP research about efficient networks?

We are encouraged by the progress that Mobile-BERT has made in leveraging ideas that are popular in the CV literature to accelerate NLP. However, we are aware of two other ideas from CV, which weren't used in MobileBERT which could be applied to accelerate NLP:

1. **Convolutions.** Since the 1980s, computer vision neural nets have relied heavily on convolutional layers (Fukushima, 1980; LeCun et al., 1989). Convolutions are quite flexible and well-optimized in software, and they can implement things as simple as a 1D fully-connected layer, or as complex as a 3D dilated layer that performs upsampling or downsampling.

2. **Grouped convolutions.** A popular technique in modern mobile-optimized neural networks is grouped convolutions (see Section 3). Proposed by Krizhevsky *et al.* in the 2012 winning submission to the ImageNet image classification challenge (Krizhevsky et al., 2011, 2012; Russakovsky et al., 2015), grouped convolutions disappeared from the literature from some years, then re-emerged as a key technique circa 2016 (Chollet, 2016; Xie et al., 2017) and today are extensively used in efficient CV networks such as MobileNet (Howard et al., 2017), ShuffleNet (Zhang et al., 2018), and Efficient-Net (Tan and Le, 2019). While common in CV literature, we are not aware of work applying grouped convolutions to NLP.

1.3 SqueezeBERT: Applying lessons learned from CV to NLP

In this work, we describe how to apply convolutions and particularly grouped convolutions in the design of a novel self-attention network for NLP,

---

[2]Note that BERT-base (Devlin et al., 2019), RoBERTa-base (Liu et al., 2019), and ELECTRA-base (Clark et al., 2020) all use the same self-attention encoder architecture, and therefore these networks incur approximately the same latency on a smartphone.

which we call SqueezeBERT. Empirically, we find that SqueezeBERT runs at lower latency on a smartphone than BERT-base, MobileBERT, and several other efficient NLP models, while maintaining competitive accuracy.

2 Implementing self-attention with convolutions

In this section, first, we review the basic structure of self-attention networks. Next, we identify that their biggest computational bottleneck is in their position-wise fully-connected (PFC) layers. We then show that these PFC layers are equivalent to a 1D convolution with a kernel size of 1.

2.1 Self-attention networks

In most BERT-derived networks there are typically 3 stages: the embedding, the encoder, and the classifier (Devlin et al., 2019; Liu et al., 2019; Clark et al., 2020; Sun et al., 2020; Lan et al., 2019).[3] The embedding converts preprocessed words (represented as integer-valued tokens) into learned feature-vectors of floating-point numbers. The encoder is comprised of a series of self-attention and other layers. The classifier produces the network's final output. As we will see later in Table 1, the embedding and the classifier account for less than 1% of the runtime of a self-attention network, so we focus our discussion on the encoder.

We now describe the encoder that is used in BERT-base (Devlin et al., 2019). The encoder consists of a stack of blocks. Each block consists of a three position-wise fully-connected (PFC) layers, then a self-attention module, and finally a stack of three position-wise fully-connected layers, known as feed-forward network (FFN) layers. The initial three PFC layers, are used to generate the *query* (Q), *key* (K), and *value* (V) activation vectors for each position in the feature embedding. Each of these Q, K, and V layers applies the same operation to each position in the feature embedding independently. While neural networks traditionally multiply weights by activations, a distinguishing factor of attention neural networks is that they multiply activations by other activations, enabling dynamic weighting of tensor elements to adjust based on the input data. Further, attention networks allow modeling of arbitrary dependencies regardless

Table 1: **How does BERT spend its time?** This is a breakdown of computation (in floating-point operations, or FLOPs) and latency (on a Google Pixel 3 smartphone) in BERT-base. The sequence length is 128.

Stage	Module type	FLOPs	Latency
Embedding	Embedding	0.00%	0.26%
Encoder	Self-attention calculations	2.70%	11.3%
Encoder	PFC layers	97.3%	88.3%
Final Classifier	PFC layers	0.00%	0.02%
Total		100%	100%

of their distance in the input or output (Vaswani et al., 2017). The self-attention module proposed by Vaswani *et al.* (Vaswani et al., 2017) (which is also used by GPT (Radford et al., 2018), BERT (Devlin et al., 2019), RoBERTa (Liu et al., 2019), ELECTRA (Clark et al., 2020) and others) multiplies the Q, K, and V activations together using the equation $softmax(\frac{QK^T}{\sqrt{d_k}})V$, where d_k is the number of channels in one attention head.[4]

2.2 Benchmarking BERT for mobile inference

To identify the parts of BERT that are time-consuming to compute, we profile BERT on a smartphone. Specifically, we measure the neural network's latency using PyTorch (Paszke et al., 2019) and TorchScript on a Google Pixel 3 smartphone, with an input sequence length of 128 and a batch size of 1. This is a reasonable sequence length for text messages, instant messages, short emails, and other messages that are commonly written and read by smartphone users. In Table 1, we show the breakdown of FLOPs and latency among the main components of the BERT network, and we observe that the self-attention calculations (i.e. $softmax(\frac{QK^T}{\sqrt{d_k}})V$) account for only 11.3% of the total latency. However, PFC layers account for 88.3% of the latency.

2.3 Replacing the position-wise fully connected (PFC) layers with convolutions

Given that PFC layers account for the overwhelming majority of the latency, we now focus on reducing the PFC layers' latency. In particular, we intend to replace the PFC layers with grouped convolutions, which have been shown to produce significant speedups in computer vision networks. As

---

[3]Some self-attention networks such as (Vaswani et al., 2017; Radford et al., 2018) also have "decoder" stage. The decoder typically uses a similar neural architecture as the encoder, but is auto-regressive.

[4]For example, in BERT-base, the self-attention module has 768 channels and 12 heads, so $d_k = \frac{768}{12} = 64$.

a first step in this direction, we now show that the position-wise fully-connected layers used throughout the BERT encoder are a special case of non-grouped 1D convolution.

Let $\mathbf{w}$ denote the weights of the position-wise fully-connected layer with dimensions $(\mathcal{C}, \mathcal{C})$. Given an input feature vector $\mathbf{f}$ of dimensions $(\mathcal{P}, \mathcal{C})$ with P positions and $\mathcal{C}$ channels to generate an output of $(P, \mathcal{C})$ features, the operation performed by the position-wise fully-connected layer for each output channel c at position p can be defined:

$$PFC_{p,c}(\mathbf{f}, \mathbf{w}) = \sum_i \mathbf{w}_{c,i} * \mathbf{f}_{p,i}$$

Then if we consider the definition of a 1D convolution with kernel size $\mathcal{K}$ with the same input and output dimensions. Let $\mathbf{q}$ be the weights of the convolution with with dimensions $(\mathcal{C}, \mathcal{C}, \mathcal{K})$

$$Conv_{p,c}(\mathbf{f}, \mathbf{q}) = \sum_i \sum_k \mathbf{q}_{c,i,k} * \mathbf{f}_{\left(p - \frac{\mathcal{K}-1}{2} + k\right), i}$$

we observe that the position-wise fully-connected operation is equivalent to a convolution with a kernel size of $\mathcal{K} = 1$ where $\mathbf{q}_{c,i,0} = \mathbf{w}_{c,i}$

$$Conv_{p,c}(\mathbf{f}, \mathbf{q}) = \sum_i \mathbf{q}_{c,i,0} * \mathbf{f}_{p,i}$$

Thus, the PFC layers of Vaswani *et al.* (Vaswani et al., 2017), GPT, BERT, and similar self-attention networks can be implemented using convolutions without changing the networks' numerical properties or behavior.

3 Incorporating grouped convolutions into self-attention

Now that we have shown how to implement the expensive PFC layers in self-attention networks using convolutions, we can incorporate efficient grouped convolutions into a self-attention network. Grouped convolutions are defined as follows.

Given an input feature vector of dimensions $(\mathcal{P}, \mathcal{C})$ with $\mathcal{P}$ positions and $\mathcal{C}$ channels outputting a vector with dimensions $(\mathcal{P}, \mathcal{C})$, a 1d convolution with kernel size $\mathcal{K} = 1$ and $\}$ groups and weight vector $\mathbf{q}$ of dimensions $(\mathcal{C}, \frac{\mathcal{C}}{g})$ can be defined as follows. Let $\mathcal{N} = \frac{\mathcal{C}}{g}$ where $\mathcal{N}$ is the number of

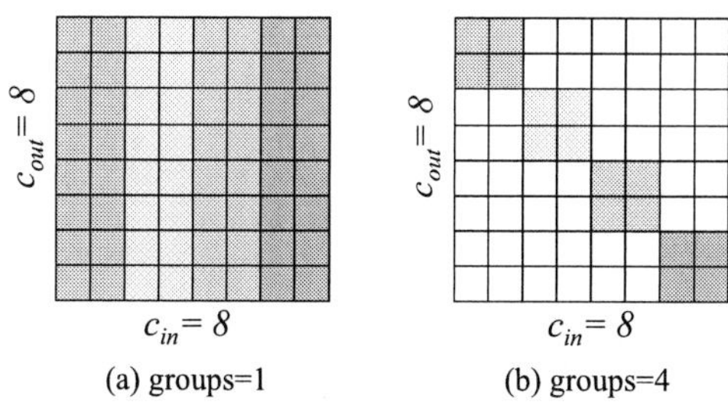

Figure 1: **Traditional vs. grouped convolutions.** In panel (a), we illustrate the weight matrix of a traditional 1D convolution with 8 input channels, 8 output channels, and a kernel size of 1. In panel (b), we illustrate a grouped convolution with $g = 4$. White cells in the grid are empty. Observe that with $g = 4$, the weight matrix has one-fourth the number of parameters as a traditional convolution.

channels in each group.

$$GConv_{p,c}(\mathbf{f}, \mathbf{q}) = \sum_i^{\frac{C}{g}} \mathbf{q}_{c,i,0} * \mathbf{f}_{p,\left(i + \lfloor \frac{c}{\mathcal{N}} \rfloor \mathcal{N}\right)}$$

This is equivalent to splitting the the input vector into g separate vectors of size $\left(P, \frac{C_{in}}{g}\right)$ along the C dimension and running g separate convolutions with independent weights each computing vectors of size $\left(P, \frac{C_{out}}{g}\right)$. The grouped convolution, however, requires only $\frac{1}{g}$ as many floating-point operations (FLOPs) and $\frac{1}{g}$ as many weights as an ordinary convolution, not counting the small (and unchanged) amount of operations needed for the channel-wise bias term that is often included in convolutional layers.[5] Finally, to complement the mathematical explanation of grouped convolutions, we illustrate the difference between traditional convolutions and grouped convolutions in Figure 1.

3.1 SqueezeBERT

Now, we describe our proposed neural architecture called SqueezeBERT, which uses grouped convolutions. SqueezeBERT is much like BERT-base, but with PFC layers implemented as convolutions, and grouped convolutions for many of the layers. Recall from Section 2 that each block in the BERT-base encoder has a self-attention module that ingests the activations from 3 PFC layers, and the block also has 3 more PFC layers called feed-forward network layers (FFN$_1$, FFN$_2$, and FFN$_3$). The FFN layers have the following dimensions: FFN$_1$ has $C_{in} = C_{out} = 768$, FFN$_2$

---

[5]Note that the grouped convolution with $g = 1$ is identical to an ordinary convolution.

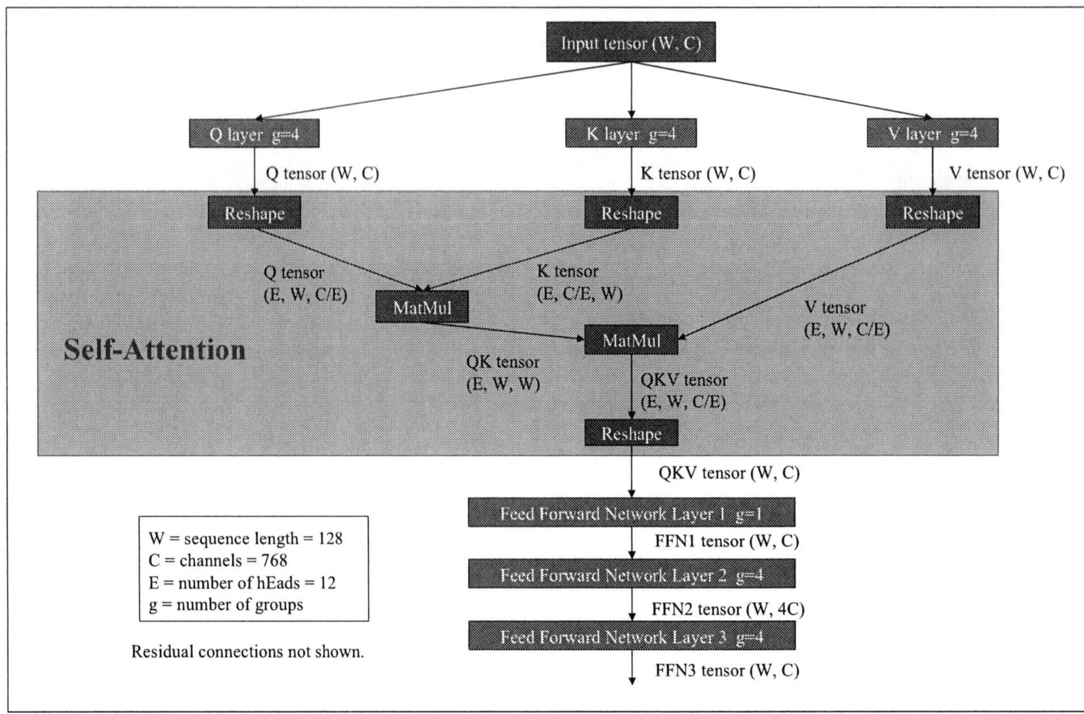

Figure 2: **One block of the SqueezeBERT encoder.** The SqueezeBERT encoder consists of a stack of 12 of these modules.

has $C_{in} = 768$ and $C_{out} = 3072$, and FFN_3 has $C_{in} = 3072$ and $C_{out} = 768$. In all PFC layers of the self-attention modules, and in the FFN_2 and FFN_3 layers, we use grouped convolutions with $g = 4$. To allow for mixing across channels of different groups, we use $g = 1$ in the less-expensive FFN_1 layers. Note that in BERT-base, FFN_2 and FFN_3 each have 4 times more arithmetic operations than FFN_1. However, when we use $g = 4$ in FFN_2 and FFN_3, now all FFN layers have the same number of arithmetic operations. We illustrate one block of the SqueezeBERT encoder in Figure 2.

Finally, the embedding size (768), the number of blocks in the encoder (12), the number of heads per self-attention module (12), the Word-Piece tokenizer (Schuster and Nakajima, 2012; Wu et al., 2016), and other aspects of SqueezeBERT are adopted from BERT-base. Aside from the convolution-based implementation and the adoption of grouped convolutions, the SqueezeBERT architecture is identical to BERT-base.

4 Experimental Methodology

4.1 Datasets

Pretraining Data. For pretraining, we use a combination of Wikipedia and BooksCorpus (Zhu et al.,

2015), setting aside 3% of the combined dataset as a test set. Following the ALBERT paper, we use Masked Language Modeling (MLM) and Sentence Order Prediction (SOP) as pretraining tasks (Lan et al., 2019).

Finetuning Data. We finetune and evaluate SqueezeBERT (and other baselines) on the General Language Understanding Evaluation (GLUE) set of tasks. This benchmark consists of a diverse set of 9 NLU tasks; thanks to the structure and breadth of these tasks (see supplementary material for detailed task-level information), GLUE has become the standard evaluation benchmark for NLP research. A model's performance across the GLUE tasks likely provides a good approximation of that model's generalizability (especially for text classification tasks).

4.2 Training Methodology

Many recent papers on efficient NLP networks report results on models trained with bells and whistles such as distillation, adversarial training, and/or transfer learning across GLUE tasks. However, there is no standardization of these training schemes across different papers, making it difficult to distinguish the contribution of the model from the contribution of the training scheme to the final accuracy number. Therefore, we first train Squeeze-BERT using a simple training scheme (described in Section 4.2.1, with results reported in Section 5.1), and then we train SqueezeBERT with distillation and other techniques (described in Section 4.2.2, with results reported in Section 5.2).

4.2.1 Training without bells and whistles

We pretrain SqueezeBERT from scratch (without distillation) using the LAMB optimizer, and we employ the hyperparameters recommended by the LAMB authors: a global batch size of 8192, a learning rate of 2.5e-3, and a warmup proportion of 0.28 (You et al., 2020). Following the LAMB paper's recommendations, we pretrain for 56k steps with a maximum sequence length of 128 and then for 6k steps with a maximum sequence length of 512.

For finetuning, we use the AdamW optimizer with a batch size of 16 without momentum or weight decay with $\beta_1 = 0.9$ and $\beta_2 = 0.999$ (Loshchilov and Hutter, 2019). As is common in the literature, during finetuning for each task, we perform hyperparameter tuning on the learning rate and dropout rate. We present more details on this in the supplementary material. In the interest of a fair comparison, we also train BERT-base using the aforementioned pretraining and fine-tuning protocol.

4.2.2 Training with bells and whistles

We now review recent techniques for improving the training of NLP networks, and we describe the approaches that we will use for the training and evaluation of SqueezeBERT in Section 5.2.

Distillation approaches used in other efficient NLP networks. While the term "knowledge distillation" was coined by Hinton *et al.* to describe a specific method and equation (Hinton et al., 2015), the term "distillation" is now used in reference to a diverse range of approaches where a "student" network is trained to replicate a "teacher" network. Some researchers distill only the final layer of the network (Sanh et al., 2019), while others also distill the hidden layers (Sun et al., 2019a, 2020; Xu et al., 2020). When distilling the hidden layers, some apply layer-by-layer distillation warmup, where each module of the student network is distilled independently while downstream modules are frozen (Sun et al., 2020). Some distill during pretraining (Sun et al., 2020; Sanh et al., 2019), some distill during

finetuning (Xu et al., 2020), and some do both (Sun et al., 2019a; Jiao et al., 2019).

Bells and whistles used for training Squeeze-BERT (for results in Section 5.2). Distillation is not a central focus of this paper, and there is a large design space of potential approaches to distillation, so we select a relatively simple form of distillation for use in SqueezeBERT training. We apply distillation only to the final layer, and only during finetuning. On the GLUE sentence classification tasks, we use soft cross entropy loss with respect to a weighted sum of the teacher's logits (Ψ_t) and a one-hot encoding of the ground-truth (Ψ_g). The weighting between the teacher logits and the ground-truth is controlled by a hyperparameter α. Formally, we write this weighted sum as:

$$\Psi = (1 - \alpha)\Psi_t + \alpha\Psi_g$$

Also note that GLUE has one regression task (STS-B text similarity), and for this task we replace the soft cross entropy loss with mean squared error. In addition to distillation, inspired by STILTS (Phang et al., 2018) and ELECTRA (Clark et al., 2020), we apply transfer learning from the MNLI GLUE task to other GLUE tasks as follows. The Squeeze-BERT student model is pretrained using the approach described in Section 4.2.1, and then it is finetuned on the MNLI task. The weights from MNLI training are used as the initial student weights for other GLUE tasks except for CoLA.[6] Similarly, the teacher model is a BERT-base model that is pretrained using the ELECTRA method and then finetuned on MNLI. The teacher model is then finetuned independently on each GLUE task, and these task-specific teacher weights are used for distillation.

5 Results

We now turn our attention to comparing Squeeze-BERT to other efficient neural networks.

5.1 Results *without* bells and whistles
In the upper portions of Tables 2 and 3, we compare our results to other efficient networks on the dev and test sets of the GLUE benchmark. Note that relatively few of the efficiency-optimized networks report results without bells and whistles, and most such results are reported on the development

---

[6]For CoLA, the student weights are pretrained (per Section 4.2.1) but not finetuned on MNLI prior to task-specific training.

Table 2: Comparison of neural networks on the **development** set of the GLUE benchmark. For tasks that have 2 metrics (e.g. MRPC's metrics are Accuracy and F1), we report the average of the 2 metrics. †denotes models trained by the authors of the present paper. Bells and whistles are: A = adversarial training; D = distillation of final layer; E = distillation of encoder layers; S = transfer learning across GLUE tasks (a.k.a. STILTs (Phang et al., 2018)); W = per-layer warmup. In GLUE accuracy, a dash means that accuracy for this task is not provided in the literature.

Model	Bells & Whistles	MNLI-m	MNLI-mm	QQP	QNLI	SST-2	CoLA	STS-B	MRPC	RTE	Average	#MParams	GFLOPs	Latency (ms)	Speedup
*Results **without** bells and whistles*															
BERT-base†	-	85.2	84.8	89.9	92.2	92.7	62.8	90.7	91.2	76.5	85.1	109	22.5	1690	1.0x
MobileBERT (Sun et al., 2020)	-	80.8	-	-	88.2	90.1	-	-	84.3	-	-	25.3	5.36	572	3.0x
ALBERT-base (Lan et al., 2019)	-	81.6	-	-	-	90.3	-	-	-	-	-	12.0	22.5	1690	1.0x
SqueezeBERT†	-	82.3	82.9	89.4	90.5	92.0	53.7	89.4	89.8	71.8	82.4	51.1	7.42	390	4.3x
*Results **with** bells and whistles*															
DistilBERT 6/768 (Sanh et al., 2019)	D	82.2	-	88.5	89.2	91.3	51.3	86.9	87.5	59.9	-	66	11.3	814	2.1x
Turc 6/768 (Turc et al., 2019)	D	82.5	83.4	89.6	89.4	91.1	-	-	87.2	66.7	-	67.5	11.3	814	2.1x
Theseus 6/768 (Xu et al., 2020)	DESW	82.3	-	89.6	89.5	91.5	51.1	88.7	89.0	68.2	-	66	11.3	814	2.1x
MobileBERT (Sun et al., 2020)	DEW	84.4	-	-	91.5	92.5	-	-	87.0	-	-	25.3	5.36	572	3.0x
SqueezeBERT†	DS	82.5	82.9	89.5	90.9	92.2	53.7	90.3	92.0	80.9	84.0	51.1	7.42	390	4.3x

Table 3: Comparison of neural networks on the **test** set of the GLUE benchmark. †denotes models trained by the authors of the present paper. Bells and whistles are: A = adversarial training; D = distillation of final layer; E = distillation of encoder layers; S = transfer learning across GLUE tasks (a.k.a. STILTs (Phang et al., 2018)); W = per-layer warmup.

Model	Bells & Whistles	MNLI-m	MNLI-mm	QQP	QNLI	SST-2	CoLA	STS-B	MRPC	RTE	WNLI	GLUE score	#MParams	GFLOPs	Latency (ms)	Speedup
*Results **without** bells and whistles*																
BERT-base†	-	84.4	84.2	80.5	91.4	92.8	51.3	86.9	87.9	70.7	65.1	79.0	109	22.5	1690	1.0x
BERT-base (Devlin et al., 2019)	-	84.6	83.4	80.2	90.5	93.5	52.1	86.5	86.9	66.4	65.1	78.3	109	22.5	1690	1.0x
SqueezeBERT†	-	82.0	81.1	80.1	90.1	91.0	46.5	84.9	86.1	66.7	65.1	76.9	51.1	7.42	390	4.3x
*Results **with** bells and whistles*																
TinyBERT 4/312 (Jiao et al., 2019)	DE	82.5	81.8	-	87.7	92.6	43.3	79.9	-	62.9	65.1	-	14.5	1.2	118	14x
ELECTRA-Small++ (Clark et al., 2020)	AS	81.6	-	-	88.3	91.1	55.6	84.6	84.9	63.6	65.1	-	14.0	2.62	248	6.8x
PKD 6/768 (Sun et al., 2019a)	DE	81.5	81.0	79.8	89.0	92.0	-	-	82.5	-	65.1	-	67.0	11.3	814	2.1x
Turc 6/768 (Turc et al., 2019)	D	82.8	82.2	79.7	89.4	91.8	-	-	84.3	65.3	65.1	-	67.5	11.3	814	2.1x
Theseus 6/768 (Xu et al., 2020)	DESW	82.4	82.1	80.5	89.6	92.2	47.8	84.9	85.4	66.2	65.1	77.1	66	11.3	814	2.1x
MobileBERT (Sun et al., 2020)	DEW	84.3	83.4	79.4	91.6	92.6	51.1	85.5	86.7	70.4	65.1	78.5	25.3	5.36	572	3.0x
SqueezeBERT†	DS	82.0	81.1	80.3	90.1	91.4	46.5	86.7	87.8	73.2	65.1	78.1	51.1	7.42	390	4.3x

(not test) set of GLUE. Fortunately, the authors of MobileBERT – a network which we will find in the next section compares favorably to other efficient networks with bells and whistles enabled – do provide development-set results without distillation on 4 of the GLUE tasks.[7] We observe in the upper portion of Table 2 that, when both networks are trained without distillation, SqueezeBERT achieves higher accuracy than MobileBERT on all of these tasks. This provides initial evidence that the techniques from computer vision that we have adopted can be applied to NLP, and reasonable accuracy can be obtained. Further, we observe that SqueezeBERT is 4.3x faster than BERT-base, while MobileBERT is 3.0x faster than BERT-base.[8]

Due to the dearth of efficient neural network results on GLUE without bells and whistles, we also provide a comparison in Table 2 with the ALBERT-base network. ALBERT-base is a version of BERT-base that uses the same weights across multiple attention layers, and it has a smaller encoder than BERT. Due to these design choices, ALBERT-base has 9x fewer parameters than BERT-base. However, ALBERT-base and BERT-base have the same number of FLOPs, and we observe in our measurements in Table 2 that ALBERT-base does not offer a speedup over BERT-base on a smartphone.[9] Further, on the two GLUE tasks where the ALBERT authors reported the accuracy of ALBERT-base, MobileBERT and SqueezeBERT both outperform the accuracy of ALBERT-base.

5.2 Results *with* bells and whistles

Now, we turn our attention to comparing Squeeze-BERT to other models, all trained with bells-and-whistles. Note that the bells-and-whistles come at the cost of extra training time, but the bells-and-whistles do not change the inference time or model-size. In the lower portion of Table 3, we first ob-

serve that when trained with bells-and-whistles MobileBERT matches or outperforms the accuracy of the other efficient models (except SqueezeBERT) on 8 of the 9 GLUE tasks. Further, on 4 of the 9 tasks SqueezeBERT outperforms the accuracy of MobileBERT; on 4 of 9 tasks MobileBERT outperforms SqueezeBERT; and on 1 task (WNLI) all models predict the most frequently occurring category.[10] Also, SqueezeBERT achieves an average score across all GLUE tasks that is within 0.4 percentage-points of MobileBERT. Given the speedup of SqueezeBERT over MobileBERT, we think it is reasonable to say that SqueezeBERT and MobileBERT each offer a compelling speed-accuracy tradeoff for NLP inference on mobile devices.

6 Related Work

Quantization and Pruning. Quantization is a family of techniques which aims to reduce the number of bits required to store each parameter and/or activation in a neural network, while at the same time maintaining the accuracy of that network. This has been successfully applied to NLP in such works as (Shen et al., 2020; Zafrir et al., 2019). Pruning aims to directly eliminate certain parameters from the network while maintaining accuracy, thereby reducing the storage and potentially computational cost of that network; for an application of this to NLP, please see Sanh et al. (2020). These methods could be applied to SqueezeBERT to yield further efficiency improvements, but quantization and pruning are not a focus of this paper.

Addressing long sequence-lengths. In work such as SqueezeBERT and MobileBERT, the inference FLOPs and latency are evaluated using a sequence length of 128. This is a reasonable sequence length for use-cases such as classifying text messages, instant-messages, and short emails. However, if the goal is to classify longer-form texts such as book chapters or even an entire book, then the typical sequence length is much longer. While the positionwise fully-connected (PFC) layers in BERT scale linearly in the sequence length, the self-attention calculations scale quadratically in the sequence length. So, when classifying a long sequence, the self-attention calculations are the dominant factor in the FLOPs and latency of the neural

---

[7]Note that some papers report results on only the development set or the test set, and some papers only report results on a subset of GLUE tasks. Our aim with this evaluation is to be as inclusive as possible, so we include papers with incomplete GLUE results in our results tables.

[8]In our measurements, we find MobileBERT takes 572ms to classify one length-128 sequence on a Pixel 3 phone. This is slightly faster than the 620ms reported by the MobileBERT authors in the same setting (Sun et al., 2019b). We use the faster number in our comparisons. Further, all latencies in our results tables were benchmarked by us.

[9]However, reducing the number of parameters while retaining a high number of FLOPs can present other advantages, such as faster distributed training (Lan et al., 2019; Iandola et al., 2016a) and superior energy-efficiency (Iandola and Keutzer, 2017).

[10]Note that data augmentation approaches have been proposed to improve accuracy on WNLI; see (Kocijan et al., 2019). For fairness in comparing against our baselines, we choose not to use data augmentation to improve WNLI results.

network. Several recent projects have worked to address this problem. For instance, Funnel Transformer downsamples the sequence length in the first few layers of the network, and it upsamples the sequence length in the final few layers of the network (Dai et al., 2020). This approach is similar to computer vision models for semantic segmentation such as U-Net (Ronneberger et al., 2015). In addition, Longformer reduces the number of FLOPs by introducing structured sparsity into the self-attention tensors (Beltagy et al., 2020). Further, Linformer projects long sequences into shorter fixed-length sequences (Wang et al., 2020b). Finally, Tay et al. (2020) provide an extensive survey of approaches for redesigning self-attention networks to efficiently classify long sequences.

Self-attention networks with dynamic computational cost. DeeBERT (Xin et al., 2020), FastBERT (Liu et al., 2020), and Schwartz et al. (2020) each describe a method to dynamically adjust the amount of computation for different sequences. The intuition is that some sequences are easier to classify than others, and the "easy" sequences can be correctly classified by only computing the first few layers of a BERT-like network.

Convolutions in self-attention networks for language-generation tasks. In this paper, our experiments focus on natural language understanding (NLU) tasks such as sentence classification. However, another widely-studied area is natural language generation (NLG), which includes the tasks of machine-translation (e.g., English-to-German) and language modeling (e.g., automated sentence-completion). While we are not aware of work that adopts convolutions in self-attention networks for NLU, we *are* aware of such work in NLG. For instance, the Evolved Transformer and Lite Transformer architectures contain self-attention modules and convolutions in separate portions of the network (So et al., 2019; Wu et al., 2020). Additionally, LightConv shows that well-designed convolutional networks without self-attention produce comparable results to self-attention networks on certain NLG tasks (Wu et al., 2019b). Also, Wang *et al.* sparsify the self-attention matrix multiplication using a pattern of nonzeros that is inspired by dilated convolutions (Wang et al., 2020a). Finally, while not an attention network, Kim applied convolutional networks to NLU several years before the development of multi-head self-attention (Kim, 2014).

7   Conclusions & Future Work

In this paper, we have studied how grouped convolutions, a popular technique in the design of efficient computer vision neural networks, can be applied to natural language processing. First, we showed that the position-wise fully-connected layers of self-attention networks can be implemented with mathematically-equivalent 1D convolutions. Further, we proposed SqueezeBERT, an efficient NLP model which implements most of the layers of its self-attention encoder with 1D grouped convolutions. This model yields an appreciable >4x latency decrease over BERT-base when benchmarked on a Pixel 3 phone. We also successfully applied distillation to improve our approach's accuracy to a level that is competitive with a distillation-trained MobileBERT and with the original version of BERT-base.

We now discuss some possibilities for future work in the design of computationally-efficient neural networks for NLP. As we observed in Section 6, in recent months numerous approaches have been proposed for reducing the computational cost of self-attention neural architectures for natural language processing. These approaches include new model structures (e.g. MobileBERT), rethinking the dimensions of attention calculations (e.g. Linformer), grouped convolutions (SqueezeBERT), and much more. Further, once the neural architecture has been selected, approaches such as quantization and pruning can further reduce some of the costs associated with self-attention neural network inference. The combination of all of these potential techniques opens up a broad search-space of neural architecture designs for NLP. This motivates the application of automated neural architecture search (NAS) approaches such as those described in (Shaw et al., 2019; Wu et al., 2019a) to further improve the design of neural networks for NLP.

Acknowledgements

K. Keutzer's research is supported by Alibaba, Amazon, Google, Facebook, Intel, and Samsung. We would like to thank the EMNLP SustaiNLP Workshop's reviewers for their helpful comments on this paper.

References

Abrar Al-Heeti. 2018. WhatsApp: 65B messages sent each day, and more than 2B minutes of calls. *CNET*.

Iz Beltagy, Matthew E. Peters, and Arman Cohan. 2020. Longformer: The long-document transformer. *arXiv:2004.05150*.

Luisa Bentivogli, Ido Dagan, Hoa Trang Dang, Danilo Giampiccolo, and Bernardo Magnini. 2009. The fifth pascal recognizing textual entailment challenge. In *Text Analysis Conference (TAC)*.

Daniel Cer, Mona Diab, Eneko Agirre, Inigo Lopez-Gazpio, and Lucia Specia. 2017. Semeval-2017 task 1: Semantic textual similarity-multilingual and cross-lingual focused evaluation. In *Eleventh International Workshop on Semantic Evaluations*.

Zihan Chen, Hongbo Zhang, Xiaoji Zhang, and Leqi Zhao. 2018. Quora question pairs.

Francois Chollet. 2016. Xception: Deep learning with depthwise separable convolutions. In *IEEE Conference on Computer Vision and Pattern Recognition (CVPR)*. https://arxiv.org/abs/1610.02357.

Kevin Clark, Minh-Thang Luong, Quoc V. Le, and Christopher D. Manning. 2020. ELECTRA: Pre-training text encoders as discriminators rather than generators. In *International Conference on Learning Representations (ICLR)*.

Zihang Dai, Guokun Lai, Yiming Yang, and Quoc V. Le. 2020. Funnel-transformer: Filtering out sequential redundancy for efficient language processing. *arXiv:2006.03236*.

Jacob Devlin, Ming-Wei Chang, Kenton Lee, and Kristina Toutanova. 2019. BERT: Pre-training of deep bidirectional transformers for language understanding. In *Conference of the North American Chapter of the Association for Computational Linguistics (NAACL)*.

William B. Dolan and Chris Brockett. 2005. Automatically constructing a corpus of sentential paraphrases. In *Proceedings of the International Workshop on Paraphrasing*.

Gordon Donnelly. 2018. 75 super-useful facebook statistics for 2018. https://www.wordstream.com/blog/ws/2017/11/07/facebook-statistics.

Kunihiko Fukushima. 1980. Neocognitron: A self-organizing neural network model for a mechanism of pattern recognition unaffected by shift in position. *Biological Cybernetics*.

Kaiming He, Xiangyu Zhang, Shaoqing Ren, and Jian Sun. 2016. Deep residual learning for image recognition. In *IEEE Conference on Computer Vision and Pattern Recognition (CVPR)*.

Geoffrey Hinton, Oriol Vinyals, and Jeff Dean. 2015. Distilling the knowledge in a neural network. *arXiv:1503.02531*.

Andrew G. Howard, Menglong Zhu, Bo Chen, Dmitry Kalenichenko, Weijun Wang, Tobias Weyand, Marco Andreetto, and Hartwig Adam. 2017. MobileNets: Efficient convolutional neural networks for mobile vision applications. *arXiv:1704.04861*.

Forrest Iandola and Kurt Keutzer. 2017. Small neural nets are beautiful: Enabling embedded systems with small deep-neural-network architectures. In *ESWEEK Keynote*.

Forrest N. Iandola, Khalid Ashraf, Matthew W. Moskewicz, and Kurt Keutzer. 2016a. FireCaffe: near-linear acceleration of deep neural network training on compute clusters. In *CVPR*.

Forrest N. Iandola, Song Han, Matthew W. Moskewicz, Khalid Ashraf, William J. Dally, and Kurt Keutzer. 2016b. SqueezeNet: Alexnet-level accuracy with 50x fewer parameters and <0.5mb model size. *arXiv:1602.07360*.

Xiaoqi Jiao, Yichun Yin, Lifeng Shang, Xin Jiang, Xiao Chen, Linlin Li, Fang Wang, and Qun Liu. 2019. TinyBERT: Distilling bert for natural language understanding. *arXiv:1909.10351*.

Nitish Shirish Keskar, Bryan McCann, Lav R. Varshney, Caiming Xiong, and Richard Socher. 2019. Ctrl: A conditional transformer language model for controllable generation. *arXiv:1909.05858*.

Yoon Kim. 2014. Convolutional neural networks for sentence classification. In *Conference on Empirical Methods in Natural Language Processing (EMNLP)*.

Vid Kocijan, Ana-Maria Cretu, Oana-Maria Camburu, Yordan Yordanov, and Thomas Lukasiewicz. 2019. A surprisingly robust trick for winograd schema challenge. In *ACL*.

Alex Krizhevsky, Ilya Sutskever, and Geoffrey E. Hinton. 2012. ImageNet Classification with Deep Convolutional Neural Networks. In *NeurIPS*.

Alex Krizhevsky et al. 2011. cuda-convnet. https://code.google.com/archive/p/cuda-convnet.

Zhenzhong Lan, Mingda Chen, Sebastian Goodman, Kevin Gimpel, Piyush Sharma, and Radu Soricut. 2019. ALBERT: A lite bert for self-supervised learning of language representations. In *ICLR*.

Y. LeCun, B. Boser, J. S. Denker, D. Henderson, R. E. Howard, W. Hubbard, and L. D. Jackel. 1989. Back-propagation applied to handwritten zip code recognition. *Neural Computation*.

Hector J Levesque, Ernest Davis, and Leora Morgenstern. 2012. The winograd schema challenge. In *Proceedings of the Thirteenth International Conference on the Principles of Knowledge Representation and Reasoning*.

Weijie Liu, Peng Zhou, Zhe Zhao, Zhiruo Wang, Haotang Deng, and Qi Ju. 2020. Fastbert: a self-distilling bert with adaptive inference time. *arXiv:2004.02178*.

Yinhan Liu, Myle Ott, Naman Goyal, Jingfei Du, Mandar Joshi, Danqi Chen, Omer Levy, Mike Lewis, Luke Zettlemoyer, and Veselin Stoyanov. 2019. RoBERTa: A robustly optimized bert pretraining approach. *arXiv:1907.11692*.

Ilya Loshchilov and Frank Hutter. 2019. Decoupled weight decay regularization. In *ICLR*.

Lovely Mobile News. 2017. Mobile has largely displaced other channels for email.

NVIDIA. 2020a. APEX - A PyTorch Extension: Tools for easy mixed precision and distributed training in pytorch. https://github.com/NVIDIA/apex.

NVIDIA. 2020b. Deep learning examples for tensor cores. https://github.com/NVIDIA/DeepLearningExamples.

Adam Paszke, Sam Gross, Francisco Massa, Adam Lerer, James Bradbury, Gregory Chanan, Trevor Killeen, Zeming Lin, Natalia Gimelshein, Luca Antiga, Alban Desmaison, Andreas Köpf, Edward Yang, Zach DeVito, Martin Raison, Alykhan Tejani, Sasank Chilamkurthy, Benoit Steiner, Lu Fang, Junjie Bai, and Soumith Chintala. 2019. PyTorch: An imperative style, high-performance deep learning library. In *NeurIPS*.

Jason Phang, Thibault Févry, and Samuel R. Bowman. 2018. Sentence encoders on stilts: Supplementary training on intermediate labeled-data tasks. *arXiv:1811.01088*.

Quora. 2017. Quora question pairs.

Alec Radford, Karthik Narasimhan, Tim Salimans, and Ilya Sutskever. 2018. Improving language understanding by generative pretraining. https://s3-us-west-2.amazonaws.com/openai-assets/research-covers/language-unsupervised/language_understanding_paper.pdf.

Alec Radford, Jeff Wu, Rewon Child, David Luan, Dario Amodei, and Ilya Sutskever. 2019. Language models are unsupervised multitask learners. https://d4mucfpksywv.cloudfront.net/better-language-models/language_models_are_unsupervised_multitask_learners.pdf.

Olaf Ronneberger, Philipp Fischer, and Thomas Brox. 2015. U-net: Convolutional networks for biomedical image segmentation. In *International Conference on Medical image computing and computer-assisted intervention*.

Olga Russakovsky, Jia Deng, Hao Su, Jonathan Krause, Sanjeev Satheesh, Sean Ma, Zhiheng Huang, Andrej Karpathy, Aditya Khosla, Michael Bernstein, Alexander C. Berg, and Li Fei-Fei. 2015. ImageNet Large Scale Visual Recognition Challenge. *International Journal of Computer Vision*.

Victor Sanh, Lysandre Debut, Julien Chaumond, and Thomas Wolf. 2019. DistilBERT, a distilled version of BERT: smaller, faster, cheaper and lighter. *arXiv:1910.01108*.

Victor Sanh, Thomas Wolf, and Alexander M. Rush. 2020. Movement pruning: Adaptive sparsity by fine-tuning. *arXiv:2005.07683*.

David Sayce. 2019. The number of tweets per day in 2019. https://www.dsayce.com/social-media/tweets-day/.

Jeff Schultz. 2019. How much data is created on the internet each day?

Mike Schuster and Kaisuke Nakajima. 2012. Japanese and korean voice search. In *International Conference on Acoustics, Speech and Signal Processing (ICASSP)*.

Roy Schwartz, Gabriel Stanovsky, Swabha Swayamdipta, Jesse Dodge, and Noah A. Smith. 2020. The right tool for the job: Matching model and instance complexities. *arXiv:2004.07453*.

Albert Shaw, Daniel Hunter, Forrest Iandola, and Sammy Sidhu. 2019. SqueezeNAS: Fast neural architecture search for faster semantic segmentation. In *ICCV Neural Architects Workshop*.

Sheng Shen, Zhen Dong, Jiayu Ye, Linjian Ma, Zhewei Yao, Amir Gholami, Michael W. Mahoney, and Kurt Keutzer. 2020. Q-BERT: Hessian based ultra low precision quantization of bert. In *AAAI*.

David R. So, Chen Liang, and Quoc V. Le. 2019. The evolved transformer. In *ICLR*.

Richard Socher, Alex Perelygin, Jean Wu, Jason Chuang, Christopher D. Manning, Andrew Ng, and Christopher Potts. 2013. Recursive deep models for semantic compositionality over a sentiment treebank. In *EMNLP*.

Siqi Sun, Yu Cheng, Zhe Gan, and Jingjing Liu. 2019a. Patient knowledge distillation for BERT model compression. In *Conference on Empirical Methods in Natural Language Processing and the International Joint Conference on Natural Language Processing (EMNLP-IJCNLP)*.

Zhiqing Sun, Hongkun Yu, Xiaodan Song, Renjie Liu, Yiming Yang, and Denny Zhou. 2019b. MobileBERT: Task-agnostic compression of BERT by progressive knowledge transfer. *OpenReview submission*.

Zhiqing Sun, Hongkun Yu, Xiaodan Song, Renjie Liu, Yiming Yang, and Denny Zhou. 2020. MobileBERT: a compact task-agnostic BERT for resource-limited devices. In *Annual Meeting of the Association for Computational Linguistics (ACL)*. ArXiv:2004.02984.

Mingxing Tan and Quoc V. Le. 2019. EfficientNet: Rethinking model scaling for convolutional neural networks. In *International Conference on Machine Learning (ICML)*.

Yi Tay, Mostafa Dehghani, Dara Bahri, and Donald Metzler. 2020. Efficient transformers: A survey. *arXiv:2009.06732*.

Templatify. 2017. How many emails are sent every day? top email statistics for business.

Iulia Turc, Ming-Wei Chang, Kenton Lee, and Kristina Toutanova. 2019. Well-read students learn better: On the importance of pre-training compact models. *arXiv:1908.08962*.

Ashish Vaswani, Noam Shazeer, Niki Parmar, Jakob Uszkoreit, Llion Jones, Aidan N. Gomez, Lukasz Kaiser, and Illia Polosukhin. 2017. Attention is all you need. In *Conference on Neural Information Processing Systems (NeurIPS)*.

Alex Wang, Amanpreet Singh, Julian Michael, Felix Hill, Omer Levy, and Samuel R. Bowman. 2018. GLUE: A multi-task benchmark and analysis platform for natural language understanding. *arXiv:1804.07461*.

Chenguang Wang, Zihao Ye, Aston Zhang, Zheng Zhang, and Alexander J. Smola. 2020a. Transformer on a diet. *arXiv:2002.06170*.

Sinong Wang, Belinda Z. Li, Madian Khabsa, Han Fang, and Hao Ma. 2020b. Linformer: Self-attention with linear complexity. *arXiv:2006.04768*.

Alex Warstadt, Amanpreet Singh, and Samuel R. Bowman. 2019. Neural network acceptability judgments. In *Transactions of the Association for Computational Linguistics*.

Adina Williams, Nikita Nangia, and Samuel R. Bowman. 2018. A broad-coverage challenge corpus for sentence understanding through inference. In *Conference of the North American Chapter of the Association for Computational Linguistics (NAACL)*.

Thomas Wolf, Lysandre Debut, Victor Sanh, Julien Chaumond, Clement Delangue, Anthony Moi, Pierric Cistac, Tim Rault, Rémi Louf, Morgan Funtowicz, and Jamie Brew. 2019. Huggingface's transformers: State-of-the-art natural language processing. *arXiv:1910.03771*.

Bichen Wu, Xiaoliang Dai, Peizhao Zhang, Yanghan Wang, Fei Sun, Yiming Wu, Yuandong Tian, Peter Vajda, Yangqing Jia, and Kurt Keutzer. 2019a. FBNet: Hardware-aware efficient convnet design via differentiable neural architecture search. In *IEEE Conference on Computer Vision and Pattern Recognition (CVPR)*.

Felix Wu, Angela Fan, Alexei Baevski, Yann N. Dauphin, and Michael Auli. 2019b. Pay less attention with lightweight and dynamic convolutions. In *ICLR*.

Yonghui Wu, Mike Schuster, Zhifeng Chen, Quoc V. Le, Mohammad Norouzi, Wolfgang Macherey, Maxim Krikun, Yuan Cao, Qin Gao, Klaus Macherey, Jeff Klingner, Apurva Shah, Melvin Johnson, Xiaobing Liu, Łukasz Kaiser, Stephan Gouws, Yoshikiyo Kato, Taku Kudo, Hideto Kazawa, Keith Stevens, George Kurian, Nishant Patil, Wei Wang, Cliff Young, Jason Smith, Jason Riesa, Alex Rudnick, Oriol Vinyals, Greg Corrado, Macduff Hughes, and Jeffrey Dean. 2016. Google's neural machine translation system: Bridging the gap between human and machine translation. *arXiv:1609.08144*.

Zhanghao Wu, Zhijian Liu, Ji Lin, Yujun Lin, and Song Han. 2020. Lite transformer with long short term attention. In *ICLR*.

Saining Xie, Ross Girshick, Piotr Dollár, Zhuowen Tu, and Kaiming He. 2017. Aggregated residual transformations for deep neural networks. In *IEEE Conference on Computer Vision and Pattern Recognition (CVPR)*.

Ji Xin, Raphael Tang, Jaejun Lee, Yaoliang Yu, and Jimmy Lin. 2020. Deebert: Dynamic early exiting for accelerating bert inference. In *ACL*.

Canwen Xu, Wangchunshu Zhou, Tao Ge, Furu Wei, and Ming Zhou. 2020. Bert-of-theseus: Compressing bert by progressive module replacing. *arXiv:2002.02925*.

Yang You, Jing Li, Sashank Reddi, Jonathan Hseu, Sanjiv Kumar, Srinadh Bhojanapalli, Xiaodan Song, James Demmel, Kurt Keutzer, and Cho-Jui Hsieh. 2020. Large batch optimization for deep learning: Training bert in 76 minutes. In *ICLR*.

Ofir Zafrir, Guy Boudoukh, Peter Izsak, and Moshe Wasserblat. 2019. Q8BERT: Quantized 8bit bert. *arXiv:1910.06188*.

Xiangyu Zhang, Xinyu Zhou, Mengxiao Lin, and Jian Sun. 2018. ShuffleNet: An extremely efficient convolutional neural network for mobile devices. In *CVPR*.

Yukun Zhu, Ryan Kiros, Rich Zemel, Ruslan Salakhutdinov, Raquel Urtasun, Antonio Torralba, and Sanja Fidler. 2015. Aligning books and movies: Towards story-like visual explanations by watching movies and reading books. In *IEEE International Conference on Computer Vision (ICCV)*.

Analysis of Resource-efficient Predictive Models for Natural Language Processing

Raj Ratn Pranesh
Birla Institute of Technology,
Mesra
raj.ratn18@gmail.com

Ambesh Shekhar
Birla Institute of Technology,
Mesra
ambesh.sinha@gmail.com

Abstract

In this paper, we presented an analyses of the resource efficient predictive models, namely Bonsai, Binary Neighbor Compression(BNC), ProtoNN, Random Forest, Naive Bayes and Support vector machine(SVM), in the machine learning field for resource constraint devices. These models try to minimize resource requirements like RAM and storage without hurting the accuracy much. We utilized these models on multiple benchmark natural language processing tasks, which were sentimental analysis, spam message detection, emotion analysis and fake news classification. The experiment results shows that the tree-based algorithm, Bonsai, surpassed the rest of the machine learning algorithms by achieve higher accuracy scores while having significantly lower memory usage.

1 Introduction

In last few years, large pretrained language models have gained a lot of popularity. These models were able to achieve state-of-the-art performance on various natural language processing tasks. But due to the higher resource requirement such as time and computation power, researchers have shifted their focus on developing more efficient and sustainable language models.

Devices like Arduino board, ATmega328 etc. which are essential in IoT infrastructures like health care, smart grids, wearables, etc, have very limited computational resources. Therefore, mostly these devices transfer data to cloud to extract some information and are dependent on them. These devices need models that can run without depending on cloud computing since cloud connectivity is not present everywhere, in a network data security can be compromised, it takes time to compute and transfer data which might not be good for real time analysis. So we need models that can run locally and need limited resources as well as do not hamper the accuracy of the task.

There have been many advances in this field like reducing the prediction cost of KNN with prototype based methods like ProtoNN (Gupta et al., 2017) and BNC(Binary Neighbour Compression) (Zhong et al., 2017) where you learn prototypes to reduce model size, SNC(Stochastic Neighbour compression) (Kusner et al., 2014) where you learn very small synthetic dataset to perform KNN, Tree based methods like bonsai tree where under constraints model learns non-linear decision rules at each node (Kumar et al., 2017), pruning the random forests based on resource constraints (Pal, 2005).

In this paper, we present an analysis of various resource efficient machine learning algorithm for performing NLP tasks, such as, sentiment and emotion classification, fake news and spam message detection. We used six models, namely, Bonsai, Binary Neighbor Compression(BNC), ProtoNN, Random Forest, Naive Bayes and Support vector machine(SVM) and reported their performance accuracy and memory usage for each task. We observed that the Bonsai model performed the best by achieving significantly higher accuracy scores than other models at the cost of minimum memory usage. We believe that our generated insights would be very useful in designing and developing IoT for NLP-based application purposes.

2 Methods

In this section, we discussed about the various models used in our analysis.

2.1 Naive Bayes

Naive Bayes (Rish et al., 2001) is based on supervised machine learning methods that uses the primitive or naive approach by applying Bayes' theorem between pair of features present in a text data point.

Proceedings of SustaiNLP: Workshop on Simple and Efficient Natural Language Processing, pages 136–140
Online, November 20, 2020. ©2020 Association for Computational Linguistics

Naive Bayes states the conditional probabilty between pair of words in a given sentence. Based on naive conditional independence assumption for x feature with y labels given, therefore for all i, this relationship is simplified to

$$P(y|x_1, ..., x_n) = \frac{P(y)\Pi_{i=1}^n P(x_i|y)}{P(x_1, ..., x_n)}$$

Since $P(y|x_1, ..., x_n)$ is the given input to the model, for classification process the predicted is

$$\hat{y} = \underset{y}{argmax} P(y)\Pi_{i=1}^n P(x_i|y)$$

Therefore for each text data point we have in our dataset, this machine learning algorithm calculates the conditional propbabilty for pairs of words and therefore based on the domain specific training it quantifies each data point to its respective classes.

2.2 Support Vector Machine

Support Vector Machine (Suykens and Vandewalle, 1999) is also a supervised learning methods majorly used in classification and outliers detection. Due to their performance with high dimensional space or higher features handling irrespective of the dimension of samples and available kernels functions for specified functions makes this model best in handling text data. If we pass a sparse matrix generated using TF-IDF function to a SVM classifier, it maximizes the decision boundary by minimizing $|||w||$ to find an optimal hyperplane for all the classification tasks:

$$min f : \frac{1}{2}||w||^2$$

$$\hat{y}^{(i)} = (w^t x^{(i)} + b) \geq 1, i = 1, ..., m \quad (1)$$

where w is the weight vector, for all i, x is input features matrix with b as the bias, with a resulting $\hat{y}$.

2.3 ProtoNN

ProtoNN (Gupta et al., 2017) is kNN based model that uses compressed model and prototypes for prediction. Prototypes are learned from the the data along with the estimation of projection matrix jointly, due to which it avoids pruning after the model is learnt to fit the model in desired memory. Prototypes are points that represent the entire data. The projection matrix is sparse matrix estimated by performing SGD and iterative hard-thresholding. Since number of prototypes are far

less than number of inputs and number of features are less the model is comparatively small. ProtoNN gives nearly the same accuracy as most popular models that take a huge amount of RAM with very small amount of memory used , which makes it fit for our use in resource constrained IoT devices. ProtoNN tries to optimize the following loss function:

$$\mathcal{L}_i(Z, B, W) = \mathcal{L}(y_i, \sum_{j=1}^m z_j K_\gamma(b_j, W x_i)) \quad (2)$$

This is for each data point i. B is prototypes and Z is its corresponding score vector. W is low dimensional projection matrix. K_γ is RBF similarity kernel function used in the paper, any other kernel function can be used as well. The optimizing problem they obtained is non-convex but alternating optimization works in this case. Each of the parameters (B, Z, W) are learnt alternately using the algorithm provided with sparsity constraints.

2.4 BNC

Another simple model which is similar to the one described above is Binary Neighbor Compression (BNC) (Zhong et al., 2017). Here a KMeans clustering is performed on each class and number of clusters from each class are given by $k_y = \beta N_y$ where $\beta \in (0, 1)$ and N_y is the number of points that belong to class y. In this way we create a matrix of prototypes C of size m $\times$ d, where m is the total number of prototypes, and d is the dimension of the data. Then we initialize a matrix W of size d $\times$ r randomly, where r is the new dimension of data. Using this we convert the Prototypes to lower dimension representation and also binary form as: $B = sign(CW)$. Hence B will be of the size m $\times$ r. After this we learn B and W alternately, using the loss function below which is similar to multi-class hinge loss:

$$\underset{W,B}{min} \frac{1}{N} \sum_{i=1}^N [\alpha - \underset{j:z_j=y_i}{max} (tanh(\gamma W^T x_i)^T b_j)$$

$$+ \underset{j:z_j \neq y_i}{max} (tanh(\gamma W^T x_i)^T b_j)] + \lambda \sum_{k \in [r]} (||w_k||^2 - 1)^2$$

where tanh is used instead of sign function, as sign is not differentiable. So as $\gamma \rightarrow \infty, tanh(\gamma W^T x_i) \rightarrow (W^T x_i)$. Here $[x]_+ = max\{0, x\}$ and α is a hyper-parameter. Also a regularization is applied on W. Prediction is made by computing the similarity of projected test point

Dataset	#Train	#Test	#Features	#Classes
SMS-Span Collection	4218	1032	1226	2
Fake and Real News	1600	400	756	2
Sentiment-140	3200	800	1362	3
The Emotion in Text	3116	780	1542	14

Table 1: Dataset Statistics

with all the prototypes, and the label of the prototype which has highest similarity is assigned to the test point.

2.5 Bonsai Tree

Based on the paper (Kumar et al., 2017) unlike normal trees which learn axis aligned decision rules bonsai learns a non linear decision rule at every node. It first projects the data into low dimensional space(can be done in streamlined fashion), then projected features are traversed through the tree with each node scoring the output in their own way and sum of all scores is used as net score.

Scoring Function Bonsai learns a single, shallow sparse tree whose predictions for a point x is given by :

$$y(x) = \sum_k I_k(x) W_k^T Z x \odot tanh(\sigma V_k^T Z x) \quad (3)$$

where $\odot$ denotes the element wise Hadamard product, σ is a hyper-parameter, Z is a sparse projection matrix and $I_k(x)$ is an indicator function taking the value 1 if node k lies along the path traversed by x and 0 otherwise and W_k and V_k are sparse scoring vectors learnt at node k.

Branching Function Bonsai tree computes I_k by learning a sparse vector θ_k at each internal node such that the sign of $\theta_k^T Z x$ determines whether data object x should be branched to the left or right child. Optimizing the I_k is hard problem so it is relaxed as follows:

$$I_{k>1} = 0.5 \times I_j(x)(1 + (-1)^{k-2j} tanh(\sigma_I \theta_j^T Z x))$$
$$(4)$$

where, j^{th} node is parent of kth node.

Optimization Problem The optimization problem can be formulated with any empirical loss function (e.g categorical cross entropy loss), as follows :

$$min_{\Theta}\{\mathcal{L}(y, x, \Theta) + \frac{\lambda_\theta}{2} Tr(\theta^T \theta)$$
$$+ \frac{\lambda_W}{2} Tr(W^T W) + \frac{\lambda_V}{2} Tr(V^T V)$$
$$+ \frac{\lambda_Z}{2} Tr(Z^T Z)\}$$

All the parameters are simultaneously optimized in alternating fashion. This model now can be trained using gradient descent approach, newton method etc. the original implementation used gradient descent with IHT(iterative hard thresholding) constraints over the parameters.

2.6 Random Forest

Random Forest is designed as an ensemble learning based classifier that combines different decision tree classifiers to perform class prediction (Injadat et al., 2016). The model is consists of multiple decision trees and the training of each of the decision tree is done using random subsets of features. In the Random Forest model, the final prediction is given through the majority voting of generated predictions from all the trees in the forest. As described by the author in (Malik et al., 2011), the Random Forest algorithm can be formulated as following:

(i) T number of trees are selected

(ii) For dividing each node m number of variables are selected, m<<M, where M represents total number of input variables.

(iii) Tree is populated by using the following methods:

- Given N training samples, a sample of size N is created while growing and replacing a tree from the produced sample.

- To obtain finest split, randomly choose m variable from m while populating each node in the tree.

- The tree is left for growing without any hindrance.

(iv) For the classification of node X, majority voting is utilized to predict the class label.

3 Dataset

We have used four textual datasets(see table 1) for different natural language processing classification task, namely, Sentiment140 dataset (Go et al., 2009) for sentiment analysis, the SMS Spam Collection dataset[1] for spam classification, the The Emotion in Text (Mohammad and Bravo-Marquez, 2017) dataset for emotion analysis and the Fake and Real news[2] dataset for fake new classification task. These datasets hold clean textual data with

---

[1] https://archive.ics.uci.edu/ml/datasets
[2] https://www.kaggle.com/c/nlp-getting-started

Datasets / Models	Sentiment-140	SMS-Span-Collection	Fake-News	The Emotion in Text
Naive-Bayes	59.66(2kB)	86.85(2kB)	78.16(2kB)	53.88(3kB)
SVM-Linear	59.83(137kB)	88.19(15.89kB)	89.66(18.37kB)	56.15(51.6kB)
SVM-poly	60.63(131kB)	88.64(64kB)	81.00(121kB)	55.52(144kB)
SVM-rbf	60.46(115kB)	88.64(18kB)	89.33(43.27kB)	57.22(125kB)
Random Forest	56.08(34kB)	88.19(1.61MB)	89.50(549kB)	60.74(812kB)
BNC	60.71(5.8kB)	90.71(3.9kB)	92.85(3.8kB)	62.41(5.0kB)
ProtoNN	62.45(3.5kB)	90.87(3.5kB)	94.17(3.5kB)	**68.97(3.5kB)**
Bonsai	**64.38(2kB)**	**94.91(2kB)**	**97.29(2kB)**	67.20(2kB)

Table 2: Models performance on datasets. For each model, accuracy(%) along with Memory usage is provided

their corresponding labels for supervised learning tasks.

Sentiment140: This contains 1.6M tweets text data extracted using twitter API. Each tweet has been annotated with labels neutral, negative, and positive to express their sentiment.

SMS Spam Collection: A collection of 5,574 English non-encoded messages annotated spam or ham(legitimate). The dataset contains 425 SMS manually extracted from the Grumbletext website, and a subset 3375 SMS randomly chosen legitimate messages of the NUS SMS corpus.

The Emotion in Text: It is a collection of 40,000 manually labelled tweets dataset for emotion detection and classification tasks. The dataset has 14 emotion categories.

Fake and Real news dataset: This contains 38,729 English news text data annotated with fake and true labels denoting whether they are fake or not. development in NLP tasks.

4 Experiment

We experimented with six machine learning models on four benchmark natural language dataset for different tasks. We used Tf-Idf as our text-features conversions, where we randomly selected the number of features to be considered while conversion. For each of the dataset, as seen in the figure 1, we used a specific number of features. We fixed the number of features so that we can evenly compare and evaluate the machine learning models. For SMS-Spam dataset, we used a subset consisting of 5120 instances of dataset with 1226 features. For Fake-News data, we used 2000 instances of dataset with 756 features. For Sentiment-140 dataset, we used 4000 instances of the total dataset with 1362 features. For The Emotion in Text dataset, we used 3896 instances of dataset with 1542 feature count.

Each dataset was splitted into train and validation dataset with a ration of 80/20. The hyperparameter setting of all the models was done based on their best performance on the validation dataset. We used ADAM (Kingma and Ba, 2014) and Gradient Descent optimization for the models.

5 Result and Discussion

We have reported the model performance in the table 2. We can clearly see that the Bonsai model was able to outperform other model in majority of the tasks which makes it suitable for IoT based applications. Bonsai achieved an accuracy of 97.29, 64.38 and 68.97 over the classification task in fake-news, sentiment-140 and SMS-spam dataset with 2kB of memory usage. The ProtoNN model was able to beat Bonsai in the The Emotion in Text dataset task by gaining an improvement of 2.56% on the Bonsai model. Being said that, even with lesser accuracy, the Bonsai model performed the classification task in just 2kB memory while ProtoNN took 4.2kB. On an average, these two light weight models, ProtoNN and Bonsai Tree, outperformed other models on average by 4.83% and 7.06% respectively. Out of Naive-Bayes, SVM and Random Forest, with significantly higher memory consumption, Random Forest surpassed other models with better performance. On the other hand, Naive-Bayes's accuracy to memory conception ratio was higher than SVM and Random Forest. This suggest that the Naive-Bayes is capable of getting accuracy with lesser memory consumption.

6 Conclusion

In this paper, we presented a comparative analysis of various machine learning model for performing NLP tasks. We investigated the models performance based on accuracy achieved and memory required for performing a NLP task. We found that Bonsai model was able to surpass other models with higher accuracy and lesser memory consumption. We also conclude that these models can be trained on a laptop and can be transferred to IoT devices satisfying resource requirements of model. Through our work, we aim at contributing towards the goal of sustainable NLP by developing more resource efficient NLP methods.

References

Alec Go, Richa Bhayani, and Lei Huang. 2009. Twitter sentiment classification using distant supervision. *CS224N project report, Stanford*, 1(12):2009.

Chirag Gupta, Arun Sai Suggala, Ankit Goyal, Harsha Vardhan Simhadri, Bhargavi Paranjape, Ashish Kumar, Saurabh Goyal, Raghavendra Udupa, Manik Varma, and Prateek Jain. 2017. Protonn: Compressed and accurate knn for resource-scarce devices. In *International Conference on Machine Learning*, pages 1331–1340.

MohammadNoor Injadat, Fadi Salo, and Ali Bou Nassif. 2016. Data mining techniques in social media: A survey. *Neurocomputing*, 214:654–670.

Diederik P Kingma and Jimmy Ba. 2014. Adam: A method for stochastic optimization. *arXiv preprint arXiv:1412.6980*.

Ashish Kumar, Saurabh Goyal, and Manik Varma. 2017. Resource-efficient machine learning in 2 kb ram for the internet of things. In *International Conference on Machine Learning*, pages 1935–1944.

Matt Kusner, Stephen Tyree, Kilian Weinberger, and Kunal Agrawal. 2014. Stochastic neighbor compression. In *International Conference on Machine Learning*, pages 622–630.

Arif Jamal Malik, Waseem Shahzad, and Farrukh Aslam Khan. 2011. Binary pso and random forests algorithm for probe attacks detection in a network. In *2011 IEEE Congress of Evolutionary Computation (CEC)*, pages 662–668. IEEE.

Saif M Mohammad and Felipe Bravo-Marquez. 2017. Emotion intensities in tweets. *arXiv preprint arXiv:1708.03696*.

Mahesh Pal. 2005. Random forest classifier for remote sensing classification. *International journal of remote sensing*, 26(1):217–222.

Irina Rish et al. 2001. An empirical study of the naive bayes classifier. In *IJCAI 2001 workshop on empirical methods in artificial intelligence*, volume 3, pages 41–46.

Johan AK Suykens and Joos Vandewalle. 1999. Least squares support vector machine classifiers. *Neural processing letters*, 9(3):293–300.

Kai Zhong, Ruiqi Guo, Sanjiv Kumar, Bowei Yan, David Simcha, and Inderjit Dhillon. 2017. Fast classification with binary prototypes. In *Artificial Intelligence and Statistics*, pages 1255–1263.

Towards Accurate and Reliable Energy Measurement of NLP Models

Qingqing Cao, Aruna Balasubramanian, Niranjan Balasubramanian
Department of Computer Science
Stony Brook University
Stony Brook, NY 11794, USA
{qicao,arunab,niranjan}@cs.stonybrook.edu

Abstract

Accurate and reliable measurement of energy consumption is critical for making well-informed design choices when choosing and training large scale NLP models. In this work, we show that existing software-based energy measurements are not accurate because they do not take into account hardware differences and how resource utilization affects energy consumption. We conduct energy measurement experiments with four different models for a question answering task. We quantify the error of existing software based energy measurements by using a hardware power meter that provides highly accurate energy measurements. Our key takeaway is the need for a more accurate energy estimation model that takes into account hardware variabilities and the non-linear relationship between resource utilization and energy consumption. We release the code and data at https://github.com/csarron/sustainlp2020-energy.

1 Introduction

State-of-the-art NLP models of today (Devlin et al., 2019; Liu et al., 2019; Raffel et al., 2020) consume large amounts of energy. Such high-levels of energy consumption adds to the worsening global warming and can cause significant social health and safety impacts (Glo; Rolnick et al., 2019). Recent studies have raised awareness of the carbon footprints and potential energy impacts and suggest ways to estimate and reduce consumption (Strubell et al., 2019; Schwartz et al., 2019).

The success of these and future efforts depend on our ability to accurately and reliably estimate the energy consumption of NLP models. A common technique to predict the energy consumption is to measure the utilization of hardware components involved in the computation—the CPU, the GPU, and memory. Each of these components is associated with a single power counter value that is provided by the underlying hardware; this power counter represents the power drawn of a given component. The total energy consumption is computed as the sum of the (utilization × power counter) of the CPU, GPU, and memory, which is then adjusted by a compensation constant (Henderson et al., 2020; Strubell et al., 2019). We call this technique software-based power measurement.

However there are two potential sources of inaccuracies in the software-based power measurement techniques. First, the software tools are known to be inaccurate because they only consider the energy consumed by three specific hardware components, which may not reflect the energy consumption of the entire system. Second, accurately mapping hardware utilization to the energy consumption is a difficult problem. The mapping depends on the underlying hardware make and type, energy is not always linearly related to the utilization (Pathak et al., 2011, 2012), and energy consumption often continues even after the NLP model has finished running (Burtscher et al., 2014).

In this work, we use a hardware power meter to measure ground truth energy consumption, which is more accurate. Our goal is to quantify how far software-based measurements are from the hardware energy measurements. We compare the energy estimates obtained using prior software based models for four Transformer-based NLP models fine-tuned for a question answering (QA) task.

In the experiments, we find that (1) software energy estimates can differ from the hardware power measurements by 20% on average. Further, the standard deviations are 2× larger than hardware power meters. (2) Power-models need to take into account the underlying hardware, make, and configuration. Hardware-agnostic energy measurements results in large errors, for example, when applied to machines with different configurations (e.g. dif-

Proceedings of SustaiNLP: Workshop on Simple and Efficient Natural Language Processing, pages 141–148
Online, November 20, 2020. ©2020 Association for Computational Linguistics

ferent GPU models, # of GPUs used).

Finally, we show the importance of accurate power-models to make the right accuracy/energy trade-off. Ground-truth energy measurements using a hardware meter show that RoBERTa-base incurs 13% more energy on average. But RoBERTa-base can answer 2.2% more questions correctly over BERT-base. However, existing power-models estimate the additional power consumption of RoBERTa-base to be 25%. Such inaccuracies can lead to wrong conclusions and poor optimizations for model practitioners. The results in this paper suggests that we need better estimation models that are calibrated to account for hardware variabilities and the non-linear relationship between power consumption and resource utilization.

2   Experiments Methodology

In this section, we describe our setup and methodology for energy measurements. We focus on energy consumption of inference for a QA task using a hardware power meter. For comparison purposes, we track software reported energy values as well.

2.1   Setup

Devices: We use 2 GPU-equipped desktop PCs as the target hardware for running our models. See Table 1 for details.

We fine-tune and perform inference in all 4 models on the SQuAD v1.1 question answering dataset (Rajpurkar et al., 2016) using PyTorch (Paszke et al., 2019) v1.6 through the HuggingFace Transformers (Wolf et al., 2020) library. The four models we study are — BERT-base (Devlin et al., 2019), RoBERTa-base (Liu et al., 2019), MobileBERT (Sun et al., 2020), and DistillBERT (Sanh et al., 2020).

Specification	PC1	PC2
CPU	Intel i9-7900X	Intel i7-6800K
Memory	32 GiB	32 GiB
GPU	2× GTX 1080 Ti	2× GTX 1070
GPU Memory	11.2 GiB per GPU	8 GiB per GPU
Storage	1 TiB SSD	1 TiB SSD

Table 1: Target hardware specifications.

Hardware-based Measurements We use the WattsUP power meter (Wat)[1] to measure *all* of

energy consumed by a PC. The WattsUpMeter is used to power the computer, and the power meter records the passthrough current and voltage values every 1 second. This allows us to accurately measure the power draw at a 1 second granularity. Figure 1 shows the energy measurement setup. We obtain current, voltage, and timestamp values from the power meter's built-in USB port. The energy (e) consumed during a time period is then calculated using the sampled current (I_t) and voltage (V_t) values in that period: $e = \sum_t V_t I_t$.

Software-based Measurements: For comparisons, we use the software-based energy measurements provided by the *experiment-impact-tracker* framework (Henderson et al., 2020) which estimates energy as a function of the GPU, CPU, and memory utilization. More details about the model can be found in §3.2.

2.2   Methodology

For each NLP model, we obtain the energy measurements over a random sample of 1000 questions from the SQuAD 1.1 dev split. We repeat these measurements over 10 runs and report the average and standard deviation of energy values. We use 1 GPU to run all experiments, but show the energy measurements accuracy for multiple GPUs in §3.2. Since it is common to batch process inputs on GPUs, we benchmark batch size 1 and batch sizes from 2 to 16 with step 2 [2].

To guarantee the consistency and reliability of the hardware energy measurement, we cool down the PCs after each experiment finishes to avoid potential overheating issue that can cause subsequent energy distortions. We measure the standby power consumption (when the CPU load is $< 0.1\%$) and ensure before running the experiments that the PC does not draw more than the standby power. Further, no other application is running during our experiments.

We record the start and end timestamp of the benchmarked program, and extract the energy values by comparing and aligning the timestamps from the power meter logs. All the energy and latency numbers are end to end, except in §3.4 where we extract the numbers for the prediction part only. In §3.4, we study the latency speedups for model prediction, whereas the latency numbers for data

---

[1]The device is available on Amazon `https://amzn.to/2EoP0tU`

[2]We tried larger batch sizes, but found the energy and latency values to be similar for batch sizes between 18 and 32, therefore, we omit numbers with batch size larger than 16 for brevity.

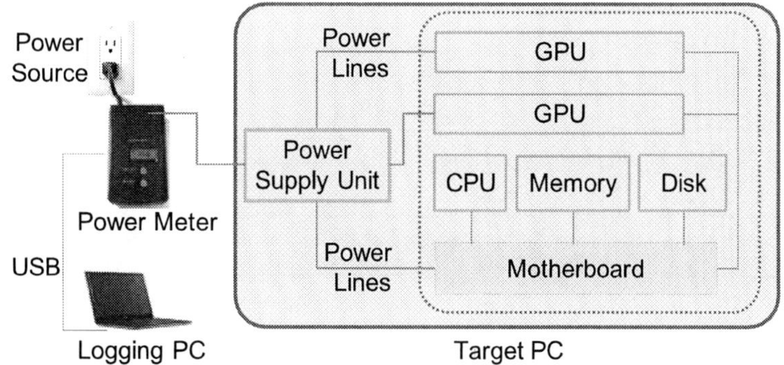

Figure 1: Illustration of the energy measurement setup using a hardware power meter.

loading, startup and cleanup are often comparable to model inference given that we only run for
1000 questions. In the real case, the startup and
cleanup costs will be amortized if running millions
or billions of the model inference.

3 Energy Results of NLP Models

In this section, we discuss the energy results of the
four Transformer-based NLP models on a question
answering task.

3.1 Existing Software-Based Energy Measurements Are Not Accurate

We use the energy values recorded by the hardware
power meter as ground truth, and report both error
percentage (|true energy - software-based energy
measurement|/true energy) and standard deviations
of the software energy measurements for all four
NLP models.

Figure 2a shows that the error of the software
measurements ranges from 2% to as much as 47%.
In more than 90% of the runs the error is at least
20%, and for a fifth of the runs the error is at least
30%. On average the error percentages are substantial for all models — error on BERT-base is
26%, RoBERTa-base is 47%, MobileBERT is 30%,
and DistilBERT is 36%. While there are some
settings where software measurements is accurate
(for example, the error is only 2.7% for RoBERTa-
base model with batch size 2), it is not accurate in
general.

Figure 2b shows that the standard deviations for
software energy measurements are twice as large
as that of hardware-based energy measurements.
Large deviations for different runs of a model in the
same setting makes the measurements unreliable.

The main takeaway here that existing software-

based energy measurements can be substantially
inaccurate. However, they are more convenient to
estimate energy consumption compared to using
hardware power meters. Going forward, we need
to design more accurate software measurements
that come close to the ground truth.

3.2 Energy Measurements Using Hardware Agnostic Parameters Is Suboptimal

Why are existing software-based energy measurements (Strubell et al., 2019; Henderson et al.,
2020) not accurate? The software-based energy
model computes energy by aggregating resource usage as follows: $e_{total} = PUE \sum_p (p_{dram} e_{dram} +
p_{cpu} e_{cpu} + p_{gpu} e_{gpu})$, where $p_{resource}$ [3] are the per-
centages of each system resource used by the at-
tributable processes relative to the total in-use resources and $e_{resource}$ is the energy usage of that
resource. The constant for power usage effectiveness (PUE) compensates for extra energy used to
cool or heat data centers.

There are two potential problems in this linear
energy model. First, different hardware devices
(e.g. different CPU or GPU models, different number of GPUs connected, etc.) can have different
cooling or heating effects causing large variations
in the amounts of energy consumed. However, the
energy model uses the PUE constant as a hardware agnostic parameter, which does not account
for such differences in device specifications. This
makes the final energy measurements less reliable.
Second, assigning energy credits based on process
resources is not always reliable. CPUs and GPUs
often have power lags, power distortions, and tail
energy especially during starting new processes or
finishing existing processes (Burtscher et al., 2014;

---

[3] $resources$ can be $dram, cpu, gpu$

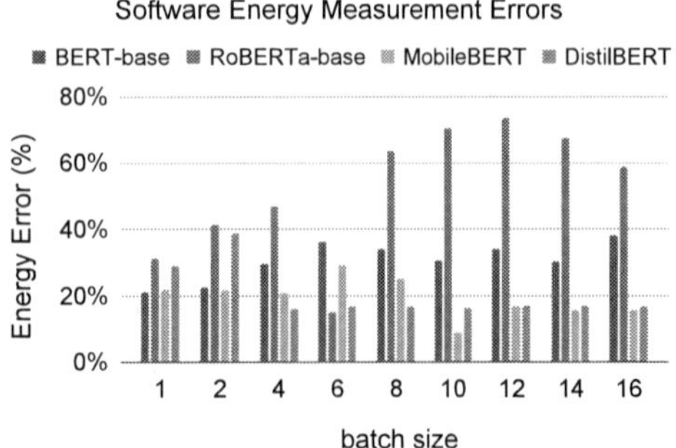

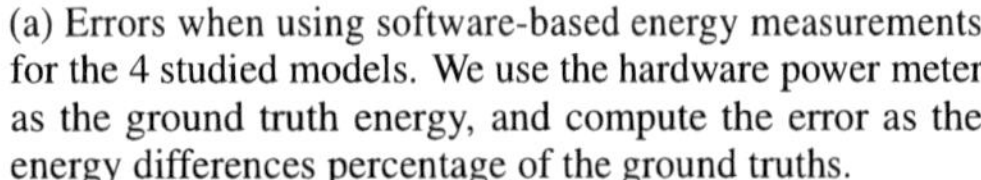

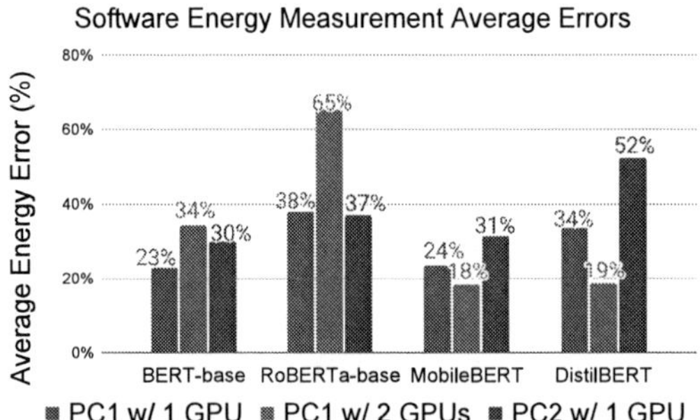

(a) Errors when using software-based energy measurements for the 4 studied models. We use the hardware power meter as the ground truth energy, and compute the error as the energy differences percentage of the ground truths.

(b) Standard deviations of both energy measured using hardware power meter and using software energy estimates. We compute the standard deviation across 10 runs for the 4 studied models.

Figure 2: Accuracy and robustness comparison between hardware and software based energy measurements. We use 1 GPU on PC1 for all the experiments.

Krzywda et al., 2018).

We conducted two empirical experiments to study these problems: (1) measuring the energy consumption of running the 4 NLP models on two different machines – **PC1** and **PC2**. The detailed device information is described in §2. (2) Use two GPUs on **PC1** to perform inference for the 4 NLP models instead of a single GPU.

Figure 3 shows that the energy errors are prominent when using two GPUs for inference compare to one-GPU setting or using a different GPU model. This is likely because the linear energy estimate model cannot easily take into account the above energy factors (power lag, distortion and tail energy) that affect GPU resources usage. Variable PUE can possibly address this, but that requires careful calibration based on the ground truth energy from the hardware power meters. Figure 4 shows the standard deviation when using existing software-based energy measurements.

3.3 Software-Based Energy Measurements Can Lead to Bad Design Choices

The inaccuracy and robustness issues in software-based measurements can adversely impact model choices when considering energy and effectiveness trade-offs. To demonstrate this we consider two decision problems. One where we want to choose between BERT-base with RoBERTa-base, and another problem where we want to choose between MobileBERT and DistilBERT. Table 2 summarizes the performance scores of these models on the SQuAD 1.1 QA dataset. Figure 5a

Figure 3: Average energy error of the software measurements for the 4 studied models using different hardware device configurations. The error patterns are different across all 3 settings, for example, (1) using two GPUs (instead of one) on the same machine can cause more errors; (2) using the same number of GPUs but with different hardware specifications may lead to different energy errors. (i.e., compare using 1 GPU on PC2 to 1 GPU on PC1)

shows that RoBERTa-base correctly answers an additional 2.2% questions over BERT-base but it incurs 13% more energy on average. Similarly, MobileBERT answers 3.5% more questions correctly with 13% more energy budget compared to DistilBERT. Moreover, for MobileBERT and DistilBERT, batching questions help close the relative gap of energy costs.

If we instead use software-based energy measurements, however, presents a misleading picture. According to software energy measurements shown in Figure 5b, RoBERTa even consumes less energy than BERT (batch sizes 6 and 8), and MobileBERT

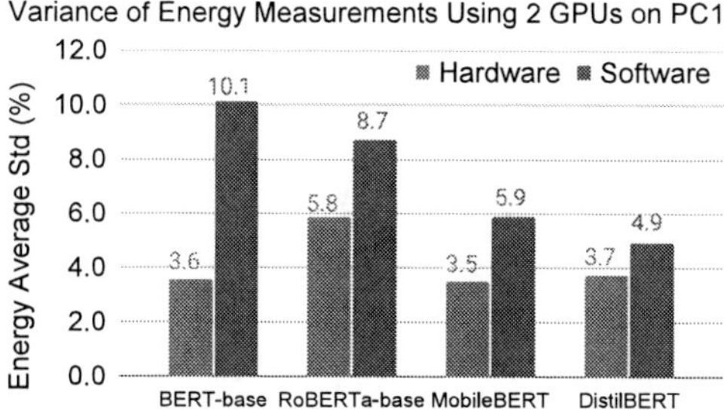

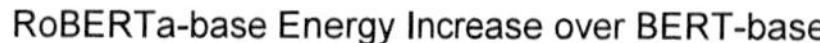
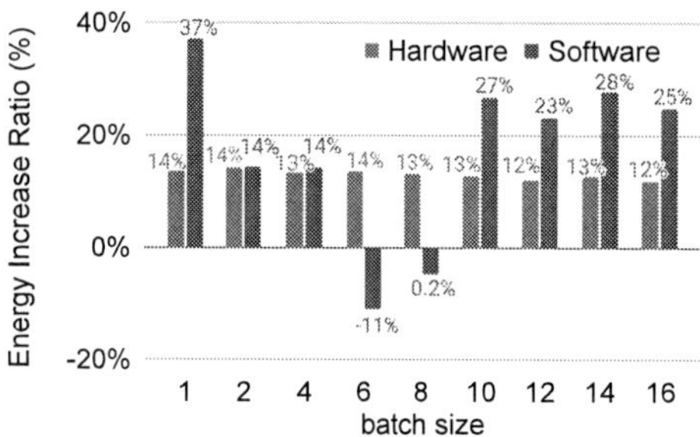

(a) Standard deviations of the hardware power meter measurements and software energy measurements using 2 GPUs on PC1 to perform inference.

(a) Energy increase ratios from DistilBERT to MobileBERT.

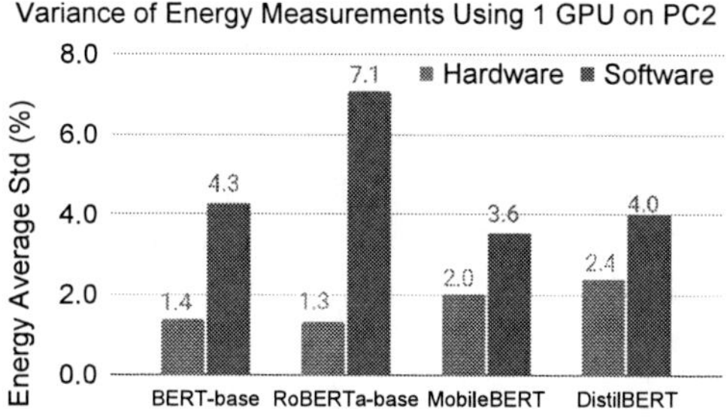

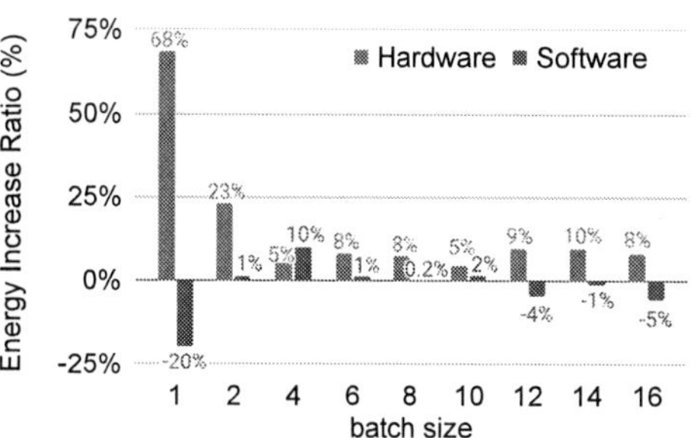

(b) Standard deviations of the hardware power meter measurement and software energy measurements 1 GPU on PC2 to perform inference.

(b) Energy increase ratios from BERT-base to RoBERTa-base.

Figure 4: Comparing the standard deviation in energy estimates under different hardware device configurations.

Figure 5: Energy increase ratio comparison using hardware and software measurements.

can be more energy efficient than DistillBERT for many batch sizes (1, 12, 14, 16). Neither conclusion is true.

Model	EM	F1-score
BERT-base	80.8	88.2
RoBERTa-base	83.0	90.4
MobileBERT	82.6	90.0
DistilBERT	79.1	86.8

Table 2: SQuAD 1.1 task performance scores of the 4 studied models.

3.4 Interactions between Inference Latency and Energy Consumption Are Non-trivial

With the more accurate hardware energy measurements, we investigate the relationship between latency and energy consumption. In particular, we correlate the model energy consumption with its inference latency and task-specific performance.

Note that, in this section, to better characterize the model inference latency and energy interactions, we do not use the end to end latency and energy numbers. Instead, we focus on the model prediction process, i.e. right before the model runs prediction and after the model finishes the prediction of all examples.

Figure 6 shows the inference latency speedup versus energy savings of MobileBERT and Distil-BERT models over the RoBERTa-base model. We can see that smaller batch sizes (< 10) give more energy benefits compared to latency improvement, but as the inference batch size increases, the latency and energy savings are approximately proportional. This is beneficial to mobile settings where smaller batch sizes happen more frequently (e.g., users ask a question at a time instead of asking many questions simultaneously).

4 Related Work and Discussion

Energy estimation is an important research topic in both the machine learning and system community.

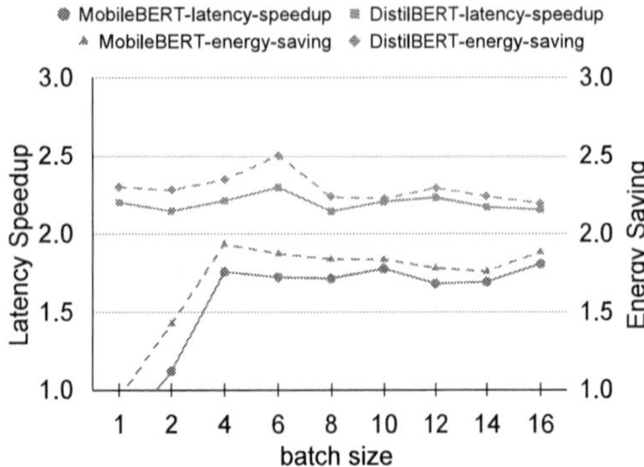

Figure 6: Latency speedup versus energy savings. All numbers are relative to the RoBERTa-base model. We report the hardware based energy values. Since the *experiment-impact-tracker* software does not sample sufficient energy values, we cannot extract the software energy for the prediction process only, hence omit comparison.

We discuss two threads of research related to energy estimation for NLP models:

Energy estimation in machine learning and NLP. Henderson et al. (2020) use a software framework called *experiment-impact-tracker* to report the aggregated energy of benchmark programs. The *experiment-impact-tracker* collects hardware resources statistics, and uses a simple linear model (Strubell et al., 2019) to estimate the total energy where the coefficients are fixed to a constant without considering the actual hardware device configurations. We have shown in the experiments that such software based energy estimation methods are neither accurate nor robust. We recommend using hardware power meters to measure the energy consumption, and then possibly calibrate the software energy values. (Zhou et al., 2020) presents an energy efficient benchmark for NLP models. However, they only report the time (hours) and cost (dollars) for training and testing NLP models, the actual energy numbers remain unknown. The Green AI (Schwartz et al., 2019) work suggests using metrics like floating point operations (FPO) to measure energy efficiency. However, Henderson et al. (2020) argues such metrics alone cannot accurately reflect energy consumption. García-Martín et al. (2019) provide a comprehensive survey of energy estimation methods in machine learning, but no energy measurements for NLP models were reported.

Energy modeling for systems and applications. Energy estimation for battery powered devices such as mobile phones is critical since mobile applications utility can be limited by the battery life. Previous work (Pathak et al., 2011, 2012; Yoon et al., 2012; Cao et al., 2017) study various fine-grained system-level power modeling and profiling techniques to help understand energy drain of applications. NLP models essentially power many emerging applications such as personal assistants with mobile intelligence. However, the energy implications for these NLP models are not studied. It is unclear how to apply the existing energy estimation methods for mobile applications to NLP models. We believe it is important to understand the computational semantics in NLP models before leveraging these existing power modeling methods. Using fine-grained power estimation models and profiling techniques could further improve our understanding of how NLP models consume energy and is an interesting future work.

Limitations. In this work, we collect the energy values every 1 second, which can reflect the total amount of energy consumed for batched inferences that often last over 10 seconds. However, if one needs to understand the energy spent inside the model for a single inference, the energy values are still coarse-grained, we will explore fine-grained energy measurement solutions to study this issue in the near future. More complex energy issues like tail power, energy distortion (Burtscher et al., 2014; Pathak et al., 2011) also affect hardware power meters if analyzing the energy spent inside the model. Further, it is not clear yet which machine component (CPU, GPU or memory reads/writes) takes how much energy for the NLP models. We leave this to future work.

5   Conclusions

As NLP models keep getting larger, reducing the energy impact of deploying these models is critical. Recent work has enabled estimating and tracking the energy of these NLP models. These works design a software-based technique to estimate energy consumption by tracking resource utilization. However, we show that currently used software-based measurements method is not accurate. We use a hardware power meter to accurately measure energy and find that this measurement method has an average error of 20% and can lead to making inaccurate design choices. Going forward, we hope this paper encourages the NLP community to build on current systems research to design more accurate energy models that take into account the underlying power dynamics and device variabilities.

References

Global Warming of 1.5 °C.

WattsUp Meter Pro.

Martin Burtscher, Ivan Zecena, and Ziliang Zong. 2014. Measuring GPU Power with the K20 Built-in Sensor. In *Proceedings of Workshop on General Purpose Processing Using GPUs*, GPGPU-7, pages 28–36, New York, NY, USA. Association for Computing Machinery.

Yi Cao, Javad Nejati, Muhammad Wajahat, Aruna Balasubramanian, and Anshul Gandhi. 2017. Deconstructing the Energy Consumption of the Mobile Page Load. *Proceedings of the ACM on Measurement and Analysis of Computing Systems*, 1(1):6:1–6:25.

Jacob Devlin, Ming-Wei Chang, Kenton Lee, and Kristina Toutanova. 2019. BERT: Pre-training of Deep Bidirectional Transformers for Language Understanding. In *Proceedings of the 2019 Conference of the North American Chapter of the Association for Computational Linguistics: Human Language Technologies, Volume 1 (Long and Short Papers)*, pages 4171–4186, Minneapolis, Minnesota. Association for Computational Linguistics.

Eva García-Martín, Crefeda Faviola Rodrigues, Graham Riley, and Håkan Grahn. 2019. Estimation of energy consumption in machine learning. *Journal of Parallel and Distributed Computing*, 134:75–88.

Peter Henderson, Jieru Hu, Joshua Romoff, Emma Brunskill, Dan Jurafsky, and Joelle Pineau. 2020. Towards the Systematic Reporting of the Energy and Carbon Footprints of Machine Learning. *arXiv:2002.05651 [cs]*.

Jakub Krzywda, Ahmed Ali-Eldin, Trevor E. Carlson, Per-Olov Östberg, and Erik Elmroth. 2018. Power-performance tradeoffs in data center servers: DVFS, CPU pinning, horizontal, and vertical scaling. *Future Generation Computer Systems*, 81:114–128.

Yinhan Liu, Myle Ott, Naman Goyal, Jingfei Du, Mandar Joshi, Danqi Chen, Omer Levy, Mike Lewis, Luke Zettlemoyer, and Veselin Stoyanov. 2019. RoBERTa: A Robustly Optimized BERT Pretraining Approach. *arXiv:1907.11692 [cs]*.

Adam Paszke, Sam Gross, Francisco Massa, Adam Lerer, James Bradbury, Gregory Chanan, Trevor Killeen, Zeming Lin, Natalia Gimelshein, Luca Antiga, Alban Desmaison, Andreas Kopf, Edward Yang, Zachary DeVito, Martin Raison, Alykhan Tejani, Sasank Chilamkurthy, Benoit Steiner, Lu Fang, Junjie Bai, and Soumith Chintala. 2019. PyTorch: An Imperative Style, High-Performance Deep Learning Library. In H. Wallach, H. Larochelle, A. Beygelzimer, F. d\textquotesingle Alché-Buc, E. Fox, and R. Garnett, editors, *Advances in Neural Information Processing Systems 32*, pages 8026–8037. Curran Associates, Inc.

Abhinav Pathak, Y. Charlie Hu, and Ming Zhang. 2012. Where is the energy spent inside my app? fine grained energy accounting on smartphones with Eprof. In *Proceedings of the 7th ACM european conference on Computer Systems*, EuroSys '12, pages 29–42, New York, NY, USA. Association for Computing Machinery.

Abhinav Pathak, Y. Charlie Hu, Ming Zhang, Paramvir Bahl, and Yi-Min Wang. 2011. Fine-grained power modeling for smartphones using system call tracing. In *Proceedings of the sixth conference on Computer systems*, EuroSys '11, pages 153–168, New York, NY, USA. Association for Computing Machinery.

Colin Raffel, Noam Shazeer, Adam Roberts, Katherine Lee, Sharan Narang, Michael Matena, Yanqi Zhou, Wei Li, and Peter J. Liu. 2020. Exploring the Limits of Transfer Learning with a Unified Text-to-Text Transformer. *Journal of Machine Learning Research*, 21(140):1–67.

Pranav Rajpurkar, Jian Zhang, Konstantin Lopyrev, and Percy Liang. 2016. SQuAD: 100,000+ Questions for Machine Comprehension of Text. In *Proceedings of the 2016 Conference on Empirical Methods in Natural Language Processing*, pages 2383–2392, Austin, Texas. Association for Computational Linguistics.

David Rolnick, Priya L. Donti, Lynn H. Kaack, Kelly Kochanski, Alexandre Lacoste, Kris Sankaran, Andrew Slavin Ross, Nikola Milojevic-Dupont, Natasha Jaques, Anna Waldman-Brown, Alexandra Luccioni, Tegan Maharaj, Evan D. Sherwin, S. Karthik Mukkavilli, Konrad P. Kording, Carla Gomes, Andrew Y. Ng, Demis Hassabis, John C. Platt, Felix Creutzig, Jennifer Chayes, and Yoshua Bengio. 2019. Tackling Climate Change with Machine Learning. *arXiv:1906.05433 [cs, stat]*.

Victor Sanh, Lysandre Debut, Julien Chaumond, and Thomas Wolf. 2020. DistilBERT, a distilled version of BERT: smaller, faster, cheaper and lighter. *arXiv:1910.01108 [cs]*.

Roy Schwartz, Jesse Dodge, Noah A. Smith, and Oren Etzioni. 2019. Green AI. *arXiv:1907.10597 [cs, stat]*.

Emma Strubell, Ananya Ganesh, and Andrew McCallum. 2019. Energy and Policy Considerations for Deep Learning in NLP. In *Proceedings of the 57th Annual Meeting of the Association for Computational Linguistics*, pages 3645–3650, Florence, Italy. Association for Computational Linguistics.

Zhiqing Sun, Hongkun Yu, Xiaodan Song, Renjie Liu, Yiming Yang, and Denny Zhou. 2020. MobileBERT: a Compact Task-Agnostic BERT for Resource-Limited Devices. *arXiv:2004.02984 [cs]*.

Thomas Wolf, Lysandre Debut, Victor Sanh, Julien Chaumond, Clement Delangue, Anthony Moi, Pierric Cistac, Tim Rault, Rémi Louf, Morgan Funtowicz, Joe Davison, Sam Shleifer, Patrick von Platen, Clara Ma, Yacine Jernite, Julien Plu, Canwen Xu, Teven Le Scao, Sylvain Gugger, Mariama Drame, Quentin Lhoest, and Alexander M. Rush. 2020. HuggingFace's Transformers: State-of-the-art Natural Language Processing. *arXiv:1910.03771 [cs]*.

Chanmin Yoon, Dongwon Kim, Wonwoo Jung, Chulkoo Kang, and Hojung Cha. 2012. AppScope: application energy metering framework for android smartphones using kernel activity monitoring. In *Proceedings of the 2012 USENIX conference on Annual Technical Conference*, USENIX ATC'12, page 36, USA. USENIX Association.

Xiyou Zhou, Zhiyu Chen, Xiaoyong Jin, and William Yang Wang. 2020. HULK: An Energy Efficiency Benchmark Platform for Responsible Natural Language Processing. *arXiv:2002.05829 [cs]*.

FastFormers: Highly Efficient Transformer Models
for Natural Language Understanding

Young Jin Kim
Microsoft
One Microsoft Way
Redmond, WA 98052, USA
`youki@microsoft.com`

Hany Hassan Awadalla
Microsoft
One Microsoft Way
Redmond, WA 98052, USA
`hanyh@microsoft.com`

Abstract

Transformer-based models are the state-of-the-art for Natural Language Understanding (NLU) applications. Models are getting bigger and better on various tasks. However, Transformer models remain computationally challenging since they are not efficient at inference-time compared to traditional approaches. In this paper, we present *FastFormers*, a set of recipes to achieve efficient inference-time performance for Transformer-based models on various NLU tasks. We show how carefully utilizing knowledge distillation, structured pruning and numerical optimization can lead to drastic improvements on inference efficiency. We provide effective recipes that can guide practitioners to choose the best settings for various NLU tasks and pretrained models. Applying the proposed recipes to the Super-GLUE benchmark, we achieve from 9.8x up to 233.9x speed-up compared to out-of-the-box models on CPU. On GPU, we also achieve up to 12.4x speed-up with the presented methods. We show that *FastFormers* can drastically reduce cost of serving 100 million requests from 4,223 USD to just 18 USD on an *Azure F16s_v2*[1] instance. This translates to a sustainable runtime by reducing energy consumption 6.9x - 125.8x according to the metrics used in the SustaiNLP 2020 shared task.

1 Introduction

Since *BERT* (Devlin et al., 2018) has been introduced, Transformer (Vaswani et al., 2017)-based pretrained language models have dominated the Natural Language Understanding (NLU) field. Transformer models have provided unprecedented accuracy improvement compared to traditional models (Devlin et al., 2018; Liu et al., 2019). However, the models' computational cost at inference time is prohibitively challenging to be widely

adopted in real world production scenarios which requires low latency, fast inference and low serving costs. In this work, we present *FastFormers*, a set of methods and recipes that provides highly efficient inference for Transformer models which enables deployment in large scale production scenarios. We specifically focus on the inference time efficiency since it mostly dominates the cost of production deployment.

Mainly, we utilize three methods: Knowledge Distillation, Structured Pruning and Model Quantization. First, we investigate the efficacy of various Knowledge Distillation techniques to significantly reduce the size of the models with respect to the depth and hidden state sizes while preserving the accuracy. Second, we explore Structured Pruning that further reduces the size of the models by reducing the number of self-attention heads and the number of intermediate hidden states in the feed-forward layers to achieve more efficiency while trying to preserve the accuracy as well. Finally, we explore Model Quantization which enables faster model executions by optimally utilizing hardware acceleration capabilities. On CPU, 8-bit integer quantization method is applied to utilize the most efficient CPU instructions available: *Vector Neural Network Instructions (VNNI)*. On GPU, all the model parameters are converted into 16-bit floating point data type to maximally utilize efficient *Tensor Cores*. Furthermore, computational graph optimizations which fuse multiple graph nodes are performed by utilizing *onnxruntime*[2] library. In addition, we explore optimal settings of allocating CPU and GPU resources to achieve better utilization.

The proposed methods are optimized and evaluated on both CPUs and GPUs which are the most commonly available hardware platforms. Per-

---

[1] `https://docs.microsoft.com/en-us/azure/virtual-machines/fsv2-series`

[2] `https://github.com/microsoft/onnxruntime`

Proceedings of SustaiNLP: Workshop on Simple and Efficient Natural Language Processing, pages 149–158
Online, November 20, 2020. ©2020 Association for Computational Linguistics

formance evaluations are conducted on Super-GLUE (Wang et al., 2019) which is one of the general purpose open domain NLU benchmarks. For the efficiency measurement, wall clock times and energy efficiency are measured while performing inferences on the test sets of *BoolQ, CB, COPA, MultiRC, ReCoRD, RTE* and *WiC* tasks from SuperGLUE. The energy efficiency is measured by an open source python library called *experiment-impact-tracker* proposed in (Henderson et al., 2020). To make sure the optimized models preserve similar accuracy, the accuracy of all the models is measured together.

The contributions of this paper are presenting a set of recipes for efficient inference of Transformer NLU models, analyzing the effect of various optimization techniques and finally making the code publicly available [3] to facilitate utilizing *FastFormers* for efficient inference of Transformers models.

The rest of the paper is organized as follows: Section 2 presents Knowledge Distillation techniques, Section 3 presents Structured Pruning techniques, Section 4 discusses Model Quantization approaches, Section 5 presents runtime optimization techniques, Section 6 presents results on various tasks and finally Section 7 concludes the findings and future directions.

2 Knowledge Distillation

Knowledge distillation (Hinton et al., 2015) is a well known model compression technique where the large model is used as a teacher for a smaller student model. The knowledge distillation is the process of training the student model to mimic the behaviour of the larger teacher model. Knowledge distillation has been shown to improve the efficiency of the Transformer-based architectures for the NLU tasks (Sanh et al., 2019; Jiao et al., 2019) as well as natural language generation tasks such as machine translation (Kim et al., 2019).

Knowledge distillation methods: We utilize two different distillation approaches, namely *task-specific* and *task-agnostic* distillation. In the task-specific distillation, we distill fine-tuned teacher models into smaller student architectures following the procedure proposed by *TinyBERT* (Jiao et al., 2019). In the task-agnostic distillation approach, we directly apply fine-tuning on general distilled

models to tune for a specific task. These two methods are illustrated in Figure 1. In the illustration, the preceding number attached to each arrow means the order of distillation steps. We use soft cross-entropy function as the knowledge distillation loss function in all our experiments as used in (Sanh et al., 2019; Jiao et al., 2019).

As teacher models, we choose 12 stacked layer *BERT*(Devlin et al., 2018) and *RoBERTa*(Liu et al., 2019) models with 768 hidden state dimension and 12 self-attention heads. This is referred as *Base* size from the original BERT paper. In particular, we use HuggingFace's pretrained BERT and RoBERTa [4] models.

In *task-specific* scenario, we observe that the initialization of the student models affects the final accuracy of the distilled models. We utilize open domain pre-distilled models, namely *distilroberta-base*[5] and *TinyBERT*[6] as the initializers for the corresponding student models. Those models have been distilled with one of the original BERT model's pretraining objective which is masked language model. So, they are not specific to any task and can be considered as smaller generic pretrained models.

Knowledge distillation results: The main goal of the knowledge distillation process is to acquire the smallest possible student model while preserving the accuracy of the teacher model. Since we are experimenting with various NLU tasks, the capacity of the optimal student model that preserves accuracy may vary with varying level of task's difficulty. Therefore, we experiment with distilling various sized student models; then, we pick the smaller model among the distilled models that can offer higher accuracy than the original BERT model for each task.

In our experiments, we have observed that distilled models do not work well when distilled to a different model type. Therefore, we restricted our setup to avoid distilling RoBERTa model to BERT or vice versa. The major difference between the two model groups is the input token (sub-word) embedding. We think that different input embedding spaces result in different output embedding spaces,

---

[3] https://github.com/microsoft/
fastformers

[4] https://github.com/huggingface/
Transformers

[5] https://huggingface.co/
distilroberta-base

[6] https://github.com/huawei-noah/
Pretrained-Language-Model/tree/master/
TinyBERT

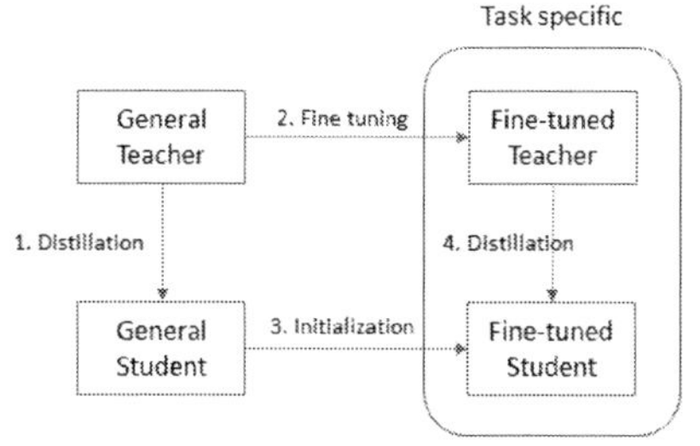

(a) Task specific distillation to general distill models

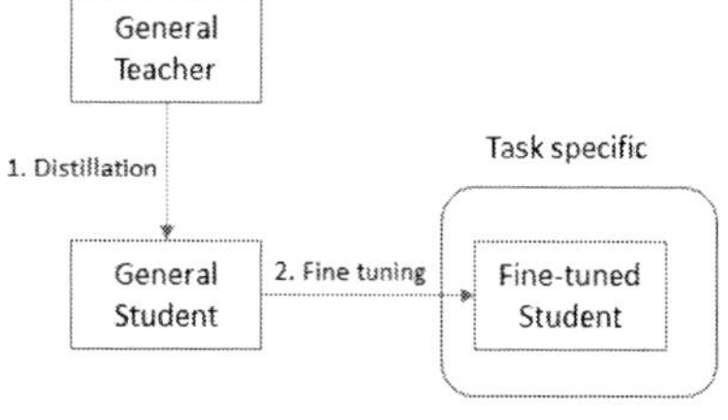

(b) Fine-tuning of general distilled models

Figure 1: Knowledge distillation methods

Model	BoolQ	CB	COPA	MultiRC	ReCoRD	RTE	WiC
BERT[†] (Reference, 12L, 768)	72.7	80.7	57.0	41.8	54.9	65.7	65.6
BERT (Teacher, 12L, 768)	75.99	87.96	64.00	42.00	64.81	69.68	72.41
BERT (Student, 6L, 768)	76.06	90.12	69.00	37.47	64.47	68.59	71.79
BERT (Student, 4L, 312)	72.63	87.63	64.00	36.71	33.68	64.62	65.20
RoBERTa (Teacher, 12L, 768)	81.59	89.34	56.00	50.30	79.66	79.06	71.63
RoBERTa (Student, 6L, 768)	75.19	90.68	57.00	42.90	67.33	66.43	65.83

Table 1: Accuracy of teacher and student models on the validation data set for each task of SuperGLUE benchmark with knowledge distillation. Model marked with † represents accuracy numbers on the test set provided by SustaiNLP organizers.

and knowledge transfer with different spaces does not work well.

The result of the knowledge distillation on the tasks are summarized in Table 1 together with the teacher models' accuracy numbers on the validation data sets. It also includes the accuracy values on test data set for BERT model presented by SustaiNLP 2020 organizers[7]. We train both *cased* and *uncased* models using both task-specific and task-agnostic approaches, and present the model with higher accuracy values. For the more challenging tasks such as MultiRC and ReCoRD, we observe that RoBERTa based models provide better accuracy than BERT based models.

3 Structured Pruning

There has been a significant amount of research on model's weights pruning approaches inspired by *The Lottery Ticket Hypothesis* (Frankle and Carbin, 2018). Furthermore, there are various papers published to apply this pruning strategy to Transformer models including: (Yu et al., 2019; Sanh et al., 2020; Gordon et al., 2020). Most of such approaches focused on random pruning to reduce the number of parameters following the lottery ticket

hypothesis. While this can reduce the size of the model on the computer storage, it may not improve the inference performance since it is not focusing on better utilization of the computing resources. Since our main focus in *FastFormers* is to improve inference efficiency, randomly pruning a subset of the model's parameters may not improve performance. In this work, we focus on structured pruning which directly reduces the computation requirements.

Voita et al. (2019); Michel et al. (2019); Hou et al. (2020) proposed methods to prune some of the *heads* of Multi-Head Attention (MHA) in Transformer architecture. *DynaBERT* (Hou et al., 2020) additionally proposed pruning intermediate hidden states in feed-forward layer of Transformer architecture together with rewiring of these pruned attention module and feed-forward layers. In the paper, we define a target model size in terms of the number of heads and the hidden state size of feed-forward network, and use the pruning/distillation approach proposed in DynaBERT as a model compression method. This effectively reduces the dimensions of Transformer models.

Structured pruning methods: The first step of our structured pruning method is to identify the least important *heads* in MHA and the least im-

[7]https://sites.google.com/view/
sustainlp2020/shared-task?authuser=0

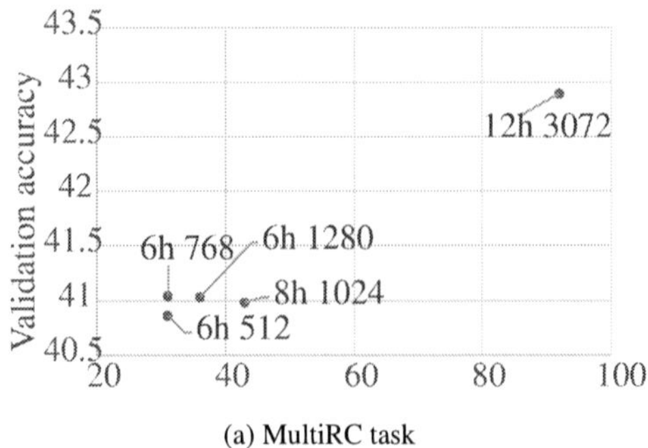

(a) MultiRC task

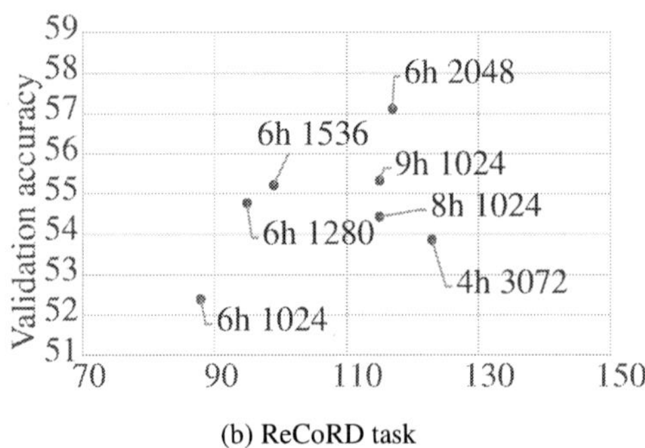

(b) ReCoRD task

Figure 2: Structured pruning - inference time versus accuracy. Each data point indicates a pruned model with the number of remaining heads and the number of remaining intermediate hidden states of feed-forward layers.

portant hidden states in the feed-forward layers. We use a first order method for computing the importance score, which utilizes the first order gradient information proposed by Michel et al. (2019); Sanh et al. (2020); Hou et al. (2020) instead of using magnitude based pruning (Frankle and Carbin, 2018; Gordon et al., 2020). Before doing the importance score computation, we add a mask variable to each attention head for the gradient computation of the heads. Next, we run forward and backward passes of the model on the entire validation data set, then the absolute values of the gradients are accumulated. These accumulated values are used as importance scores which we use to sort the importance of the heads and the intermediate hidden states. Based on the target model size, we select a given number of top heads and top hidden states from the network. Once the sorting and selection steps are done, we re-group and reconnect the remaining heads and hidden states which result in a smaller sized model. When heads and hidden states are pruned, we use the same pruning ratio across different layers. This enables further optimizations to work seamlessly with the pruned models. In our experiments, we observed that the pruned model can get better accuracy when it goes through another round of knowledge distillation; this has also been noted in Hou et al. (2020). Therefore, we do one more knowledge distillation by using the non-pruned model as a teacher model and the pruned model as an initializer of student model.

Structured pruning results: We apply the structured pruning method mainly to MultiRC and ReCoRD tasks. For the other tasks, the test sets are not that big; therefore, knowledge distillation and other optimizations could make the models quite efficient. In both MultiRC and ReCoRD tasks, the base model is RoBERTa based distilRoberta-base[8] which has 6 stacked layers with 768 hidden states, 12 self-attention heads and 3072 hidden states in feed-forward layer. The structured pruning method brings better efficiency by trading off the accuracy. So, it is important to pick a reasonable model size that doesn't compromise the accuracy of the task. Figure 2 presents trade-off between inference speed and accuracy on MultiRC and ReCoRD validation data sets. For the MultiRC task, we could get 2.97x speed-up while losing 1.9 point of accuracy by pruning 50% of heads and 75% of intermediate hidden states from 12 heads and 3072 hidden sizes. For the ReCoRD task, we got 1.95x speed-up while trading off 12.1 point of accuracy by pruning 50% of heads and 50% of hidden states in feed-froward layer. In both cases, they are still exceeding the teacher sized BERT model's accuracy.

4   Low Precision Inference

After knowledge distillation and structured pruning compression, models can benefit form more efficient numerical computations by quantizing the model parameters on CPU and GPU (Rodriguez et al., 2018). It has been shown that the accuracy of Transformer models doesn't get severely compromised when utilizing 8-bit or 16-bit lower precision arithmetic (Devlin, 2017; Kim et al., 2019; Bhandare et al., 2019; Zafrir et al., 2019; Shen et al., 2020; Fan et al., 2020; Aji and Heafield, 2020). Modern CPUs and GPU accelerators are capable of computing those lower numerical arithmetic efficiently. For example, Cascade Lake CPUs have a special 8-bit vector instruction set called AVX (Advanced Vector eXtensions)-512-VNNI and V100

---

[8]`https://huggingface.co/distilRoberta-base`

GPUs can utilize its efficient Tensor Cores with 16-bit floating point data.

8-bit quantized matrix multiplications on the CPU: 8-bit quantized matrix multiplication brings a significant amount of speed-up compared to 32-bit floating point arithmetic, thanks to the relieved memory bandwidth bottleneck and reduced number of CPU instructions. Efficient utilization of the vector registers and CPU cache memories requires that the parameter weight matrix to be tiled and transposed in a cache efficient layout. This is referred as *packing* operation in the matrix multiplication. Packing itself is a non-negligible operation and repeated packing operation could cancel out all the benefits from the quantized matrix multiplications. Therefore, the result of the packing operation needs to be properly cached to get efficient performance. Moreover, some of the matrix products should stay 32-bit floating point to avoid repeated packing operations. Therefore, we do not use 8-bit matrix product for the Q, K inner product because both matrices are not constant. All the other matrix products have constant weight matrix, so we utilize 8-bit matrix products for them with cached weight packing. For the 8-bit quantized matrix product API, we utilize an open source quantized matrix multiplication library FBGEMM[9] which we have integrated into the onnxruntime framework. It provides various quantization methods and a separate matrix packing functionality explicitly. We use dynamic quantization method which decides the quantization range of input matrix dynamically every time[10]. This enables the quantized values to effectively represent all the values in the input matrix. The weight matrix' quantization range is selected for each column separately and the quantization range for the input matrix is selected for entire input tensor. In our experiments, this 8-bit quantization brings up to around 3.0x speed-up on Cascade Lake CPUs for the Transformer models by trading off small amount of accuracy loss.

16-bit model conversion for the GPU: V100 GPU supports full 16-bit operations for the Transformer architecture. Also, 16-bit floating point operations do not require special handling of inputs and outputs except for having smaller value ranges. The impact of the numerical overflow due to the smaller range in 16-bit float points is minimal at inference time, so we have not observed any differences in accuracy. Therefore, the model can be fully converted into 16-bit floating point data type before the model is utilized for inference. This 16-bit model conversion brings quite significant speed gain, since the Transformer models are memory bandwidth bound workload. We observe up to 3.53x speed-up depending on the model settings. V100 GPU also supports 8-bit quantized arithmetic, but it is not supported with its efficient Tensor cores; hence we do not utilize 8-bit quantization on GPUs.

5 Runtime Optimization

On top of the structural and numerical optimizations applied, we can utilize various ways to further optimize the computations. In particular, we focus on multi-processing optimizations and computational graph optimization.

Multi-processing optimization: The evaluation machine for the SustaiNLP 2020 shared task has two Cascade Lake 6248 CPUs with 40 physical cores. The default execution engines for HuggingFace's transformers including PyTorch[11] and TensorFlow[12] usually use all available CPU cores for a single operator. This is not the optimal way of utilizing available CPU cores for several reasons. The operators in compressed Transformer architectures are not big enough to fully utilize the parallelism of 40 CPU cores. Therefore, the overheads of parallelizing the operation significantly overshadow the actual gains from the parallelism. Another important factor is that the parallelization to all cores reduces the cache locality and degrades the overall efficiency of CPU utilization. Therefore, we implement a multiple instance inference by leveraging multiprocessing module of python[13] programming language. It is preferable to use multi-threading instead of multi-processing to avoid additional copy of program memory, but python's multi-threading cannot really utilize multiple threads due to the Global Interpreter Lock (GIL)[14]. Even with this limitation, multi-instance inference with multiprocessing brings much more efficient computation.

---

[9]https://github.com/pytorch/FBGEMM

[10]https://pytorch.org/tutorials/recipes/recipes/dynamic_quantization.html

[11]https://github.com/pytorch/pytorch

[12]https://github.com/tensorflow/tensorflow

[13]https://docs.python.org/3/library/multiprocessing.html

[14]https://wiki.python.org/moin/GlobalInterpreterLock

Number of inference instances	Time (sec)	Speed-up
Baseline (no thread control)	433	1.00x
1 instance (20 threads/instance)	319	1.36x
2 instances (10 threads/instance)	243	1.78x
4 instance (5 threads/instance)	247	1.75x
5 instance (4 threads/instance)	255	1.70x
10 instance (2 threads/instance)	300	1.44x
20 instance (1 thread/instance)	351	1.23x

Table 2: Speed comparison of different number of inference instances with thread control - time to perform inference on 1,000 ReCoRD validation data samples.

To maximize the cache locality, each inference instance is pinned to specific physical cores using *Linux' taskset* command. Utilizing hyper-threading harms the cache utilization, so we always keep the total number of utilized threads (the number of threads per one inference instance multiplied by the number of instances) not exceeding the number of physical cores in the machine. The optimal number of multiple processes for the best efficiency varies by the model, hardware settings and the data set. We conduct experiment with all target tasks and investigate the best setting for each task. Table 2 shows one example of the speed-up achieved by optimized multi-instance inference on 1,000 samples of validation data set of ReCoRD task.

Computational graph optimizations: Computational graph optimization can further improve the efficiency of the neural network inference by pruning unused graph nodes and fusing multiple operations together. In particular, graph node fusion reduces additional memory allocation and copy which potentially degrade the efficiency. Also, graph node fusion potentially improves parallelism by increasing the size of individual operators. We replace Gaussian Error Linear Units (GELU) with Rectified Linear Units (ReLU) for the computational efficiency while model is distilled without losing any accuracy. We fuse ReLU and bias addition operations followed by matrix multiplications into FBGEMM's fused post processing operation. Moreover, we utilize multi-head attention node fusion provided by onnxruntime. We use a customized onnxruntime based on v1.3.1.

6 Results

6.1 Combined results

Table 3 and Figure 3 present how the proposed methods work together on BoolQ task using CPU.

For the ablation study, an Azure F16s_v2 instance which has Intel(R) Xeon(R) Platinum 8168 CPUs (8 physical cores) is utilized. When all the optimizations are applied, it could achieve around 233x speed-up while only losing 1.2 of accuracy. First, it is worth noting that the batch generation code in many frameworks including HuggingFace's transformers uses fixed sequence length for the input. Whenever there comes a shorter sentence than the fixed length for the inference, additional zeros are padded at the end of each input sentence. This degrades CPU performance greatly which has relatively small parallelism than GPU. We modify the batch generation to support dynamic sequence length for each batch to avoid such redundant computation. By doing this dynamic shape batching, we could get around 3.51x speed-up on the test CPU. On top of the dynamic shape batching, all the optimization techniques introduced are applied. As described in Section 2, knowledge distillation brings a significant speed-up which is more than 9 times faster than the original teacher model while preserving the accuracy. One thing to note is that the compressible student model size varies with the task. In this BoolQ example, 4 stacked layers with smaller hidden size (312) model could learn original teacher model's knowledge without losing any accuracy score on the validation data set. 8-bit quantization together with onnxruntime graph optimization brings around 2.26x speed-up on the 4 layer distilled model. This is lower than 3.0x speed-up acquired when the same methods is applied to 12 layer base size models mentioned in Section 4, because the system is already compressed into a smaller size. By using 8 concurrent and independent instances for inference instead of one inference instance with 8 threads, more than 1.7x additional speed-up could be achieved. Finally, by pruning heads in multi-head attentions and intermediate hidden states in feed-forward layers, another speed-up from 1.38x to 1.81x could be accomplished while trading off the accuracy. One interesting observation is that the structured pruning approach brings better speed-up when it is combined with multi-instance inference which is up to 1.81x. The same pruned model brings at most 1.26x speed-up when it is used with one inference instance. This indicates that multi-instance inference gets more performance benefits when each individual model size gets smaller.

Optimization methods added	Time (sec)	Cumulative speed-up	Speed-up	Accuracy	USD for 100 M queries
Baseline (PyTorch out-of-the-box, 12L, 768)	734.35	1.00x	-	74.01	$4,223
+ dynamic sequence length	209.29	3.51x	3.51x	74.01	$1,204
+ knowledge distillation (4L, 312)	22.5	32.64x	9.30x	74.04	$129
+ 8-bit quantization + graph optimization	9.97	73.66x	2.26x	73.43	$57
+ multi-instance inference	5.68	129.29x	1.76x	73.43	$33
+ structured pruning					
25% heads and 25% hidden states pruned	4.11	178.67x	1.38x	73.36	$24
33% heads and 50% hidden states pruned	3.14	233.87x	1.81x	72.81	$18

Table 3: An ablation study of CPU inference speed-up on BoolQ validation data set with batch size 1. All performance numbers are measured on an Azure F16s-v2 instance.

6.2 Shared task submissions

We submit our optimized *FastFormers* systems to SustaiNLP 2020 shared task; four systems for track 1 and two systems for track 3. For track 1, we have GPU-only submissions and hybrid submissions which utilize both CPUs and GPUs. We observe that the inference time for ReCoRD only exceeds the inference time of the other tasks all together. Therefore, for the hybrid systems, we use GPUs for ReCoRD task inference and CPUs for all the other tasks. Those CPU and GPU inferences can be executed in parallel for the best throughput. For track 3, we only use CPUs for all tasks as indicated in the shared task description. For the GPU inference, we always limit the number of GPUs we utilize to one. Our highly optimized and compressed models can be executed on a single GPU fast enough. And, the scaling of multiple GPUs is sub-linear (3.0x with 4 GPUs and 1.8x with 2 GPUs) which indicates a single GPU inference is most energy efficient. We apply different types of optimization depending on the time consumed to run the task. For most time consuming tasks, MultiRC and ReCoRD, all compression and optimization techniques mentioned above are applied. All GPU inference uses batch size of 256 which gives the highest throughput and the best efficiency. On the other hand, a single batch works better for most of the cases on CPUs. We use batch size of 1 for all tasks except for CB (batch size of 4) and COPA (batch size of 8).

Table 4 summarizes the accuracy, speed-up numbers and energy savings of *FastFormers* systems prepared for the shared task. For GPUs, CB, COPA and WiC data sets are quite small, so the initial performance without any optimization took 1 or 2 seconds close to the resolution (1 second) of the wall clock time measurement. Therefore, it was hard to observe big speed improvements for those data sets. For the other tasks, we acquire a good amount of speed-up ranging from 5.8x to 12.4x by our optimization. On CPUs, model compression gives more benefits all across the board in terms of speed. The smallest gain is 9.8x for WiC data set which could not utilize onnxruntime optimization due to the control 'for' loop in the output layer. This is currently not supported in onnxruntime. For the other tasks, we observe up to 40.3X speed-up. On the other hand, the energy savings while preserving BERT model accuracy measured by the shared task organizers range from 6.9X up to 125.8X. When combining all the tasks, our best systems save 22.1x energy on CPUs and 21.6x energy on GPUs.

7 Conclusion

In this paper, we have introduced *FastFormers*, which achieves efficient inference-time performance for Transformer-based models on various NLU tasks. We showed that utilizing knowledge distillation, structured pruning and numerical optimization can lead to drastic improvements on inference efficiency. We showed that the improvements can be up to 200X speed-up and results in more than 200X inference cost saving with 22X energy saving. We open source *FastFormers* for the community hoping it can drive more sustainable optimizations for Transformers models. For future directions, some other methods such as early exiting (Xin et al., 2020; Liu et al., 2020; Schwartz et al., 2020; Zhou et al., 2020) and linear time complexity self-attention models (Shen et al., 2018; Wang et al., 2020) could be added to the proposed recipes and possibly improve the efficiency further.

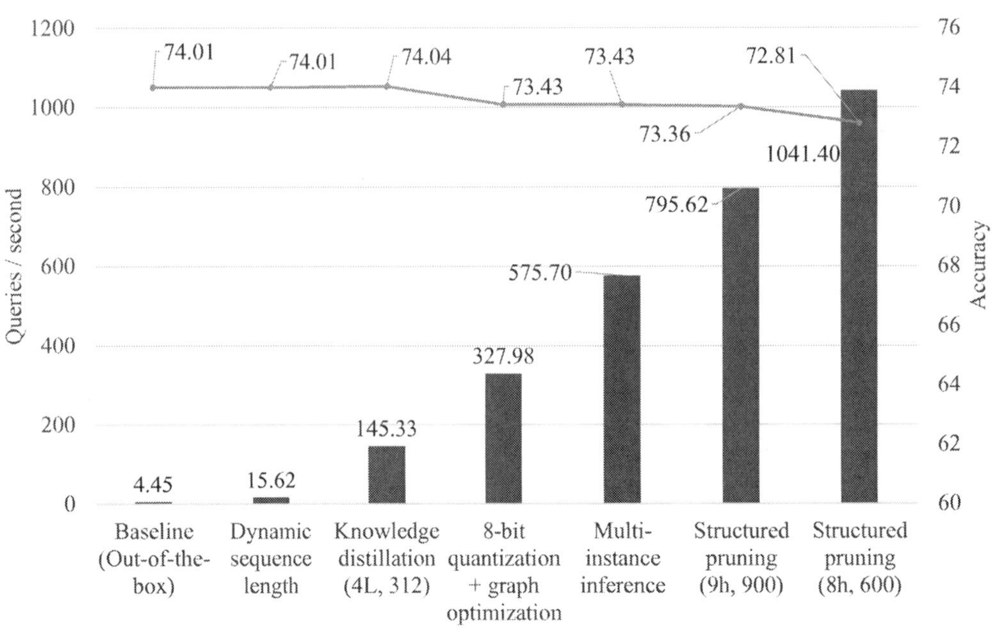

Figure 3: Accuracy versus queries per second with various optimizations on CPU.

Submitted systems	BoolQ	CB	COPA	MultiRC	ReCoRD	RTE	WiC	Overall
BERT[†] (Reference, 12L, 768)	72.7	80.7	57.0	41.8	54.9	65.7	65.6	62.6
Inference time speed-up	1.0x	1.0x	1.0x	1.0x	1.0x	1.0x	1.0x	1.0x
Energy savings	1.0x	1.0x	1.0x	1.0x	1.0x	1.0x	1.0x	1.0x
System 1 (GPU only)	74.0	82.7	58.0	41.8	56.2	66.4	66.0	63.6
Inference time speed-up	5.8x	2.0x	2.0x	9.1x	**12.4x**	9.0x	2.0x	11.3x
Energy savings	11.0x	57.9x	**125.8x**	6.9x	23.9x	20.5x	28.7x	20.3x
System 2 (GPU only)	74.0	82.7	58.0	43.2	56.2	66.4	66.0	63.8
Inference time speed-up	5.8x	2.0x	2.0x	9.1x	**12.4x**	9.0x	2.0x	11.3x
Energy savings	11.9x	58.3x	80.1x	8.1x	25.0x	15.9x	22.4x	**21.6x**
System 3 (CPU/GPU hybrid)	73.7	82.7	58.0	43.0	56.2	66.9	65.9	63.8
Inference time speed-up	**40.3x**	22.0x	38.0x	25.0x	12.4x	22.4x	9.8x	**14.5x**
Energy savings	13.4x	49.4x	**92.8x**	13.8x	23.0x	32.7x	30.4x	16.5x
System 4 (CPU/GPU hybrid)	73.7	82.7	58.0	43.1	56.2	66.9	65.9	63.8
Inference time speed-up	**40.3x**	22.0x	38.0x	17.5x	12.4x	22.4x	9.8x	**14.5x**
Energy savings	13.2x	45.8x	75.4x	11.8x	23.5x	34.0x	28.4x	16.1x
System 5 (CPU only)	73.7	82.7	58.0	43.0	56.6	66.9	65.9	63.8
Inference time speed-up	**40.3x**	22.0x	38.0x	25.0x	15.5x	22.4x	9.8x	**16.6x**
Energy savings	14.0x	41.1x	75.0x	15.3x	22.5x	34.7x	26.2x	**22.1x**
System 6 (CPU only)	73.7	82.7	58.0	43.1	56.6	66.9	65.9	63.8
Inference time speed-up	**40.3x**	22.0x	38.0x	17.5x	15.5x	22.4x	9.8x	16.1x
Energy savings	11.4x	22.4x	27.2x	9.2x	16.0x	**85.5x**	13.5x	15.6x

Table 4: Accuracy numbers with speed-up and energy savings on the test data set of submitted systems to the SustaiNLP 2020 shared task. Model marked with † was accuracy numbers on the test set provided by organizers.

Acknowledgments

We would like to thank the organizers of SustaiNLP 2020 for their various efforts and the reviewers for the thoughtful and helpful suggestions.

References

Alham Fikri Aji and Kenneth Heafield. 2020. Compressing neural machine translation models with 4-bit precision. In *Proceedings of the Fourth Workshop on Neural Generation and Translation*, pages 35–42.

Aishwarya Bhandare, Vamsi Sripathi, Deepthi Karkada, Vivek Menon, Sun Choi, Kushal Datta, and Vikram Saletore. 2019. Efficient 8-bit quantization of transformer neural machine language translation model. *arXiv preprint arXiv:1906.00532*.

Jacob Devlin. 2017. Sharp models on dull hardware: Fast and accurate neural machine translation decoding on the cpu. *arXiv preprint arXiv:1705.01991*.

Jacob Devlin, Ming-Wei Chang, Kenton Lee, and Kristina Toutanova. 2018. Bert: Pre-training of deep bidirectional transformers for language understanding. *arXiv preprint arXiv:1810.04805*.

Angela Fan, Pierre Stock, Benjamin Graham, Edouard Grave, Rémi Gribonval, Hervé Jégou, and Armand Joulin. 2020. Training with quantization noise for extreme model compression. *arXiv Prepr. arXiv2004*, 7320:1–18.

Jonathan Frankle and Michael Carbin. 2018. The lottery ticket hypothesis: Finding sparse, trainable neural networks. *arXiv preprint arXiv:1803.03635*.

Mitchell A Gordon, Kevin Duh, and Nicholas Andrews. 2020. Compressing bert: Studying the effects of weight pruning on transfer learning. *arXiv preprint arXiv:2002.08307*.

Peter Henderson, Jieru Hu, Joshua Romoff, Emma Brunskill, Dan Jurafsky, and Joelle Pineau. 2020. Towards the systematic reporting of the energy and carbon footprints of machine learning. *arXiv preprint arXiv:2002.05651*.

Geoffrey Hinton, Oriol Vinyals, and Jeffrey Dean. 2015. Distilling the knowledge in a neural network. In *NIPS Deep Learning and Representation Learning Workshop*.

Lu Hou, Lifeng Shang, Xin Jiang, and Qun Liu. 2020. Dynabert: Dynamic bert with adaptive width and depth. *arXiv preprint arXiv:2004.04037*.

Xiaoqi Jiao, Yichun Yin, Lifeng Shang, Xin Jiang, Xiao Chen, Linlin Li, Fang Wang, and Qun Liu. 2019. Tinybert: Distilling bert for natural language understanding. *arXiv preprint arXiv:1909.10351*.

Young Jin Kim, Marcin Junczys-Dowmunt, Hany Hassan, Alham Fikri Aji, Kenneth Heafield, Roman Grundkiewicz, and Nikolay Bogoychev. 2019. From research to production and back: Ludicrously fast neural machine translation. In *Proceedings of the 3rd Workshop on Neural Generation and Translation*, pages 280–288.

Weijie Liu, Peng Zhou, Zhe Zhao, Zhiruo Wang, Haotang Deng, and Qi Ju. 2020. Fastbert: a self-distilling bert with adaptive inference time. *arXiv preprint arXiv:2004.02178*.

Yinhan Liu, Myle Ott, Naman Goyal, Jingfei Du, Mandar Joshi, Danqi Chen, Omer Levy, Mike Lewis, Luke Zettlemoyer, and Veselin Stoyanov. 2019. Roberta: A robustly optimized bert pretraining approach. *arXiv preprint arXiv:1907.11692*.

Paul Michel, Omer Levy, and Graham Neubig. 2019. Are sixteen heads really better than one? In *Advances in Neural Information Processing Systems*, pages 14014–14024.

Andres Rodriguez, Eden Segal, Etay Meiri, Evarist Fomenko, Y Jim Kim, Haihao Shen, and Barukh Ziv. 2018. Lower numerical precision deep learning inference and training. *Intel White Paper*, 3.

Victor Sanh, Lysandre Debut, Julien Chaumond, and Thomas Wolf. 2019. Distilbert, a distilled version of bert: smaller, faster, cheaper and lighter. *arXiv preprint arXiv:1910.01108*.

Victor Sanh, Thomas Wolf, and Alexander M Rush. 2020. Movement pruning: Adaptive sparsity by fine-tuning. *arXiv preprint arXiv:2005.07683*.

Roy Schwartz, Gabi Stanovsky, Swabha Swayamdipta, Jesse Dodge, and Noah A Smith. 2020. The right tool for the job: Matching model and instance complexities. *arXiv preprint arXiv:2004.07453*.

Sheng Shen, Zhen Dong, Jiayu Ye, Linjian Ma, Zhewei Yao, Amir Gholami, Michael W Mahoney, and Kurt Keutzer. 2020. Q-bert: Hessian based ultra low precision quantization of bert. In *AAAI*, pages 8815–8821.

Zhuoran Shen, Mingyuan Zhang, Haiyu Zhao, Shuai Yi, and Hongsheng Li. 2018. Efficient attention: Attention with linear complexities. *arXiv preprint arXiv:1812.01243*.

Ashish Vaswani, Noam Shazeer, Niki Parmar, Jakob Uszkoreit, Llion Jones, Aidan N Gomez, Łukasz Kaiser, and Illia Polosukhin. 2017. Attention is all you need. In *Advances in neural information processing systems*, pages 5998–6008.

Elena Voita, David Talbot, Fedor Moiseev, Rico Sennrich, and Ivan Titov. 2019. Analyzing multi-head self-attention: Specialized heads do the heavy lifting, the rest can be pruned. *arXiv preprint arXiv:1905.09418*.

Alex Wang, Yada Pruksachatkun, Nikita Nangia, Amanpreet Singh, Julian Michael, Felix Hill, Omer Levy, and Samuel Bowman. 2019. Superglue: A stickier benchmark for general-purpose language understanding systems. In *Advances in Neural Information Processing Systems*, pages 3266–3280.

Sinong Wang, Belinda Li, Madian Khabsa, Han Fang, and Hao Ma. 2020. Linformer: Self-attention with linear complexity. *arXiv preprint arXiv:2006.04768*.

Ji Xin, Raphael Tang, Jaejun Lee, Yaoliang Yu, and Jimmy Lin. 2020. Deebert: Dynamic early exiting for accelerating bert inference. *arXiv preprint arXiv:2004.12993*.

Haonan Yu, Sergey Edunov, Yuandong Tian, and Ari S Morcos. 2019. Playing the lottery with rewards and multiple languages: lottery tickets in rl and nlp. *arXiv preprint arXiv:1906.02768*.

Ofir Zafrir, Guy Boudoukh, Peter Izsak, and Moshe Wasserblat. 2019. Q8bert: Quantized 8bit bert. *arXiv preprint arXiv:1910.06188*.

Wangchunshu Zhou, Canwen Xu, Tao Ge, Julian McAuley, Ke Xu, and Furu Wei. 2020. Bert loses patience: Fast and robust inference with early exit. *arXiv preprint arXiv:2006.04152*.

A comparison between CNNs and WFAs for sequence classification

Ariadna Quattoni
Universitat Politècnica de Catalunya
Campus Nord, Barcelona
aquattoni@cs.upc.edu

Xavier Carreras
IIIA-CSIC
Campus UAB, Bellaterra
xavierc@iiia.csic.es

Abstract

We compare a classical CNN architecture for sequence classification involving several convolutional and max-pooling layers against a simple model based on weighted finite state automata (WFA). Each model has its advantages and disadvantages and it is possible that they could be combined. However, we believe that the first research goal should be to investigate and understand how do these two apparently dissimilar models compare in the context of specific natural language processing tasks. This paper is the first step towards that goal. Our experiments with five sequence classification datasets suggest that, despite the apparent simplicity of WFA models and training algorithms, the performance of WFAs is comparable to that of the CNNs.

1 Introduction

In the latter years CNNs have been proposed as models for sequence classification and it has been shown that they can give competitive results, even when compared to more complex models (Kim, 2014; Zhang and Wallace, 2017; Kalchbrenner et al., 2014; Johnson and Zhang, 2015; Goldberg, 2016). They typically combine various convolutional filters with max-pooling layers.

Because they have several interacting layers, it is in general is hard to interpret exactly what is it that they are learning. But most likely their success relies on the fact that their convolutional filters have the ability to capture arbitrary features of the input sequence.

On the other hand, non-deterministic weighted automata (WFAs) are recurrent models that only use linear activation functions.Essentially, WFAs can be regarded as recurrent neural networks where the function that predicts the dynamic state representation from previous states is linear.

For more details about the relations between linear activation RNNs and WFAs, we refer the reader to (Rabusseau et al., 2019). Several algorithms based on low rank matrix decompositions have been proposed (Hsu et al., 2009, 2012; Bailly et al., 2009; Balle et al., 2011; Cohen et al., 2012; Balle et al., 2014).

In addition to being easily trainable, WFAs offer other advantages. The main advantage is that they are classical computer science models that have been intensively researched in the theoretical community. Because of this they are relatively well understood and we know how to efficiently perform important computations. For example, consider a WFA computing a distribution over strings, there are simple and efficient algorithms to compute marginal probabilities for prefixes, infixes and suffixes. Furthermore another advantage of these models is that there are well known and understood algorithms for transforming them into deterministic automata. The resulting deterministic automata can be used to interpret the computation performed by WFAs.

Both CNNs and WFAs are general models, and the exact architecture can be specified to solve different tasks such as language modeling, or sequence classification which is the focus of this paper. Each model has its advantages and disadvantages and it is possible that they could be combined.

However, we believe that the first research goal should be to investigate and understand how do these two apparently dissimilar models compare in the context of specific natural language processing tasks.

This paper is the first step towards that goal. We focus on the task of sequence classification and compare the performance of WFAs and CNNs trained under the same initial conditions, over five different data sets.

To a certain extent a similar comparison between

Proceedings of SustaiNLP: Workshop on Simple and Efficient Natural Language Processing, pages 159–163
Online, November 20, 2020. ©2020 Association for Computational Linguistics

WFAs and neural models was made by (Quattoni and Carreras, 2019) in the context of language modeling. But to our knowledge this is the first empirical comparison of CNNs and WFAs for sequence classification.

2   WFAs for Sequence Classification

2.1   Preliminaries: WFAs for sequence modelling

We will use weighted finite state automata (WFAs) as elementary building blocks to build our sequence prediction model.

More precisely, a WFA takes as input a sequence and outputs a real number, that is: $f : \Sigma^\star \to \mathbb{R}$ where $x = x_1 \cdots x_n$ is sequence of length n over some finite alphabet Σ.

We denote as $\Sigma^\star$ the set of all finite sequences, and we use it as a domain of our functions. A WFA with k states is defined as a tuple:

$$A = \langle \boldsymbol{\alpha}_0, \boldsymbol{\alpha}_\infty, \{\mathbf{A}_\sigma\}_{\sigma \in \Sigma} \rangle \qquad (1)$$

where: $\boldsymbol{\alpha}_0, \boldsymbol{\alpha}_\infty \in \mathbb{R}^k$ are the initial and final weight vectors; and $\mathbf{A}_\sigma \in \mathbb{R}^{k \times k}$ are the transition matrices associated to each symbol $\sigma \in \Sigma$.

The function $f_A : \Sigma^\star \to \mathbb{R}$ realized by a WA A is defined as:

$$f(x) = \boldsymbol{\alpha}_0^\top \mathbf{A}_{x_1} \cdots \mathbf{A}_{x_n} \boldsymbol{\alpha}_\infty \qquad . \qquad (2)$$

Probabilistic Non-Deterministic Finite Automata (PNFA) are WFAs that compute a probabilistic distribution over strings. One can easily transform a PNFA into another automata that computes substring expectations via simple transformations of the model parameters, and the reverse is also true, see Balle et al. (2014) for details.

In this paper we will directly learn and use automata that compute expectations. To train the WFAs we will use the classical spectral learning method by described in Balle et al. (2014), using the scalability techniques by Quattoni et al. (2017).

2.2   WFA Classifier Ensemble

We will now describe how we combine class specific WFAs to build a sequence classifier. Let's assume that we have a set $L = \{1, \ldots, l\}$ of target class labels and a training set $D = \{(x_1, y_1), \ldots, (x_n, y_n)\}$ of n labeled samples where $x \in \Sigma^\star$ is an input sequence and $y \in L$

is an output label. Our goal is to use D to learn a function mapping sequences to class labels, i.e. a classifier $c : \Sigma^\star \to L$.

We start by partitioning the training set D into l training sets $(d_1, \ldots d_l)$, one for each target class. Then for each training set d_l we train a corresponding WFA: $f_l(x) : \Sigma^\star \to \mathbb{R}$ using the spectral method. We can think that this model is computing an approximation of the expected number of times of observing a subsequence x from a sequence sampled from the distribution of sequences of class l. More generally, one can regard $f_l(x)$ as a real valued score that measures the compatibility between a subsequence x and a label l. Intuitively, think of x as an ngram feature.

With the scores computed by the class-specific WFAs we will build a prediction function. The idea is quite simple, we will run the scoring function over all ngrams up to a given length and aggregate the outputs to compute a single score measuring the compatibility of a sequence and a target class.

More precisely, we define a maximum ngram length parameter t. Given a sequence x we denote the set of all ngrams of x up to length t as $W_x = (w_1, \ldots, w_m)$. The aggregate prediction score is simply defined as:

$$z(x, l) = \sum_{w \in W_x} \frac{f_l(w)}{\sum_{l' \in L} f_{l'}(w)} \qquad . \qquad (3)$$

We can regard

$$\frac{f_l(w)}{\sum_{l' \in L} f_{l'}(w)} \qquad (4)$$

as an approximation of the conditional distribution $P(l|w)$, since $f_l(w)$ is an approximation of an expectation and therefore is a non-negative score.

Given the aggregate scoring function $z(x, l)$ the prediction of the WFA ensemble is simply: $\text{argmax}_l z(x, l)$. Essentially, we are using the generative models in a *discriminative* manner.

A natural question to ask is why not to use the Naive Bayes score:

$$z(x, l) = \log P(l) + \sum_{w \in W_x} \log P(w|l) \qquad (5)$$

where we approximate $P(w|l)$ by $f_l(w)$. To do so, instead of the expectation WFA, we would use a WFA that computes probabilities (which can be easily obtained from the WFA that computes expectations (Balle et al., 2014)). We have indeed tried this approach but it performed poorly since the generative model cannot capture the discriminative ngrams of the data.

On the other hand we realized that the simple modification of using the generative models to make a discriminative prediction resulted in good performance.

3 Experiments

We conducted experiments on five sequence classification data sets:

- MR: This is a movie review data set where the task is to classify a sentence as positive or negative review. There are two classes and the average sentence length is 20. The total number of samples is 106,662 and the vocabulary size 18,765 (Pang and Lee, 2005).

- SST-2: This is a sentiment treebank, where the task is to predict a positive or negative sentiment label. There are two classes and the average sentence length is 19. The total number of samples is 9,613 and the vocabulary size 16,185 (Socher et al., 2013).

- Subj: This is a subjectivity data set were the task is to predict if a sentence is subjective or objective.There are two classes and the average sentence length is 23. The total number of samples is 10,000 and the vocabulary size 21,323 (Pang and Lee, 2004).

- TREC: This is a question classification data set. The task is to classify a question into six question types (e.g. a question about a location, a person, etc.). There are six classes and the average sentence length is 10. The total number of samples is 5,952 and the vocabulary size 9,592 (Li and Roth, 2002).

- CR: This data set contains reviews written by customers about various products. The task is to predict the review is positive or negative. There are two classes and the average sentence length is 19. The total number of samples is 3,775 and the vocabulary size 5,340 (Hu and Liu, 2004).

The WFA models have two parameters: the number of states k and the maximum window size t, both parameters were validated using a validation set. For k we tried [50, 100, 200] and for t we tested [2, 3, 4, 5].

DATA	CNN	WFA
MR	76.1	**77.3**
SST-2	**82.7**	81.6
Subj	89.6	**91.9**
TREC	**91.2**	90.1
CR	**79.8**	79.5
average	83.9	**84.1**

Table 1: Results of the WFA classifier against a baseline CNN.

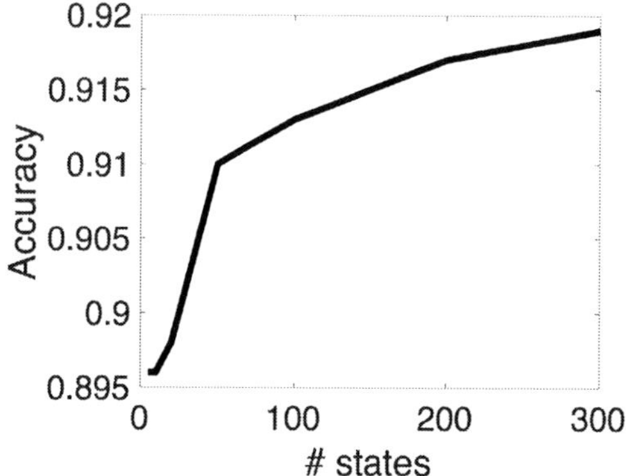

Figure 1: Performance as a function of the number of states of the model for the SUBJ dataset.

When a standard train-development-test partition was not provided in the original data set we performed 10 fold cross validation and report mean performance.

We will compare the performance of the ensemble WFA with a classical CNN architecture for sequence classification. More specifically, we compare against the model described in (Kim, 2014). The model has 100 convolutional filters run over ngrams of size: [3, 4, 5], a max-pooling layer and a fully connected softmax layer. The word embeddings are randomly initialized and then modified during training. The model was trained using 0.5 drop-out and $l2$ regularization.

We performed experiments on the 5 sequence classification datasets and report the results on Table 1. As we can see the results show that the performance of the WFA model is comparable to that of the CNN. Figure 1 shows accuracy as a function of the number of states of the model for the SUBJ dataset, as we can see even with only 5 states the model shows reasonable performance, around 89.5.

4 Discussion

In the surface CNNs and WFAs for sequence classification might seem quite dissimilar. The performance of the CNNs relies on learning good discriminative ngram features via their convolutional filters. In contrast the WFA ensemble focuses on learning good estimates of the moments distributions of each class.

However, if we look closer into the WFAs we realize that implicitly the WFA can also capture arbitrary features of the input sequences via its latent states (i.e. the latent states can remember any regular pattern of the input sequence).

The ability to induce patterns seems to be confirmed by our experiments. Our results show that by simply making a discriminative prediction out of the outputs of the class specific WFAs we can get very close to matching the performance of the CNNs.

Both CNNs and WFAs have their advantages and disadvantages. The main advantage of the CNNs is that they are very flexible and can induce arbitrary patterns. However, training them can be computationally expensive and the resulting model might be hard to interpret.

On the other hand WFAs can be easily trained with the classical spectral method. Most of the models reported in these experiments were trained in less than five minutes in a regular machine with four CPUs. In addition, because the relation between inputs and latent-state is more transparent (i.e. just a linear function) they might be interpreted more easily.

The main disadvantage of WFAs is that they lack the modeling flexibility of CNNs. This is because it is harder to incorporate arbitrary loss functions. While there have been extensions of spectral methods that can exploit any convex loss function (Quattoni et al., 2014) this usually results in optimizations that are significantly more costly. And therefore the resulting training algorithms loose part of the practical appeal of the classical spectral method.

Finally, another potential limitation of WFAs is that because the latent state dynamics is linear, they might need more states than models that can make use on non-linear dynamics.

Most likely the best model would combine the best of both worlds. But the first step is to understand their similarities and differences in the context of concrete NLP tasks. We believe our results are a first tiny step towards that goal.

5 Future Work

In many ways our experiments are crippled. The most evident limitation is that none of the models exploit external features such as pre-trained word embeddings, as it is well known that such features are essential to improve the performance of sequence prediction models.

As we already said this is just a first comparison, and we focused on the simplest possible configuration of both models. In the future, we plan to make comparisons of models that incorporate word embeddings.

Notice that WFAs have also been defined for real valued inputs (Recasens and Quattoni, 2013) and therefore they can also incorporate pre-trained word embedding vectors.

Furthermore, the comparison is relatively unfair in the sense that the WFAs are trained in a generative fashion. There have been proposals for discriminative training or discriminative refinements that we plan to explore in the future (Quattoni and Carreras, 2019; Quattoni et al., 2014).

Finally, in this paper we focus on comparisons against CNNs. But it would be interesting to expand the study to other models such as RNNs and LSTMS.

Acknowledgements

This work is supported by the European Research Council (ERC StG INTERACT 853459).

References

Raphaël Bailly, François Denis, and Liva Ralaivola. 2009. Grammatical inference as a principal component analysis problem. In *Proceedings of the 26th Annual International Conference on Machine Learning*, ICML '09, pages 33–40, New York, NY, USA. ACM.

Borja Balle, Xavier Carreras, Franco M. Luque, and Ariadna Quattoni. 2014. Spectral Learning of Weighted Automata: A Forward-Backward Perspective. *Machine Learning*, 96(1):33–63.

Borja Balle, Ariadna Quattoni, and Xavier Carreras. 2011. A spectral learning algorithm for finite state transducers. In *Proceedings of the 2011th European Conference on Machine Learning and Knowledge Discovery in Databases - Volume Part I*, ECMLPKDD'11, pages 156–171, Berlin, Heidelberg. Springer-Verlag.

Shay B. Cohen, Karl Stratos, Michael Collins, Dean P. Foster, and Lyle Ungar. 2012. Spectral learning of latent-variable pcfgs. In *Proceedings of the 50th Annual Meeting of the Association for Computational Linguistics (Volume 1: Long Papers)*, pages 223–231, Jeju Island, Korea. Association for Computational Linguistics.

Yoav Goldberg. 2016. A primer on neural network models for natural language processing. *Journal of Artificial Intelligence Research*, 57(1):345420.

Daniel Hsu, Sham M Kakade, and Tong Zhang. 2012. A spectral algorithm for learning hidden markov models. *Journal of Computer and System Sciences*, 78(5):1460–1480.

Daniel J. Hsu, Sham M. Kakade, and Tong Zhang. 2009. A spectral algorithm for learning hidden markov models. In *COLT 2009 - The 22nd Conference on Learning Theory, Montreal, Quebec, Canada, June 18-21, 2009*.

M. Hu and B. Liu. 2004. Minning and summarizing customers reviews. In *Proceedings of ACL SIGKDD 2004*.

Rie Johnson and Tong Zhang. 2015. Effective use of word order for text categorization with convolutional neural networks. In *Proceedings of the 2015 Conference of the North American Chapter of the Association for Computational Linguistics: Human Language Technologies*, pages 103–112, Denver, Colorado. Association for Computational Linguistics.

Nal Kalchbrenner, Edward Grefenstette, and Phil Blunson. 2014. A convolutional neural network for modelling sentences. In *Proceedings of the 52th Annual Meeting on Association for Computational Linguistics*.

Yoon Kim. 2014. Convolutional neural networks for sentence classification. In *Proceedings of the 2014 Conference on Empirical Methods in Natural Language Processing (EMNLP)*, Doha, Qatar. Association for Computational Linguistics.

X. Li and D. Roth. 2002. Learning questions classifiers. In *Proceedings of ACL 2002*.

B. Pang and L. Lee. 2004. A sentimental eduction: Sentiment analysis using subjectivity summarization based on minimum cuts. In *Proceedings of the Annual Meeting on Association for Computational Linguistics*.

B. Pang and L. Lee. 2005. Seeing starts: Exploiting class relationships for sentiment categorization with respect to rating scales. In *Proceedings of the Annual Meeting on Association for Computational Linguistics*.

Ariadna Quattoni, Borja Balle, Xavier Carreras, and Amir Globerson. 2014. Spectral regularization for max-margin sequence tagging. In *Proceedings of the 31st International Conference on Machine Learning (ICML-14)*, pages 1710–1718. JMLR Workshop and Conference Proceedings.

Ariadna Quattoni and Xavier Carreras. 2019. Interpolated spectral NGram language models. In *Proceedings of the 57th Annual Meeting of the Association for Computational Linguistics*, pages 5926–5930, Florence, Italy. Association for Computational Linguistics.

Ariadna Quattoni, Xavier Carreras, and Matthias Gallé. 2017. A maximum matching algorithm for basis selection in spectral learning. In *Proceedings of the 20th International Conference on Artificial Intelligence and Statistics (AISTATS)*, volume 54 of *JMLR Proceedings*.

Guillaume Rabusseau, Tianyu Li, and Doina Precup. 2019. Connecting weighted automata and recurrent neural networks through spectral learning. In *Proceedings of Machine Learning Research*, volume 89, pages 1630–1639. PMLR.

Adria Recasens and Ariadna Quattoni. 2013. Spectral learning of sequence taggers over continuous sequences. In *Machine Learning and Knowledge Discovery in Databases*, pages 289–304. Springer Berlin Heidelberg.

R. Socher, A. Perelygin, J. Wu, J. Chuang, C. Manning, A. Ng, and C. Potts. 2013. Recursive deep models for semantic compositionality over a sentiment treebank. In *Proceedings of EMNLP 2013*.

Ye Zhang and Byron Wallace. 2017. A sensitivity analysis of (and practitioners' guide to) convolutional neural networks for sentence classification. In *Proceedings of the Eighth International Joint Conference on Natural Language Processing (Volume 1: Long Papers)*.

Label-Efficient Training for Next Response Selection

Seungtaek Choi[*]
Yonsei University
hist0613@yonsei.ac.kr

Myeongho Jeong[*]
Yonsei University
wag9611@yonsei.ac.kr

Jinyoung Yeo
Yonsei University
jinyeo@yonsei.ac.kr

Seung-won Hwang[†]
Yonsei University
seungwonh@yonsei.ac.kr

Abstract

This paper studies label augmentation for training dialogue response selection. The existing model is trained by "observational" annotation, where one observed response is annotated as gold. In this paper, we propose "counterfactual augmentation" of pseudo-positive labels. We validate that the effectiveness of augmented labels are comparable to positives, such that ours outperform state-of-the-arts without augmentation.

1 Introduction

This paper studies the problem of response selection of the most appropriate answer given the dialogue history (or, context). A key challenge in this task is annotations being limited to "observational", most frequently annotating only one of such valid answers. Meanwhile, linguistically diverse datasets are critical to ensure the robustness of machine learning models, though augmenting diverse expert annotations are often too costly to sustain, both in terms of (1) annotation and (2) training cost. For the first challenge of keeping annotation cost sustainable, there have been two directions:

- (a) Crowdsourcing: A training resource `Advising-1` (Yoshino et al., 2019), collecting dialogues for advising students on which classes to take, is observational, but 1-5 alternatives to the observed answer can be crowdsourced to increase linguistic diversity, which we denote as `Advising-3`.

- (b) Paraphrase generator: Paraphrase generation is typically trained from sentence-level paraphrase pairs. For example, a gold response *"Cheap please."*, can be augmented

with its paraphrase *"Could you find me a cheap restaurant?"*. However, when considering the context of asking *"Do you prefer a cheap or expensive restaurant?"*, the latter may not be a counterfactual alternative as argued in (Gao et al., 2020).

In this direction, Unsupervised Data Augmentation (UDA) (Xie et al., 2019a) of adding noises to unlabeled text x to keep model prediction invariant, known as consistency training. Ours is fundamentally different that we keep x intact, and thus keep training cost unchanged, and orthogonal to these approaches adding training instances (and cost). Considering our focus keeping training cost low, we report UDA variant (of "selecting" and not generating noised x) instead.

Figure 1(a) and (b) visualize crowd-sourced and paraphrased positive, as a blue and yellow polygon, respectively. Figure 1(a) incurs human-annotation overhead while Figure 1(b) requires no such cost but suffers a limited overlap. Our goal is to combine the strength of the two, and propose Figure 1(c) with comparable coverage to (a), but with no annotation overhead as in (b). Specifically, our technical contributions are:

- Contextual paraphrase selection: We mine contextual paraphrase pairs, by selecting responses to the same context. Unlike crowdsourcing, this would neither incur any annotation, nor increase the training dataset size.

- Multi-Reference Training: Some noisy paraphrase selection by (c, c') may incorrectly augment response with r'. We thus aim to eliminate such noise by a context-response matching model $s(c, r') < \epsilon$. To this model, we add an auxiliary task of generating soft-labels suggesting soft-selection of multiple

---

[*]The authors contribute equally to this paper.
[†]corresponding author

164

Proceedings of SustaiNLP: Workshop on Simple and Efficient Natural Language Processing, pages 164–168
Online, November 20, 2020. ©2020 Association for Computational Linguistics

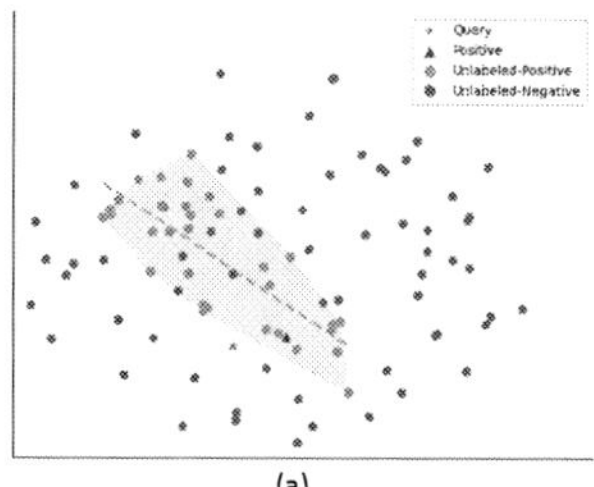
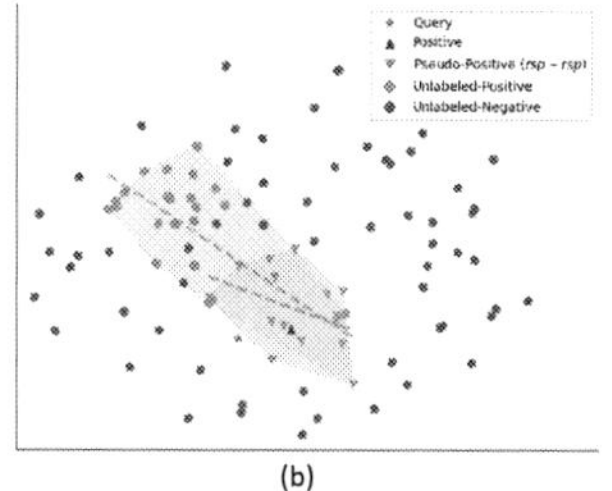
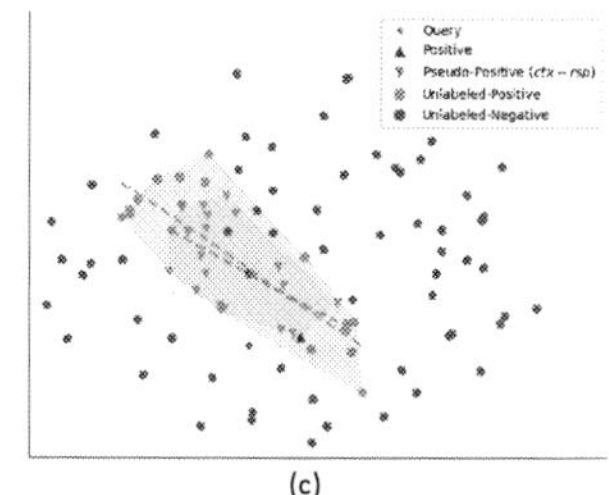

Figure 1: t-SNE visualization for `DailyDialog` dataset in Section 3.2. **(a)** shows a single observational positive (blue triangle), or, an observed answer "Yeah." to "Are you an American?". Blue polygon shows the distribution of crowd annotation that is clearly distinct from that of unlabeled points. **(b)** shows an automated pseudo-positive labeling using response similarity. We can observe that the distribution (and also regression line) of blue and yellow polygon do not align. Finally, **(c)** visualizes our pseudo-positives that align better, with examples such as "No. I am Canadian. Are you Chinese?", or "No, I'm a Britisher. Where do you come from?".

alternative references r', or replacing the original observational distribution with an approximated multi-reference couterfactual distribuitions (Zhao and Kawahara, 2020).

Figure 1(c) illustrates the effectiveness of these contributions. We empirically validate our models, using public benchmark datasets for next response selection task: `Advising` and `DailyDialog`.

This work builds on and extends (Jeong et al., 2020) by reporting how our model generalizes to `Advising-1` and DSTC8 competition results.

2 Background

In this section, we first define the response selection task and describe widely used baselines, namely Bi-encoder (Humeau et al., 2019) architectures.

2.1 Response Selection Task

The objective of the response selection task is developing dialogue agents that select proper utterances from candidates for given conversation context (Humeau et al., 2019; Zhang et al., 2018; Lowe et al., 2015; Dinan et al., 2019). Given a dataset $\mathcal{D} = \{(c_i, R_i)\}_{i=1}^{N}$, where c_i represents a conversation context, and R_i is a set of response candidates. Let $R_i = \{(r_{i,k}, y_{i,k}\}_{k=1}^{T}$, where T is the number of response candidates, determined in task setting. Each $r_{i,k}$ is the k-th response candidate and $y_{i,k} \in \{0, 1\}$ denotes a label with $y_{i,k} = 1$ indicating $r_{i,k}$ is a correct response for context c_i and $y_{i,k} = 0$ otherwise. We propose to augment $\mathcal{D}$ into $\mathcal{D}'$.

The response selection task thus aims to learn a matching model $s(\cdot, \cdot)$ from $\mathcal{D}$. For any context-response pair (c, r), the matching model gives a score $s(c, r)$ that reflects the matching degree between c and r, and thus allows one to rank a set of response candidates R_i according to the corresponding scores for response selection.

2.2 Base Architecture: BERT Bi-Encoder

We use Bi-encoder (Humeau et al., 2019) for context-response matching $s(c, r)$, where input context and the candidate response are encoded into vectors with BERT (Devlin et al., 2018):

$$\bar{c}_i = \text{BERT}_c(c_i) \tag{1}$$

$$\bar{r}_{i,k} = \text{BERT}_r(r_{i,k}) \tag{2}$$

where BERT_c and BERT_r are two transformers, pre-trained as described in (Humeau et al., 2019). A key advantage is that c and r can be pre-computed of the embeddings of all contexts (and responses).

The score of a response candidate $r_{i,k}$ is given by the dot-product $\hat{s}(c_i, r_{i,k}) = \bar{c}_i \cdot \bar{r}_{i,k}$. In BERT fine-tuning, the function is trained to minimize a cross-entropy loss $\mathcal{L}$ in which the logits are $\hat{s}(c_i, r_{i,1}), ..., \hat{s}(c_i, r_{i,T})$, where $r_{i,1}$ is the only correct response:

$$\mathcal{L} = \sum_{\mathcal{D}} y_{i,k} \log \hat{s}(c_i, r_{i,k}) \tag{3}$$

Following (Humeau et al., 2019), all other gold responses of other contexts in the same batch are treated as negative responses in training.

3 Multi-Refrence Training

Our proposed approach has a base architecture of (Jeong et al., 2020), which adopts noisy student training paradigm (Xie et al., 2019b; Park

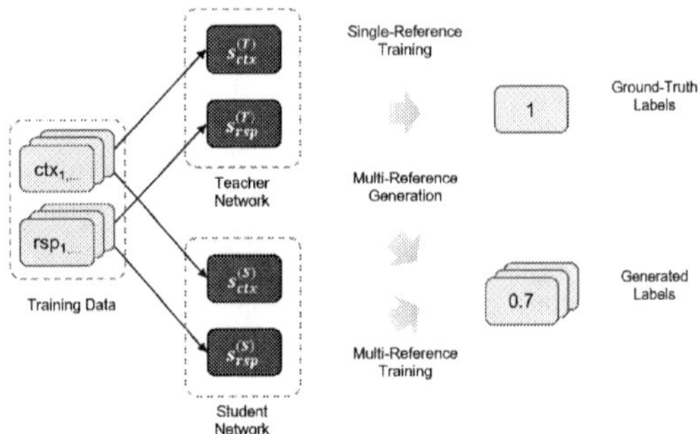

Figure 2: Illustration of multi-referenced training.

et al., 2020). Recall that the observed annotation is $\mathcal{D} = \{(c_i, R_i)\}_{i=1}^{N}$ where for each context c_i, R_i consists of one gold annotation, denoted as $r_{i,1}$, and $T - 1$ negatively sampled examples. Our goal is to expand $\mathcal{D}$, a $N \times T$ matrix, into counterfactual observations of $N \times N$ matrix, where each context may have up to P positive labels.

1. Train teacher model $s^{(T)}$ on labeled dataset $\mathcal{D}$

2. Expand $\mathcal{D}$ into noisy paraphrases $\mathcal{D}'$

3. Filter $\mathcal{D}'$ by context-response matching $s^{(T)}$

4. Train student model $s^{(S)}$ on the mix of $\hat{s}^{(T)}(\mathcal{D}')$ and $\mathcal{D}$.

5. Trained student model can be a teacher for another iteration, but we report one iteration result for sustainable training.

3.1 Teacher: Contextual Paraphase Selection

Following (Jeong et al., 2020), we compute a pairing matrix $M^{\text{ctx}} \in \mathbb{R}^{N \times N}$ comparing c_i and c_j as:

$$M_{ij}^{\text{ctx}} = \begin{cases} \text{sim}(\bar{c}_i, \bar{c}_j), & \text{if } \text{sim}(\bar{c}_i, \bar{c}_j) > \epsilon, \\ 0, & \text{otherwise,} \end{cases} \quad (4)$$

where we empirically set the threshold ϵ to 0.6. Here we only use context encoder out of two (bi-) encoders, which we argue as a distinction from self-training approaches of using the entire teacher architecture.

M can viewed as a soft expansion of $\mathcal{D}$ into $\mathcal{D}'$, with the maximum number of augmented responses T tuned as a hyper-parameter. For sustainable training, we select top-T similar paraphrases from N.

3.2 Student: Context-Response Matching

Based on the soft labels of the teacher trained on $\mathcal{D}$ and $\mathcal{D}'$, we can train student to mimic $\bar{y}_{i,k} = \hat{s}^{(T)}(c_i, r_{j,1})$. This student network can be evaluated with classification (identifying multiple positive responses) and ranking (finding one response), such as `Advising-3` and `Advising-1` tasks.

$$\mathcal{L} = \sum_{\mathcal{D}'} \bar{y}_{i,k} \log \hat{s}^{(S)}(c_i, r_{i,k}), \quad (5)$$

where $\hat{s}^{(S)}$ denotes the student network and $\bar{y}_{i,k}$ is the soft-labels from the teacher model $s^{(T)}$.

4 Experiments

The goal of our experiments is answering the following research questions.

- **RQ1:** Is automated augmentation comparable to human annotation in classification?

- **RQ2:** Does augmentation improve ranking?

4.1 Datasets

- **Advising** (Yoshino et al., 2019): This dataset collects multiple observational golds (avg: 3.6), which are semantically identical in the given context (*i.e.*, contextual paraphrases).

  `Advising-1` aims to rank the only gold response out of 100 candidates, while `Advising-3` requires to classify all positive responses.

  The training split is constructed by the same strategy introduced in (Lowe et al., 2015). With this dataset, we compare **Oracle** using human annotation, with our proposed **Sustainable** using one sampled answer. **Oracle** is reported as an upper bound accuracy.

- **DailyDialog** (Gupta et al., 2019): `DailyDialog` is constructed to evaluate semantic diversity of *generated* responses, which we repurpose as a selection task. As there are no available training annotations for classifying multiple positives, this dataset naturally motivates a sustainable augmentation scenario: Such annotations exist only for evaluation– 5 gold responses out of given 100 candidates.

  For evaluation, we employ generally used metrics: mean average precision (MAP), recall at position k for classification, and mean reciprocal rank (MRR) for ranking.

Train Data	Advising-1			Advising-3			DailyDialog		
	MRR	R@1	R@10	MAP	R@1	R@10	MAP	R@1	R@10
Oracle									
ESIM (Chen and Wang, 2019)	0.3197	0.2040	0.5780	0.3862	0.0973	0.5462	-	-	-
BERT (a)	0.3926	0.2600	0.6860	0.4585	0.1191	0.6310	-	-	-
Sustainable									
BERT no-aug	0.2992	0.1760	0.5240	0.3836	0.1308	0.5183	0.7838	0.1868	0.8575
BERT (b)	0.3514	0.2200	0.6340	0.4344	**0.1327**	0.6038	0.7809	0.1862	0.8541
BERT (c)– ours	**0.3664**	**0.2280**	0.6400	**0.4485**	0.1264	**0.6149**	**0.8024**	**0.1884**	**0.8702**
BERT-UDA	0.3614	0.2220	**0.6460**	0.4311	0.1227	0.6036	0.7806	0.1860	0.8543

Table 1: First two rows trained on **Oracle** annotations for valid responses (upper bound), and the rest is for **Sustainable** scenario.

4.2 Implementation Details

In experiments below, we leverage bi-encoder with strictly following original setting of public implementation[1], specifically using `bi_model_huge_reddit` pre-trained weights.

However, as BERT architecture requires large GPU memories, we modify the batch size and the number of response candidates to fit in our experimental environments. For bi-encoder, we modify batch size 512 to 32, processing 32 dialogue contexts in a batch. However, to prevent performance drop from a reduced number of candidates, we additionally sample negative candidates from other contexts having up to 224 candidates for one context. For cross-encoder, we keep batches to 16 elements, during providing negatives with random sampling.

We use AdaMax (Kingma and Ba, 2014) optimizer with 5e-05 learning rate for training on `Advising-3` dataset, Adam (Kingma and Ba, 2014) optimizer with 5e-05 learning rate on `DailyDialog` dataset and Adam with weight decay of 0.01 on `Advising-1` dataset.

4.3 RQ1: Classification

We first evaluate how our conditional augmentation compares to **Oracle**, using all human annotations for multiple valid annotations for training. Our work samples only one gold response and still performs comparably, with our proposed augmentation. In Table 1, we report BERT Bi-encoder with (a) oracle annotation, (b) augmented by contextual paraphrasing, (c) our proposed counterfactual augmentation, each of which corresponds to Figure 1(a)-(c) respectively. Ours achieves

0.4485 MAP, comparable with BERT (a) with oracle augmentation, while improving 6.49% point gains from BERT without augmentation (no-aug) in `Advising-3`. These observations were consistent in `DailyDialog` task. We also add BERT-UDA, a variant of UDA of selecting a likely augmentation based on response similarity. Those were not as effective as ours, but comparable in terms of increasing recall@10. Finding an effective way to merge it with ours would be an interesting future topic.

4.4 RQ2: Ranking

In Table 1, we compare the BERT cross-encoder with and without our proposed augmentation, in the ranking task of `Advising-1`. Our proposed augmentation significantly improves BERT ranker in terms of MRR and R@1: BERT (c) achieves 0.3664 MRR and 0.2280 R@1. A similar discussion was in (Lin, 2019) showing regularization effect from pseudo-positive augmentation contributes to ad-hoc ranking, which is consistent with our results. We also validated the robustness of our method in DSTC 8[2], by being ranked the 2nd and the 3rd in DSTC8 Track 2 Sub-task 1 (Team 5 and 12 in Ubuntu).

5 Conclusion

This paper studies the problem of label augmentation for response selection. Our empirical results validate its effectiveness in both ranking and classification tasks.

---

[1] https://github.com/facebookresearch/ ParlAI/tree/master/projects/polyencoder

[2] Link to DSTC8 Leaderboard

References

Qian Chen and Wen Wang. 2019. Sequential attention-based network for noetic end-to-end response selection. *arXiv preprint arXiv:1901.02609*.

Jacob Devlin, Ming-Wei Chang, Kenton Lee, and Kristina Toutanova. 2018. Bert: Pre-training of deep bidirectional transformers for language understanding. In *NAACL*.

Emily Dinan, Varvara Logacheva, Valentin Malykh, Alexander Miller, Kurt Shuster, Jack Urbanek, Douwe Kiela, Arthur Szlam, Iulian Serban, Ryan Lowe, et al. 2019. The second conversational intelligence challenge (convai2). *arXiv preprint arXiv:1902.00098*.

Silin Gao, Yichi Zhang, Zhijian Ou, and Zhou Yu. 2020. Paraphrase augmented task-oriented dialog generation. *arXiv preprint arXiv:2004.07462*.

Prakhar Gupta, Shikib Mehri, Tiancheng Zhao, Amy Pavel, Maxine Eskenazi, and Jeffrey P Bigham. 2019. Investigating evaluation of open-domain dialogue systems with human generated multiple references. *arXiv preprint arXiv:1907.10568*.

Samuel Humeau, Kurt Shuster, Marie-Anne Lachaux, and Jason Weston. 2019. Poly-encoders: Transformer architectures and pre-training strategies for fast and accurate multi-sentence scoring. *arXiv preprint*.

Myeongho Jeong, Seungtaek Choi, Hojae Han, Kyungho Kim, and Seungwon Hwang. 2020. Conditional response augmentation for dialogue using knowledge distillation. In *INTERSPEECH*.

Diederik P Kingma and Jimmy Ba. 2014. Adam: A method for stochastic optimization. *arXiv preprint*.

Jimmy Lin. 2019. The neural hype and comparisons against weak baselines. In *ACM SIGIR Forum*.

Ryan Lowe, Nissan Pow, Iulian Serban, and Joelle Pineau. 2015. The ubuntu dialogue corpus: A large dataset for research in unstructured multi-turn dialogue systems. In *SIGDIAL*.

Daniel S Park, Yu Zhang, Ye Jia, Wei Han, Chung-Cheng Chiu, Bo Li, Yonghui Wu, and Quoc V Le. 2020. Improved noisy student training for automatic speech recognition. *arXiv preprint arXiv:2005.09629*.

Qizhe Xie, Zihang Dai, Eduard Hovy, Minh-Thang Luong, and Quoc V Le. 2019a. Unsupervised data augmentation for consistency training. *arXiv preprint arXiv:1904.12848*.

Qizhe Xie, Eduard Hovy, Minh-Thang Luong, and Quoc V Le. 2019b. Self-training with noisy student improves imagenet classification. *arXiv preprint arXiv:1911.04252*.

Koichiro Yoshino, Chiori Hori, Julien Perez, Luis Fernando D'Haro, Lazaros Polymenakos, Chulaka Gunasekara, Walter S Lasecki, Jonathan K Kummerfeld, Michel Galley, Chris Brockett, et al. 2019. Dialog system technology challenge 7. *arXiv preprint*.

Saizheng Zhang, Emily Dinan, Jack Urbanek, Arthur Szlam, Douwe Kiela, and Jason Weston. 2018. Personalizing dialogue agents: I have a dog, do you have pets too? In *Proceedings of the 56th Annual Meeting of the Association for Computational Linguistics (Volume 1: Long Papers)*, pages 2204–2213.

Tianyu Zhao and Tatsuya Kawahara. 2020. Multi-referenced training for dialogue response generation. *arXiv preprint arXiv:2009.07117*.

Do We Need to Create Big Datasets to Learn a Task?

Swaroop Mishra*   Bhavdeep Sachdeva*
Department of Computer Science, Arizona State University
{srmishr1, bssachde}@asu.edu

Abstract

Deep Learning research has been largely accelerated by the development of huge datasets such as Imagenet. The general trend has been to create big datasets to make a deep neural network learn. A huge amount of resources is being spent in creating these big datasets, developing models, training them, and iterating this process to dominate leaderboards. We argue that the trend of creating bigger datasets needs to be revised by better leveraging the power of pre-trained language models. Since the language models have already been pretrained with huge amount of data and have basic linguistic knowledge, there is no need to create big datasets to learn a task. Instead, we need to create a dataset that is sufficient for the model to learn various task-specific terminologies, such as 'Entailment', 'Neutral', and 'Contradiction' for NLI. As evidence, we show that RoBERTA is able to achieve near-equal performance on $\sim 2\%$ data of SNLI. We also observe competitive zero-shot generalization on several OOD datasets. In this paper, we propose a baseline algorithm to find the optimal dataset for learning a task.

1   Introduction

Large scale datasets such as Imagenet (Russakovsky et al., 2015) in Vision, and SQUAD (Rajpurkar et al., 2016) and SNLI (Bowman et al., 2015) in NLP have accelerated our progress in deep learning. The general trend has been to create large scale datasets for various tasks such as Abductive NLI (Bhagavatula et al., 2019), DROP (Dua et al., 2019), and SWAG (Zellers et al., 2018). The process of creating big datasets involves heavy investment in resources, that further increases when models are developed in response to these datasets, and trained to top leaderboards. This makes deep learning research and development inaccessible to

communities where resources are scarce. Additionally, the heavy computation involved in training models adversely affects the environment on a broader scale (Schwartz et al., 2019). This leads us to the question: *Do we always need to create big datasets?*

We probe this question with motivation from the process by which we learn a certain topic/task. *Even though we have access to hundreds of materials available online, we do not need to go through all of them in order to learn the specific topic. In fact, we intentionally avoid certain materials which are noisy, distracting, or irrelevant to the topic.* Humans have deep background knowledge about the world which makes this possible. With the recent developments in language modelling, pre-training on huge datasets have imparted linguistic knowledge to models like BERT (Devlin et al., 2018) and RoBERTA (Liu et al., 2019). With this knowledge, models need not learn everything from scratch; instead they should just learn task specific terminologies such as 'Entailment', 'Neutral', and 'Contradiction' for NLI, which might not necessitate the use of big datasets.

There are certain other factors that recommend against creating big datasets. A growing number of recent works (Poliak et al., 2018; Geva et al., 2019; Kaushik and Lipton, 2018; Schwartz et al., 2017; Mishra et al., 2020; Bras et al., 2020) have exposed the presence of spurious bias in many popular benchmarks. Spurious bias represents unintended correlations between input and output (e.g.: the word 'not' is most often associated with the label 'contradiction'(Gururangan et al., 2018)). Spurious bias makes a task easy for models, allowing them to exploit instead of learning generalizable features like humans. Models finetuned on these benchmarks fail to generalize in Out of Distribution (OOD) and Adversarial settings. Since the sources of these spurious biases: data collection,

---

 * equal contribution

Proceedings of SustaiNLP: Workshop on Simple and Efficient Natural Language Processing, pages 169–173
Online, November 20, 2020. ©2020 Association for Computational Linguistics

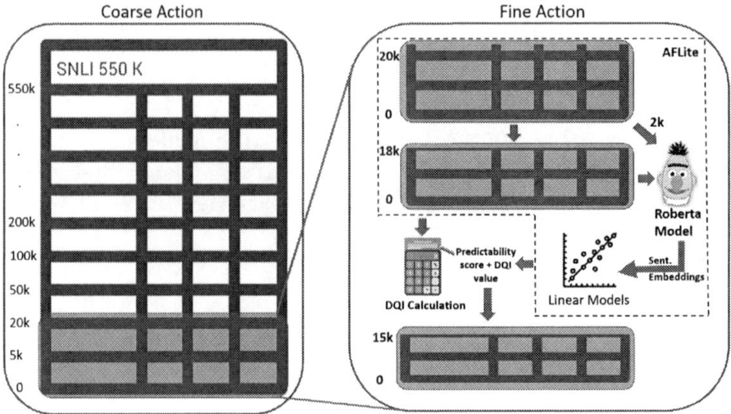

Figure 1: Proposed baseline approach to select the optimal data necessary to learn a task.

and crowdsourcing are hard to control, carefully selecting a smaller and optimal dataset may be a viable alternative.

We propose a baseline in this paper to find the optimal dataset for learning a task. Our approach is inspired by the human tendency to first make a rough estimate of the presence of relevant materials by glancing at various parts of an entire set of available materials. After selecting a slice of existing materials in the first phase, they remove redundant/easy/already known/possible distracting content from the slice. Finally, they use heuristics based on their background knowledge about the task to sort based on relevance and select the most optimal content based on the priority of the task and availability of time to learn it. We utilize several recently proposed modules in our baseline.

We prune SNLI (Bowman et al., 2015) to $\sim 2\%$ of its original size using our baseline. Our results show that RoBERTA on training with this pruned set achieves near-equal performance on the SNLI dev set and competitive zero-shot generalization on three OOD datasets (i) NLI Diagnostics (Wang et al., 2018), (ii) Stress Tests (Naik et al., 2018), (iii) Adversarial NLI (Nie et al., 2019). Our analysis shows that big datasets not only prevent generalization, but also impact IID testset performance. Interestingly, we find the annotation of those data to be correct and not noisy. This indicates that, certain data samples might be distracting a model by acting against the inductive bias created by rest of the dataset. Our finding opens up the possible existence of such distractors in real datasets, encouraging NLP community to explore the optimal selection of certain samples in a dataset instead of trying to dominate a leaderboard with the entire dataset.

2 Proposed Algorithm

We mimic the relevant material selection process in humans to propose algorithm for selecting the optimal dataset necessary to learn a task, as illustrated in Figure 1. We use robotics terminology (Rauch et al., 2019) to explain the stages of learning (i) coarse action (ii) fine action. Algorithm 1 details our approach. We briefly explain each stage below.

Formalization: Let D represent the entire dataset, s represent samples, M be the model, S be the pruned set, $E(s)$, $C(s)$ and $P(s)$ be the evaluation score, correct evaluation score and predictability score of each sample s respectively. In this preliminary work, we just explore the first term of DQI_{c1}. Expanding this to other terms will be the immediate future work.

Coarse Action: We start with a random subset of $a\%$ of dataset (D), train model (M) on it and calculate accuracy on the IID testset. We iteratively append a random subset of $b\%$ of data from the rest of D, train M on the combined data and calculate accuracy on the testset. We continue adding $b\%$ of data until the testset accuracy stops increasing. L1-L8 of algorithm 1 explains coarse action.

Fine Action: We use two key modules (i) AFLite (Bras et al., 2020; Sakaguchi et al., 2019) and (ii) DQI (Mishra et al., 2020) for fine action on the data selected after coarse action. AFLite is a recent technique for adversarial filtering of dataset biases, whereas DQI has a method to quantify quality of samples with or without annotation.

AFLite: In our setup, AFLite randomly selects 10% of data (selected after coarse action) for fine tuning on M, and then discards them. It randomly partition the data into train and test set, and does it in parallel several times. It trains linear models (logistic regression and SVM) with the train data, and evaluate on the test data. It combines parallel sessions by calculating predictability score ($P(s)$) of every data as the number of time it has been correctly predicted ($C(s)$) divided by the number of times it has been evaluated ($E(s)$). It then shortlists samples for which predictability score is greater than a threshold (tau).

DQI: DQI stands for Data Quality Index. It is a compilation of various linguistic parameters related to dataset biases. It has seven components –(i) Vocabulary, (ii) Inter-Sample N-gram Frequency and Relation, (iii) Inter-Sample STS (Semantic Textual Similarity), (iv) Intra-Sample Word Similarity, (v) Intra-Sample STS, (vi) N-Gram Frequency per Label, (vii) Inter-Split STS – that cover various possible inter/intra-sample interactions (a subset of which leads to biases) in an NLP dataset. DQI has a total of 20 subcomponents and 133 terms. Higher DQI is meant to indicate lower existence of spurious bias and higher generalizable features.

Leveraging AFLite and DQI in Fine Action: We use DQI in the pruning step of AFLite; instead of sorting samples based on the predictability score, we sort them based on the DQI values. L9-L34 and L34-36 of algorithm 1 explain the usage of AFLite and DQI respectively in fine action.

Size	Performance on IID test set
5000	36.77
10000	77.45
15000	81.69
20000	**84.69**
25000	80.96

Table 1: Coarse Action results on SNLI dataset

3 Results

Hyperparameters: We use $a = 5000, b = 5000$ and use other hyperparameters from AFLite (Bras et al., 2020) and DQI (Mishra et al., 2020) papers.

Analysis: Table 1 shows that IID testset accuracy decreases after 20k, so we stop there and proceed for fine action with 20k data. With fine action, we

prune 20k data further to the size of 5k-15k, as shown in Table 2. Our results in Table 2 shows that the pruned datasets achieves near equal performance on IID testset and competitive performance on various sections of three OOD datasets. Since we have included just the first term of DQI_c1, we perform ablation study of that specific term. Our results in Table 3 shows that the first term of DQI_{c1} helps in improving performance on most of the cases. Interestingly we observe that, 20k data has lower IID testset accuracy than 5k, 8k, 10k, 12k and 15k datasets, as shown in Table 2.

Algorithm 1: Optimal Sample Selection

Result: Input: Dataset D, Hyper-Parameters a, b, m, n, t and tau and Output: Pruned dataset S

1 **for** $a < 100$ **do**
2   Randomly Select $a\%$ of samples from D and Check IID testset accuracy of model M;
3   **if** *IID accuracy is increasing* **then**
4   a=a+b
5   **else**
6   break
7   **end**
8 **end**
9 $D = a\%$ of samples from D;
10 Fine tune RoBERTA on 10 % of D and get the embeddings of rest of the dataset D. Discard 10 % of D used in Training.;
11 $S = D$;
12 $E(s) = 0$ and $C(s) = 0$ for all s in S ;
13 **while** $\|S\| > n$ **do**
14   **forall** $i \in m$ **do**
15   *Randomly select trainset of size t from S ;*
16   *Train Logistic Regression on t and evaluate on rest of S i.e. V ;*
17   **forall** $s \in V$ **do**
18             $E(s) = E(s) + 1$;
19   **if** *model prediction is correct* **then**
20                 $C(s) = C(s) + 1$
21   **end**
22   **end**
23   *Train SVM on t and evaluate on V ;*
24   **forall** $s \in V$ **do**
25             $E(s) = E(s) + 1$;
26   **if** *model prediction is correct* **then**
27                 $C(s) = C(s) + 1$
28   **end**
29   **end**
30   **end**
31   **forall** $s \in S$ **do**
32         $P(s) = C(s)/E(s)$
33   **end**
34   *Shortlist instances for which $P(s) > tau$;*
35   *Sort shortlisted instances based on DQI values and delete k instances with lowest DQIs*
36 **end**
37

---

4 Discussion

We perform a preliminary analysis on the 15k samples retained using our algorithm and observe that the 15k retained data contains 4939, 5058 and 4983

Size	IID Test	OOD ANLI			OOD NLI Diagnostics				OOD Stress Combined		
		R1	R2	R3	Knowl.	LS	Logic	PAS	Comp.	Distraction	Noise
550k	**89.64**	36.6	30.5	31.33	**57.64**	**62.23**	53.8	66.51	**51.63**	72.13	**79.52**
20k	84.69	33.1	32.2	30.42	39.93	51.9	39.95	63.21	33.79	57.77	61.84
5k	87.47	32.6	31.8	28	50.35	61.14	48.37	**67.45**	35.29	65.72	73.97
8k	87.54	34.7	31.5	28.92	51.74	55.98	51.63	65.57	40.21	68.99	75.08
10k	87.93	34.5	**33**	**31.67**	55.9	61.14	53.26	66.75	45.94	**74.88**	74.62
12k	88.56	32.6	32.7	30.67	49.31	57.61	50.82	66.27	39.03	67.84	73.67
15k	88.95	**37.2**	28.3	29.17	56.6	56.79	**54.62**	65.8	45.94	70.66	77.71

Table 2: Fine Action on the selected subset of SNLI post coarse action: Highlighted points have best performances. First row represent the original SNLI dataset of size 550k, second row represents the dataset of size 20k selected after coarse action. Last five rows (5k-15k) represent the dataset retained after pruning in fine action.

Size	IID Test	OOD ANLI			OOD NLI Diagnostics				OOD Stress Combined		
		R1	R2	R3	Knowl.	LS	Logic	PAS	Comp.	Distraction	Noise
5k	**86.76**	34.4	**29.8**	27.75	**50.04**	**56.52**	**47.01**	**65.33**	38.1	66.14	**72.01**
8k	87.08	33.1	31.2	28.42	46.18	56.52	47.01	65.57	37.93	68.91	71.85
10k	88.39	**33.5**	31.6	30.42	53.47	60.05	47.28	66.27	40.05	67.02	73.26
12k	88.38	33.9	**31.1**	29.17	51.04	57.42	50.27	66.98	38.81	69.42	76.32
15k	88.92	35.4	33.9	28.5	49.31	57.88	51.9	67.22	50.24	70.45	75.07

Table 3: Ablation Study for DQI_{c1}: Highlighted points show sections of various datasets where addition of DQI has resulted in higher performance

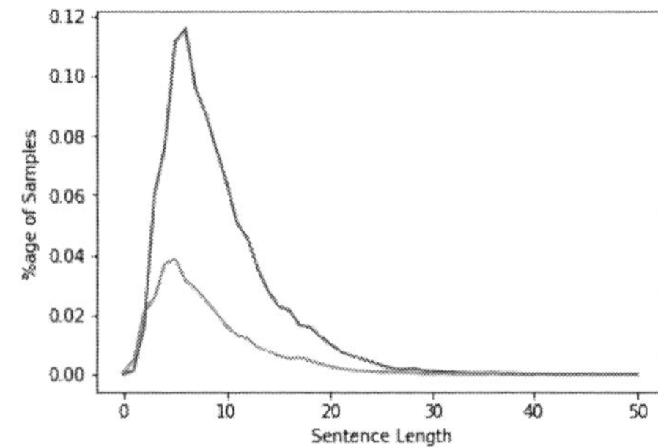

Figure 2: Sentence length vs. percentage of samples for the dataset retained (15k, Blue) and removed (5k, Red) after fine action

samples of contradiction, entailment and neutral respectively. This is similar to the distribution of the original SNLI dataset which has around 183k samples for each class. However, figure 2 illustrates that sentence length of retained and removed samples follow different distributions.

5 Conclusion

We propose a baseline approach to find the optimal set of samples required to learn a task. Our approach mimics humans in identifying relevant materials for learning a task. In the first stage, our algorithm finds a rough estimate as part of the coarse action. The second stage leverages two recently proposed modules AFLite (for adversarial filtering of dataset biases) and DQI (for quantifying the quality of data) to perform fine action. We show the efficacy of our baseline by pruning SNLI to 2% of its original size. Our results show that RoBERTA on training with this pruned set achieves near-equal performance on the SNLIdev set and competitive zero-shot generalization on three OOD datasets. Our analysis shows that big datasets not only prevent generalization, but also impact IID performance. Our findings about distracting samples will encourage community to look for the possible existence of such distractors in real datasets and subsequently explore the optimal selection of samples in a dataset instead of trying to dominate a leaderboard with the entire dataset. Studying the effect of our algorithm on model training time, memory footprint, model interpretation research and better understanding of how deep learning models work in general are some of the potential future directions to explore.

References

Chandra Bhagavatula, Ronan Le Bras, Chaitanya Malaviya, Keisuke Sakaguchi, Ari Holtzman, Hannah Rashkin, Doug Downey, Scott Wen-tau Yih, and Yejin Choi. 2019. Abductive commonsense reasoning. *arXiv preprint arXiv:1908.05739*.

Samuel R Bowman, Gabor Angeli, Christopher Potts, and Christopher D Manning. 2015. A large annotated corpus for learning natural language inference. *arXiv preprint arXiv:1508.05326*.

Ronan Le Bras, Swabha Swayamdipta, Chandra Bhagavatula, Rowan Zellers, Matthew E Peters, Ashish Sabharwal, and Yejin Choi. 2020. Adversarial filters of dataset biases. *arXiv preprint arXiv:2002.04108*.

Jacob Devlin, Ming-Wei Chang, Kenton Lee, and Kristina Toutanova. 2018. Bert: Pre-training of deep bidirectional transformers for language understanding. *arXiv preprint arXiv:1810.04805*.

Dheeru Dua, Yizhong Wang, Pradeep Dasigi, Gabriel Stanovsky, Sameer Singh, and Matt Gardner. 2019. Drop: A reading comprehension benchmark requiring discrete reasoning over paragraphs. *arXiv preprint arXiv:1903.00161*.

Mor Geva, Yoav Goldberg, and Jonathan Berant. 2019. Are we modeling the task or the annotator? an investigation of annotator bias in natural language understanding datasets. *arXiv preprint arXiv:1908.07898*.

Suchin Gururangan, Swabha Swayamdipta, Omer Levy, Roy Schwartz, Samuel R Bowman, and Noah A Smith. 2018. Annotation artifacts in natural language inference data. *arXiv preprint arXiv:1803.02324*.

Divyansh Kaushik and Zachary C Lipton. 2018. How much reading does reading comprehension require? a critical investigation of popular benchmarks. *arXiv preprint arXiv:1808.04926*.

Yinhan Liu, Myle Ott, Naman Goyal, Jingfei Du, Mandar Joshi, Danqi Chen, Omer Levy, Mike Lewis, Luke Zettlemoyer, and Veselin Stoyanov. 2019. Roberta: A robustly optimized bert pretraining approach. *arXiv preprint arXiv:1907.11692*.

Swaroop Mishra, Anjana Arunkumar, Bhavdeep Sachdeva, Chris Bryan, and Chitta Baral. 2020. Dqi: Measuring data quality in nlp. *ArXiv*, abs/2005.00816.

Aakanksha Naik, Abhilasha Ravichander, Norman Sadeh, Carolyn Rose, and Graham Neubig. 2018. Stress test evaluation for natural language inference. *arXiv preprint arXiv:1806.00692*.

Yixin Nie, Adina Williams, Emily Dinan, Mohit Bansal, Jason Weston, and Douwe Kiela. 2019. Adversarial nli: A new benchmark for natural language understanding. *arXiv preprint arXiv:1910.14599*.

Adam Poliak, Jason Naradowsky, Aparajita Haldar, Rachel Rudinger, and Benjamin Van Durme. 2018. Hypothesis only baselines in natural language inference. *arXiv preprint arXiv:1805.01042*.

Pranav Rajpurkar, Jian Zhang, Konstantin Lopyrev, and Percy Liang. 2016. Squad: 100,000+ questions for machine comprehension of text. *arXiv preprint arXiv:1606.05250*.

Christian Rauch, Vladimir Ivan, Timothy Hospedales, Jamie Shotton, and Maurice Fallon. 2019. Learning-driven coarse-to-fine articulated robot tracking. In *2019 International Conference on Robotics and Automation (ICRA)*, pages 6604–6610. IEEE.

Olga Russakovsky, Jia Deng, Hao Su, Jonathan Krause, Sanjeev Satheesh, Sean Ma, Zhiheng Huang, Andrej Karpathy, Aditya Khosla, Michael Bernstein, et al. 2015. Imagenet large scale visual recognition challenge. *International journal of computer vision*, 115(3):211–252.

Keisuke Sakaguchi, Ronan Le Bras, Chandra Bhagavatula, and Yejin Choi. 2019. Winogrande: An adversarial winograd schema challenge at scale. *arXiv preprint arXiv:1907.10641*.

Roy Schwartz, Jesse Dodge, Noah A Smith, and Oren Etzioni. 2019. Green ai. *arXiv preprint arXiv:1907.10597*.

Roy Schwartz, Maarten Sap, Ioannis Konstas, Li Zilles, Yejin Choi, and Noah A Smith. 2017. The effect of different writing tasks on linguistic style: A case study of the roc story cloze task. *arXiv preprint arXiv:1702.01841*.

Alex Wang, Amanpreet Singh, Julian Michael, Felix Hill, Omer Levy, and Samuel R Bowman. 2018. Glue: A multi-task benchmark and analysis platform for natural language understanding. *arXiv preprint arXiv:1804.07461*.

Rowan Zellers, Yonatan Bisk, Roy Schwartz, and Yejin Choi. 2018. Swag: A large-scale adversarial dataset for grounded commonsense inference. *arXiv preprint arXiv:1808.05326*.

Overview of the SustaiNLP 2020 Shared Task

Alex Wang
New York University
alexwang@nyu.edu

Thomas Wolf
HuggingFace
thomas@huggingface.co

Abstract

We describe the SustaiNLP 2020 shared task: efficient inference on the SuperGLUE benchmark (Wang et al., 2019). Participants are evaluated based on performance on the benchmark as well as energy consumed in making predictions on the test sets. We describe the task, its organization, and the submitted systems. Across the six submissions to the shared task, participants achieved efficiency gains of $20\times$ over a standard BERT (Devlin et al., 2019) baseline, while losing less than an absolute point in performance.

1 Introduction

While ever-larger pretrained language models have led to impressive gains across a variety of natural language processing (NLP) tasks, there is growing concern about the environmental impact of training and deploying these models (Strubell et al., 2019; Schwartz et al., 2019). In response, there has been a growing body of research focusing on making these large models smaller and more efficient with minimal sacrifice to performance (Sanh et al., 2019; Michel et al., 2019, i.a.).

The SustaiNLP 2020 shared task focuses on the development of computationally and energy efficient NLP systems. The task uses the SuperGLUE benchmark (Wang et al., 2019), a standard benchmark for natural language understanding. Systems are evaluated on both the benchmark score as well as the energy consumed in evaluating the system on the benchmark. Participants are therefore incentivized to develop models that are energy efficient while maintaining the high performance of recent models. The shared task received six submissions that employed a large variety of optimizations to improve system efficiency. Overall, the submitted systems were on average $20\times$ more efficient than a standard baseline using pretrained language models while nearly matching baseline performance.

2 Shared Task Description

2.1 Task

The shared task centers on the SuperGLUE benchmark, a suite of eight diverse NLU tasks designed to test a system's ability to perform a broad range of language understanding capabilities. The tasks vary substantially in task type, input size, and textual domain. We use seven of the eight SuperGLUE tasks, as the extremely small nature of the Winograd Schema Challenge (WSC) makes it challenging to obtain meaningful performance while improving the efficiency of the system. We briefly describe the seven tasks used here; see Wang et al. (2019) for an in-depth discussion of the tasks.

- Boolean Questions (BoolQ; Clark et al., 2019) is a question answering (QA) dataset where each example consists of a paragraph and a yes/no question about that paragraph. The test set consists of 3245 examples, and the evaluation metric is accuracy.

- CommitmentBank (CB; De Marneffe et al., 2019) is a natural language inference (NLI) task where each example consists of a short text containing an embedded clause. The task is to determine if the embedded clause is entailed or contradicted by the original text. The test set consists of 250 examples, and the evaluation metrics are accuracy and F1.

- Choice of Plausible Alternatives (COPA; Roemmele et al., 2011) is a causal reasoning dataset where each example consists of a premise sentence and the task is to determine a likely cause or effect of the premise from among two choices. The test set consists of 500 examples, and the evaluation metric is accuracy.

Proceedings of SustaiNLP: Workshop on Simple and Efficient Natural Language Processing, pages 174–178
Online, November 20, 2020. ©2020 Association for Computational Linguistics

- Multi-Sentence Reading Comprehension (MultiRC; Khashabi et al., 2018) is a QA dataset where each example consists of a paragraph and a variable number of multiple choice questions about the paragraph. Each questions can have one or more valid answers. The test set consists of 1800 examples, and the evaluation metrics are F1 over all answer choices as well as exact match of answer sets.

- Reading Comprehension with Commonsense Reasoning Dataset (ReCoRD; Zhang et al., 2018) is a QA dataset where each example consists of a news article and a Cloze question about the article whose answer choices are entities in the article. If an entity appears multiple times in the article, all mentions are considered correct. The test set consists of 10K examples, and the evaluation metrics are maximum token-level F1 (over all mentions) and exact match.

- Recognizing Textual Entailment (RTE; Dagan et al., 2006; Bar Haim et al., 2006; Giampiccolo et al., 2007; Bentivogli et al., 2009) is a collection of NLI datasets where each example consists of a premise sentence and a hypothesis sentence. The task is to determine if the premise entails, contradicts, or is neutral to the hypothesis. The test set consists of 300 examples, and the evaluation metric is accuracy.

- Words in Context (WiC) is a word sense disambiguation task where each example consists of a pair of sentence that each contain the same marked word. The task is to determine if the word has the same sense in both sentences. The test set consists of 1400 examples, and the evaluation metric is accuracy.

To participate, each submission produces predictions on the test set of each task and is scored according to the task evaluation metrics. The overall task performance is determined by averaging performance metrics for each task. For tasks with multiple evaluation metrics, we first average within each task.

2.2 Efficiency

As the workshop focuses on developing computationally efficient systems, we additionally evaluate systems by how efficiently they produce predictions on the test set. We focus on measuring efficiency during inference rather than training, as, in the current paradigm, models are trained only a handful of (expensive) times but used for inference many more times. Additionally, measuring efficiency during training is complicated by the widespread reliance on pretrained model components.

Though there are many metrics for measuring efficiency, we follow the recommendation of Henderson et al. (2020) and measure efficiency by the power consumed throughout the course of inference. To do so, we use the `experiment-impact-tracker` library Henderson et al. (2020).

2.3 Organization

We consider two[1] tracks: one using GPUs and one restricted to CPU only. All systems were welcome to use any programming language or libraries, but were run on standardized hardware environments. For the GPU track, participants had four Nvidia V100s (32GB) available to them, but all participants chose to use only one GPU due to the cost of parallelization overhead. We run all submissions three times and report the mean task and efficiency scores.

3 Submissions

We provided participants with a simple baseline that follows the standard paradigm of finetuning a pretrained language model to each task. For pretrained models, we use BERT-base (Devlin et al., 2019) and RoBERTa-large (Liu et al., 2019), as provided by the HuggingFace Transformers library (Wolf et al., 2019).

There were six submissions to the shared task, four submissions to the GPU track and two submissions to the CPU track. All submissions were provided by Kim and Hassan (2020). We provide a brief description of the six submissions below; see Kim and Hassan (2020) for in-depth descriptions. Systems 1-* are submissions to the GPU track and systems 3-* are submissions to the CPU track.

- 1-1: This submission employs optimizations at all levels. The model is first trained using

---

[1]Originally, we considered three tracks: one CPU track and two GPU tracks separated by performance thresholds. However, we only received submissions to two of the three tracks

	system	total	BoolQ	CB	COPA	MultiRC	ReCoRD	RTE	WiC
GPU	BERT-base	328.781	7.035	1.334	1.299	20.380	290.650	5.350	0.734
	RoBERTa-large	752.935	16.020	2.734	4.014	43.278	667.607	13.126	6.156
	1-1	16.169	0.639	0.230	0.010	2.972	12.170	0.260	0.095
	1-2	15.248	0.594	0.023	0.016	2.524	11.632	0.337	0.122
	1-3	19.953	1.615	0.046	0.049	4.559	12.661	0.677	0.345
	1-4	20.477	1.641	0.050	0.060	5.356	12.348	0.653	0.369
CPU	BERT-base	1449.018	21.698	2.296	4.515	62.951	1324.910	22.182	10.466
	3-1	65.570	1.548	0.056	0.060	4.111	58.756	0.639	0.399
	3-2	92.797	1.911	0.102	0.166	6.830	82.750	0.259	0.778

Table 1: Energy consumption ($\times 1000$) in kWh for various systems.

system	avg	BoolQ	CB	COPA	MultiRC	ReCoRD	RTE	WiC
BERT-base	64.5	76.5	82.2/87.6	50.8	69.5/18.6	58.1/57.4	68.5	69.1
1-1	63.6	74.0	79.3/86.0	58.0	65.7/17.9	56.6/55.8	66.4	66.0
1-2	63.8	74.0	79.3/86.0	58.0	67.5/18.8	56.6/55.8	66.4	66.0
1-3, 3-1	63.6	73.7	79.3/86.0	58.0	65.8/18.1	56.6/55.8	66.9	65.9
1-4, 3-2	63.8	73.7	79.3/86.0	58.0	67.6/18.4	56.6/55.8	66.9	65.9

Table 2: Task performance for various systems. For BoolQ, COPA, RTE, and WiC, the evaluation metric is accuracy. For CB, the evaluation metrics are accuracy and F1. For MultiRC, the evaluation metrics are answer-level F1 and exact match. For ReCoRD, the evaluation metrics are token-level F1 and exact match. The overall task performance is an unweighted average of performance across tasks.

both task-specific and task-agnostic knowledge distillation (Hinton et al., 2015) from the pretrained and finetuned BERT model. They then reduce the model sizes via network pruning (Karnin, 1990) and further decrease the memory footprint by using 16-bit precision. Finally, they improve the runtime by fusing specific operations using onnxruntime and using a large evaluation batch size.

- 1-2: This submission is the same as 1-1 except they use a modified model for MultiRC.

- 1-3: This submission is a hybrid system that uses the GPU only for ReCoRD due to its much larger size and CPU for all other tasks. It uses the same optimizations as 1-1.

- 1-4: This submission is the same as 1-3 except it uses the modified MultiRC model.

- 3-1: This submission uses the same models as 1-3, but runs only on CPUs. It includes additional CPU-specific optimizations such as 8-bit quantization for some matrix multiplications and optimzed number of CPU processes per task.

- 3-2: This submission uses the same models as 1-4, but only uses CPUs. It uses the same optimizations as 3-1.

4 Results

Energy and task results are respectively presented in Tables 1 and Table 2.

We find that the submitted systems are able to substantially improve total energy consumption over the baseline systems, as much as $20\times$ in both the GPU and CPU settings, while trading off less than one point average task performance. The differences tend to be larger in the CPU setting than the GPU setting, likely because large, unoptimized pretrained language models were developed to be run on GPUs. The improvements of the submitted systems vary wildly between tasks, and do not scale linearly in the size of the test set. On CB and COPA, two of the smallest datasets, the improvements are as much as $50-100\times$ in the GPU setting. On WiC and BoolQ, the improvements are a more modest $10\times$. Similarly, the improvements do not seem to scale in the size of the inputs, as improvements on the paragraph-input tasks (BoolQ, MultiRC, and ReCoRD) are frequently matched and dwarfed by improvements on the sentence-level tasks.

Among the systems, we find that the hybrid submissions (1-3, 1-4) consistently consume more power than the GPU-only counterparts (1-1, 1-2). All of the submissions that use a GPU (1-*) substantially outperform those that do not (3-*), which is in large part due to the large test set for ReCoRD. We observe fairly high variance between similar systems (1-1 and 1-2; 1-3 and 1-4; 3-1 and 3-2). In the worst case, systems 3-1 and 3-2 only differ by the MultiRC model, but the energy consumption varies significantly. We attribute this variance to runtime differences in the environment.

Task performances are consistently around 2 absolute points lower in the submitted systems than the baseline, except for COPA, where the submitted systems outperform the baseline. However, given the large efficiency improvements over the baseline, this tradeoff seems favorable.

5 Conclusion

We describe the results of the SustaiNLP 2020 Shared Task. The six submissions were able to substantially improve over the baseline systems, obtaining improvements $20\times$ in energy consumption while only losing a point in performance. To achieve these results, the submissions employed efficiency optimizations at numerous levels, including model architecture, storage, and runtime, which hints at the rich design space for efficient machine learning models.

Acknowledgments

We thank Peter Henderson for developing the `experiment-impact-tracker` library and for guidance on using the library.

References

Roy Bar Haim, Ido Dagan, Bill Dolan, Lisa Ferro, Danilo Giampiccolo, Bernardo Magnini, and Idan Szpektor. 2006. The second PASCAL recognising textual entailment challenge.

Luisa Bentivogli, Ido Dagan, Hoa Trang Dang, Danilo Giampiccolo, and Bernardo Magnini. 2009. The fifth PASCAL recognizing textual entailment challenge.

Christopher Clark, Kenton Lee, Ming-Wei Chang, Tom Kwiatkowski, Michael Collins, and Kristina Toutanova. 2019. BoolQ: Exploring the surprising difficulty of natural yes/no questions. In *Proceedings of NAACL-HLT 2019*.

Ido Dagan, Oren Glickman, and Bernardo Magnini. 2006. The PASCAL recognising textual entailment challenge. In *Machine learning challenges. evaluating predictive uncertainty, visual object classification, and recognising tectual entailment*, pages 177–190. Springer.

Marie-Catherine De Marneffe, Mandy Simons, and Judith Tonhauser. 2019. The Commitment-Bank: Investigating projection in naturally occurring discourse. To appear in proceedings of Sinn und Bedeutung 23. Data can be found at https://github.com/mcdm/CommitmentBank/.

Jacob Devlin, Ming-Wei Chang, Kenton Lee, and Kristina Toutanova. 2019. BERT: Pre-training of deep bidirectional transformers for language understanding. In *Proceedings of the Conference of the North American Chapter of the Association for Computational Linguistics: Human Language Technologies (NAACL-HLT)*. Association for Computational Linguistics.

Danilo Giampiccolo, Bernardo Magnini, Ido Dagan, and Bill Dolan. 2007. The third PASCAL recognizing textual entailment challenge. In *Proceedings of the ACL-PASCAL workshop on textual entailment and paraphrasing*, pages 1–9. Association for Computational Linguistics.

Peter Henderson, Jieru Hu, Joshua Romoff, Emma Brunskill, Dan Jurafsky, and Joelle Pineau. 2020. Towards the systematic reporting of the energy and carbon footprints of machine learning. *arXiv preprint 2002.05651*.

Geoffrey Hinton, Oriol Vinyals, and Jeff Dean. 2015. Distilling the knowledge in a neural network. *arXiv preprint 1503.02531*.

Ehud D Karnin. 1990. A simple procedure for pruning back-propagation trained neural networks. *IEEE transactions on neural networks*, 1(2):239–242.

Daniel Khashabi, Snigdha Chaturvedi, Michael Roth, Shyam Upadhyay, and Dan Roth. 2018. Looking beyond the surface: A challenge set for reading comprehension over multiple sentences. In *Proceedings of the 2018 Conference of the North American Chapter of the Association for Computational Linguistics: Human Language Technologies, Volume 1 (Long Papers)*, pages 252–262.

Young Jin Kim and Hany Hassan. 2020. Fastformers: Highly efficient transformer models for natural language understanding. In *First Workshop on Simple and Efficient Natural Language Processing*.

Yinhan Liu, Myle Ott, Naman Goyal, Jingfei Du, Mandar Joshi, Danqi Chen, Omer Levy, Mike Lewis, Luke Zettlemoyer, and Veselin Stoyanov. 2019. Roberta: A robustly optimized bert pretraining approach. *arXiv preprint 1907.11692*.

Paul Michel, Omer Levy, and Graham Neubig. 2019. Are sixteen heads really better than one? In *Advances in Neural Information Processing Systems*, pages 14014–14024.

Melissa Roemmele, Cosmin Adrian Bejan, and Andrew S. Gordon. 2011. Choice of plausible alternatives: An evaluation of commonsense causal reasoning. In *2011 AAAI Spring Symposium Series*.

Victor Sanh, Lysandre Debut, Julien Chaumond, and Thomas Wolf. 2019. Distilbert, a distilled version of bert: smaller, faster, cheaper and lighter. *arXiv preprint 1910.01108*.

Roy Schwartz, Jesse Dodge, Noah A Smith, and Oren Etzioni. 2019. Green ai. *arXiv preprint arXiv:1907.10597*.

Emma Strubell, Ananya Ganesh, and Andrew McCallum. 2019. Energy and policy considerations for deep learning in nlp. In *Proceedings of the 57th Annual Meeting of the Association for Computational Linguistics*, pages 3645–3650.

Alex Wang, Yada Pruksachatkun, Nikita Nangia, Amanpreet Singh, Julian Michael, Felix Hill, Omer Levy, and Samuel Bowman. 2019. Superglue: A stickier benchmark for general-purpose language understanding systems. In *Advances in Neural Information Processing Systems*, pages 3266–3280.

Thomas Wolf, Lysandre Debut, Victor Sanh, Julien Chaumond, Clement Delangue, Anthony Moi, Pierric Cistac, Tim Rault, Rémi Louf, Morgan Funtowicz, Joe Davison, Sam Shleifer, Patrick von Platen, Clara Ma, Yacine Jernite, Julien Plu, Canwen Xu, Teven Le Scao, Sylvain Gugger, Mariama Drame, Quentin Lhoest, and Alexander M. Rush. 2019. Huggingface's transformers: State-of-the-art natural language processing. *ArXiv*, abs/1910.03771.

Sheng Zhang, Xiaodong Liu, Jingjing Liu, Jianfeng Gao, Kevin Duh, and Benjamin Van Durme. 2018. ReCoRD: Bridging the gap between human and machine commonsense reading comprehension. *arXiv preprint 1810.12885*.

Association for Computational Linguistics
209 N. Eighth Street
Stroudsburg, Pennsylvania 18360

ISBN 978-1-7138-2005-5